BOLIVIA

Coimbra

PARAGUAY

BRAZIL

Potosí

R. Pilcomayo

TERR. OF MISIONES

TERR. OF FORMOSA

R. Bermejo

R. Paraná

JUJUY
Humahuaca

TERR. OF THE CHACO

CORRIENTES

SALTA

LOS ANDES

SANTIAGO DEL ESTERO

TUCUMÁN

R. Saladillo

R. Salado

SANTA FÉ

ENTRE RIOS

URUGUAY

Paraná

CATAMARCA

Copiapó

LA RIOJA

CÓRDOBA

Rosario

Campaña

Buenos Aires

La Plata

SAN JUAN

SAN LUIS

Chacabuco

Aconcagua

Uspallata Pass

Maipó

MENDOZA

ARGENTINA

BUENOS AIRES

Mar del Plata

TERR. OF THE PAMPAS

Pavon

R. Colorado

Bahia Blanca

TERR. OF THE NEUQUÉN

Cañel

TERR. OF THE RIO NEGRO

L. Nahuel Huapí

Great Plateau of Patagonia

TERR. OF THE CHUBUT

Rivadavia

Puerto Deseado

TERR. OF SANTA CRUZ

FALKLAND ISLANDS

PACIFIC OCEAN

ATLANTIC OCEAN

Strait of Magellan

TIERRA DEL FUEGO

Uschuaia

SCALE OF MILES

0   100   200   300   400

ARGENTINA

THE LIFE STORY OF A NATION

Argentina

The Life Story of a Nation

JOHN W. WHITE

1942

THE VIKING PRESS · NEW YORK

TO
That Great Argentine Democrat
DR. ALFREDO L. PALACIOS
Senator, Gentleman, and Knight of his Ideals

CONTENTS

ILLUSTRATIONS

FOREWORD

MY FIRST sight of the great city of Buenos Aires was through a heavy rain from the rail of the ill-fated *S. S. Vauban* a long time ago. Little did I dream that I was to spend a whole adult lifetime there. As the two tugs ushered us up the shallow, muddy Rio de la Plata, there was nothing attractive or inviting about the low-lying, sprawled-out city without a skyline that lay shrouded in the rain and the mist ahead of us. Only two buildings in the whole city were tall enough to stand up above the rest—the Railway Exchange Building and the dome of the Congressional Palace. I was a rather young and probably insufferably conceited vice consul, excited and enthusiastic over having been promoted to this important post, and I was plying an "old-time" American with questions. One of the basic troubles in our relations with Argentina is that any American who has lived there as long as eight years is considered by the other Americans to be an "old-timer." This particular old-timer was filling me with a lot of misinformation which I had to get rid of soon after landing. I remember asking him the meaning of the letters "M.O.P." on the channel buoys. He said they were the initials of the Argentine national motto—*Mañana ó pasado*, tomorrow or the next day.

I lived in Argentina long enough to learn that the letters on the channel buoys stand for *Ministerio de Obras Públicas* (Ministry of Public Works) and that while Argentines probably never will abandon their exasperating tendency to do things *mañano ó pasado*, they manage to get a great deal of effective work done within the tempo set by that phrase. In the meantime, their professional and business men find time to live and to acquire a standard of culture considerably higher than that of Americans in the same income brackets. They always seem to be able to find time for at least part of a late afternoon concert, or to hear a lecture, or to drop in at one of the several art expositions along the Calle Florida. Consequently, at any social gathering any average Argentine can keep up his end of an interesting conversation without once mentioning the stock market or last Wednesday's golf score. The big, busy, modern, very beautiful and abominably noisy city of Buenos Aires stands as a monument to their ability to get things done efficiently in spite of taking time out to live.

On my last trip up the river to Buenos Aires, knowing that I was leaving it within a few days, I got up at sunrise to have a last look at it.

When the sun came up majestically out of the muddy waters of the Mar Dulce, as its discoverer christened the apparently boundless river, its brilliant rays danced and glistened on the many tall white apartment houses and office buildings of the third metropolis of the western world until it appeared to be a great silvery, make-believe city of the stage, set against the heavy backdrop of the still dark sky in the west. If poor old Pedro de Mendoza could rise from his watery grave for a moment and look at Buenos Aires in all its silvery glory at sunrise, and could make himself believe that what he saw was real, perhaps he would go back to sleep feeling that it was all worth while, after all.

For more than a generation, Argentina has rather prided herself on being a thorn in the flesh of the United States. It is not pleasant to realize that we are the most heartily disliked of all foreigners in one of the most cosmopolitan capitals of the world. Much more important than personal feelings, however, is the fact that our inability to get onto a solid basis of understanding and mutual regard with the No. 1 republic of South America has weakened continental defense at one of its most vital spots. Yet there was a time when the relations between Argentina and the United States were so cordial as to be almost lyrical; when the young republic of the south looked to the United States for both political guidance and economic strength and received both in great abundance; and when trade flowed freely in both directions, to the mutual profit of both Americans and Argentines.

A change so abrupt from this former situation to the present one is not one of those things that just happens. It has deep and far-reaching causes and truth compels the confession that most of the fault is ours, as can be learned from even a superficial study of history.

The situation existing between the United States and the Argentine Republic proves better than any of our other South American relationships that understanding between countries is not exclusively a matter for governmental action. It is vitally necessary that the people themselves understand one another; that John Citizen and Juan Pueblo not only know each other but that they have sufficient regard for each other to find some real satisfaction in folding their arms on top of the fence and looking upon each other not only as good neighbors but as "real folks," as they express it in Virginia.

This book attempts to introduce Argentina to American readers; to give an all too brief review of the country's fascinating history; and to discuss some of the problems involved in our relationship with the Argentines. If the Argentine point of view instead of the American seems

to be stressed in discussing some of these problems it is because I feel
that the American viewpoint already is known to Americans and that
they probably will be interested in knowing why the Argentines sometimes look at the same problems from other, and often opposite, angles.
The book does not pretend to be complete. No single volume could be.
An interesting book could be written on practically every one of the
twenty-nine chapter headings into which this effort has been divided.
This book will have achieved its purpose if it contributes something
to better understanding between Argentina and the United States by
awakening a livelier American interest in the Argentine Republic and its
people.

I am very grateful to the several friends who were so helpful in the
gathering and selection of material, either by allowing me the privilege
of using their libraries or in personally undertaking valuable research
work for me. Some of these friends are in government positions; others
are prominent in other activities. Their assistance was largely in the historical and economic fields and as they are in no way responsible for
my conclusions in the political field, with some of which they may disagree, it seems desirable to leave them anonymous while here expressing
publicly my appreciation of their generous co-operation.

I also want to acknowledge publicly my deep obligation to Senator
Alfredo L. Palacios for extending to me his friendship, his home, and
his political support at a moment when I was being made the victim
of a dictator's whim.

My thanks also go to my friends Messrs. Marval, Rodríguez Larreta,
and O'Farrell for their kind permission to reproduce from their valuable compilation in English of all the Argentine legal codes, the text of
the Argentine Constitution that appears in Appendix VII and is liberally
quoted from in Chapter XII.

And to my many Argentine friends: *Salud!*

J. W. W.

Mexico City, June, 1942.

ARGENTINA

THE LIFE STORY OF A NATION

1. THE LAND

THE visitor who makes his first contact with the Argentine Republic through the proud, arrogant, and wonderful city of Buenos Aires, as most new arrivals do, misses something of the great charm of the country which he never can quite capture. So magnificent is the capital that it eclipses the rest of the country. The deep impression remains, no matter how far into the interior one goes, inducing continual unfair comparisons. Argentina should be approached the first time by one of the several routes which take the visitor across the land and through the inland cities and enable him to see and feel the country before Buenos Aires absorbs him. From Bolivia, for instance, southward through the mighty Humahuaca Canyon, down through Jujuy and the sugar cane of the garden province of Tucumán, and then across the wide, fertile pampas to the capital. Or from Chile, following the historic Uspallata Pass through the very heart of the tremendous Andes to the fragrant vineyards of Mendoza and then out across the dreary, dusty San Luis desert onto the green pampas. Or through the Chilean lake district across wild, windy Patagonia, and then up through the Queen Province of Buenos Aires. When one sees it that way for the first time, there is a charm and a beauty, almost a bewitchment, about the whole Argentine Republic, from north to south and from west to east, that gets into the heart and stays there forever in spite of Buenos Aires. For Argentina is one of the most attractive lands on earth. Its majestic mountains and wide, lazy rivers, its green pastures and golden fields stretching to the horizon, even its gray, dusty deserts all weave over one who has known them intimately a spell which is difficult to shake off, no matter how long the miles or how many the years by which the separation is measured. Argentines always warn foreigners that once they learn to like maté as the *criollos* drink it, through a silver tube from a gourd cup, they never again will be able to get the spell of the country out of their blood.

Stretching 2300 miles through 33½ degrees of latitude, the Argentine Republic has almost all the different climates and geographic panoramas that there are—from the bleak Tibetan plateau in the extreme northwest, down through the subtropical Chaco, the boundless pampas, and the western deserts, to the charming Swiss region of blue lakes and low mountains in the south, where Llao-Llao on Lake Nahuel Huapi rapidly is winning international renown as a resort for skiing and other winter sports. La Quiaca, on the Bolivian frontier, is inside the Torrid Zone, approximately 100 miles north of the Tropic of Capricorn and 70 miles north of Rio de Janeiro. The southern tip is at Beagle Channel on the 55th parallel, and the near-by prison colony at Ushuaia is the world's most southerly settlement. The greatest breadth is 905 miles, but over most of the area it is much narrower than that.

With an area of 1,080,550 square miles,[1] Argentina is more than one-third the size of the United States (38 per cent) and occupies the entire southern half of the South American continent, except for the narrow strip west of the Andes that comprises Chile, and the tiny Republic of Uruguay on the east. If this long, wedge-shaped country were super-imposed on the North American continent, in reversed position corresponding to the reversed latitudes and seasons, it would extend from torrid Tampico, Mexico, to Winnipeg, Canada, which is well within the cold Labradorean latitudes. The widest area would stretch from Memphis to Amarillo, Texas, and Buenos Aires would be on the latitude of Cape Hatteras.

It is not generally known that the entire territory of Argentina lies east of the longitude of New York City. The Andean frontier between Chile and Argentina lies directly south of Boston, and Buenos Aires is about 400 miles east of the longitude of Halifax. Buenos Aires, in fact, is seven degrees east of Bermuda.

The reversal of the latitudes and seasons in the Southern Hemisphere produces a whole world of strange contrasts to which American and European residents in Argentina never become completely reconciled. Christmas in mid-summer! Easter at the beginning of a cold, rainy autumn! The Fourth of July in mid-winter! It is from the north that the hot winds blow in summer, and the south from which come the cold winds of winter. The cold mornings of August find lawns and window-panes whitened with frost. The September equinox brings in spring with its riot of wistaria, japonica, and orange blossoms. October's warm breezes are laden with the heavy perfume of jasmine and of the clustered blooms of the paraiso trees. Early November finds Argentina's inimitable golden sunshine scintillating on mile after mile of smooth, pale-blue carpets of flowering flax which within a few weeks will produce more than half the world's supply of linseed oil. In sultry December, when the flowering jacarandá trees become soft blue clouds bordering the main streets and avenues of Buenos Aires, city dwellers pack up their belongings and flock to the seaside in search of cooler air.

---

[1] For detailed figures of area and population see Appendix I.

A VIEW OF THE PAMPAS

AERIAL VIEW OF AN ESTANCIA

OMBÚ TREE, KNOWN AS "THE LIGHTHOUSE OF THE PAMPAS"

LLAMAS IN PATAGONIA

Buenos Aires gives the impression of being the metropolis of a rich and highly developed industrial nation. But this is because the capital selfishly absorbs unto itself the wealth of the whole country, as though the nation existed solely for the city's aggrandizement. The result is a tremendously large, beautiful, and cultured head supported by a rickety, undernourished, and not always clean body. Buenos Aires is one of the half-dozen leading cities of the world. Argentina is a backward agricultural and grazing land where the people live and think very much as they did a hundred years ago. The marked contrast between the wealth and beauty of busy, up-to-date Buenos Aires and the drab poverty and neglect of the backward interior causes a shock of incredulity when first met. This contrast between the capital and the interior, between wealth and poverty, between progress and backwardness, between highly developed culture and almost animal ignorance, pervades the whole pattern of the country's political, economic, and social life.

Argentina is one of the wealthiest agricultural countries on the globe, but its farming wealth is produced by less than 10 per cent of its total area, only 60,000,000 acres being under cultivation out of an aggregate of 691,552,000 acres. With a territory almost as large as Europe, excluding Russia, the nation's life and wealth are concentrated in an area about the combined size of Missouri, Kansas, and Iowa. This is the expanse of boundless, fertile plains that have become famous in song and story as the pampas. These grassy, treeless plains, virtually without a stone or a gravel, extend in a semi-circle around the city of Buenos Aires with an average radius of 350 miles, embracing the provinces of Buenos Aires and Santa Fé, the southern part of Córdoba and San Luis, and a part of the Territory of La Pampa. The whole pampa area is only one-fifth of the country's total area and contains the wide grazing lands as well as the cultivated fields, yet it produces 90 per cent of the grain and 60 per cent of the livestock, except sheep. The soil of the pampas, miraculously fertile, has been described by American and European experts as the best in all the world. It is a rich black alluvial deposit varying in depth from seven to eleven feet. Eleven feet of alluvial top-soil!

The pampas put on one of their most beautiful shows in early March, when the pampa grass is in bloom. Then for mile after mile the landscape is brightened by the great cream and white tassels swaying in the breeze on top of the long, slender green stalks that have been sent eight to ten feet into the air from thick tussocks which themselves grow to a height of two or three feet.

There is a rare fascination about the pampas. Stretching perfectly level and unbroken to the horizon in all directions, they have a strange air of the sea, as though the sea suddenly had turned to solid earth. Flights of white-breasted gulls, of a species that has left the ocean and established itself on land, follow the plows and swoop down for worms and grubs with the characteristic motions of their marine cousins who still follow ships at sea. This illusion of the ocean is increased at sunrise and sunset when the magnificent colorings and cloud effects are fully as spectacular as any seen at sea. The illusion is even more real at night, especially on moonless nights when the cool breezes blow across the wide pampas and the big, brilliant stars shine down as though alive out of the black dome that seems just beyond reach.

By day the pampas form another world. The intimacy with the night and the earth is gone, and man again feels small and lost in space. At long intervals across the endless fields and boundless pastures, the monotonous skyline is broken by great squares of huge, shaggy eucalyptus trees and tall, stately Lombardy poplars—the alamos which gave their name to the historic Texas mission. These trees form the windbreaks that have been planted around the acres set apart as the park surrounding the palatial residence of the owner of an *estancia*. Within this park are polo fields, tennis courts, and swimming pools; and both inside and outside the house are the comforts that money can buy. Outside the park, often farther than the eye can see, are the miles and miles of open pastures and cultivated fields belonging to the *estanciero*. Here and there on these fields are small clusters of three or four trees which provide a bit of shade for the grass-thatched, floorless, windowless mud hut, or *rancho*, which houses the family, the pigs, and the chickens of the *colono*, or tenant farmer. With the exception of the lonely ombú, no tree grows wild on the pampas, so that a small clump of shade trees is always the sign of a habitation.

When property owners began to grow rich in the latter years of the nineteenth century, they imported trees from Europe by the hundreds of thousands and set them out on their estancias. Beautiful Palermo Park in Buenos Aires was once an estancia belonging to the dictator Rosas and most of its thousands of trees were imported from Europe.

With the exception of the Japanese cherry tree, no plant has such an important place in the traditions of a people as the ombú has in the songs and stories of the Argentines. The ombú has an enormous trunk, and its great spreading branches shade an immense space of ground; its knotted roots protrude from the ground in strange shapes, forming convenient resting places for tired horsemen. Argentine poets have called the ombú the lighthouse of the pampas because in the days of the gaucho it frequently was the only object to be seen for miles and miles on the sea-like plains.

Ombú wood is entirely worthless, even as fuel, and the tree has no usefulness except for its welcome shade, but it is the best loved of all trees in Argentina, probably because of its associations with past centuries. Some of these ombús are associated with great historic events in the life of the country. The Ombú of Hope, for example, is so called because San Martín and two other eminent men of his day, Juan Martin De Pueyrredon and Tomás Guido, seated on its enormous roots, made a solemn vow to perfect the independence they were struggling to obtain. The Ombú of Pedriel was a mute witness to one of the important battles of the English invasions. Several others in various parts of the country were named for the treaties which were signed in their shade during the period of the civil wars.

No one seems to know how long the ombú lives; many that witnessed historic events more than a hundred years ago are still flourishing. Argentines say that no one has ever seen an ombú that was decayed by age. Cyclones cannot blow them down and neither drought nor fire destroys them, their roots being so stored with nourishment as to enable them to resist flame itself. It is impossible to count the age of an ombú by its rings because it grows like a gigantic weed, producing more than ten rings a year. One of the oldest known ombús is the Viceroy's Ombú, named for Viceroy Vertiz because it stood in his *quinta* in Olivos, a suburb of Buenos Aires, in 1779. The authorities of the Argentine Forestal Society made a careful study of this tree in 1914 and decided that it was at least five hundred years old.

Botanists have determined that the ombú is Argentina's only indigenous tree and that it seems to have originated in the region of Lake Iberá in the Province of Corrientes. There are a few ombús in Andalusia, Spain, where they are known as *bellasombra*, or beautiful shade, but they were sent there from Argentina in 1775.

Since Argentina has attained its world-wide fame from the wealth of the pampas, the outside world has come to think of it as a land of flat open plains. But Argentina has six mountains that are higher than Mount McKinley, the king of them all being majestic Aconcagua, whose rounded peak, 23,081 feet high, whitened with eternal ice, lords it over all the peaks of the Western Hemisphere. Aconcagua and its five neighbors stand on the mighty cordillera of the Andes, which forms a wall along the entire western edge of the country. Over most of its length this cordillera is an awe-inspiring mass of bare, rocky ranges and ice-capped peaks which spurn man and make him feel insignificant. At Para-millo, at an altitude of 9800 feet on the route from Mendoza to Chile, is one of the most spectacular mountain views in the world, as a hundred miles of the great main ridge of ice and snow spread out to view. In the south the mountains are lower and the panorama is as friendly, inviting, and beautiful as any in Switzerland. Here the rich green vegetation climbs up the mountains and meets the low snowline, and huge splendid blue lakes spread their fiord-like arms in and out among the hills.

In Argentina, as in most of the rest of South America, Nature is not man's friend. It is too big and overwhelming and forbidding for man ever to get close to it. Instead of low, friendly hills, there are mountains so tremendous that they make man feel small. The River Plate, instead of being a friendly stream flowing along to the ocean, stretches to the horizon, a muddy sea which grows as rough and boisterous as any other sea when the wind blows. Even the pampas crush man with their great distances and lonely spaces. No matter where man turns, Nature awes him instead of inviting or inspiring him.

North of the pampas is the subtropical Chaco district, which extends northward into the Chaco Boreal, where Bolivia and Paraguay fought the Chaco War. This is a region of unnavigable meandering streams, in-habited in its unsettled portions by jaguars, alligators, snakes, and mi-gratory birds, causing the Indians to call it *chaco*, which is Quechua for "hunting grounds." The northern part of this region produces fine hardwoods in great abundance and is the center of the quebracho indus-try which produces tannin extract for the tanneries of the United States and Europe. The southern part, where the timber has been cleared away, is the region of Argentina's cotton and tobacco fields.

Northeast of the pampas is another very productive but much smaller agricultural region which is known as the "Mesopotamia" country, lying between the rivers Paraná and Uruguay and embracing the provinces of Entre Rios and Corrientes and the Territory of Misiones. These two provinces produce the best and cleanest wool in the country and also considerable linseed and fruit. Misiones, thrust like a threatening thumb into Brazilian territory, produces most of Argentina's yerba-maté tea.

In the Province of Mendoza, at the foot of the Andes, and along the Rio Negro in northern Patagonia, irrigation has conquered the deserts and produced two wonderfully rich fruit and wine centers.

The windswept, stony desert of Patagonia extends from the Rio Negro southward to the Strait of Magellan, embracing the territories of

Rio Negro, Chubut, and Santa Cruz and rising gradually from the Atlantic to the foothills of the Andes. Parts of central Patagonia are devoted to sheep-raising; the extreme southern part is covered with heavy forests; and on the Atlantic seaboard in the vicinity of Comodoro Rivadavia are to be found Argentina's largest petroleum fields.

But it is on the pampas that Argentina lives. This one-fifth of the nation's territory has been endowed with an almost ideal combination of fertile soil, warm sunshine, and abundant rainfall which has made the country wealthy with very little effort on the part of those who control the wealth. Production costs of high-grade meats, grain, and wool are so low that the world's buyers compete for them, and in normal times Argentina has only to sit on its own doorstep and wait for buyers' offers. Many sources of wealth have not been tapped yet because it is so much easier to produce the meats and grains and wool for which markets already exist.

Seventy per cent of the country's population of 13,000,000 live in the city of Buenos Aires and on or just around the pampas. The five principal cities border this area, but there are no important towns on the pampas themselves. The land is owned by a comparatively few individuals and 85 per cent of the acreage is cultivated by tenant farmers, whose standard of living is extremely low. Formerly, when there were no government restrictions on the remittance of funds, the landlords and their large families lived abroad, mostly in Paris, and it was their lavish spending of unearned wealth that first made the name Argentine known in Europe.

Generally, the owner of a big estate, or estancia, devotes himself to cattle-raising and leaves the growing of grain to the colonos. As a result of this system there exist on the pampas immense livestock ranches which cannot be equaled anywhere else, either in size or in development. Some of the largest herds of pure-bred stock in the world are to be found on these estancias.

The colono occupies the social position in Argentina's agricultural economy that the Indian and the roto, or mestizo, occupy in the metal-producing countries of the South American continent. In the metal-producing countries, the elite upper class has solved its problems by making the Indians and the rotos work in the mines while the gente fina, or the people who count, run the governments and live off the royalties and export taxes paid by the foreigners to whom the mines had been sold or leased. In Argentina the landowners wax rich by collecting from one-third to one-half of what the worker produces.

More than half of Argentina's grain is produced on small tracts of rented land averaging less than 300 acres. The colono does not own the land he works. The word means colonist, but he is a roving sharecropper. He contracts to till a piece of land, usually 100 to 150 hectares (247 to 370 acres), for a period varying from two to five years. He turns over to the landlord from one-fourth to one-half, usually one-third, of what he produces. The colono is not a farmer. He is a grower of grain. He buys his potatoes and other vegetables as well as his meat. Since any improvements which he might make on the property have to be left for the landlord without compensation when he moves off the land, he does not make any improvements. He and his family live on a plane only slightly above that of animals.

The colono plows his land in April and then lets it lie untouched until June, when he plants his wheat. From June until November, when the harvest begins, he does little but wait for the wheat to ripen. He sees and handles money only once a year, when he sells his crop. But before he gets it he usually owes it all to the *acopiador*. The colono lives as a slave to the acopiador, the middleman who finances him during the year and so is able to corner all the crops in his district before they are sold to the big exporting firms. The acopiador usually owns the general store in the nearest town and in return for financing the colono he requires him to buy everything at his store at whatever prices he chooses to charge. The crop has to be delivered in new jute bags and the colono has to buy these from the acopiador, who also owns the threshing machine which he rents to the colono at so much a bushel. Since the colono is heavily in debt by the time his grain is threshed, he has to sell it at once. Because all the other colonos are doing the same thing, this is the moment at which prices are at their lowest level of the year. The acopiador stores the grain in his warehouse or piles it in huge stacks near the railroad station and holds it until prices rise to a level that assures him a good profit. Meanwhile the colono considers himself lucky if he has been able to pay off his debts and begin the new year penniless but without a carryover of old debts to be worked off. If he has two or three bad years in succession, as often happens, he accumulates a burden of debt that makes his situation hopeless—in which case he abandons the land he is working and wanders off to some other part of the country to try again. But the acopiador and the landowner never lose. They cannot lose because the whole game is rigged in their favor.

The importation of jute from India for the manufacture of grain bags is one of the most important items in British trade with Argentina. The

British-owned railroads can hardly be blamed, therefore, for their refusal to build elevators that would do away with the bag business and thus ruin the jute trade. In 1935 the Argentine government began the construction of more than 300 country and terminal elevators to cost $28,000,000 and to be owned and operated by the government. When completed, these elevators were to advance negotiable warrants against the grain delivered to them, and the government hoped that the elevators and the National Grain Board eventually would be able to relieve the plight of the colono, especially his economic slavery to the acopiador.

Argentina has 3000 wealthy families. It is the only South American country which has a middle class that lives more or less comfortably. But nine-tenths of the people are poor. As in all Spanish countries, there is an immense spread between extreme wealth and extreme poverty. For the wealthy, life is easy and cheap. Even for the poor, poverty does not entail the suffering and privation that it does in colder climates and in countries where food is scarce or costly. The poorest workman can afford a rib of beef and a small loaf of excellent bread for his lunch, because the beef, which he roasts himself over an open fire, costs him only 20 centavos (9 cents) and the bread 5 centavos (1¼ cents). For another 20 centavos he can have a pint of red wine. Argentina's poor suffer from inadequate housing, insufficient clothing, and the other lacks from which the poor suffer everywhere, but there is little hunger, even among the poorest.

When the belligerently progressive twentieth century dawned, Argentina was living a slow, easy, and contented life, so little known by the outside world that even her geographical situation was hazy, except to her nearest South American neighbors. In less than forty years the country has skyrocketed from obscurity to world prominence in a manner so spectacular as to be without parallel in modern history. During the first twenty-five years of the century Argentina achieved international economic importance by becoming one of the largest producers of foodstuffs, especially meats and grains. From 1930 to 1940 the country assumed a leading position in the world's political affairs, and the names of her leading statesmen became as well known as those of the leading Europeans.

It was Argentina that organized the conference of American neutrals and stopped the three-year Chaco War after the League of Nations had failed in its attempts to do so. It was Argentina that sent a warship to Spain at the time of the Civil War to force both sides in the conflict to recognize the principle of political asylum, which always has been sacred to the South American republics. It is Argentina that always stands up and opposes the United States at Pan-American conferences.

More correctly, it is the city of Buenos Aires, rather than Argentina, that has achieved this political prominence. Buenos Aires always has dominated the country. There are only eight other cities of any considerable size and their combined population is only 1,544,000, or somewhat more than half that of Buenos Aires. Argentina has been known by several names, viz., the River Plate, Buenos Aires, the United Provinces of South America, the United Provinces of the River Plate, the Argentine Confederation, the Argentine Republic, and its present official name, as given in the Constitution, the Argentine Nation. In the twenty years between 1810 and 1829 the country had eleven constitutions and other pacts designed to set up a stable system of government, and changed its name with most of these agreements. But Buenos Aires always has been Buenos Aires. For more than two hundred years Buenos Aires was the visible expression of everything Argentine. Even after the establishment of independence, foreign governments spoke of the "government of Buenos Aires," "the diplomatic agent of Buenos Aires," "the Congress of Buenos Aires," and even "the President of Buenos Aires." The city and Province of Buenos Aires outweighed all the rest of the country, and the entire country expressed itself through Buenos Aires even during those troublesome times when it was refusing to recognize Buenos Aires as the seat of centralized government. Political leaders who wanted to make themselves heard or obeyed had to establish themselves in Buenos Aires.

The great city of Buenos Aires stands proudly on the edge of the pampas; so close, in fact, that there are several places where departing trains and automobiles are on the pampas before they pass the city limits. Yet the life of Buenos Aires could hardly be more remote from the life of Argentina if it were on another continent. Buenos Aires turns its face to Europe—to Paris—and keeps its back to the interior, which supplies its strength and lifeblood. The people of Buenos Aires live the same sort of life that people live in New York, except that they live it more leisurely. They attend cocktail parties, play bridge, like the movies (which end at one a.m.) and go to bed late. And at the very door of the city are the boundless plains over which galloping horsemen still measure distances in leagues.

Buenos Aires is one of the world's largest, busiest, and most splendid cities. A census taken in October 1936, on the occasion of the four-hundredth anniversary of the first founding of the city, showed it to have a population of 2,388,646. It is the eleventh largest city in the world, the largest south of the Equator, and the third on the American continent, being surpassed only by New York and Chicago. It is the second largest Latin city, being exceeded only by Paris. The 1936 census included only those people who sleep in the city proper and omitted more than 1,000,000 others who work in the city but live in the suburbs. It is estimated that 4,000,000 people live in the Greater Buenos Aires area, or nearly one-third of the country's population. The rapid growth of Buenos Aires has been even more remarkable than that of the country at large. In 1880, three hundred years after its second founding, the city had only 300,000 inhabitants. Fifteen years later it had 663,000, and in 1900 it had 800,000. In the sixty years following 1880, the population doubled three times, and in 1941 it was estimated at 2,524,624.

Today there is nothing Spanish or "South American" about Buenos Aires except the language—no air of romance, no two-hour closing of shops and offices for the mid-day siesta, no carefully preserved relics of old colonial days. Buenos Aires has ruthlessly thrown off and destroyed everything that might remind it that there ever could have been a time when it was anything except the same big, sophisticated, tremendously noisy capital that it is today.

Although situated 172 miles from the sea, Buenos Aires is the second most important port in the Western World; only New York surpasses it. In normal times 9000 overseas vessels and 6000 river vessels enter the port every year and nearly 10,000,000 tons of freight pass through it. From the port radiate 20,000 miles of the country's 26,800 miles of railroad. The city has one of the busiest suburban train services in the world, 1800 trains arriving and departing daily at the 5 railroad stations. City transportation is provided by 5 subways, 86 street-car lines, and 119 bus lines. One-fourth of the 3,500,000 people who travel in the city every day are transported by small busses, called *colectivos*, which accommodate from 10 to 12 passengers and race through the streets like mad.

Buenos Aires is one of the most cosmopolitan of cities, since the wealthy Argentines draw on virtually every country in Asia and Europe, as well as on the United States, for their luxury goods, snobbishly looking down their noses at their own products. It also is one of the most beautiful cities in the world. Its 6 public gardens, 21 parks, and 130 plazas provide 3400 acres of trees, flowers, and open space, and cost 425,000,-000 pesos. Many of the principal streets and avenues are bordered with beautiful flowering trees, and in one four-year period in the late 1930's 90,000 trees were set out. The streets literally are jammed with 10,000 taxicabs and 27,000 private cars, largely because the taxi drivers cruise slowly along in quest of fares and block traffic, stubbornly refusing to accelerate their speed or to wait for passengers at parking stands.

Some of the city's 145 churches are very old, the one of San Ignacio de Loyola at the corner of Calles Alsina and Bolívar, for example, having been there since 1722. But the churches are the only ancient landmarks that have escaped the city's feverish growth and renovation. Modern office buildings have replaced everything else in the downtown district and only the Avenida de Mayo retains the architecture and atmosphere of the early years of the twentieth century. The finest embassy residence in the city is that of the United States and the finest office building is that of the First National Bank of Boston. The new diagonal Avenida Roque Saenz Peña, with its uniform skyline and uniform architecture, is destined to be a surpassingly beautiful thoroughfare when building is completed. Up-to-date, air-conditioned apartment houses are replacing the old residence buildings and radically altering the Argentine's mode of life. Most of the new office structures provide basement garages and there is a municipal underground garage providing free parking space for 2000 cars under the Avenida 9 de Julio, the world's widest avenue and the shortest.

Despite all this rapid growth and modernization, experienced travelers usually describe Buenos Aires as one of the saddest cities in the world, a criticism which always annoys Argentines intensely. The people sit around small tables on the sidewalks, hoping they look Parisian, but there is no gay laughter as there used to be in Paris. The coffee drinker in Buenos Aires almost invariably is engaged in a very solemn discussion, or a heated one, of some form of money-making, and the word "pesos" is the one that is most frequently caught in those small snatches of conversation that are overheard in the street. As for the sadly overrated night life, it would be difficult to imagine anything duller than an Argentine cabaret.

2. THE PEOPLE

THE contrast between the people of Buenos Aires and those of the interior is fully as striking as the contrast between the capital and the country. The people of Buenos Aires proudly call themselves *porteños*, or people of the port, to distinguish themselves from all other Argentines. The people of the interior just as proudly call themselves criollos, that they be not mistaken for the people of Buenos Aires. The porteños and the criollos are as different as though they were men of separate races, as, indeed, they are. As far back as the seventeenth century the people of Buenos Aires prided themselves that they were not like other men. They were of pure Spanish stock, proud and arrogant as only men of Castile and Aragon could be. They were not conquistadors, but merchants and lawyers and notaries, and they had gone to the New World to trade in the products of the land that was being opened by the adventurers they despised. They considered themselves infinitely superior to the new race of gauchos which was being born on the pampas, fathered by the conquistadors and mothered by the brown-skinned girls of the conquered Indian tribes. Their sense of superiority extended also to the criollo, who was a locally born Spaniard of pure-white stock.

By the time of the revolution against Spain in 1810, the two centuries of constant crossing of white blood with the mixed race in the interior had produced a new white race *sui generis,* the members of which also became known as criollos. As Dr. Juan José Guaresti, Jr., puts it in his *Economy and Finances of the Argentine Nation,* "The Spaniards united with the Indian women, giving rise to a new ethnical type—the mestizo. These mestizos were designated by the common name of criollos, a term which also was applied to the native sons of Europeans, to the sons of Europeans and mestizos, and to the sons of mestizos and mestizas. This criollo type, which was undoubtedly superior to the European, was the nerve, the brain, and the arm of the emancipation of the Americas. Also, he has been and still is the vital element of our democracy."

The Pampa Indians have long since been exterminated or pushed far back into Patagonia, and great tides of Spanish and Italian immigration have given the white man's blood a predominance in Argentina which it does not enjoy in any other South American country except Uruguay. But the people of Buenos Aires still are proud and stiff and arrogant. And they still live and wax wealthy by trading in the grains and meat,

13

the hides and wool produced by the criollos and the Spaniards and Italians of the interior. As for the criollo, it would be difficult to find in any land a more congenial, friendly, and hospitable person. His friendship is warm and genuine and he really likes people, though he still is inclined to be a bit suspicious of the porteño. The farther one goes from Buenos Aires into the interior, the more congenial and friendly the people become. It usually is the man of Buenos Aires, however, who is seen abroad and who has come to be considered the representative of his country, just as the city of Buenos Aires always has stood for Argentina.

Argentines, both men and women, are almost without exception handsome and well groomed. European experts have described the men as the best dressed in the world, and in the matter of feminine attire Buenos Aires is recognized universally as second only to Paris. Argentine women seem to be born with a knack for wearing clothes smartly. Argentine men are taller and bigger than other South Americans and there are more blonds, among both the men and the women, than in the other South American countries. One of the handsomest masculine types anywhere is the fine big Irish porteño, a mixture of Irish and Spanish blood. Many of them are in the carefully picked presidential guard of Mounted Grenadiers, one of the world's finest cavalry regiments.

The people of Buenos Aires are no longer predominantly Spanish. There is a strong strain of Italian and other European bloods in the Argentine city dwellers. Although foreign races are not assimilated as rapidly in Argentina as in the United States, there is gradually but surely being produced a distinct Argentine type, just as there is a distinct American type. This type already has evolved to a stage where the Argentine is more easily identifiable in a crowd than any other South American.

But what distinguishes Argentines from all other Latins is the seriousness with which they take their pleasures. The Argentine is so concerned with maintaining his dignity that he forgets to be gay. He has no sense of humor, never laughs at himself, and Heaven help the man who laughs at him! He dances the tango with a set face and an air of grim determination that is not seen in any other dance. The tango itself is the saddest and most forlorn music to be found anywhere, although its rhythm represents the slow, easy lope of the gaucho's horse and the pampa wind blowing past his ears. The lyrics monotonously concern themselves with abandoned love—unmarried love, of course—which gives the unimaginative song writers their opportunity to use their invariable rhyming

TYPICAL HUT OF COWBOYS ON THE PAMPAS

THE COLÓN THEATER CROWDED FOR A PIANO RECITAL
BY ALEXANDER BRAILOWSKY

A STREET IN JUJUY, NORTHERNMOST CITY OF ARGENTINA

MAR DEL PLATÁ, ARGENTINA'S ATLANTIC CITY

of the unrequited *pasión* with the broken *corazón*. Blind beggars sit on the sidewalks throughout Latin America, as far north as Mexico, wailing Argentine tangos to tear the heart out of the passer-by and a coin out of his pocket.

The tango offers a striking example of the Argentine's snobbish acceptance of anything that comes from abroad, especially from Europe, in preference to anything produced at home. When the twentieth century dawned, no one would have dared play a tango in an Argentine ballroom. It was considered a rather shameful inheritance from the city-despised gaucho and was danced only in brothels. But when the *nouveau riche* families began going to Paris to spend their money, their sons introduced the tango there and it immediately became popular. Women find it exciting. By becoming the rage in Paris, the tango had been refined and made perfectly proper for any young Argentine lady to dance in public, so it was imported back from Europe and immediately replaced the waltz, the polka, and the other old-fashioned dances of the nineteenth century.

Much as they would resent being told so, the Argentines in many ways are more like the people of the United States than is any other people. For one thing, they have developed to a higher degree than any of the other Latin Americans most of those traits which they so persistently criticize in North Americans. They are materialistic, imperialistic, hypocritical, overbearing, and insincere—the five major crimes they charge against the *Yanquis*. Like North Americans they are money-conscious and are forever talking about the price of things. Like North Americans they talk too loudly in public places, as though afraid they will not be seen unless heard. Like North Americans, the Argentines are intense individualists, full of zest and spontaneity, and ready to fight at the least slight, real or imaginary, and they stubbornly refuse to be disciplined. Argentines bump into one another at every few steps on the sidewalks rather than abide by any rule to keep to the right or the left. They crowd railroad and theater ticket offices and all other public offices, barging into one another like sheep and struggling to get ahead of someone else. Forming a line would be much more comfortable and quicker, of course, but it also would imply a recognition of the right of someone else to be ahead just because he got there first, a right which no self-respecting Argentine could possibly recognize. Toward those he knows, an Argentine can be a most courteous and charming person, but he seems to lack any sense of public politeness toward those he does not know. Joaquín V. González, notable

Argentine educator and publicist and founder of the University of La Plata, in his *Patria y Democracia* (*Homeland and Democracy*), says that hatred is a congenital disease of the Argentine people and that the hatred in the Argentine character hinders energy and nullifies constructive effort.

It should be easier for Americans to understand the Argentines than any other of the South American peoples, because the attitude of the Argentines toward themselves, their country, and international affairs is almost identical with the attitude of Americans toward themselves and their country. Or is it this very similarity of ideas and goals that causes the conflict? Argentines are impelled by the same patriotic motives that inspire North Americans—an intense pride in their country and a strong faith in its national destiny. The latter is accompanied by a rather haughty but perfectly natural desire for leadership, especially in Latin American affairs.

The late Marcelo T. de Alvear, former President of Argentina, in a newspaper interview a year after the outbreak of war in Europe, described the character of his countrymen as follows:

The Argentines refuse to accept any truth which makes them inferior to anyone else. Theirs is the greatest city in the world, their frontier mountains are the highest and their pampas the widest; theirs the most beautiful lakes, the best cattle, the richest vineyards, and the loveliest women. They accept no qualifications, nor will they accept the fact that there might be some other country which surpasses them in anything. . . . Perhaps it is this overwhelming pride of the Argentines that leads them to believe that they can live aloof from any interdependence of nations; that they are self-sufficient without possessing even the elementary industries; and that they need have no fear of whatever changes may come.

Argentines like to think of themselves as idealists, while looking upon the Yankees as materialists. This is the result of the vivid Latin imagination, since the Argentines are the most materialistic of all South Americans. After the revolution against Spain in 1810, Bolivia, Paraguay, and Uruguay refused to remain in the Argentine Federation. Although the Argentines have convinced themselves that they magnanimously consented to the separation, the truth is that all three republics won their independence from Argentina on the battlefield. Like North Americans, the Argentines love slogans and have coined some very effective ones. Among the most popular is "America for humanity," as opposed to Monroe's "America for Americans." "Victory confers no rights" is another one. Having loyally practiced their own preaching on this latter

By 1942 this social conflict was making itself felt most strongly in the revolt of women against their Moorish seclusion. With their growing sense of liberty they also were demanding legal and economic emancipation and the right to think for themselves. Highly significant of this latter demand was the fact that they were reading much more than ever before. Also, they were flaunting their revolt against the old customs in the only way that is open to women in that difficult period of "kicking over the traces" before they have won their social freedom: they were priding themselves on doing all the things that were considered "shocking" by the old patriarchal tradition. Before the First World War married women seldom danced, because it meant being in the arms of a man other than their husband. By the latter 1930's they not only were dancing, but doing it in a manner to set wagging the tongues of scandalized elders. Also, they were drinking and smoking in public places, something undreamed of in the early 1920's. Although they did not quite dare yet to go about alone, they gathered in groups of five or six to smoke and drink cocktails in places where a few years earlier the only women to be seen were the mistresses of their fathers and brothers.

By 1942, Argentine women were at an extremely interesting crossroads. Impelled by fashion and the American movies to be more daring and audacious, they constantly were being pulled back toward conservatism by the influences of the Church and the home. Falling back on fashion for their excuse and ignoring the admonitions of their confessors, they were displaying the most daring bathing suits they could find. But they never wandered out of range of *mamá's* protective watchfulness. At night they frequented the *boîtes* and gambling casinos, trying so very hard to ape the demimondaines of the picture shows. But two or three brothers or cousins always were close enough to protect them from anyone who might be so silly as to accept them for what they were trying to appear. All this, of course, evoked the usual masculine protest. Indignant writers, lecturers, and radio commentators in their horrified fifties waxed furious in their campaign of support for those two old fetishes of the conservative male—the virtue of womanhood and the sanctity of the home. The growth of nationalism and reaction made the political outlook of Argentina in 1942 one of confusion and uncertainty. But there was little doubt that the social revolt of women would go along serenely on its way, completely heedless of protesting males, until the women got what they wanted, as they always do. And when they got it, it also is certain that their virtue, their motherhood, and the sanctity of their homes would be on a much more sounder basis than it was before the 1930's.

The emancipation of women in Argentina, although not likely to reach the extremes that it has reached in England and the United States, certainly will free them from the rigid old customs of sixteenth-century Spain which hitherto have imprisoned them. Eventually a sane balance between the two extremes undoubtedly will be achieved. Argentine women have shown little interest in suffrage and have not responded to the efforts of those organizations which are trying to get the vote for them. But while ignoring politics they have been keenly awake to their civil and social status, and in 1938 prevented a man-made Congress from passing a law which would have returned them to the days when they were the economic slaves of their husbands by depriving them of any legal status before the courts, prohibiting their working without the consent of their husbands, and requiring them to turn all their own funds over to their husbands to be applied to household expenses. Young women are engaging more and more in such outdoor sports as golf, tennis, riding, and swimming, and this naturally tends toward social freedom. The dominance and the unquestioned authority of the men of the family are reluctantly following the gaucho into oblivion.

Newcomers in Buenos Aires always are impressed by the large number of men and women wearing black. This is the result of the strict etiquette of mourning. A widow or a daughter must wear unrelieved black for two years, including every piece of underwear. Mourning is also worn for uncles, aunts, and second cousins, and as the families usually are large it is not uncommon for people to wear mourning for ten or fifteen years without interruption. Often, when the interruption does come, another death of a distant relative causes a return to black. This social situation has been very ably handled in the Colon Theater, where eight heavily grilled boxes permit people who are in mourning to enjoy the opera and see what dresses their friends and enemies are wearing without being seen themselves. Access to these mourning boxes is from a dark street on the other side of the theater from the gaily lighted entrance. The strictness of mourning etiquette is another of the old traditions that are destined to be broken down as women acquire more freedom.

Horse-racing is the national sport and soccer football the national game. More than 15,000,000 pesos are bet on horse-races every month at the dozen or more tracks in all parts of the country. An average of 1,500,000 pesos is bet every Sunday and every holiday at the famous

Palermo track in Buenos Aires. Four million pesos are played every month in the national lottery, in addition to which there are half a dozen provincial lotteries to satisfy the Argentine's gambling instinct. This urge to gamble is carefully catered to in a great variety of ways from early childhood. The schoolboy, instead of spending his penny and being handed a piece of candy, is given a chance on a wheel of fortune which always is at the school gate. Professional football is the most popular spectacle, with an average attendance of 8600 at the 273 games that are played each year. In addition to the organized games, every Saturday, Sunday, and holiday finds thousands of men and boys playing football on vacant lots, just as American men and boys play baseball.

Argentines pretend to be great lovers of music, but they arrive late and chatter all through the performance. At concerts and recitals the most beautiful passages of violin or voice solos are ruined by people in the audience hissing at their neighbors to cease whispering. The opera is well attended because it is a place to be seen and to see others, just like the afternoon stroll in the Calle Florida. But Argentines are very poor patrons of concerts and recitals, and the audiences are made up largely of foreign residents. Movies are extremely popular, especially between six and eight. "Nice" girls can attend the shows at these hours without chaperons, but they must go in groups of three or four.

The most sought-after privilege an Argentine can acquire is some form of *fuero*, the old Spanish privilege which exempted its holder from complying with the law. Strangely enough, this is the first privilege granted to all lawmakers, from Congressmen down to city councilmen, with the result that as soon as a man attains a position where he is entrusted with making or enforcing the law, he is the first to break it. A young Argentine will work for weeks pulling the necessary political strings to get one of the white automobile license plates which are issued to Congressmen, councilmen, and high city officials so they may ignore the traffic laws. Lawmakers also are issued a special gold watch-fob which protects them from arrest no matter what they do. The fuero is so deeply imbedded in Argentine psychology that as soon as a man becomes an officer of a club he permits the members of his family to ignore the club rules. This tends to create that general disrespect for law and rules which is so apparent everywhere. Whenever the police of Buenos Aires or other Argentine cities try to enforce some new law or regulation there are so many people intent on exercising the exemption privilege of their fuero that everyone else refuses to obey.

This is the main reason that Buenos Aires has what undoubtedly is one of the most disorganized traffic systems in the world.

Several questions present themselves immediately to anyone who visits Argentina or attempts to study anything about it. How is it that Argentina has a white European population instead of the mestizo race that dominates all the rest of the South American continent? What was it that enabled Argentina to obtain the leading economic position in South America? What is behind Argentina's isolationist policy? Is Argentina Fascist? What is the future of democracy in Argentina? Where is Argentina going? The succeeding chapters attempt to answer these and other questions.

3. THE GREAT SILVER LEGEND

THE Spanish Conquest invaded the South American continent from two opposite directions—through Peru and the River Plate. One of these invasions was seeking gold; the other, silver. One was a dramatic and glorious success. It conquered, subjugated, and eventually destroyed a great, prosperous, and highly civilized Indian nation; sent shipload after shipload of precious metal home to the Spanish Crown; and established a vast colonial empire that was to stand for three hundred years and then in its fall set up nine of the ten South American republics we know today.

The other was a tragic and heart-breaking failure. Ferocious savages, wild jaguars, starvation, thirst, and, worst of all, hard cruel disillusion-ment killed the spirit of the River Plate conquistadors one by one, long before their tired and skinny bodies were destroyed. Their deaths were the most inglorious and miserable of all the many deaths of the Conquest: death from hunger, from vile diseases, from Indian bludgeons. Through the many years of failure and defeat, some 1500 men left their bones to bleach in the hot sun along the 1300 lonely miles that stretched between the River Plate and Potosí, the "silver-sprouting mountain" which was their goal and their inspiration.

No Prescott has yet written the story of the conquest of the River Plate, although the men who attempted it and died in the attempt per-formed, time and again, seemingly impossible feats of bravery, courage, and perseverance such as never were required of Pizarro's men. But they failed, completely and ignominiously, and when Buenos Aires eventually was founded on the west bank of the River Plate, its founder was a man who had followed Pizarro into Peru and then crossed the continent.

In no other section of the Americas did the conquistadors meet with such hostility as in the region drained by the River Plate, that fabulous stream which led to a mountain of silver and a lake of gold—Potosí and Titicaca. The Indians defended their lands with savage and brutal tenac-ity. Had the Inca Atahualpa found himself at the head of warriors such as these, Pizarro would have met a far different fate.

But even more deadly than the Indians was the hostility of the terri-tory itself. To reach Potosí and the other rich silver deposits in the cen-ter of the continent, the conquistadors had to cross the deadly Chaco Boreal, which the Paraguayan historian Manuel Dominguez has so aptly described as a giant dragon sprawled out to the west of the Paraguay

23

River to guard the silver deposits. This dragon consumed the silver hunters by the hundreds. It was not that the Chaco Boreal is a South American Sahara. True, there are times when there is no water to drink; but at
other times there is too much water and the Chaco is flooded. The dead-
liness of the Chaco Boreal lay then, as today, in the absence of navigable
streams. It is 400 miles in a straight east-west line across the Chaco from
the River Paraguay to the Andean foothills that lead up to the Bolivian
plateau on which the mountains of silver are situated. That distance had
to be covered on foot or horseback. Only a numbered few of the conquistadors ever got across. Four hundred years later, the dragon has not
yet been conquered.

But before the conquistadors could begin their fatal battle with the
dragon they had to fight the Indians. The plains of the River Plate and
its tributaries were peopled by two races of brave and savage Indians—
the Pampas and the Guaranis. Later it was to become a legend of the
Conquest that the South American Indians fled in terror at the sight of a
soldier on horseback or at the explosion of a gun. But that legend rose
far from the shores of the River Plate. The Indians of the pampas feared
neither horsemen nor guns, and their skillful use of the *boleador* forced
the Spanish invaders to abandon their horses and fight on foot.

The Pampas and the Guaranis were not united in great nations as were
the Incas. Consequently, they had not been suppressed and domesticated
like the subjects of the God-dictator at Cuzco. Although Pizarro found
his path blocked by great hordes of Indian warriors, they were docile
Indians who already had been conquered and in whom all individual initiative had been crushed. They were servilely obedient to their masters
and when those masters were killed or imprisoned, the bewildered subjects dispersed and abandoned to the invaders their homes, their temples,
and their wealth. The Spanish conquest of their lands meant simply a
change of masters—a change for the worse, it might be added, because
never since, not even under the South American governments of today,
have they regained anything approaching the standard of life which they
enjoyed under the Inca.

The conquistadors of the River Plate, on the other hand, found themselves opposed and harassed, day and night, by strong, wild, and determined Indians who were banded together in smaller armies but impelled by savage individual initiative. They were not citizens of a great
nation; they were wild men of the plains and swamps. But they were
free and determined to remain so. Their wild instinct for liberty was
later to be sown in the blood of the half-breed gaucho race which their

women mothered, and this seed was so strong that an almost savage love of liberty became the dominant trait of the gauchos of the River Plate. Three hundred years later, when the locally born white criollos demanded local self-government, it was the gauchos of the interior who formed the mounted militias which finally overthrew the great colonial empire that had spread over the continent from Peru.

The Guaranis were armed with spears and bows and arrows similar to those of the North American Indians. The Pampas were armed with spears and boleadors—two or three smooth, round stones tied to the ends of long leather thongs, the other ends of which were tied together. The Indian held one stone and swung the other two in a circle at arm's length above his head until they were spinning at high speed. Then he let go of the stone in his hand and the boleador whizzed through the air and wrapped itself tightly around the legs of the quarry. The Pampas had long used these boleadors in hunting the swift-footed guanaco and the South American ostrich. They used them with equal skill against the horses of the Spaniards. Later the boleador was to become the characteristic tool and weapon of the gauchos who roamed the plains of Argentina and Uruguay.

The Pampa Indians saw their first white men in 1516 and immediately enticed them ashore and killed them. In January of that year, Juan Diaz de Solís sailed slowly down the sunny east coast of South America, examining every inlet as he passed. He had succeeded Amerigo Vespucci as pilot-general to the Spanish king and was under commission to find a passage to the ocean that Balboa had discovered three years before. Solís arrived at what appeared to be the southern end of the continent. Rounding a cape which he christened Santa María, he headed west into what seemed to be a sea of fresh water, which he therefore named Mar Dulce.

After the extraordinary success of the Turkish armies in Europe had closed the trade routes between Europe and Asia, the only outlet lay to the west, and the two great maritime powers, Spain and Portugal, had set out to find new routes in that direction. The unknown land unexpectedly discovered by Columbus was a barrier and a nuisance. Its seemingly interminable shores extended clear across the globe, almost from Pole to Pole, cutting across the new routes and blocking them before they reached any profitable destination. The world's most daring navigators were trying to find a way through or around this barrier. The belief was growing that if they could get beyond the continent they could reach Cathay, India, and the famed Spice Islands. Solís thought he had found the way when he turned westward into the 100-mile-wide mouth of the River Plate. Keeping close to the shore of what now is Uruguay, he began to cross the Sweet-Water Sea. But the shallows soon convinced him that he was in a river, even though he could not see the opposite shore. Disappointed at his failure to find the passage he was seeking, he transshipped to his smallest vessel and started westward to explore the river, still hugging the shore. More than 100 miles upstream he found an island and landed on it to bury his chief navigator, Martín Garcia, whose name he gave to the island. Noting along the banks many Indians who appeared to be making friendly and festive gestures, Solís went ashore with six of his companions. As they walked toward the Indians with amicable overtures, they were greeted with a shower of arrows which killed them all. Whether or not the Indians roasted and ate Solís and his companions is one of those finer points over which historians have been disputing ever since.

The remaining members of Solís's expedition decided that they had had enough and set out for home. One vessel was shipwrecked off the southern coast of Brazil in one of those storms for which Santa Catharina has become famous. Eleven of the survivors reached Santa Catharina Island, and it was from them that Europe first heard of the wealth of the Incas.

The Portuguese, who had explored the shores of Brazil in 1500, always have maintained that the River Plate was discovered in 1502 by a Portuguese, Nuño Manuel. Some historians think that Solís got as far south as the River Plate in his previous voyage of 1508. At any rate, he now is generally credited with being the discoverer of the River Plate, and the history of South America can be said to begin with his christening of the Mar Dulce in 1516.

The Guaranis of southern Brazil and Paraguay, while brave warriors, were less ferocious and more approachable than those who had come in contact with the wild Pampas of the River Plate. They taught their language to the shipwrecked men on Santa Catharina Island and told them wonderful tales of a rich Indian empire far to the west. These Caracaras, said the Guaranis, were ruled over by a white king—the Rey Blanco—and their wealth in gold and silver was unlimited. This Rey Blanco was the Inca. In his empire, according to the Guaranis, there was a mountain which sprouted solid silver. It was called Potosí and was situated near a river, the Pilcomayo, which flowed into the Paraná. Close to Potosí was Porco, which contained the most celebrated mines of the whole Inca empire and which had provided most of the silver for the

Temple of the Sun at Cuzco. These two mountains of silver were situated in the territory of the Caracaras, in Charcas, the smallest of the Inca provinces and the last one to be subjugated by the sixth Inca. The Guaranis had been trading with the Caracaras for many years. They sent their old men, their women, and their children on frequent trading expeditions to Potosí and Porco to bring back the silver plaques and diadems which the Guaranis wore when at war. It was not until the white men came that the Indians learned that silver and gold are worth fighting and dying for.

Among the shipwreck survivors at Santa Catharina was a Portuguese, Alejo Garcia, who had been with Solís in the Mar Dulce. Garcia was extraordinarily audacious even for his day and among men whose daring led them anywhere against any odds. After listening for eight years to these tales of the wealth of the Rey Blanco and his people, and after seeing and handling the silver ornaments brought back by the Guaranis, Alejo Garcia finally persuaded four of his companions to accompany him to the empire of the Rey Blanco. They set out on foot early in 1524 to cross the unknown continent in one of the boldest adventures in all American history.

Garcia and his four companions walked across Brazil and reached the Paraguay River at the point where Asunción was founded thirteen years later. Garcia had learned the language of the Guaranis so well, and spoke it with such fluency and fervor in Paraguay, that he persuaded the entire male population of a Guarani settlement—2000 men—to join his expedition against the Caracaras. At the head of this army, Garcia and his companions ascended the Paraguay River 400 miles to Coimbá and then struck out westward across the Chaco Boreal into what now is Bolivia. Finally, "after many days' march," they penetrated the Andean ranges as far as Tarabuco, near Sucre, "killing and robbing," according to the chroniclers of the expedition.

So numerous were the Indians of Charcas who took up arms and confronted Garcia that he and his army retreated. They escaped injury and returned to Paraguay with large quantities of booty, leaving the whole Inca province of Charcas under arms and in terror at this raid from the east. Garcia had walked 3000 miles and had invaded the Inca empire eight years before the arrival of Pizarro. He had seen and touched the brilliant dream that had enticed him across the continent. He had proved the Silver Legend. There really was a Rey Blanco. There really was a Mountain of Silver. Two of them. The unbelievable wealth of the Caracaras was real.

Garcia decided to remain in Paraguay to organize another expedition against the Incas. He sent twelve Indian servants to Santa Catharina with two or three arrobas (50–75 pounds) of silver and with letters to his companions Melchor Ramirez and Enrique Montes, urging them to join him in Paraguay. Ramirez and Montes, after listening to the Indians' stories of the dangers and hardships that Garcia had suffered, decided to remain where they were. Later, however, they both succumbed to the temptation of the Silver Legend. Montes accompanied a Portuguese, Martim Affonso de Souza, across the continent to the Paraguay River, following Alejo Garcia's route, and then joined the expedition which Diego Garcia took to the River Plate while Cabot was there. Ramirez went to the River Plate as notary in Pedro de Mendoza's famous expedition.

Toward the end of 1525 the Guaranis killed and ate Garcia and his companions. But the story he had sent back to Santa Catharina changed the course of history. The exciting Silver Legend spread rapidly and reached Europe about the same time that news of the Inca's gold reached Spain from Panama. The two great streams of conquistadors began moving toward South America. Navigators and adventurers were interested no longer in finding a short route to the Orient. For the next generation men lived, fought, and died shouting: "On to the Mountain of Silver! On to the land of the Caracaras!" The name of Silver was used for christening everything on the eastern side of South America. Santa Catharina Island became the Island of Silver. Port Vera on the Brazilian coast in front of Santa Catharina became the Port of Potosí. There were at least five Rivers of Silver—the Pilcomayo, the Paraná, the Guapay, the Paraguay, and the Mar Dulce, or Solís's River. The men of eastern South America even called the Andes the Silver Range. All because from Santa Catharina or Solís's River or the Paraguay or the Pilcomayo it was possible to reach Potosí, Porco, and the Silver Range.

Sebastian Cabot, who had succeeded Solís as pilot-general, heard this story of silver and of Garcia's great adventure when he reached Pernambuco in June 1526 on a voyage which he had contracted to take to the Spice Islands. Magellan had proved his theory that he could reach the Spice Islands by sailing round the southern end of the American continent. He had been killed on the way, but the survivors of his expedition finally landed in the Moluccas in November 1521. Cabot had left the service of Henry VII of England after the failure of his voyage to Hudson's Bay, and Charles V had invited him to Spain to replace Magellan in colonizing the Spice Islands. He had sailed with four vessels and 200 men to follow Magellan's route around South America, his expedition having been financed by the merchants of Seville.

The story of silver which Cabot heard at Pernambuco decided him to change his destination. The silver of the Incas was much closer than the Spice Islands, and the promise of great wealth was brighter, so Cabot decided to take his four ships to Solís's River and work his way up its tributaries until he found the route to the Silver Country of the Rey Blanco. Cabot thus became the first conquistador of the River Plate region. He heard the silver story again and in more detail direct from the lips of Ramirez and Montes when he stopped at the Island of Silver in October. He christened the island after his wife Catharine, took on board three young Indians to act as interpreters, and sailed for the River Plate.

Magellan's men had christened the Mar Dulce the River of Solís when they visited it in 1519 and made certain that it was a river and not a sea. But it was becoming known, by common consent, as the Rio de la Plata, because it was known to lead up the Paraná and the Pilcomayo to Potosí, and also because the Portuguese insisted on calling it the Rio da Prata rather than recognize it as the River of Solís. Cabot was the first European to explore the River Plate and its tributaries and the first to establish a settlement in what is now Argentina, which also took its Latinized name from the Silver Legend.

River Plate, of course, is not the proper translation of Rio de la Plata. It is another of those many meaningless phrases which the British have scattered around the world in their attempts to find English equivalents for the names associated with places where they have settled. A new arrival reading the gossip columns of the English papers of Buenos Aires which list the people who have come into town from "the camp" gets the impression that there is a gigantic English camp somewhere. But "the camp" is merely the British translation of the Spanish *el campo*, meaning the country or interior. "Plate" was the nearest English equivalent for *Plata*, so the Silver River became to them the River Plate. And as such it has become accepted in shipping circles throughout the world.

When Cabot reached the mouth of the River Plate, he left two of his vessels there and sailed up the Paraná with the other two as far as the confluence of the Carcarañá, about 30 miles above the present city of Rosario. There, on May 27, 1527, he established Fort Sancti Spiritus to serve as a supply depot, shelter port, and base for his explorations farther up the river. Sancti Spiritus thus became the first European settlement in what is now Argentina. The Indians at Sancti Spiritus repeated the silver story and told Cabot that the tribes to the north in the vicinity of the Pilcomayo and the Paraguay traded with the people of the Rey Blanco.

Cabot ascended the Paraguay to a point well above the present site of Asunción and then returned downstream to explore the Pilcomayo and Bermejo rivers because they came from the west. Here Cabot encountered the Chaco Boreal. Both the Pilcomayo and the Bermejo proved to be unnavigable, and exploring parties on shore were ambushed by the Indians. So Cabot started down the Paraná to his two supply ships to see if the Spanish king had sent the reinforcements he had requested. On the way, he learned of the destruction of Sancti Spiritus and the slaughter of all the men he had left there. When he reached the two ships in the mouth of the River Plate there was no news of help from Spain.

Cabot had been seeking Potosí for more than three years; he had lost most of his men, and had neither men nor resources with which to continue his search for the route to the Inca silver. He set sail for Spain and arrived there on July 22, 1530, with only 20 of the 200 men who had left Spain with him. Bankrupt and broken in spirit, he had one ounce of silver to prove his story. He also had the three young Indian interpreters who were to accompany him back to South America on his next expedition.

But Cabot never returned to the River Plate. When he reached Spain, his patron Charles V was in Italy, where one of his generals had sacked Rome and imprisoned the Pope. Furthermore, the king had delegated all matters regarding South American explorations to the Supreme Council of the Indies, which had been set up shortly before Cabot's departure from Spain. This council showed little enthusiasm for Cabot's plans to take another expedition to the River Plate.

Cabot became involved in numerous lawsuits instituted by his creditors and his rivals. While he was fretting under all his troubles, Henry VIII died and was succeeded by Edward VI. Cabot returned to the service of England. But his reports, and the others which reached Spain from Santa Catharina Island and elsewhere, led to the outfitting of the magnificent expedition which Pedro de Mendoza took to the River Plate five years later. Three years after Cabot reached Spain, Francisco Pizarro discovered and conquered the Inca empire. Charles V returned from Rome about the time that Hernando Pizarro arrived from Panama with a cargo of Peruvian gold and silver. Charles sent Mendoza to the River Plate with instructions to invade the Inca domain from the east. While Mendoza's expedition was a failure as far as finding wealth was concerned, Pizarro continued to send gold home to the Crown. The great Silver Legend was forgotten in the gold fever which swept over all Spain, and Peru replaced the River Plate as the goal of Spanish adventure.

But the silver mirage which had enticed so many men to their death gave its name to the river, to all the country drained by the river, and to the people who inherited that country. Among the many places that had been named for silver was the city of La Plata, situated in the very heart of the Silver Range itself. La Plata eventually became known as Chuquisaca and finally as Sucre, the official capital of Bolivia. But while it was still La Plata it became the episcopal see and the seat of the royal *audiencia*, or tribunal, whose jurisdiction extended clear to the River Plate.

In the Latin, as used by the chroniclers of the Church and the audiencia, the adjective *argentinus* was applied to the city of La Plata, to its citizens and its institutions. The Rio de la Plata was Fluvius Argentinus. In the late 1570's, one Martín del Barco Centenera went out to South America and spent twenty-five years in Peru, Upper Peru (now Bolivia), Paraguay, and the River Plate country. He became well acquainted with the whole tragedy of the Silver Legend and undertook to write an epic poem of the conquest of the River Plate, obviously inspired by Ercilla's famous poem of the Chilean conquest, *La Araucana*, the first part of which had been published in 1569.

Barco Centenera transferred to the Rio de la Plata the use of the words *argentinus*, *argentino*, and *Argentina* that had been applied to the city of La Plata. In 1602, several years after he returned to the Peninsula, his poem was published in Lisbon under the title *La Argentina and the Conquest of the River Plate*. It was an ambitious work of ten thousand hendecasyllable verses, divided into twenty-eight cantos. In 1602 the word *Argentina* was merely the name of a poem, of which only the name remains today. But in the meantime the Latin chroniclers at La Plata and later the Jesuit fathers and other Church scribes in Paraguay continued to use the term Fluvius Argentinus when referring to the Rio de la Plata, and by the middle of the seventeenth century Argentinus, Argentino, and Argentina were the accepted Latin names for the country and the people as well as the river in the River Plate zone, which at that time included the land drained by the Paraná and Paraguay rivers, since these were considered part of the Rio de la Plata because they were believed to lead to the silver of the Rey Blanco.

The name Argentina was not officially adopted as the name of the country, however, until 1860, as related in the chapter entitled "Federation."

4. ARGENTINA'S TRAGIC BEGINNING

THE expedition which Don Pedro de Mendoza took to the River
Plate in 1535 and which led eventually to the founding of Buenos
Aires and Asunción was the largest and most elaborate of all the
armadas that had left Spain for the New World. Its preparation had been
begun in secret by the Crown in 1532 before receipt of the news of Pizarro's great achievement, and its principal objective was to discover
and take possession of the silver mines of the Inca before the Portuguese
got there. The Spanish spies and diplomatic agents had kept the Crown
informed constantly of Portugal's two major intentions for beating the
Spaniards in the race to the empire of the Rey Blanco. One was to occupy
the entire coast southward from Rio de Janeiro and to establish ownership over the River Plate, which was considered to be the certain route
to Potosí and which the Portuguese claimed by right of its discovery
by Nuño Manuel. The other intention was to reach the silver mines and
the lands of the Inca by penetrating the continent from the Atlantic
coast. Portugal was tempting adventurers to move overland toward the
rich provinces of the Rey Blanco by granting them strips of land 150
miles wide on the coast and without any western limit. Spain was looking for governors capable of heading off these advances of the Portuguese.

Leadership of the River Plate armada had been offered to two or three
other noblemen before it was accepted by Mendoza. The capitulations
of Miguel de Herrera, the first to whom the command was offered, authorized him to proceed to the River Plate and ascend it until he discovered the gold and silver mines. He was granted governorship over
an area 600 miles long and 450 miles wide, with the provision that if he
found that the mines were not situated within this grant he was to move
northward until he found them and then establish his colony around
them in such a way as to shut them off from invasion by the Portuguese.

Mendoza finally accepted the command of the great expedition to the
River Plate under a land grant much more extensive than that offered
to Herrera. By this time it was known in Spain that there was no treas-
ure in the River Plate country—only savage Indians and hunger. The
great problem was to reach the rich domains of the Rey Blanco in the
center of the continent. Mendoza signed his capitulations with the king
in 1534. By the terms of this agreement he was appointed *adelantado* in

return for paying all the expenses of the venture. As adelantado he was governor and captain-general, with supreme military and civil authority over the members of the expedition and over all the Indians of the territory he conquered. One-fifth of all revenue was to go to the Crown, and another fifth to the royal treasury for the expenses of the court. The capitulations also provided that Mendoza was to open roads to Peru to join up with the frontiers of the discoveries of Pizarro and Almagro and so unite the lands washed by the Atlantic and the Pacific. He was to take with him breeding animals, seeds, tools, and equipment, eight Franciscan monks, and one or more physicians, surgeons, and druggists, with everything necessary for their professions. He was to establish at least three settlements and three *ayuntamientos*, or town councils, between the River Plate and the limits of his concession, with nine *regidores* in each, he to have the rank and eminence of chief *alcalde* in each settlement in addition to his rank as supreme military chief. If some rich empire was invaded, half of everything that belonged to the conquered prince was to go to the Crown, the other half to be distributed among the conquerors. This shows that Mendoza intended to occupy some part of the Inca empire, since that was the only region where a wealthy ruler was to be found.

The fifth paragraph of the capitulations read: "You are to pay all expenses, without charging anything against the Crown, since that is why you are named adelantado; that is, lord of all the lands and riches conquered by you in the very ample territory under your government, and which will be donated in perpetuity to you and your descendants, successors, or delegates named by you in case that after three years you desire to retire and live at court."

After signing the agreement with Charles V, Mendoza was taken suddenly ill and delayed his departure for a whole year. He finally sailed from Sanlúcar on August 24, 1535, with eight vessels and 800 men. The expedition had become so famous, largely because of Mendoza's personal fame, that it was joined at Teneriffe by three vessels with 150 Germans and 300 Spaniards from the Canary Islands, under the command of Miguel Lopez Gallego, conqueror of Teneriffe. Mendoza thus had eleven ships and 1250 men under his command when he set his course for America.

The leaders of the expedition were the most illustrious men who had yet crossed the Atlantic. Mendoza was renowned throughout Spain for his military achievements, his spirit of adventure, and his great wealth. He was one of the leading nobles of the Spanish court, a knight of the

Military Order of Santiago, and a member of the personal household
of Charles V. He belonged to a distinguished family, had commanded
troops in the sack of Rome, and had profited greatly thereby. Thirty-
two persons of noble blood joined his adventure, including several ladies
of the court who refused to remain behind when their husbands sailed.
Among Mendoza's lieutenants were his brilliant master-at-arms Juan
de Osorio, who also had won fame in the recent campaign in Italy, Juan
de Ayolas, Domingo Martínez de Irala, Diego de Abreu, Felipe de Cá-
ceres, Juan de Salazar de Espinosa, Gonzalo Mendoza, and Diego de
Mendoza, brother of Pedro and admiral of the expedition.

The armada reached Rio de Janeiro in November, by which time Mendoza's health was so bad that he ordered a landing for a rest on one of the
white, sunny beaches. They remained there for fourteen days and were
overtaken by the tragedy which destroyed the morale of the whole expedition and contributed largely to its failure. Mendoza's illness was so
grave that he had been forced to delegate a great deal of authority to
Osorio. The master-at-arms was one of the best-liked men in the expedition, but he was conceited and talked rashly about himself and what
he intended to do. His authority, which increased with Mendoza's illness, aroused the jealousy of other lieutenants, particularly Ayolas, and
they filled Mendoza's ears with stories of Osorio's boast to take the command away from the adelantado as soon as they disembarked at the
River Plate. Mendoza appears to have been blood-thirsty, ill-tempered,
and vindictive even when in good health; and his illness probably aggravated this side of his character. Without giving Osorio a hearing or
even letting him know that charges had been made against him, Mendoza
sentenced him to be executed and Ayolas stabbed him to death on the
beach in full view of many witnesses.

When the expedition resumed its course for the River Plate, instead
of being urged on and inspired by the lively expectation of great adventure, it moved with heavy spirit and ruined morale. Osorio had been
very popular, not only among the noblemen of his own rank but also
among the common soldiers, most of whom he had placed under contract in person as Mendoza's agent. Depressed and bewildered by Osorio's assassination, the expedition wasted two months on the eastern side
of the river—two months of inactivity and indecision that consumed
the food supplies. It was not until there was a threat of mass desertion
back to Brazil that Mendoza, sick in spirit and in body, finally ordered
the ships moved over to the western shore. This move prevented the

desertion but plunged the expedition into its terrible disaster. As Friar Luis Miranda wrote, "There the armada was buried."

The eastern coast of the River Plate offered far better conditions for a settlement than the western. The coast was high and rocky, the river was much deeper, and there were many bays and inlets which would have made good ports. The western coast was low and swampy and the great plains of the pampas dipped very gradually into the water, with many sandbanks and much shallow water. But a settlement on the eastern bank would be open to a surprise attack by the Portuguese. Furthermore, there seems to be no evidence that Mendoza had any intention of establishing a permanent settlement where Buenos Aires now stands; his goal was farther up the river. But with supplies running low and his company demoralized, it was imperative to get the men onto land and put them to work.

Argentine historians are disagreed over the exact date and the exact site of Mendoza's settlement, but it appears to have been early in February 1536 and probably at the point where the tiny Riachuelo flows into the Plate, in what now is the Boca district of Buenos Aires. Mendoza christened the little settlement Puerto de Santa María de los Buenos Aires, in honor of Our Lady of Fair Winds, the patron saint of sailors. She stood over the altar of a little church on the island of Sardinia, which at that time belonged to the Crown of Castile, and her image was on the compass box of all Spanish and Portuguese vessels. But in the old Spanish of these days, and especially among navigators, Buenos Aires meant fair winds, not good airs. So the name was given to the settlement, not in honor of its bad climate, but in homage to the patron saint who had blessed the expedition with the fair winds that had carried it safely across the ocean.

The Indians appear to have been fairly friendly at first. Ulrich Schmidel, a German member of the expedition who has left the most detailed chronicle of what happened, says they brought fish and meat (probably guanaco) to the Spaniards in the early days of the settlement. What happened to offend the Indians is not clear, but the brutal adventurers no doubt wanted to consider them as slaves. When one day they failed to arrive, Mendoza sent three mounted men to the Indian camp to demand food. The emissaries were treated badly and obliged to return without the supplies they sought. Mendoza then sent 30 horsemen and 300 foot soldiers with orders to kill or capture all the Indians and take possession of their encampment. The Spaniards found 4000 Indians awaiting them. The battle, which took place on Corpus Christi Day, gave the Spaniards their first experience with the boleadors. Their horses were thrown and the riders killed. Schmidel says that all the cavalry would have been killed had not the infantry arrived and put the Indians to flight. Among the 30 Spaniards who were killed were Mendoza's brother Diego and three of his nephews. The Spaniards remained in the Indian camp for three days, collecting all the skins, furs, and food, and then destroyed it.

The adelantado put his men to work building a fort and stockade against an attack by the Indians. Food became so scarce that the Spaniards ate rats, mice, and serpents. Schmidel says they even ate the legs of three men who had been hanged, and there is a drawing in his book showing soldiers cutting off the legs of the men hanging on the gallows. Some time later, 20,000 Indians attacked the settlement and burned the fort. They tied hay soaked in fish oil to their boleadors, lit it, and threw the boleadors into the fort. They also hurled into the stockade burning hay tied to arrows and spearheads. The Indians continually attacked the settlement and finally burned one of the vessels as well as many of the Spanish huts. The only thing that kept the expedition going was the faith in the great riches that lay ahead. But nearly all the Spanish nobles who went to the River Plate in search of wealth met horrible deaths at the hands of the Indians.

Mendoza, who had decided that the position on the River Plate was untenable even before the Indians attacked Buenos Aires, had sent Ayolas and a company of men up the Paraná. Ayolas founded the settlement of Corpus Christi near the ruins of Cabot's Sancti Spiritus on the day that the battle took place at Buenos Aires. Mendoza, leaving 160 men at Buenos Aires, took his remaining 600 up the Paraná to a point twelve miles south of Corpus Christi. There he founded Buena Esperanza as the new base of the expedition, and it was from that base that Ayolas was sent in search of the silver of the Inca.

Ayolas left Buena Esperanza in October 1536 with three small vessels and 160 men, under orders to found a township and a fort which would serve as a safe base for operations into the interior and a secure harbor for the vessels that were to be sent up the river when the new base was established. He also was under orders to return within four months, whether or not he found the route to Peru. These instructions prove the ignorance of the conquistadors regarding the stupendous distances and difficulties that lay before them, as it required at least four months to make the one-way journey from Buena Esperanza to Paraguay in those days. At least a year was necessary for the journey to Potosí and back.

Mendoza returned to Buenos Aires to await news from Ayolas and from two ships that he had sent to Santa Catharina, under the command of Gonzalo Mendoza, to bring back fresh supplies. He found that the two ships had returned with food and many adventurers eager to join the expedition. When three months elapsed without news from Ayolas, Mendoza sent Captain Juan de Salazar and Gonzalo Mendoza with 58 men to look for him. When another three months passed without news from Salazar, Mendoza, disheartened and in constant pain, finally surrendered to his illness and made arrangements to return to Spain. He left 250 men at Buenos Aires under Francisco Ruiz Galán, appointed Juan de Ayolas chief of the expedition, and sailed for home. He died at sea on June 23, 1537, just two months short of two years from the day on which he had sailed his proud armada out of Sanlúcar, and his body was thrown overboard with those solemn, dreadful rites that are called burial at sea.

Ayolas had continued up the Paraná and the Paraguay to Lambaré, capital of the vast Guarani federation, where the Spaniards were astonished to find a large temple devoted to the worship of a serpent. Far from being an evidence of barbarity, as the Spaniards reported at the time, this really proved the high plane of civilization to which the Guaranis had attained, because serpent-worship is an advanced form of sun-worship, which has come down from the greatest antiquity.

Since the Guaranis were engaged in constant warfare with the less civilized tribes of the Chaco, Ayolas had little difficulty in persuading them to help him. Several hundred joined his expedition, and he took as his mistress the young daughter of an Indian chief, this being the customary way of sealing an alliance. He met and took with him as guide an Indian who as a boy had accompanied Alejo Garcia on his march to the empire of the Inca twelve years before. Ayolas led his men up the Paraguay to a point near Coimbá, where on February 3, 1537, he established a small base which he christened Candelaria. There he left his three boats and 33 soldiers under the command of his lieutenant, Domingo Martínez de Irala, with orders to await his return. Then he started westward over the route that Garcia had followed. On reaching Charcas he found the natives ready for war and protected by wooden forts which the Inca had ordered built after Garcia's invasion. Ayolas decided to return to Candelaria for reinforcements. With 20 Indians laden with gold and silver, they started back, marching in long, roundabout zigzags to avoid Indian settlements because they were short of ammunition. Finally he and 80 haggard survivors of his original 127 men reached Candelaria, only to find to their horror that it was deserted. The Spaniards, exhausted, starved, and disheartened, waited seven or eight days, hoping that Irala and the boats would return. At the end of a week the Indians brought them food and invited them to their huts. Ayolas's men eagerly accepted these friendly offerings and followed the Indians into the high rushes. Suddenly they were pounced upon by the Indians, two of whom held each white man while other Indians beat in his skull with wooden clubs. Ayolas died without knowing that Asunción had been founded, that Mendoza had died several months before, or that he had been appointed to succeed the adelantado. He was the second conquistador to reach the Inca empire from the east.

Salazar had left Buenos Aires on January 15, 1537, to look for Ayolas. At the end of April he arrived at the point where he later founded Asunción. Paraguay is at its best in late April. The luxuriant and fragrant vegetation seemed like a paradise after the bare, treeless pampas farther down the river, and its beauty was heightened by contrast with the barren shore of the Chaco just across the river. The warm air was soft with the perfume of wild flowers and flowering trees. The heat of the day was forgotten in the coolness of the quiet night and the early morning. The moon did fascinating things to the wide sweep of the river-bend. All the way up the river the Spaniards had been harassed by the hostility of the Indians. Here at the very heart of the Guarani country they found the Indians friendly and ready to welcome them, just as they had welcomed Ayolas when he had passed through three or four months earlier. Surely this was the most hospitable spot the white men had found since they left sunny Spain! They landed and fraternized with the Guaranis, with the help of the four interpreters they had brought with them. On learning from the Indians that Ayolas had gone up the river, Salazar decided to establish a fort and town on this spot, in order to be closer to the Silver Mountain. He and his officers made a declaration to that effect before the notary of the expedition, agreed with the Indians that the fort and town would be established upon their return, and started up the river to continue their search for Ayolas.

Irala and his band had left Candelaria and gone farther north after the hostility of the Indians had been aroused by the viciousness and the orgies of the white men. Salazar found them 90 miles above Candelaria on the day that Pedro de Mendoza died at sea. Salazar and Irala now had four boats and 90 men. They returned down the river, re-established

Irala at Candelaria, and then Salazar continued downstream to the point where he had decided to set up the new base. The foundations of the wooden fort were laid on August 15, Ascension Day, and the settlement took the name of Nuestra Señora Santa María de la Asunción. When the fort was completed, Salazar left it in charge of Gonzalo Mendoza with 30 men and returned to Buenos Aires to persuade the Adelantado to move the settlement to Asunción, being still ignorant of Mendoza's death. In 1547 Charles V authorized Salazar to use a golden tower on his coat-of-arms, in recognition of his founding of Asunción.

Irala was one of the most ambitious and unscrupulous of all the conquistadors who entered South America by way of the River Plate. He again abandoned Candelaria and took his men down to Asunción, where he assumed the governorship on the ground that he was Ayolas's successor. He refused to recognize the authority of Ruiz Galán, whom Mendoza had left as governor of Buenos Aires, or of Alonso de Cabrera, whom the late adelantado's backers sent to the River Plate with several hundred soldiers, ammunition, and supplies. Irala and his men mistreated the Indians, stole their daughters and traded them among themselves, and amused themselves by slashing the faces of any who dared oppose them. The little colony had 700 Indian women at its service in 1540, according to a report by Irala.

Cabrera joined forces with Irala, and Galán returned to Buenos Aires. Irala, fearing that new arrivals from Spain might join Galán and endanger his own power, ordered Buenos Aires abandoned and the population taken up the river to Asunción. When the people of Buenos Aires refused to obey his orders, he and Cabrera filled two vessels with soldiers, went downriver, and forcibly put his orders into effect. Galán and some of his friends escaped to Santa Catharina. Irala burned the church, the supply vessel that had been beached, and all the houses.

Five and a half years after the founding of Buenos Aires nothing remained of the settlement except the burned ruins and the horses and mares which were abandoned on the pampas.

5. FOUNDING OF BUENOS AIRES

AFTER Irala's destruction of Buenos Aires in September or October 1541, the country reverted to its primeval desolation. No other conquistador attempted to settle the River Plate since there was nothing there to attract adventurers. For more than two hundred years Asunción was to remain the seat of government. Newcomers from Spain reached Asunción by the long, dangerous overland route from Santa Catharina and the Brazilian coast. Irala continued to carry out the most daring and glorious feats in the most cruel and barbarous manner.

Cruelty marked the entire Conquest of South America. The bravest and most audacious captains, the men whose natures and characters best fitted them for brilliant leadership in the constant war against savages and privations, almost invariably were bad governors and administrators, and unbelievably cruel and evil in their own private lives. This was natural, of course, because the conquistadors belonged to a race which had developed strong fighting instincts during its long wars to expel the Moors from their seven-hundred-year occupation of the Iberian Peninsula. (The last Moorish sovereign, Boabdil, Caliph of Granada, had been deposed by the armies of Ferdinand and Isabel in the year that Columbus discovered America.) When this race united with the liberty-loving Indians, it produced a bellicose mestizo race with a strong spirit of rebellion and a savage love of independence.

During more than three hundred years this cruelty of the Spanish conquistadors was to be the dominant trait in the mestizos, aggravated by the moroseness and cunning inherited from the Indian mothers. It reached its highest expression anywhere in South America when it threw off all restraint and raged with the wild fury of a hurricane during the unspeakably barbarous civil wars which kept Argentina in anarchy for fifty years after its separation from Spain. It persists today in the cruelty and absolute lack of feeling of the lower classes toward animals. It would be difficult to find anywhere else in civilized life anything as cruel as the breaking of colts in Argentina. Men whose daily work brings them into close contact with animals are unnecessarily cruel in their handling of them, as though venting on the dumb brutes some psychological rebellion against their own frustrated lives.

But Irala's cruel rampages took him beyond the boundaries of this book when he abandoned Buenos Aires. It need only be mentioned that he led a daring expedition of 580 Spaniards and 4000 Indians across the deadly Chaco Boreal as far as the Guapay River (now called the Rio Grande), one of the Marañón's larger tributaries which forms the southern boundary of the Bolivian province of Cochabamba. This expedition of discovery was to receive world-wide publicity four hundred years later, when Paraguay put it forward at the Chaco Peace Conference in Buenos Aires as one of its primary claims to sovereignty of the Chaco.

In defense of Irala's ability as a colonial administrator, he is credited with being the first governor to create a *cabildo*, or municipal council, thus permitting the colonists of Paraguay to take part in the discussion of public affairs, and also with originating the *encomienda* system. This latter appears to have been a successful method of settling the Indians in an agricultural colony, such as the River Plate was, but it degenerated under the greed of the Spaniards and reduced the Indians to abject slavery. The encomienda took its name from the deed by which the Indians were put into the care of the conquistadors for religious conversion and employment. This deed provided: "Unto you, So-and-so, are given in trust (*se os encomiendan*) so many Indians, for you to make use of in your farms; and you are to teach them the things of the holy Catholic faith." The conversion of the Indians usually was limited to baptizing them and putting them to work as slaves. The encomienda system became the basis of Indian slavery in the mines of all the metal-producing colonies of the New World.

News of Irala's inhuman treatment of the Indians was not long in reaching the Spanish court, and when Alvar Núñez Cabeza de Vaca was appointed adelantado to succeed Pedro de Mendoza, two of his instructions were to free the Indians from the slavery in which Irala had bound them and to see that young Indian girls were no longer taken as mistresses by the Spaniards without the consent of their parents.

Eventually the title of adelantado of the River Plate fell to one Juan Ortiz de Zarate, who had entered South America at Panama on his way to Peru as a member of the retinue of Viceroy Blasco Núñez Vela. Later he worked his way down through Tarija and Cochabamba to Paraguay, acquiring much property, wealth, and political importance en route. He had taken with him to South America his fourteen-year-old nephew, Juan de Garay, whose name was to live forever as the founder of the great city of Buenos Aires.

When Zarate's appointment as adelantado reached him, Garay who was then 38 years old, was busy with two other Paraguayan captains in conquering and populating Santa Cruz de la Sierra, now a Bolivian city, which was to set up another Paraguayan claim to the Chaco. As

Zarate had to go to Spain to have his appointment confirmed and receive his instructions, he recalled Juan de Garay to Asunción and instructed him to build four vessels, fill them with men and supplies, and
take them to the "gulf" of the River Plate to meet him upon his return
from Spain.

Leaders of the colony at Asunción had long been convinced of the
necessity of re-establishing Buenos Aires to give Paraguay an outlet to
the sea and to form a convenient intermediary supply base and transfer
point for traffic with Spain. The surviving members of Mendoza's settlement, remembering the bitter hardships they had suffered, were so opposed to returning down the river that two attempts to organize an expedition had to be abandoned. Garay finally founded both Santa Fé
and Buenos Aires with young mestizos who had been born in Paraguay
and knew nothing about the earlier hardships. Of the volunteers for both
these expeditions Garay selected only the strongest and most soldierly.

Garay took 9 Spaniards, 75 of these young mestizos, and 200 Indian
families down the river, with 10 horses and equipment, and on November 15, 1573, founded Santa Fé de Vera Cruz at a point 54 miles north
of the present city of Santa Fé. Before founding the town, however, his
vessels had escorted out of the River Plate and as far up the coast as the
present port of Rio Grande do Sul the caravel *San Cristóbal de la Buena
Aventura*, the first vessel built in the River Plate to make the voyage back
to Spain.

The founding of Santa Fé opened the way for the refounding of
Buenos Aires and provided Garay with a base much closer than Asunción
to his new goal. At dawn one morning there was a great commotion
among the Indians of the little settlement, which caused Garay to fear
that he had an uprising on his hands. But the lookout reported that a
group of horsemen was chasing and riding down the Indians on the
outskirts of the settlement. Not doubting for a moment that such horsemen would be Spaniards, Garay rode out to meet them. They reported
themselves the vanguard of the forces of the governor of Tucumán,
Jerónimo Luis Cabrera, who had just founded a new settlement called
Córdoba de la Llana, and that they were taking possession of all the
territory to a point 75 miles below the ruins of Cabot's Sancti Spiritus,
on orders from the viceroy at Lima. This was the first meeting of the
two rival streams of conquistadors which had entered South America
at Lima and the River Plate.

The Lima and River Plate expeditions had been moving toward this
inevitable clash from the very beginning. In the same year, 1527, Cabot

BUENOS AIRES SOON AFTER ITS FOUNDING BY PEDRO MENDOZA
FROM A PAINTING BY L. MATTHIAS

THE CARRETA, ARGENTINA'S COVERED WAGON

A GAUCHO—ARGENTINA'S VANISHING RACE OF INDIAN COWBOYS
WITH TYPICAL ACCOUTREMENTS

A PULPERÍA SOMEWHERE IN THE INTERIOR

had established his base at Sancti Spiritus and Pizarro had established his on Gallo Island. Lima was founded in 1535 and Buenos Aires in 1536. In 1573, when the men from Peru founded Córdoba and the River Plate men founded Santa Fé, they were only 240 miles apart.

On the day that they finally met at Santa Fé, Cabrera himself rode up while Garay was talking with the horsemen and confirmed their statement that he had founded Córdoba de la Llana on July 6, 1573, and that he was under instructions from the viceroy to establish ports on the Paraná that would permit maritime commerce with Spain and thus extend the Spanish dominions "from sea to sea." The creation of such a sea-to-sea colonial empire had been one of Mendoza's specific objectives and the excuse for Irala's expedition to the boundaries of Peru.

Garay informed Cabrera that the lands of the River Plate basin had been granted by Charles V to Mendoza and that Ortiz de Zarate was expected back from Spain any day with the king's appointment as Mendoza's successor. Before Cabrera and Garay had decided who was to give way, an Indian messenger arrived to inform Garay of Zarate's arrival at the island of San Gabriel in the River Plate, in front of the present site of Buenos Aires. Garay immediately took all his men down the river to the assistance of the new adelantado, whose attempt to establish a settlement on the eastern bank of the river, where Colonia, Uruguay, now stands, was meeting with furious resistance from the same race of Indians who had killed Solís when he landed on their shores.

Zarate finally gave up his effort to settle on the eastern bank and he and Garay returned upstream to Santa Fé. The Spanish courts eventually ruled that jurisdiction belonged to the colonizers from Paraguay, but in the meantime Zarate became involved in protracted litigation with the viceroy of Peru which kept him in the presence of the audiencia at Chuquisaca for several years; and Garay, as his deputy, was head of the government in Paraguay from 1576 to his death in 1583.

In 1580 Garay at last decided to undertake the refounding of Buenos Aires. With 10 Spaniards, 54 young mestizos, and 200 Indian families he set out for Santa Fé. From that point he sent the Indians overland to the old site of Buenos Aires with 1000 horses, 200 cows, 500 sheep, and mares, oxen, carts, and equipment for founding the new city, all under guard of half his soldiers. With eleven small locally built vessels and the caravel *San Cristóbal de la Buena Aventura*, Garay and the rest of the soldiers proceeded down the river with the tools, wood, arms, munitions, and seeds.

Finding the old site low, swampy, and unsuitable for a settlement,

Garay worked back northward along the western bank for a few miles until he found high land. His monument, facing the north front of Government House just off the northeast corner of the Plaza de Mayo, marks the spot where he is supposed to have stepped out of his boat. The Jesuit historian Padre Lozano says that the city was founded and the royal standard planted in the name of Philip II on Holy Trinity Day, 1580, and for that reason Garay christened his new settlement with the glorified name of Ciudad de la Santísima Trinidad y Puerto de Santa María de Buenos Aires, or City of the Most Holy Trinity and Port of Santa María of Buenos Aires. This soon became shortened simply to Buenos Aires. The English-speaking residents have shortened it still further to the affectionate nickname "B.A."

The Argentine historian Vicente Fidel López points out that there is considerable doubt as to the exact date of Garay's arrival, since the date of the formal founding is given as June 11, 1580, which was not a Sunday and therefore could not be Holy Trinity Day. But, he says, the good Padre Lozano knew better than anyone else that Holy Trinity Day had to be a Sunday and if he reported that it also was on June 11, he, López, is not going to dispute it. But he refers his readers to other authorities who do.

In the *Acta*, or formal document recording the founding, which has been reproduced in Buenos Aires on various occasions, Garay reports the founding of the city "on this day, Saturday, the day of the feast of St. Barnabas, the eleventh day of the month of June in the year of the birth of our redeemer, Jesus Christ, one thousand five hundred and eighty." This same Acta shows that Garay, "being this day in the port of Santa María de Buenos Aires," merely founded the city in the name of the Holy Trinity and recorded that that name was to be given to both the city and the principal church. Zarate had decreed that the River Plate country should be known as Nueva Vizcaya, for no better reason than that he was from Vizcaya, in Spain. Garay intended his new city to be called Ciudad de la Trinidad, or City of the Trinity. But the names Rio de la Plata and Buenos Aires were already too well known and accepted to be changed.

Garay laid out his new settlement in 144 squares of approximately 100 by 100 yards, cut by streets 11 yards wide which crossed at right angles. The town was on a bluff overlooking the river, with 16 of these squares running along what are now Calles 25 de Mayo and Balcarce, from Calle Córdoba to Calle Chile, and extending westward for 9 squares to the present Calles Libertad and Salta. At the exact center of the waterfront one square was reserved for Garay and numbered "O." The square just west of it was designated as No. 1 and reserved for the Plaza de Armas, or principal plaza, on which were to be built the church and cabildo, or town hall. These two squares now form the Plaza de Mayo, which all through the history of Buenos Aires has been the city's heart. Of all the many beautiful plazas in the city today, the Plaza de Mayo is the only one that was purposely set out as a plaza, all the others having originally been market-places, bone-yards, or dump-heaps, most of them far outside the city limits. The very beautiful Plaza San Martín was once the slave market.

Most of the other city squares were quartered and distributed among the soldiers. Lot No. 2, a quarter-square set aside for the church, is the site of the present Cathedral. Two squares south of Garay's lot an entire square was set aside for San Francisco, and the San Francisco Church now stands there. Garay's original town plan, showing the ownership of all the lots, is still intact in the General Archives of the Indies, in Seville.

The land just around the little settlement was used for communal crops and grazing. The outlying land as far as the present towns of Zarate, Tigre, and Lujan was laid out in agricultural tracts of approximately 1½ by 3½ miles. These tracts were also given to the soldiers, and the Indian families that had been brought from Paraguay, men and women, were distributed on the land to work as slaves of the owners. Other Indians were assigned to masters as household servants. As there were not enough Indians to work all this land, Garay and his followers went out among the near-by tribes and captured others. In the region around the present town of San Isidro they found a sedentary tribe of docile Indians who since pre-Columbian days had engaged in agriculture. These Indians were easily subdued and distributed among the settlers. The name San Isidro was given to this region in honor of the patron saint of agriculture because of the unusually fertile earth thereabouts. It is indicative of the astounding fertility of the Argentine pampas that this region has been under constant cultivation for more than four hundred years without the use of fertilizers.

But the Indians along the Riachuelo, in the vicinity of Pedro de Mendoza's townsite, were just as furiously opposed to the presence of white men as they had been forty years earlier. So before they could concert any alliance with other tribes in preparation for an attack on the little settlement, Garay attacked them with all the men he had. The battle took place on the Riachuelo about twelve miles inland and the tribe was completely destroyed, so many Indians being killed that that part of the river is still called the Matanza, or Slaughter.

Two years after founding Buenos Aires, Garay felt that the settlement was sufficiently organized and secure to permit him to visit Santa Fé and Asunción. Along the way, he and his staff left the vessel one night to sleep on shore and all were killed by the Indians.

There being no mineral wealth in the vicinity, Buenos Aires at once became an agricultural colony. This set up a new social organization in South America that tended naturally toward democracy because it tended toward equality. In Peru, Mexico, and Chile, where the Spaniards were using the Indians as slaves in the mines, there were two classes of society—the rich Spaniards and the poor Indians. In Buenos Aires everyone was more or less on the same economic level, only slightly above poverty; and everyone had to work. The colonists were soon harvesting wheat which the old chroniclers described as being the equal of that of Valencia. Seventeen years after the founding of Buenos Aires the new settlement exported 1498 bushels of flour to Brazil at a value of 39,280 *reales* ($4910). The imports in that same year, 1597, were valued at 67,817 *reales*, which included the price of Negro slaves which already were being brought into the colony. The *real* was worth 12½ cents and the famous "pieces of eight," which were the forefathers of the American silver dollar, were so called because they were worth eight *reales*.

The rapidity with which horses and cattle multiplied on the pampas soon made agriculture unattractive. When Mendoza's settlement had been abandoned, seventy stallions and mares had been turned loose on the land because they could not be taken up the river. When Garay and his colonists arrived forty years later, the plains were overrun with wild horses. Before the end of the sixteenth century, Zarate's nephew and successor carried out the stipulation of Zarate's contract with the Crown to introduce cattle and sheep from his estates in Upper Peru, which is now Bolivia. These animals and the horses ran the plains in such numbers that for three hundred years Argentina lived off the export of what are known today as by-products—hides, horns, and tallow.

But for more than a hundred years Buenos Aires was little more than a stopping place on the way to Paraguay, and as late as 1716, one hundred and thirty-six years after the founding, the town had only 400 mud and straw houses. There is no record of the use of bricks until 1750, when the town had a population of less than 11,000.

In 1595 work was begun on the construction of a fort to protect the settlement from British and Dutch pirates who had arrived in the River

Plate. The fort was built on the site where the Casa Rosada (Government House) now stands. As late as 1706 there was only one notary in the town. In 1750, there were only four *pulperías*, or saloons, which paid an annual tax of 20 pesos each. In 1773, three years before Buenos Aires became the capital of the new Viceroyalty, there were only 16 horse coaches in the town.

For two hundred years, from its founding until the establishment of the Viceroyalty, Buenos Aires remained a small, dirty, unattractive colonial town. A census taken in 1744 showed that it had a population of 10,223. Of this number, 141 were Spanish property owners who formed the colonial nobility of office-holders. All the others were "the common people," offspring of Spanish men and Indian women. In the country districts around Buenos Aires there were 6083 inhabitants, and of these 186 were Spanish landlords to whom the Crown had awarded grants of land. The rest were mestizos. The Spanish government prohibited immigration into the colonies all during the colonial period, but it encouraged marriage between Spaniards and Indian women. Most of the Spaniards, however, considered themselves above marrying Indians and what slow increase took place in the population during the two hundred years before the creation of the Viceroyalty consisted almost exclusively of the offspring of their illegitimate relations with the Indian women they refused to marry.

6. THE COLONIAL PERIOD

ARGENTINA was so long in getting started on its national life that it is the youngest of the South American countries. Yet it has grown so rapidly that it has become the most important one of them all. Argentina dates its history from the revolution of May 25, 1810, against Spain, but it did not become a nation until fifty-two years later. International law defines a nation as an independent association of individuals occupying their own territory, united under the same government, and ruled by a code of common laws. Argentina could not answer that definition until 1862, for it required a half-century of barbarous civil wars, including twenty-two years of one of the most ruthless despotisms in history, to unite the so-called United Provinces of the River Plate.

Yet it is not strange that Argentina was so much later than the other South American republics in getting started. The wonder is that it could ever have become a united nation at all; for the territory that now forms the Argentine Republic was colonized between the years 1536 and 1596 by three rival invasions of Spanish conquistadors whose jealous hatred of one another was even more bitter than their hatred of the Indians who disputed their advance.

The first invasion of conquistadors went directly from Spain to colonize the region known as the River Plate, which included the territory between the 25th and 36th parallels and extended from the Atlantic to the Pacific. The second invasion was a prolongation of the conquest of Peru. It moved southward through the Humahuaca Valley, following the trail of the Incas, who had carried their empire as far south as San Carlos and Tunuyán in Mendoza Province. This colonizing stream founded the city of Santiago del Estero and later spread out over the present provinces of Tucumán, Salta, Jujuy, La Rioja, Catamarca, Santiago del Estero, Córdoba, and part of the Territory of the Chaco. The third invasion entered Argentina from Chile and divided into two branches. One of these continued the occupation of Tucumán. The other occupied the region then known as Cuyo, which included the present provinces of Mendoza, San Luis, and San Juan, and then extended itself into the Territory of Neuquén and parts of the territories of La Pampa and Rio Negro.

After the revolt against Pizarro in Peru had been crushed, Pedro de Valdivia was rewarded in 1548 for his services to the Crown by being appointed governor of Chile, which he had colonized in 1541. His grant was certified as 100 leagues wide and so extended to the 64th meridian, taking away from the River Plate conquistadors the territory already mentioned. This region, twice as large as the Province of Buenos Aires which eventually became the sphere of action for the River Plate invasion, remained under the jurisdiction of Chile for two hundred years until the establishment of the Viceroyalty of the River Plate with its capital at Buenos Aires.

When the early settlement at Buenos Aires was abandoned and the River Plate conquistadors established themselves at Asunción, they were as far away from the River Plate as St. Louis is from New Orleans, and as they were bound for the silver mines of Peru, or so they thought, they left the River Plate region completely abandoned. Apparently they had no intention at first of ever returning to colonize the country they had left behind them. When they finally did return and established the city of Buenos Aires forty years later, a dozen towns had already been founded in the west and northwest. Consequently, the colonization of Argentina can be said to have begun in the far northwest.

In 1550 an expedition which had been sent out from Lima founded a settlement called Barco near the headwaters of the Saladillo River at a point now called Río Hondo, about sixty miles southeast of the present city of Tucumán. Barco did not last long and has a place in history only because it was the first town settled by the Spaniards who entered Argentina from Peru.

The establishment of Barco aroused the ire of Valdivia in Chile, who considered that his domain was being invaded. So he sent an expedition to destroy the settlement. This expedition moved all the settlers from Barco to the River Dulce in 1553 and there founded the city of Santiago del Estero, which still stands and is the oldest city in Argentina. In 1558 another expedition was sent from Chile to take possession of what is now the Province of Tucumán. This expedition founded three towns, Cañete, Córdoba del Calchaquí, and Londres (London), the last being so christened in honor of the marriage of Philip II of Spain to the queen of England, Mary Tudor. The Indians soon destroyed all three of these settlements, but Londres was rebuilt and still stands in the Province of Catamarca as the second oldest town in Argentina.

The territorial conflict between the governor of Chile and the viceroy of Peru finally was settled by the Crown in 1563 through the issuance of a royal cedula putting Tucumán under the jurisdiction of Peru. A new colonizing expedition was sent out immediately, which founded the city of Tucumán in 1565 and made it the regional capital. From Tucumán the cities of Córdoba, Salta, La Rioja, and Jujuy were founded in 1573, 1582, 1591, and 1593, respectively. Córdoba originally was called Córdoba de la Llana (Córdoba of the Plain) to indicate that it was the first town which the men of Peru had founded outside the Andes, facing the great plains of the pampas.

In the meantime the men from Chile had been busily colonizing the region farther south. In 1561 the city of Mendoza had been founded and so named in honor of Garcia Hurtado de Mendoza, who had succeeded Valdivia as governor of Chile. These same men founded San Juan in 1562 and San Luis in 1596.

And, as noted in the previous chapter, the River Plate men, having despaired of reaching the silver of Peru, had returned southward and founded Santa Fé in 1573 and Buenos Aires in 1580.

The scene was set for the long colonial period.

The founding of Buenos Aires brought to a close the preliminary era of conquest and opened the secondary era, that of colonization. In 1591 the Crown abolished the system of *adelantazgo* by which private individuals had been permitted to colonize certain territory at their own expense in exchange for the privilege of governing it. The system had created serious conflicts between the political interests of the Crown and the private interests of the adelantado, which was demonstrated nowhere so plainly as by the abandonment of Buenos Aires and the transfer of the entire colonization movement to Paraguay as well as by the abandonment of two other River Plate settlements, Corpus Christi and Buena Esperanza. Therefore the king decided to put the colonies in charge of governors responsible directly to him and with no personal interest in the colonists, as the adelantados had.

The adelantazgo system had lasted nearly sixty years, from 1534 to 1591, and in that period the River Plate had had seventeen adelantados, some of whom attempted to govern the territory through lieutenants without even visiting it. In the next thirty years, from 1591 to 1621, there were nine governors of the River Plate. Then, by a royal cedula issued in 1617, the Crown separated Buenos Aires from Paraguay and established them as two distinct colonies, both under the jurisdiction of the viceroy at Lima.

The name River Plate had been given to a region where there was no silver, and several expeditions had proved the impossibility of reaching the wealth of Peru from Paraguay. It had therefore been decided to base the colonization of the River Plate region on the occupation of the land itself. This was a completely new departure in Spanish colonization.

In fact, the whole conquest of the River Plate differed radically from all the other Spanish conquests in South America because of the complete absence of wealth and the savagery of the Indian tribes which had to be conquered.

The men who eventually colonized Buenos Aires were less adventurous but better workers than those in Peru and Chile. While the Spaniards in Peru and Chile occupied themselves simply with looting the wealth already established by the Indians, the men of the River Plate set about producing new wealth from the land. The millions of wild cattle and horses grazing on the pampas offered comparatively easy wealth. It was merely necessary to ride out on the plains, kill the animals by the hundreds, and remove their hides and fat. The hides and tallow of Buenos Aires soon found a ready market in Europe, the first cargo of River Plate hides and Paraguayan sugar being dispatched to Spain three years after the founding of Buenos Aires.

English and Dutch filibusters lay in wait for the galleons that were carrying the silver of Mexico and the gold of Peru home to Spain, but they let pass the hides and tallow from Buenos Aires. These efforts of the River Plate colonists to trade with Europe, however, soon encountered fierce opposition from the Crown. In 1598 Philip II prohibited all trade, incoming or outgoing, through the port of Buenos Aires and in the following year decreed the death penalty for violation of this edict.

It very soon became apparent that the colonies throughout South America had been established for the sole benefit of Spain without any consideration for the colonists. They were kept in constant subjugation to the Spaniards, and all the important posts in the government, army, and Church were monopolized by the men sent out from the mother country.

As soon as the preliminary period of conquest was completed and permanent cities set up in various parts of the continent, the Spanish government decreed a strict trade monopoly, designed to keep all the profits in its own hands and to prevent any of the colonies from developing to a point where they might offer serious competition to Spain. The colonists were prohibited from engaging in industry, as that would have tended to make them economically independent of the mother country, which reaped exorbitant profits from selling them things which they could have made for themselves. The colonies were deliberately kept to the status of producers of raw materials, but even their production of these was restricted. They were not allowed to grow grapes or olives, which would have provided wine and oil at much lower prices than those imported from Spain. They were not permitted to raise flax or hemp; and trading in salt, tobacco, and gunpowder was a jealously guarded monopoly of the Crown. As Buenos Aires was the only colony interested in trade at that time, it suffered most from the monopoly restraints.

Although Buenos Aires has long since surpassed in size and beauty all the cities of Spain, one of its most critical problems–that of the narrow streets and apparently invincible traffic jam—is the consequence of this early Spanish jealousy of the colonies and a royal decree which limited the width of the streets in the South American settlements.

The trade-monopoly decree of 1599, establishing the death penalty and confiscation of property for violation, closed all the ports of South America and required the colonists to export and import from Puerto Bello on the northern shore of the Isthmus of Panama. Puerto Bello, in turn, could trade only with Seville, which was the headquarters of the Spanish monopoly. A convoy was sent out from Seville twice a year in order that the galleons might be accompanied by armed vessels in sufficient numbers to protect them from the filibusters. When these convoys reached the Caribbean they divided into two sections, one going to Mexico and the other to Puerto Bello. After unloading their cargoes and reloading, they reassembled and were convoyed home. Nothing could be shipped legally either to or from South America except by these convoys.

Merchandise for Buenos Aires, consequently, had to be unloaded at Puerto Bello, carried across the isthmus on muleback, put on coastwise vessels to Callao or Arica, and again unloaded and transferred to the backs of mules for the 2523-mile journey from Lima to the River Plate. These pack-trains usually were made up of about 200 mules, ambling along two by two, their tails tied to the necks of the ones following to prevent any of them from straying. As can easily be imagined, the price of merchandise carried in this manner reached a fabulous height by the time the goods reached Buenos Aires. The pastoral and agricultural products of the River Plate could not be exported, as only precious stones and metals, rare drugs and other articles of great value for small bulk could stand the cost of transport under such conditions.

In the latter half of the eighteenth century these mule-trains began to be replaced by an entirely new type of transport—the *carreta*. The carreta was Argentina's "covered wagon" and it occupies a position in history and legend similar to that of the covered wagon of the American plains. It was mounted on two enormous wheels with axles three or four feet from the ground to keep the cargo high and dry above the marshes and streams that had to be crossed. These carts were drawn usually by six oxen, the leading pair strung out far ahead of the others. This enabled the leaders to get across mud-holes or streams onto dry land and then drag the wheelers and their load across after them. For nearly two hundred years, well into the twentieth century, the high-riding silhouette of this "ship of the pampas," as it was called, was the most typical sight on the almost unbroken landscape of the plains. Because of their high wheels, the carretas could leave the roads and take short-cuts across the country even when muddy. Custom made it permissible to cut wire fences to permit the passage of the carreta, provided, of course, that they were put up again after the cart got through.

The carretas, which usually traveled in caravans of fourteen or sixteen, with twenty-five or thirty armed outriders, and rarely moved more than fifteen miles a day, required from eighty to ninety days for the trip between Salta and Buenos Aires. Each cart carried from a ton and a half to two tons of merchandise and so much time was lost along the way and at the ends of the journey that it usually took from ten to twelve months for a round trip, the cost of which was around $5000 for the whole caravan.

The carreta remained the chief means of carrying wheat, wool, and hides to the railroad stations until about 1920, when hard-surfaced roads began to replace the mud roads which had been passable only for carretas and horses. In more recent years the horse replaced the ox as traction power and it was customary to hitch twenty or thirty horses to a cart, ten or twelve abreast, with some of them pulling from the axles instead of the shafts. Before being replaced by the automobile, the carreta gave its name to the roads in Argentina which are called *carreteras*.

The trade monopoly during the colonial period provoked repeated protests in Buenos Aires and continual discussions over questions arising from the Crown's maritime laws and the inflexible customs regulations of Cádiz. These discussions and the constant dissatisfaction led to the growth of a strong local sentiment, a nationalism that was absent from the rest of South America; and it was this local sentiment growing out of dissatisfaction over the trade monopoly that led eventually to the revolution.

The customs regulations of Cádiz took into consideration only the interests of Spain. Buenos Aires demanded continually freedom to trade where it desired. In 1618, thirty-eight years after its founding, the colony was granted permission to send two vessels to Spain each year, but they could not be larger than 100 tons each. This was the only trade concession made to Buenos Aires in nearly a hundred years. All commercial intercourse with the other Spanish colonies in South America remained prohibited under heavy penalty.

It was humanly impossible, of course, to enforce trade laws which violated all the laws of economics, and Buenos Aires soon became a great center for smuggling, an enterprise in which the English, Dutch, and Portuguese enthusiastically co-operated. Spanish ships could not participate in this contraband trade, because they would be caught when they returned to their home ports. But the English, Dutch, and Portuguese all thrived on it. It is said that 300,000 hides were smuggled out of Buenos Aires in English ships alone in 1658. In 1661 a Spanish commissioner in Flanders watched four Dutch ships unload and certified that $3,000,000 worth of River Plate hides, wool, and wood was taken out of their holds.

Still, as far as Spain was concerned, the entire trade with her American colonies continued to be a monopoly of the merchants of Seville and Cádiz through Puerto Bello. It was not until 1774, two hundred years after the founding of Buenos Aires, that the colonies were granted permission to engage in transoceanic trade. Nine ports in Spain and twenty-four in the colonies were opened for this commerce, but the traffic was still confined exclusively to Spaniards and Spanish shipping.

The effect of this concession was immediate. Before 1774 the legal exports of hides from the River Plate did not exceed 150,000 yearly. As a result of the new regulations, the number rose to between 700,000 and 800,000 annually and in 1783 totaled 1,400,000.

But for two hundred years Buenos Aires had lived on contraband. In the Spanish language, a law, decree, or ordinance was called a *bando* and its violation was a *contrabando,* a word which in time came to be applied only to smuggling. Buenos Aires became the smuggling headquarters for South America in the late 1590's, when slaves for Peru were allowed to be landed at Buenos Aires, that being the shortest route from Africa. The captains of the slave ships smuggled other merchandise in and out of the port and when the slave license was revoked in 1609 the smuggling trade continued.

Despite all the restrictive measures of the Spanish government, Buenos Aires continued to grow commercially and politically until its importance could no longer be ignored, and the Crown finally, in 1776, created the Viceroyalty of the River Plate and put Buenos Aires on a par with Lima and Mexico City. In order to give this measure the importance it merited, the king sent the first viceroy, Pedro de Cevallos, to the

River Plate at the head of the largest expedition that ever had been seen in the southern seas. There were 116 vessels, of which 20 were ships of war. These vessels carried 10,000 men, almost equivalent to the whole population of Buenos Aires.

The viceroy's instructions were to clear the Banda Oriental, or Uruguay, of the Portuguese who had established smuggling posts at Montevideo and at Colonia, just across the river from Buenos Aires. He stopped on the way in February 1777 to take possession of Santa Catharina Island and to capture the Portuguese province of Rio Grande do Sul and then made a triumphal entry into Buenos Aires on October 15, 1777. This was one month before the Continental Congress of the thirteen American States adopted the Articles of Confederation and Perpetual Union. The viceroy's attempt to add Rio Grande do Sul to the Spanish domain was nullified by the signing of the Peace of San Ildefonso on October 1, 1777, by which Rio Grande was returned to the Portuguese in exchange for Uruguay, which was added to the Viceroyalty of the River Plate.

This great Viceroyalty, with an area of nearly 2,000,000 square miles, extended from the Strait of Magellan to the southern frontier of the present Republic of Peru and included the present republics of Argentina, Uruguay, Paraguay, and Bolivia. The establishment of the capital of the Viceroyalty at Buenos Aires necessitated the setting up of an elaborate local government with jurisdiction over the vast territory. This gave a tremendous political, economic, and social impetus to Buenos Aires, until finally all it needed was to set up its own sovereignty. When Cevallos was recalled after two years, the bond uniting Buenos Aires to the Crown was so weak that any political disturbance would have been sufficient to set up an independent River Plate State.

The Viceroyalty lasted only thirty-three years, during which there were eleven viceroys. Only one of them is buried in Buenos Aires, Pedro Melo de Portugal y Villena, who ruled from 1795 to 1797. His remains rest in the San Juan church at the corner of Calles Piedras and Alsina.

Life in Buenos Aires during the colonial period was drab and uninspiring. Outside of Buenos Aires it must have been almost insupportable. In the capital, none of the streets was paved; the houses were made of adobe; and there was no street illumination. The second viceroy, Juan José de Vertiz, introduced paving and street lighting and tried to make the city more livable, but he was in office only six years. The candle lamps which he introduced were in use until 1840, when oil lamps were installed for street lighting. Buenos Aires still pays homage to

Vertiz's civic enterprise by giving his name to one of its principal avenues, the continuation of Avenida Alvear, from Palermo Park to the
suburb of Belgrano.

When the Constituent Assembly met in 1817, it issued a proclamation
to the people recording the cruel treatment suffered during two hundred years of Spanish rule, to justify the declaration of independence.
This proclamation charged that throughout the colonial period the
Spaniards had tried to insure their domination of the colonies by exter-
minating, destroying, and degrading the colonists; that after extermi-
nating the Indian population, Spain prohibited the immigration of
foreigners and strictly limited that of Spaniards, but facilitated the immigration of criminals. Not even the prospects of wealth offered by the
development of the colonies had shaken the Crown's stubborn opposition to them. There were hundreds of unoccupied miles between cities;
entire towns had been destroyed; the teaching of the sciences was prohibited and schooling was restricted to Latin grammar, ancient philosophy, theology, and civil and canon law. Industries were prohibited lest
they tend to make the colonies independent of the mother country.
Spain did everything possible to degrade the people born in the colonies because it did not want them to rise to a position where they might
assume leadership, even in improving civilization. The colonists had no
voice, either direct or indirect, in the legislation that was drawn up in
Spain for their control or in the local governments which could have
eased the rigor of law enforcement. Government employees were always Spaniards. Of the hundred and seventy viceroys appointed in the
Americas, only four were born on the American continent. Of the six
hundred and two governors and captains-general, only fourteen were
American-born.

The governors and, later, the viceroys were appointed for only three
years, which could be extended or shortened at the pleasure of the
Crown. Of the twenty-eight governors who were sent to the River
Plate colony between 1620 and 1776, only four ruled as long as ten years
and the average was five and a half years. Of the eleven viceroys who
ruled in the name of the king between 1777 and 1810, only three remained as long as five years and seven were in office only two years or
less. Because of the brevity of their term of office, the viceroys were
unable to identify themselves very closely with the welfare of the colony, even if they had been so disposed, which most of them were not.
With the exception of Liniers, the tenth viceroy, they were all more
interested in their future relations with the Crown and in meriting the

continuance of its favors than they were in the people over whom they ruled.

By the end of the eighteenth century it needed only some jarring event to tear the River Plate Viceroyalty away from the Crown. The invasion of Spain by Napoleon and the invasion of Buenos Aires by the English set in motion the revolution that was to free Buenos Aires and all the other South American colonies from Spain.

7. THE ENGLISH INVASIONS

THE popular movement toward emancipation which led to the revolution of 1810 began in earnest with the English invasions of Buenos Aires in 1806 and 1807. Public opinion had been smoldering during the last hundred years of the colonial period and had risen to the boiling point under the viceroys. There had been repeated uprisings and democratic movements on the part of the native-born criollos as far back as the sixteenth century, and there was a pronounced public opinion in favor of independence all through the period of the viceroys. The English invasions awakened the people to their own strength and their ability to take care of themselves and handle their own affairs under the most trying circumstances. Also, the invasions brought to a climax the long-growing discontent with Spanish rule and especially with the local representatives of that rule.

For nearly two centuries the English had been engaged in the smuggling trade with Buenos Aires. But after the American Revolution and the loss of the colonies in North America, England found it imperative that the Spanish American ports be opened to English trade. Consequently, the English government and leading Englishmen had taken part in several schemes for the liberation of the South American colonies from Spain, but none of these plans materialized. England had been at war with Spain almost continuously since the American Revolution, which Spain and France had aided. In 1804 the British navy captured four Spanish ships that were homeward bound from South America. This caused Spain to join forces with France, which had been at war with England since the previous year.

The combined Spanish and French fleets were defeated at the battle of Trafalgar in 1805. Immediately after that engagement, the English sent a fleet under Sir Home Popham to capture the Dutch colony at the Cape of Good Hope, which he did in January 1806. Popham, one of the most enthusiastic supporters of the idea that England needed the trade of the South American colonies, had taken part in some of the scheming in London for the liberation of the Spanish colonies. He decided on his own responsibility to cross over to the River Plate and capture the Spanish Viceroyalty that had its capital at Buenos Aires. He took with him 1500 veteran troops under the command of General William C. Beresford. The English landed at Quilmes, ten miles south of

Buenos Aires, on June 25, 1806, and on June 27 entered the capital and ran up the English colors on the fort.

It had required only forty-eight hours for 1500 Englishmen to take the city, which by this time had grown to 45,000. By 1806 the River Plate had become the most important point in South America. Buenos Aires was the busiest port in the whole colonial empire, and European merchants were depending more and more on the export and import trade through that port. The provinces of the interior were trading through Buenos Aires, since the port had been opened by the first viceroy. More than 300 vessels were entering the port every year and the foreign trade was valued at 18,000,000 *reales* ($2,250,000). Paraguay's yerba-maté was warehoused in Buenos Aires before being distributed in the interior. More than 1,000,000 hides were being exported every year, and Buenos Aires also was the center of the slave trade for all South America. The River Plate province was the only trading colony in South America and the only one that was known throughout the world. Every important port in the world received vessels from Buenos Aires.

All this presupposed an interest on the part of the government in defending Buenos Aires, since Peru would be of no value to Spain if Buenos Aires and the River Plate were held by a foreign power. Such a power would soon eliminate Spanish trade and there already had been an example of this when the Portuguese held Colonia and smuggling flourished. But instead of defending the city at the approach of the English, the viceroy, Rafael de Sobremonte, fled to Córdoba with his staff, leaving Buenos Aires and its people to their fate, and made no attempt to return while the English were in command. He had been warned that the English fleet was off Montevideo several days before, but had refused to believe it. When he fled, he took the treasury with him, but a detachment sent in pursuit by Beresford caught up with him and the $2,000,-000 were dispatched to London. The people of Buenos Aires were furious at Sobremonte's cowardice, which left them without leadership to resist the invaders, but since no one knew where to find the arms and ammunition in the fort there was nothing to do except to stand by and watch the English take possession.

A French-born officer, Captain Santiago Liniers, who was in command of the Spanish garrison at Ensenada, near the city of La Plata, proved the hero of the occasion and won for himself an immortal place in history by his masterly recapture of Buenos Aires. Liniers made his way into the city and, after studying the strength and disposition of the English, organized a small army and then went to Montevideo and returned with 1300 men. They crossed the 35-mile-wide river from Colonia to San Isidro, where they were met by 1500 criollos from Buenos Aires under the command of Juan Martín de Pueyrredon, who was destined eight years later to become the Supreme Director of the United Provinces of the River Plate.

The recapture of Buenos Aires is one of the most brilliant episodes in Argentine history. There were only 2500 soldiers in the entire Viceroyalty, and Liniers had to enlist and train a volunteer army of men who never had been engaged in war. These were the men Pueyrredon had taken to San Isidro. This army marched the 13 miles into Buenos Aires on a dark, stormy night, re-formed at dawn in the bull-ring where the Retiro railroad station now stands, and on the morning of August 12 entered Buenos Aires, defeated the English veterans, and recaptured the city. The English lost 300 killed and wounded, the remaining 1200 surrendering. The criollos lost 200 killed and wounded, but captured 35 cannon and 1600 muskets. One of the two parallel streets by which Liniers and his army entered the city has since been known as Calle Reconquista (Reconquest). The other was later to be called Calle San Martín, in honor of the hero of the Andes.

The people tried to set up Liniers as viceroy, but Sobremonte returned from his refuge in Córdoba and resumed office. He had lost all prestige, however, and the people looked upon the high office he held with even less respect than before.

Among the English troops defeated by Liniers was the famous 71st Regiment of Royal Scottish, under the command of Colonel Pack. This was one of the most glorious regiments of the English army and had had a brilliant career in Europe, India, and Egypt, where it had been the cornerstone of the defense against Napoleon's famous army of Egypt. The defeated English officers, with the exception of Beresford and Pack, were interned in Córdoba, Mendoza, and Catamarca. Beresford and Pack were released on parole and given the freedom of the city.

This victory over the English veterans awakened an enthusiastic military spirit in the people of Buenos Aires, who up to that time had been opposed to all suggestions for the establishment of a volunteer militia. By October more than 8000 men were receiving two hours of military training a day, from six to eight in the morning. Five thousand of them were native-born criollos and three thousand were Spaniards. This criollo militia was the beginning of the patriot army that eventually was to wrest independence from Spain.

Had it not been for Liniers and his brilliant action, it is almost certain that Argentina and Uruguay today would be parts of a British dominion in South America. For there was great rejoicing in London when news arrived that Beresford had captured Buenos Aires. A fleet and an army were sent to reinforce him and enable him to retain possession of the River Plate country. Another fleet and army were sent to capture Valparaiso and Talcahuano to prevent the viceroy at Lima from sending help to Buenos Aires by way of Chile. After news reached London of the loss of Buenos Aires, the two English forces were ordered to unite and recapture the city. When they met off the mouth of the River Plate there were 20 warships, 90 transports, and 12,000 men, including three brigades of artillery and one of engineers.

The English captured Montevideo, and again the cowardly viceroy fled and left his people to fend for themselves. The English then sailed up the River Plate and disembarked at Ensenada, about 35 miles below Buenos Aires. Liniers and his criollo forces were routed at the Riachuelo and the English troops entered the city. Men, women, and children flocked to the housetops and poured boiling water on the invaders and dropped stones on their heads, while the soldiers fired from every window. After several hours of fighting, the English were defeated and surrendered. When General John Whitelocke was court martialed in London later, he declared that there was no case in all history to parallel the defense of Buenos Aires by its citizens. "Every male inhabitant, whether free or slave," he said, "fought with a resolution and perseverance which could not have been expected even from the most inveterate and implacable hostility."

This episode is known in Argentine history as the Defense and is commemorated in Calle Defensa, the continuation of Calle Reconquista south of the Plaza de Mayo, on which much of the defensive fighting took place.

The English immediately organized a larger and stronger army at Cork and put it under command of General Wellesley, later to become the Duke of Wellington and hero of Waterloo, who was popularly known as "the invincible." Before this army was ready to sail for Buenos Aires, Napoleon invaded Spain and put his brother Joseph on the throne. Spain appealed to England for help against the French, and the English, considering the defeat of Napoleon more important than the possession of Buenos Aires, sent Wellesley and his army to Spain, where it was largely responsible for the political events on the Peninsula that induced Buenos Aires to declare its independence.

During the short time that the English were in possession of Buenos

Aires they instituted freedom of trade and published a weekly news-paper in Montevideo called *Estrella del Sud* (*Star of the South*) in which they propagated their liberal ideas. After the defeat of the English, Beresford became a close friend of Liniers, and he and the other English officers spread the idea of independence under the protection of England.

The invasions had opened the eyes of the criollos to the advantage of free trade, had awakened in them a desire for independence, had enabled them to organize a democratic army in which the officers were elected, and had left them such large stores of war supplies that during the subsequent wars of independence Buenos Aires was the only revolutionary center which was not defeated by the Spanish royalists.

After the defeat of the second English invasion, the people forced Sobremonte to resign and elected Liniers viceroy. Liniers felt a deep affection for the criollos who had rallied to the defense of Buenos Aires and there began a definite split between the native-born criollos under Liniers and the Spaniards under the cabildo, or town council, which had always been closed to the people born in the country.

Although the English had been in control of Buenos Aires for less than two months, they left economic effects which led directly to the revolution. Beresford's decree of free trade had permitted the exportation at good prices of large quantities of produce that had accumulated and was destined to rot because of the impossibility of shipping it under the monopoly. In return, the colonists had received large shipments of English manufactured goods without having to pay the excessive cost of the long overland haul from Lima. Also, the invasion, by disturbing the colony's financial organization, revealed its weaknesses and held it up to criticism. Beresford had lowered the customs duties, abolished the State monopoly on salt, tobacco, and other products, and suppressed the interprovincial customs duties, proving that the public administration could be conducted without putting such a heavy burden on the community.

When the English were repulsed, the people refused to return to the former restrictions. The Spaniards in the cabildo, supported by the Spanish merchants who had been profiting under the trade monopoly, tried to re-establish the monopoly, but the criollo producers refused to accept this backward step. This led to a critical state of tension and constant conflict between the Spaniards and the criollos. Liniers began depriving the cabildo of its prerogatives and tried to reduce its duties to routine police matters. This pleased the criollos, of course, but widened the breach between the viceroy and the Spaniards.

Several projects for independence appeared in the colony immediately after the withdrawal of the English. One was independence as an English protectorate, an idea that had been implanted by Beresford. Another was to set up an independent monarchy and give the crown to Princess Carlota, wife of the regent of Brazil, on the ground that she was the sister and therefore the dynastic heir of the Spanish king, Ferdinand VII, whom Napoleon had imprisoned. This scheme fell through because the Spaniards of Buenos Aires wanted to set up a constitutional monarchy, while Carlota insisted that it be an absolute one. In 1809 the people began to demand the right to elect local government *juntas*, as had been done in Spain, and this idea finally triumphed.

In January 1809 the Spaniards in Buenos Aires and Montevideo tried to start a revolt to overthrow Liniers, but the criollos gathered in the Plaza de Mayo in such force, shouting for Liniers, that the movement failed. The Spaniards then sent complaints to the junta at Cádiz, accusing Liniers of being a traitor against the Spaniards and in league with Napoleon. The junta sent Baltazar Hidalgo de Cisneros as viceroy to the River Plate with instructions to depose Liniers, crush the criollo movement, and restore the prestige of the local Spaniards. Liniers was accorded the title of Count of Buenos Aires in recognition of his services.

Cisneros was the last viceroy of the River Plate. A naval officer who had distinguished himself at Trafalgar, he had the qualities which fitted him for his high office. But he found his territory in a state of political upheaval and economic bankruptcy and met with strong resistance from the people, who were clamoring for self-government. So bad was the economic situation that holes in the streets were being repaired by filling them with wheat.

The new viceroy went to Montevideo and dissolved the junta that had plotted the revolt against Liniers. Then he dropped the charges against everyone who had been involved in that plot, a measure by which he hoped to relieve the tension. He opened all the ports of the Viceroyalty to trade with England and Portugal, and this produced immediate and excellent results. The costs of the administration totaled 250,000 pesos a month, or 3,000,000 pesos a year, and the receipts were barely 100,000 pesos a month, resulting in a deficit of 1,800,000 pesos a year. The opening of the ports promptly produced a revenue of 5,000,000 pesos a year, which much more than paid the government's expenses.

But the people continued to insist that the Spanish government had ceased to exist and that Cádiz, which had appointed Cisneros viceroy, was merely a city, without authority to usurp the prerogatives of the Crown. The cities of Spain which were not under French domination were being ruled by local juntas, elected by popular vote, and the people of Buenos Aires insisted on their right to be ruled in the same way. Finally, a formal demand was made on the viceroy and the cabildo that they call a *cabildo abierto,* or open cabildo in which the people could take part. This was an institution provided for by the Laws of the Indies in cases of emergency.

Printed invitations were prepared for distribution to 450 leading citizens. These cards were to serve as credentials to the cabildo abierto. On the day before the cabildo abierto was to meet, some of these cards were stolen from the printer and distributed to criollos. The viceroy later reported that the criollo soldiers in the plaza refused to pass leading Spanish citizens who had been invited to the assembly, but admitted criollos who had been provided with false credentials. It was Argentina's first fraudulent election.

This meeting has come down in Argentine history as the famous cabildo abierto of May 22, 1810. One of the delegates, Juan José Paso, made the point that the people of Buenos Aires had no right to decide the form of government for the whole Viceroyalty without inviting the other cities to send delegates. This was the principle that was to cause the fifty years of anarchy which followed the declaration of independence. The assembly voted that the viceroy be deposed and that the governing power be invested in a junta to be appointed by the cabildo. Then it adjourned until the next afternoon.

The popular assembly had made a mistake in entrusting the formation of the junta to the cabildo because that body was composed of Spaniards who were favorably disposed toward the viceroy. The cabildo met the next day and framed a beautiful example of what would be called today the double-cross. First it abolished the cabildo abierto that was to have met in the afternoon. Then it ruled that although the viceroy was to be deposed, he was to remain in office until a new assembly had been called with representatives from the interior—a project that had been voted down the previous day.

On the following day, May 24, the cabildo appointed a junta, with the viceroy as president. Even the viceroy was alarmed at this turn of events and replied that the action of the cabildo did not appear to him to be in accordance with the wish of the people. As soon as this action became known, the people rose in indignation. The criollo militia stood by its arms while its officers arrested two of the members of the new junta. The viceroy and the other two members resigned that night. The stage was set for the glorious 25th of May.

8. THE GAUCHO

DURING the nearly two hundred years of the colonial period there grew up on the boundless pampas a completely new and original race of human beings who were to become known as gauchos. The gaucho was the most picturesque and romantic type of man produced on the earth in modern times. Unfortunately, he was destined to pass into oblivion. But before he disappeared he played a tremendously important part in Argentine history. It is no exaggeration, in fact, to say that it was the gaucho who made Argentina. First, he helped the Spaniards win the country from the Indians by providing an effective barrier between the civilized towns and the raiding savages. Later, he formed the mounted militias which won freedom from Spain, not only for Argentina but also for Uruguay, Chile, Bolivia, and Peru. Then after the many years of civil war he finally forced the city and province of Buenos Aires to join the federation. It was then, and not until then, that Argentina became a nation.

In Argentina, as elsewhere in South America, the conquistadors were looking for gold and silver and adventure, not for homes. With the exception of a few of the titled nobles who held high positions of leadership in the expeditions, they took no women with them. Consequently, the dark-skinned Indian girls were highly prized trophies of war. The gaucho was the son of that liaison. By the middle of the sixteenth century this mixing of white and Indian blood had become the most important consequence of the Conquest.

Many Argentine writers and lecturers insist that the gaucho was a pure-blooded offspring of Spanish parents and reject all evidence of his being a mestizo. But, as Martiniano Leguizamon points out in his *La Cuna del Gaucho (The Cradle of the Gaucho)*, there was nothing else he could be. True, he was distinct from the mestizo of the metal-producing colonies of Mexico, Peru, and Bolivia. And with the successive crossing of the races, the gaucho gradually developed into a white, because, as Manuel Dominguez explains in *El Alma de la Raza (The Soul of the Race)*, the white race reappears in the fifth generation. Demersay, in his *Historia del Paraguay*, insists that the physical characteristics of the Indian disappear in the third generation, but this is a bit optimistic.

It should be noted that not all the conquistadors in the River Plate country were Spaniards. There were many Bavarians, Italians, Portuguese, and even some Arabs; and many others who were not required to state their nationality or reveal their pasts when joining the expeditions. The continual crossing of the blood of these white adventurers with that of the half-breed girls of the earlier generations eventually produced a white race *sui generis* which contained much of the Spaniard, much of the Indian, and much of something else which was not to be found, or at least was not visible, in either of the parent races. As Ribot points out in his *Psychological Inheritance*, new characteristics and new aptitudes were revealed, as when two bodies are combined in chemistry to form a third which has new properties not found in either of the two component parts. The gaucho was Spanish in his strong individualism, Moorish in his fatalism, and Indian in his close identification with the soil.

But the gaucho was a great deal more than merely a romantic figure. He was the real Argentine, as distinguished from the people of Buenos Aires. He was a nomad horseman who slept in the open, using his saddle as a pillow. Sitting alone night after night under the stars of the pampas and brooding about himself and those stars as his Moorish forefathers had done for centuries before him on the deserts of Africa and Arabia, he became something of a mystic and had the mystic's contracted features. By day he was not a herdsman or a breeder who counted his cattle or looked after their sustenance or improved their breed, but simply a wild, ignorant, lawless hunter of the wild horses and cattle that roamed the pampas by the million. Yet in the fifty years of his glory, just before he disappeared, he reached heights of great heroism and nobility that have few parallels in history.

The gaucho was strong and handsome, with an olive complexion tanned by sun and wind. He was of medium height and somewhat bent. Since he was virtually inseparable from his horse, his constant riding made him muscular and vigorous. He had black piercing eyes accustomed to seeking out distant landmarks on the horizons of the pampas. Although he looked and acted like a centaur when mounted, his living on horseback and galloping over those immeasurable distances prevented him from being a notable figure on foot, when he was slightly stoop-shouldered and bow-legged. But when he was on a horse, galloping like the wind in pursuit of a fleeing ostrich, his poncho flying straight out behind him and his right arm swinging the boleadors high above his head, he was an inspiring and exciting spectacle. No wonder the women adored him!

The gaucho was the peculiar product of the environment into which he was born, an environment of boundless plains and wild cattle. When

Mendoza's settlement on the banks of the River Plate was abandoned, the horses and mares were turned loose on the pampas. Forty years later, when Garay arrived to establish the town of Buenos Aires, he found the plains overrun with wild horses. Cattle were introduced into the new settlement from ranches which the Spaniards had laid out in the Cochabamba Valley of southern Bolivia and multiplied so rapidly under the favorable conditions of the pampas that the settlers stopped trying to keep track of them as private property and turned them out onto the plains. By 1780 the pampas were so thickly populated with wild horses and cattle that they roamed as far south as the Rio Negro and westward through Santa Fé, Córdoba, and Mendoza to the Andes. The colonial historian Azara reports that in 1780 there were approximately 42,000,000 head of wild horses and cattle roaming over 48,000 leagues (276,480,000 acres), or almost one-third the total area of what is today Argentine territory.

During the entire colonial period the commerce of the River Plate region consisted almost exclusively of the hides and tallow of these animals. When the gaucho needed money he rode out onto the plains and killed as many animals as he desired, removed the hides, and left the carcasses to rot in the sun. His only weapons and tools were the boleadors, his lasso, and a long, silver-handled sharp knife called a *facón*, which he carried stuck under the back of his belt. The facón was an inheritance from his Moorish forefathers, the word itself coming from the Andalusian *faca*, which in turn is derived from the Arabian *farjá*.

The gaucho was wildly independent and shunned the towns as much as possible. Above everything else he wanted freedom. Since avoiding civilization deprived him of the means of living which civilization would have offered him, he took to habits of his own. If he had a home at all, it was a wretched adobe hut with a grass roof. His wealth, when he had any, was displayed in the rich silver ornaments he lavished on his bridle and saddle. Work was beneath his dignity as a man, so he left it to his woman, who was called a *china* (pronounced "chee-na"), a Quechua word which means simply *hembra*, or female in the sense in which the word is applied to animals. *China* has since acquired a somewhat more affectionate meaning and still is applied to girls of the lower classes in the interior. But as a rule the gaucho avoided tying himself down to a hut or one woman. One of his favorite sports was to ride up to a timid *china*, snatch her up onto the saddle in front of him, and gallop out on the pampas with her.

The gaucho's idle time was spent mainly in repairing his boleadors or his lasso, or in tinkering with his bridle and saddle. But most of his time was spent on horseback. He began his day just before dawn by mounting his horse, as a city man begins his by shaving. Then he would think of where the horse could take him. His only serious aims in life were to ride better, to mount and dismount a galloping horse, to throw and tame a wild colt single-handed, and to gallop across the roughest ground at the utmost speed he could get out of his horse. All this gave him a childish delight in the consciousness of his mastery over animals.

The thought of being thrown from his horse was one that never entered the gaucho's mind. His idea of a rider was a man who could ride an untamed colt and alight on his own feet when the animal fell. In *The Voyage of the Beagle* Darwin tells of seeing a gaucho riding a very stubborn horse. Three times the horse reared so high that it fell over backward with great violence. The rider judged with uncommon coolness the exact moment for slipping off, and landed each time on his feet. As soon as the horse got up, he jumped on its back.

In all his exploits the gaucho never appeared to exert any muscular effort. Darwin describes watching a good rider with whom he was galloping along at a rapid pace, and says that he thought to himself: "Surely if the horse starts, you appear so careless on your seat, you must fall." At that moment a male ostrich sprang from his nest directly under the horse's nose, and the young colt bounded to one side like a stag. As for the gaucho, all that could be said of him was that he started and took fright with his horse.

The gaucho wore black, baggy pantaloons called *chiripás*, a waterproof poncho of vicuña hair, and long white underdrawers finished with a deep fringe of lace. His boots usually were made from the entire hide of a calf's hindleg, the knee-joint forming the heel of the boot. His hat was a jaunty *chambergo* of soft black felt which turned up in front like the hat of a musketeer. On his boots he wore a pair of very large, very heavy spurs, sometimes made of silver. His black hair was allowed to grow to his shoulders; he usually had a large, flowing mustache, and sometimes a beard. When he was a man of sufficient means to afford silver ornaments on his bridle and saddle he presented an imposing picture which gave rise to a proverb which is still popular in Argentina, *al gaucho van las prendas* (finery is becoming to the gaucho), which by a play of words also means that he is attractive to women.

J. M. Estrada, in his *Historia de la Argentina*, says:

The gaucho was the product of a system of government that stimulated neither agriculture nor commerce and which had neither schools nor incentives for civilization. Isolated from the crude civilization of the cities, he was pushed into the open life of the pampas in a struggle with the desert and with misery. There he became a barbarian. He had no recourse to science in case of illness, nor a church or home in affliction.

Throughout the colonial period the gauchos were despised by the Spaniards of the towns as wild outlaws only slightly better than Indians, and the contemporary chronicles contain frequent depreciatory references to them as a malignant and dangerous pest, disgraceful and without shame. The very name gaucho originally was a term of disparagement, being a corruption of the Quechua *huaco*, a lost animal without a mother, consequently an orphan or an outcast. It was not until General Martín Miguel de Güemes used the word affectionately in referring to his soldiers during the wars of independence that "gaucho" ceased to be a term of opprobrium. The first official document in which the word gaucho was used was the dispatch of Francisco Fernando de la Cruz, dated in Tucumán, June 1, 1814, forwarding Güemes's report that a party of his gauchos had defeated a detachment of Spanish royalists. After that, they figured prominently and heroically in the wars of independence. At the most critical period of the revolution, the gauchos on the northwestern frontier with Bolivia (then called Upper Peru), maintained a continual guerrilla warfare against a much larger and stronger royalist force with such effectiveness that the Spaniards were kept on the defense and held at bay for seven months until the surrender of Montevideo to the patriot army and the defeat of the Spanish fleet in the River Plate permitted the dispatch of 4000 troops from Buenos Aires to Upper Peru. The royalists retired at the approach of this patriot army, and General San Martín began the preparations for his famous crossing of the Andes and the liberation of Chile and Peru.

The Spanish general, Garcia Gamba, reported that the gauchos were extraordinary in their handling of the horse, expert in the use of all kinds of arms, individually valiant, and clever in dispersing and re-forming for attack, with a confidence, agility, and sang-froid which aroused the admiration of the European officers; that they were equal, if not superior, to the Cossacks, and capable of keeping up an accurate and effective fire either from horseback or on foot, with conspicuous ability for surprise attacks and guerrilla warfare.

The gaucho became a well-defined type, ethnically, politically, and socially, in the latter part of the eighteenth century, shortly before the River Plate colonies declared their independence from Spain. Throughout the colonial period the gauchos had resisted the authority of the agitation for the establishment of a locally elected government. The original intention seems to have been not to declare independence from Spain, but merely to insist on the right of the people to a voice in their local government. But since the beginning of the century, and more especially since the English invasions, there had been an ever-widening split between the criollos, who were demanding freedom to trade with all the countries of the world without restrictions on their exports, and the Spaniards, the traditionalists, who were insisting on compliance with the customs regulations of Cádiz.

The leaders of the revolutionary secret society were Mariano Moreno, Nicolás Rodriguez Peña, Juan José Paso, Hipólito Vieytes, and Juan José Castelli. Colonel Cornelio Saavedra, commander of the regiment of nobles known as the Patricios, pledged his support whenever the opportune moment for revolt should arrive. It was agreed that this moment would be when the French finally suppressed the junta at Cádiz, which was the last of the Spanish juntas pretending to represent the authority of the imprisoned king, Ferdinand VII. Being protected by the guns of the English fleet, Cádiz held out longer than any of the other Spanish municipalities against the Napoleonic invasion.

In 1808 the people of Cádiz revolted against the junta, assassinated the governor, and dragged his corpse through the streets. In the confusion that followed, a group of reactionaries set themselves up as a regency to rule in the name of Ferdinand. One of the first acts of this regency was to annul the decree of Viceroy Cisneros that opened the port of Buenos Aires to commerce. Just about the time that the people of Buenos Aires learned of this, two English brigantines arrived at Montevideo with the news that Napoleon himself, at the head of an army of 300,000, had swept southward across the Peninsula and occupied Seville and Cádiz. The moment agreed upon for the revolution had arrived.

The viceroy tried frantically to keep the news secret, but it soon was known throughout Buenos Aires. On May 18 he issued a rather feeble and pathetic proclamation admitting the fall of Cádiz and calling upon the people to remain loyal. But the leaders of the secret society had been spreading the theory that since there was no king there could be no viceroy, or vice-king, and they led the colony in insisting on its right of petition, which led to the open cabildo of May 22 and thus to the revolution. The people were determined that the viceroy should go, and that the local governing power should be invested in a popularly elected junta.

The morning of May 25 dawned cold and drizzling—one of those miserable, melancholy autumnal days for which May in Buenos Aires is noted. The cabildo was to meet at eight o'clock in the morning to act on the resignation of the junta which it had appointed on the 23rd, following the open cabildo of the previous day. Long before eight o'clock the Plaza de Mayo was filled with people whose hostility to the cabildo was plainly apparent. In a belligerent attitude, they demanded to know what was going on, giving rise to a popular phrase that has since been repeated whenever there has been a conflict between the government and the people: *el pueblo quiere saber de qué se trata*, "the people want to know what is going on."

Two young criollos made themselves prominent in the plaza that morning and were later to become famous in Argentine history. One was Domingo French, a letter-carrier; the other was Antonio Luis Berutti, a clerk in the Treasury. While the cabildo was deliberating behind locked doors, French and Berutti bought up all the white and blue ribbon they could find in one of the shops on the plaza. Berutti stuck these colors in his hat-band, and he and French then distributed pieces of the ribbons to the patriots assembled in the plaza. These were the colors that had been worn by the regiment of nobles during the English invasions, and the action of French and Berutti in the plaza that morning led to their adoption for the Argentine flag.

In 1812 Belgrano ordered cockades of these colors to be worn by two regiments which he had organized at Rosario and the cockades were approved by the Triumvirate. But when Belgrano made a blue and white flag for his troops, the Triumvirate reprimanded him severely and ordered him not to use it. Eventually his flag was adopted as the national banner by the Congress of Tucumán which drew up the declaration of independence in 1816.

French and Berutti were members of the revolutionary secret society, and after distributing the colors they demanded entrance into the session of the cabildo, where they presented a petition from the people requesting the appointment of a junta made up of men whose names were given in the petition. In view of this petition and the threatening attitude of the crowd, the cabildo sent for the troops to clear the plaza, but the officers replied that they were with the people. Members of the cabildo then stepped out onto a balcony overlooking the plaza, read the petition to the people, and asked them if that was what they wanted. They shouted back that it was, and the city councilors returned to the assembly room to draw up the legal document recording what had taken place.

The main portion of the historic old cabildo building still stands on the west side of the Plaza de Mayo, although parts of the north and south wings were cut away to make room for the Avenida de Mayo and Avenida Julio A. Roca. In the tower hangs the Liberty Bell which called the people to the plaza.

Tradition has it that at the moment the people shouted their answer back to the members of the cabildo the sun forced its way through a rift in the leaden clouds and shone down on the scene. This sun has become known as the *sol de Mayo*, sun of May, and appears in the center of the Argentine flag and on the coat-of-arms.

A little while later, the cabildo announced the appointment of a "Provisional Governing Junta of the River Plate," consisting of the men whose names were on the petition presented by French and Berutti. They were Cornelio Saavedra, President; Mariano Moreno and Juan José Paso, secretaries; Juan José Castelli, Manuel Belgrano, Miguel Azcuénaga, Manuel Alberti, Domingo Matheu, and Juan Larrea. This council is known as the *Primera Junta*, or First Junta, and governed the Viceroyalty from May 25 to December 18, 1810.

As Bartolomé Mitre has pointed out, "The revolution was effected without bayonets or violence, by pure pressure of public opinion, triumphant on the grounds of reason, law, and public welfare; abstaining from persecutions, it with dignity removed the chains which had bound the nation and assumed the rights of sovereignty with uprightness and moderation."

This first junta was to rule the Viceroyalty until a general junta could be formed with delegates from all the other municipalities of the Viceroyalty. There immediately began a keen conflict between the Spaniards and the criollos to control the elections of delegates to the general junta. One of the first acts of the new junta was to send an army into the interior, under Balcarce, and another to Paraguay, under Belgrano, to prevent royalist influence over the elections. The former viceroy, Liniers, joined the governor of Córdoba in leading a counter-revolution under the royal colors. He was overtaken by Balcarce and tried by a summary court-martial presided over by Castelli, who had begun a reign of terror similar to that of the French Revolution, and was immediately executed.

Balcarce and Castelli, who were leading the revolutionary forces against Peru, continued northward and on November 7, 1810, defeated the Spanish army from Lima at Suipacha, just beyond the Argentine frontier with Bolivia. This was the first victory of the South American revolution. Castelli ordered the execution of the three Spanish generals who had been defeated and the execution took place at Potosí. The whole region known as Upper Peru rose in rebellion against the Spaniards and they were forced to retire beyond the Desaguadero River, which was the boundary of the Viceroyalty of the River Plate.

When the revolution broke out, the Viceroyalty of the River Plate had an area of approximately 2,300,000 square miles, or about one-third of the area of the South American continent. The dismemberment of the Viceroyalty during the war of independence set up four independent States—Argentina, Bolivia, Paraguay, and Uruguay—and left Argentina with 1,080,550 square miles, or approximately half the territory that was being ruled from Buenos Aires when the viceroy was overthrown. Paraguay, Uruguay, and Peru, including Bolivia, refused to recognize the junta at Buenos Aires and reaffirmed their allegiance to the regency at Cádiz. Paraguay seceded from the United Provinces in 1811; Uruguay was invaded and occupied by the Portuguese from Brazil; and the war of independence between the patriots of Buenos Aires and the royalists of Peru settled down to a long tug-of-war in the northwestern provinces. Eventually Bolivia established itself as an independent nation in 1825 and Uruguay in 1828.

In 1810 the total population of the Viceroyalty was estimated at 720,000, composed of 421,000 mestizos, 210,000 Indians, 60,000 mulattoes, 20,000 Negroes, 6000 European whites, and 3000 native-born whites. About 60 per cent of this population was in what is today Argentina. Most of the whites and nearly all the Negroes and mulattoes were in Argentina and Uruguay, while the population of Peru and Bolivia was mostly Indian and mestizo. The population of the city of Buenos Aires at the time of the revolution was 45,000.

A month after the victory at Suipacha, the junta was enlarged by the addition of twelve members from the provinces and immediately proved too unwieldy to be of any use either in administration or in debate. Moreno resigned and in the following September the junta admitted the hopelessness of its situation, declared itself dissolved, and set up a Triumvirate which managed to save the State from shipwreck.

On March 9, 1812, the English frigate *George Canning* arrived at Buenos Aires. One of its passengers was Colonel José de San Martín, who was to be the hero of the Argentine revolution and the liberator of Chile and Peru. San Martín had been born in Yapeyú, Misiones, on February 25, 1778, two years after the formation of the Viceroyalty of the River Plate, so was thirty-four years old when he returned to Buenos Aires. His father had been lieutenant-governor of the Department of Yapeyú. When San Martín was eight years old his family took him to Spain and placed him in the Seminary of Nobles. Before he was twelve he had joined the Murcia Regiment as a cadet, and when only fifteen took part in a campaign against the Moors. Eventually, San Martín was in command of the troops at Cádiz on the day the governor was assassinated and dragged through the streets. For the rest of his life he had a horror of mobs and governments which relied on them.

When Napoleon was expelled from Spain, San Martín was mentioned in the order of the day, was promoted to the rank of lieuenant-colonel and awarded a gold medal. He returned to Buenos Aires and offered his services to the patriot government, then organized a troop of mounted grenadiers who eventually were to march across the Andes with him and liberate Chile and Peru. Descendants of those grenadiers, still wearing the showy uniform that San Martín designed, form the carefully picked regiment which acts as the Presidential Guard and posts sentinels at all the entrances of Government House.

San Martín began at once to take a leading part in the revolutionary movement, declaring that it was silly and futile to keep up the fiction of loyalty to Spain and demanding the establishment of an independent State. On October 8, 1812, he and his mounted grenadiers led a revolution that overthrew the first Triumvirate because of its weak and vacillating policy in conducting the war.

In 1813 the Spanish governor at Montevideo sent eleven ships and 400 men up the Paraná River in search of provisions for Montevideo, which was being besieged by Argentine and Uruguayan patriots. San Martín with his 125 grenadiers followed the enemy as they ascended the river, keeping hidden, and arrived at San Lorenzo, fifteen miles north of Rosario, two hours after the Spaniards had arrived there. At sunrise San Martín watched the disembarking of the Spaniards from his hiding place in the chapel. He divided his men into two companies behind the convent walls and ordered them to keep out of sight until the Spaniards approached and then to attack them only with sword and lance. When the Spaniards had got very close, the grenadiers charged furiously and engaged the enemy hand to hand. San Martín's horse was shot and fell on his rider. A Spaniard was just about to run his lance through San Martín when one of his soldiers did the same to the Spaniard. Sergeant

Juan Bautista Cabral rushed up and dragged San Martín from under his horse and was killed while protecting his commandant with his own body. He died exclaiming, "I die content. We have won!" As the historian Levene remarks, Cabral saved not only the life of San Martín but the independence of half a continent. Sergeant Cabral's name has been given to a short street running westward from the Plaza San Martín, and the battle has been commemorated in the "San Lorenzo March." The action had an importance entirely out of proportion to the number of troops involved, because it put an end to the Spanish raids against river towns and had a tremendous effect on the morale of the patriots.

In November 1813 San Martín was sent to Tucumán to assist Belgrano, who had been forced to fall back after his defeat at Vilcapiego, a defeat that was due to his having been too magnanimous after defeating the Spaniards at Salta in February and permitting them to depart after receiving their pledge not to take up arms against the patriot cause. By this time San Martín had become convinced that independence could never be won until the Spaniards were pushed out of Chile, Peru, and other colonies from which they could carry on a never-ending war against any patriot government that might be set up at Buenos Aires. While in Tucumán, he made up his mind that the patriot army in the northwest was not sufficient to carry on an offensive war against the Spanish power entrenched in Peru. So he persuaded the government at Buenos Aires to take up a purely defensive position, which he entrusted to General Martín de Güemes and his gauchos in Salta while he went to Mendoza to organize an army to cross the Andes against the Spaniards in Chile and Peru.

Güemes and his gauchos carried on a nerve-racking guerrilla war against the Spaniards which kept them continually on the defensive and prevented them from sending reinforcements to Chile. One of the very unmilitary but highly successful innovations of the gauchos was to tie large bunches of straw to the tails of wild horses they had rounded up and then light this straw and stampede the crazed animals into the Spanish encampment at midnight. For a year and a half the Spaniards were harassed with this kind of warfare.

In the meantime San Martín had so imbued the people with a passion for liberty that every man in the west and northwest was either fighting or helping San Martín in his preparations to invade Chile. It seems incredible that he could have kept his plans secret for a year and a half while so near the Chilean frontier. But he had organized a highly efficient spy system which informed him of everything the Spaniards were doing, towns. The perpetual danger from Indian raids had compelled them to band together in semi-military organizations for their own protection. The man strong enough to hold the respect of the gauchos in his locality and command them in war became the *caudillo*, or chieftain, of that locality. For two hundred years most of the interior had been under the rule of these strong local caudillos. When independence from Spanish rule was declared and the city of Buenos Aires arrogated to itself the right to represent all the people living in the Viceroyalty and to act in their name, it met with the unanimous opposition of the gaucho caudillos of the interior, who saw their power threatened. As a result, Argentina's history has been the story of a continuous conflict between the city of Buenos Aires and the interior, and the story of caudillo politics.

The nomadic, freedom-loving gaucho simply could not understand the situation that arose after the declaration of independence, particularly the tyranny of the town authorities who replaced the Spanish authorities he had helped to overthrow. The upper classes owned everything. They had bought or seized all the land not still in possession of the Indian tribes. And while it is true that the gauchos were nomads by choice, it also is true that neither the law, customs, nor the new, independent government gave them an acre of land they could call their own or on which they might live in peace. Yet, although they had no home, if they wanted to go from one place to another they had to obtain a passport to show that they had the right to travel in their own land. So they turned on the townspeople and fought them just as fiercely as they had fought the Spaniards.

The whole course of Argentine history probably was changed, leading to the adoption of the federal instead of the unitarian form of government, as the result of a single dexterous throw of a gaucho's boleadors. When Juan Manuel de Rosas was made governor of the Province of Buenos Aires in 1822, the one man whose military genius probably would have prevented Rosas from obtaining supreme power was General José Maria Paz, leading caudillo in the Province of Córdoba. Rosas sent a strong force to Córdoba with orders to suppress this chieftain who refused to submit to the governor of Buenos Aires.

The force under General Paz was weaker than the force sent by Rosas, but Paz evidently had few qualms about the result of the encounter and he was so foolhardy as to reconnoiter the enemy position personally on the evening before the engagement was to take place. Mounted on a fast horse, he rode out onto the plain to satisfy himself on some point about the disposition of Rosas's troops, and in an unwary

moment permitted a group of enemy gauchos to get within striking distance. As his horse was swift enough to carry him to safety, the adventure probably would have ended satisfactorily had it not been for
the fatally accurate aim of a gaucho named Zeballos, whose boleadors
wrapped themselves around the legs of General Paz's horse and brought
the animal to earth so suddenly that the rider was made prisoner. Paz
languished in prison during the years that Rosas little by little acquired
the supremacy that enabled him to rule the country as a tyrannical dictator from 1830 to 1852.

Paz had been a nineteen-year-old, third-year law student at the University of Córdoba when the liberating army from Buenos Aires marched
into the provinces after the revolution of May 1810. He joined the army
and spent the rest of his life as a soldier. After the overthrow of Rosas
at the battle of Caseros, Paz went to Buenos Aires and died there in 1854.

In the time of Rosas the gaucho still was the buffer between the
civilized settlements and the savage Indians. It needed only a word or a
signal to change the soft-spoken, apparently emotionless mystic into a
hard-riding, hard-fighting warrior. He could not tolerate town life,
and as civilization moved out across the pampas the gaucho moved also,
always in the vanguard of civilization but never quite a part of it. As a
result, he was constantly at war with the Indians who were being en-
croached upon, and the Indians were always lying in wait just beyond
the horizon. When the hour of the *malón* was at hand, they sprang out
of the silence, lanced the gaucho and his sons and carried off the women
and girls, dispersed the cattle, and fled, their hair and the manes of their
horses stained with blood and flying in the wind. Today, in the best
Argentine society, a surprise party is a malón.

Fifty years after the boleadors captured Paz, General Julio A. Roca
led a gaucho army in one last grand campaign against the Pampa Indians
and pushed them back beyond the Rio Negro into Patagonia. The campaign was a great sweep along the whole course of the Rio Negro, capturing men, women, and children and bringing back great numbers of
them as prisoners to be used in the agricultural colonies of Santa Fé and
Entre Rios. Later, as President, Roca stimulated the immigration of
farmers from Europe; fences were built across the plains; the plow
turned up the grazing lands and replaced them with wheat fields; and
the romance of the pampas slowly faded away.

The last generation of gauchos hung on until the early years of the
twentieth century, working as cowboys on the large estancias. But the
old gaucho still found it difficult to settle down inside the confines of

fences. He was inclined to wander from ranch to ranch, driving twelve or fifteen horses of his own before him. These he expected to pasture on his employer's land and usually could do so until the last twenty or thirty years of the last century. He was loyal to the *patrón* and depended on the patrón to get him out of his frequent trouble with the police. A strict gaucho code of unwritten law grew up on the pampas. It was a crime to steal a horse. It was all right to borrow one without the owner's knowledge, because when it was turned loose it would return home. It was also acceptable to kill another man's cow for food, but honor required that the owner of the animal get its hide.

The gaucho also had a deep, inborn sense of hospitality. He never under any circumstances refused a meal and lodging to anyone who might ask for it, even when he knew his guest was a hunted criminal. And, of course, he never admitted to the police who his lodger had been. No stranger ever got out of his saddle in front of a shack on the pampas without first calling out "*Ave Maria*" and waiting to be invited to dismount. If he responded to the greeting "*Buenas tardes*" ("Good afternoon") with "*Buenos días*" ("Good morning"), that meant he had had no lunch, and food was prepared for him at once, no matter what the time of day. Throughout Argentina today, people still say "Good afternoon" at eleven in the morning and "Good morning" at three in the afternoon, according to whether or not they have had their mid-day meal.

The gaucho reached his most romantic type in the *payador*, or trouba-dour, who wandered from one estancia to another with his guitar, im-provising witty and ironic couplets which he sang to his own accompani-ment. His appearance on an estancia was the occasion for a fiesta. When two of these payadores met and got into a contest of singing back and forth at each other, the fiesta almost invariably wound up in the vicious *duelo criollo* with the long, sharp facones, against which the only shield was the poncho draped around the left arm. Much of Argentina's folk-lore comes down from these payadores.

But the last gaucho has galloped across the far-away horizon of the pampas and into the twilight of history, and Argentina has lost its most characteristic and attractive citizen. His successor is a poor, miserable, underpaid peon who is called a *paisano* but never a gaucho, and nothing makes an Argentine quite so angry as to have a gushing young American tourist ask him to show her a gaucho.

9. INDEPENDENCE

IT was the French Revolution, rather than the American, that inspired the Buenos Aires revolution of May 25, 1810, which was to liberate the entire South American continent from Spanish rule. The revolt of the English colonies in North America served as an example that such a break could be made successfully, but the whole ideology of the South American movement was French. The French inspiration is still commemorated in the Argentine coat-of-arms, in which the Phrygian liberty cap appears above the clasped hands of the great republican slogan—Liberty, Equality, Fraternity—which was adopted from the French Revolution as the slogan of the Argentine uprising.

At the beginning of the nineteenth century, Buenos Aires was fortunate enough to possess a group of very intelligent writers and thinkers who enjoyed considerable prestige in the community. The universities of Córdoba and Charcas, with their high scholastic standards, had prepared several generations of conscientious thinkers, some of whom had completed their education by traveling in Europe. Among the most notable of these men were Mariano Moreno, who became virtual mentor of the liberating movement; Bernardino Rivadavia, who became the first President; Manuel Belgrano, a sincere and enthusiastic patriot whose failure as an emergency military leader cost the loss of Paraguay; and a score of others whose names will live forever in Argentine history.

These men were all earnest students of the French Encyclopedists and inspired by their ideas. Moreno had translated into Spanish Rousseau's *Social Contract*, except that part of it which he said "got off the track on the question of religion." Belgrano had obtained permission from Pope Pius VI to read the works of Voltaire, Montesquieu, Diderot, and Rousseau, and was deeply impressed by their democratic ideas. Copies of the works of these great French thinkers were circulating surreptitiously throughout the Spanish colonies at the beginning of the century and in Mexico a prominent patriot had been imprisoned for translating and circulating *The Rights of Man*.

The salon was the popular social activity in Buenos Aires, just as in France, and this small group of democratically inclined thinkers propagated their ideas orally during the animated conversations that were the *raison d'être* of these social gatherings. By 1809, revolution was obviously in the air and the intellectuals formed a secret society to direct the agitation for the establishment of a locally elected government. The original intention seems to have been not to declare independence from Spain, but merely to insist on the right of the people to a voice in their local government. But since the beginning of the century, and more especially since the English invasions, there had been an ever-widening split between the criollos, who were demanding freedom to trade with all the countries of the world without restrictions on their exports, and the Spaniards, the traditionalists, who were insisting on compliance with the customs regulations of Cádiz.

The leaders of the revolutionary secret society were Mariano Moreno, Nicolás Rodriguez Peña, Juan José Paso, Hipólito Vieytes, and Juan José Castelli. Colonel Cornelio Saavedra, commander of the regiment of nobles known as the Patricios, pledged his support whenever the opportune moment for revolt should arrive. It was agreed that this moment would be when the French finally suppressed the junta at Cádiz, which was the last of the Spanish juntas pretending to represent the authority of the imprisoned king, Ferdinand VII. Being protected by the guns of the English fleet, Cádiz held out longer than any of the other Spanish municipalities against the Napoleonic invasion.

In 1808 the people of Cádiz revolted against the junta, assassinated the governor, and dragged his corpse through the streets. In the confusion that followed, a group of reactionaries set themselves up as a regency to rule in the name of Ferdinand. One of the first acts of this regency was to annul the decree of Viceroy Cisneros that opened the port of Buenos Aires to commerce. Just about the time that the people of Buenos Aires learned of this, two English brigantines arrived at Montevideo with the news that Napoleon himself, at the head of an army of 300,000, had swept southward across the Peninsula and occupied Seville and Cádiz. The moment agreed upon for the revolution had arrived.

The viceroy tried frantically to keep the news secret, but it soon was known throughout Buenos Aires. On May 18 he issued a rather feeble and pathetic proclamation admitting the fall of Cádiz and calling upon the people to remain loyal. But the leaders of the secret society had been spreading the theory that since there was no king there could be no viceroy, or vice-king, and they led the colony in insisting on its right of petition, which led to the open cabildo of May 22 and thus to the revolution. The people were determined that the viceroy should go, and that the local governing power should be invested in a popularly elected junta.

The morning of May 25 dawned cold and drizzling—one of those miserable, melancholy autumnal days for which May in Buenos Aires is noted. The cabildo was to meet at eight o'clock in the morning to act on the resignation of the junta which it had appointed on the 23rd, following the open cabildo of the previous day. Long before eight o'clock the Plaza de Mayo was filled with people whose hostility to the cabildo was plainly apparent. In a belligerent attitude, they demanded to know what was going on, giving rise to a popular phrase that has since been repeated whenever there has been a conflict between the government and the people: *el pueblo quiere saber de qué se trata*, "the people want to know what is going on."

Two young criollos made themselves prominent in the plaza that morning and were later to become famous in Argentine history. One was Domingo French, a letter-carrier; the other was Antonio Luis Berutti, a clerk in the Treasury. While the cabildo was deliberating behind locked doors, French and Berutti bought up all the white and blue ribbon they could find in one of the shops on the plaza. Berutti stuck these colors in his hat-band, and he and French then distributed pieces of the ribbons to the patriots assembled in the plaza. These were the colors that had been worn by the regiment of nobles during the English invasions, and the action of French and Berutti in the plaza that morning led to their adoption for the Argentine flag.

In 1812 Belgrano ordered cockades of these colors to be worn by two regiments which he had organized at Rosario and the cockades were approved by the Triumvirate. But when Belgrano made a blue and white flag for his troops, the Triumvirate reprimanded him severely and ordered him not to use it. Eventually his flag was adopted as the national banner by the Congress of Tucumán which drew up the declaration of independence in 1816.

French and Berutti were members of the revolutionary secret society, and after distributing the colors they demanded entrance into the session of the cabildo, where they presented a petition from the people requesting the appointment of a junta made up of men whose names were given in the petition. In view of this petition and the threatening attitude of the crowd, the cabildo sent for the troops to clear the plaza, but the officers replied that they were with the people. Members of the cabildo then stepped out onto a balcony overlooking the plaza, read the petition to the people, and asked them if that was what they wanted. They shouted back that it was, and the city councilors returned to the assembly room to draw up the legal document recording what had taken place.

The main portion of the historic old cabildo building still stands on the west side of the Plaza de Mayo, although parts of the north and south wings were cut away to make room for the Avenida de Mayo and Avenida Julio A. Roca. In the tower hangs the Liberty Bell which called the people to the plaza.

Tradition has it that at the moment the people shouted their answer back to the members of the cabildo the sun forced its way through a rift in the leaden clouds and shone down on the scene. This sun has become known as the *sol de Mayo*, sun of May, and appears in the center of the Argentine flag and on the coat-of-arms.

A little while later, the cabildo announced the appointment of a "Provisional Governing Junta of the River Plate," consisting of the men whose names were on the petition presented by French and Berutti. They were Cornelio Saavedra, President; Mariano Moreno and Juan José Paso, secretaries; Juan José Castelli, Manuel Belgrano, Miguel Azcuénaga, Manuel Alberti, Domingo Matheu, and Juan Larrea. This council is known as the *Primera Junta*, or First Junta, and governed the Viceroyalty from May 25 to December 18, 1810.

As Bartolomé Mitre has pointed out, "The revolution was effected without bayonets or violence, by pure pressure of public opinion, triumphant on the grounds of reason, law, and public welfare; abstaining from persecutions, it with dignity removed the chains which had bound the nation and assumed the rights of sovereignty with uprightness and moderation."

This first junta was to rule the Viceroyalty until a general junta could be formed with delegates from all the other municipalities of the Viceroyalty. There immediately began a keen conflict between the Spaniards and the criollos to control the elections of delegates to the general junta. One of the first acts of the new junta was to send an army into the interior, under Balcarce, and another to Paraguay, under Belgrano, to prevent royalist influence over the elections. The former viceroy, Liniers, joined the governor of Córdoba in leading a counter-revolution under the royal colors. He was overtaken by Balcarce and tried by a summary court-martial presided over by Castelli, who had begun a reign of terror similar to that of the French Revolution, and was immediately executed.

Balcarce and Castelli, who were leading the revolutionary forces against Peru, continued northward and on November 7, 1810, defeated the Spanish army from Lima at Suipacha, just beyond the Argentine frontier with Bolivia. This was the first victory of the South American revolution. Castelli ordered the execution of the three Spanish generals who had been defeated and the execution took place at Potosí. The whole region known as Upper Peru rose in rebellion against the Spaniards and they were forced to retire beyond the Desaguadero River, which was the boundary of the Viceroyalty of the River Plate.

When the revolution broke out, the Viceroyalty of the River Plate had an area of approximately 2,300,000 square miles, or about one-third of the area of the South American continent. The dismemberment of the Viceroyalty during the war of independence set up four independent States—Argentina, Bolivia, Paraguay, and Uruguay—and left Argentina with 1,080,550 square miles, or approximately half the territory that was being ruled from Buenos Aires when the viceroy was overthrown. Paraguay, Uruguay, and Peru, including Bolivia, refused to recognize the junta at Buenos Aires and reaffirmed their allegiance to the regency at Cádiz. Paraguay seceded from the United Provinces in 1811; Uruguay was invaded and occupied by the Portuguese from Brazil; and the war of independence between the patriots of Buenos Aires and the royalists of Peru settled down to a long tug-of-war in the northwestern provinces. Eventually Bolivia established itself as an independent nation in 1825 and Uruguay in 1828.

In 1810 the total population of the Viceroyalty was estimated at 720,000, composed of 421,000 mestizos, 210,000 Indians, 60,000 mulattoes, 20,000 Negroes, 6000 European whites, and 3000 native-born whites. About 60 per cent of this population was in what is today Argentina. Most of the whites and nearly all the Negroes and mulattoes were in Argentina and Uruguay, while the population of Peru and Bolivia was mostly Indian and mestizo. The population of the city of Buenos Aires at the time of the revolution was 45,000.

A month after the victory at Suipacha, the junta was enlarged by the addition of twelve members from the provinces and immediately proved too unwieldy to be of any use either in administration or in debate. Moreno resigned and in the following September the junta admitted the hopelessness of its situation, declared itself dissolved, and set up a Triumvirate which managed to save the State from shipwreck.

On March 9, 1812, the English frigate *George Canning* arrived at Buenos Aires. One of its passengers was Colonel José de San Martín, who was to be the hero of the Argentine revolution and the liberator of Chile and Peru. San Martín had been born in Yapeyú, Misiones, on February 25, 1778, two years after the formation of the Viceroyalty of the River Plate, so was thirty-four years old when he returned to Buenos Aires. His father had been lieutenant-governor of the Department of Yapeyú. When San Martín was eight years old his family took him to Spain and placed him in the Seminary of Nobles. Before he was twelve he had joined the Murcia Regiment as a cadet, and when only fifteen took part in a campaign against the Moors. Eventually, San Martín was in command of the troops at Cádiz on the day the governor was assassinated and dragged through the streets. For the rest of his life he had a horror of mobs and governments which relied on them.

When Napoleon was expelled from Spain, San Martín was mentioned in the order of the day, was promoted to the rank of lieuenant-colonel and awarded a gold medal. He returned to Buenos Aires and offered his services to the patriot government, then organized a troop of mounted grenadiers who eventually were to march across the Andes with him and liberate Chile and Peru. Descendants of those grenadiers, still wearing the showy uniform that San Martín designed, form the carefully picked regiment which acts as the Presidential Guard and posts sentinels at all the entrances of Government House.

San Martín began at once to take a leading part in the revolutionary movement, declaring that it was silly and futile to keep up the fiction of loyalty to Spain and demanding the establishment of an independent State. On October 8, 1812, he and his mounted grenadiers led a revolution that overthrew the first Triumvirate because of its weak and vacillating policy in conducting the war.

In 1813 the Spanish governor at Montevideo sent eleven ships and 400 men up the Paraná River in search of provisions for Montevideo, which was being besieged by Argentine and Uruguayan patriots. San Martín with his 125 grenadiers followed the enemy as they ascended the river, keeping hidden, and arrived at San Lorenzo, fifteen miles north of Rosario, two hours after the Spaniards had arrived there. At sunrise San Martín watched the disembarking of the Spaniards from his hiding place in the chapel. He divided his men into two companies behind the convent walls and ordered them to keep out of sight until the Spaniards approached and then to attack them only with sword and lance. When the Spaniards had got very close, the grenadiers charged furiously and engaged the enemy hand to hand. San Martín's horse was shot and fell on his rider. A Spaniard was just about to run his lance through San Martín when one of his soldiers did the same to the Spaniard. Sergeant

Juan Bautista Cabral rushed up and dragged San Martín from under his horse and was killed while protecting his commandant with his own body. He died exclaiming, "I die content. We have won!" As the historian Levene remarks, Cabral saved not only the life of San Martín but the independence of half a continent. Sergeant Cabral's name has been given to a short street running westward from the Plaza San Martín, and the battle has been commemorated in the "San Lorenzo March." The action had an importance entirely out of proportion to the number of troops involved, because it put an end to the Spanish raids against river towns and had a tremendous effect on the morale of the patriots.

In November 1813 San Martín was sent to Tucumán to assist Belgrano, who had been forced to fall back after his defeat at Vilcapiego, a defeat that was due to his having been too magnanimous after defeating the Spaniards at Salta in February and permitting them to depart after receiving their pledge not to take up arms against the patriot cause. By this time San Martín had become convinced that independence could never be won until the Spaniards were pushed out of Chile, Peru, and other colonies from which they could carry on a never-ending war against any patriot government that might be set up at Buenos Aires. While in Tucumán, he made up his mind that the patriot army in the northwest was not sufficient to carry on an offensive war against the Spanish power entrenched in Peru. So he persuaded the government at Buenos Aires to take up a purely defensive position, which he entrusted to General Martín de Güemes and his gauchos in Salta while he went to Mendoza to organize an army to cross the Andes against the Spaniards in Chile and Peru.

Güemes and his gauchos carried on a nerve-racking guerrilla war against the Spaniards which kept them continually on the defensive and prevented them from sending reinforcements to Chile. One of the very unmilitary but highly successful innovations of the gauchos was to tie large bunches of straw to the tails of wild horses they had rounded up and then light this straw and stampede the crazed animals into the Spanish encampment at midnight. For a year and a half the Spaniards were harassed with this kind of warfare.

In the meantime San Martín had so imbued the people with a passion for liberty that every man in the west and northwest was either fighting or helping San Martín in his preparations to invade Chile. It seems incredible that he could have kept his plans secret for a year and a half while so near the Chilean frontier. But he had organized a highly efficient spy system which informed him of everything the Spaniards were doing, and he saw to it that they got only such documents as had been specially prepared to deceive them.

The Chilean revolution had collapsed and its leader, Bernardo O'Higgins, had fled to Mendoza, where he joined San Martín. But the Chilean patriots organized themselves into small voluntary bands and waited for leadership.

The organization of the Army of the Andes and its crossing of the mountains was one of the greatest feats in history. Military experts describe it as a much more daring exploit than Napoleon's crossing of the Alps and it is studied in all military colleges. During its organization, the army was supported by patriotic subscriptions, gratuitous services, and special taxes. The people of the three Cuyo provinces bore the brunt of the maintenance of the army. The ladies of Mendoza contributed their jewels to pay for cannon and powder and have come down in history as the *Patricias Mendocinas*. San Martín entrusted the organization of an arsenal to a mendicant friar, Luis Beltrán, who soon had 300 men working for him. They produced cannon and shot, melting church bells when they could not get anything else, and made horseshoes and bayonets, knapsacks and shoes. A powder factory was built and made sufficient powder for the campaign. A cloth factory was established and the women of Mendoza made uniforms free of charge.

Early in 1817 San Martín had an army of 4000 ready. There were 3000 infantry, 700 mounted grenadiers, 250 artillerymen with ten six-pounders, two howitzers, and nine four-pound mountain guns. In addition there were 1200 mounted gaucho militia and a host of muleteers, artisans, and 120 miners to keep the mountain roads in repair. The army was divided into three sections, each of which was complete in itself. Two of these marched across the Andes by way of Los Patos Pass and the artillery went through the Uspallata Pass.

The army was ready to start its historic march on January 17, 1817. It was a great holiday in Mendoza. The whole army marched to salute the Virgin of Carmen as its patron saint and there received a serge flag that had been made by the ladies of Mendoza. While this flag was blue and white, it differed considerably from the flag that had been adopted as the national standard, having one blue and one white band, running vertically, and a golden sun embroidered in the center. It is carefully guarded in the museum at Mendoza.

The River Plate patriots played a vitally important part in the emancipation of the rest of the continent and it is almost certain that except for San Martín's expedition to the Pacific the entire revolutionary movement would have been crushed. There were two main centers of revolt, one at Buenos Aires and the other at Caracas, with the Spanish base in between them at Lima, from which point Spanish armies were sent south or north against whichever revolutionary movement was the more threatening at the moment.

In December 1813 Napoleon had released Ferdinand and withdrawn all his forces from Spain to defend France against the invasion of his enemies. Ferdinand re-established his absolutist monarchy and immediately took steps to put down the rebellion in South America at all costs. The years from 1814 to 1817 were extremely dangerous ones for the patriotic movement, which finally seemed to be on the verge of complete collapse, with the Spanish royalists victorious from Mexico to Chile.

It was at this critical moment that San Martín led his army across the Andes. The two detachments that took the northern route through Los Patos Pass marched 300 miles. The artillery was dragged nearly 200 miles over almost impassable mountain trails, across an altitude of 12,000 feet, and down into the Aconcagua Valley on the Chilean side. After eighteen days of hard marching and great difficulties, the three sections of the army united on the heights of Chacabuco. Meanwhile, small detachments had been sent through several other passes to the north and south to confuse the Spaniards, who dispersed their forces, as San Martín intended they should do.

The battle of Chacabuco, which took place on February 12, resulted in a disastrous defeat for the Spaniards, who lost 500 dead, 600 prisoners, a large quantity of arms, and seven flags, three of which were sent to Buenos Aires. On the 14th San Martín entered Santiago, which the Spanish commander had abandoned. On the same day, and almost at the same hour, the Portuguese sacked and burned Yapeyú, the town in which San Martín was born. It never has been restored.

Chacabuco was the turning point of the revolution and had very important political results, as well as military. From the military point of view, it crowned with success San Martín's long preparations and signalized the beginning of a continental offensive war on the part of the patriots. Politically, it removed the danger of a Spanish invasion of the River Plate, paralyzed the royalist operations against Buenos Aires in what is now Bolivia, and encouraged the Chileans to renewed efforts by freeing Santiago of Spanish domination.

The Spanish forces in Chile were definitely defeated and dispersed a year later in the battle of Maipó, which was the first really big battle in South America and a model of military operations. Here San Martín showed his military genius, for the battle was what military scholars call an oblique engagement, of which there had been only two known examples up to that time. One was led by Epaminondas of Thebes at Leuctra and the other was won by Napoleon at Austerlitz. The Spaniards lost 1000 dead and a total of 2362 prisoners, including 162 officers. The patriots lost 1000 dead and wounded. After Maipó the Spanish power was restricted to Peru. When news of San Martín's victory reached Europe, most of the governments and public men of the Old World became convinced that Spain's colonial empire was finished. The Holy Alliance toyed with the idea of helping Ferdinand get his colonies back, but dropped it when England persuaded France not to support the project.

San Martín refused the post of Supreme Director which the Chileans wanted to confer upon him, and the post was given to O'Higgins. San Martín spent the next two years organizing an army of Argentines and Chileans to liberate Peru.

By this time Argentina was in a state of anarchy. There was no constituted central government, and each province was a small republic recognizing no authority except its own. San Martín was called several times to return to Buenos Aires to put down these insurrections, but refused. He knew that the independence of the Argentine provinces would never be secure until the Spaniards were repulsed from their last foothold in South America; he believed that anarchy was the result of the people's own unfitness for self-government and that it could not be cured by an army; so he took upon himself the great responsibility of preparing the invasion of Peru on his own authority. The expedition left Valparaiso on August 20, 1820, in sixteen transports, escorted by eight warships. The army totaled 4450 men, of whom 2313 were Argentines and 1805 Chileans, in addition to which there were 332 of other nationalities, including American and English. There were 1600 men in the navy, of whom 500 were Englishmen.

The transports of the expedition were under the command of Captain Paul Delano, of Boston, who had taken the 28-gun sloop *Curiacio* to Valparaiso after its purchase by the Chilean government. Captain Delano was related to the ancestors of President Franklin Delano Roosevelt and later established the Delano family which has been prominent in the Chilean navy down to the present. The *Curiacio* was christened *Independencia* after its arrival in Chile and became famous in Chilean history for capturing the royalists' *Esmeralda* in Callao Bay.

San Martín defeated the Spaniards in Peru and was acclaimed Protector of Peru. He designed the Peruvian flag which is still in use. On July 26, 1822, San Martín met the other great American liberator, Simón Bolívar, at Guayaquil. Bolívar, who was inspired much more by personal ambition than was San Martín, desired to finish the liberating campaign by himself. Also, he wanted to establish a republic in Peru, while San Martín was convinced that all the South American people were unfit for self-government and that independent monarchies should be established under European princes. San Martín was absolutely without personal ambition, however. He had devoted ten years of hard and thankless work to the mission of winning independence for three South American countries. When he saw that his own person was likely to become an issue, he retired from public life. In bidding farewell to Peru, he said, "My promise to the countries for which I fought is fulfilled: to secure their independence, and to leave them to select their own governments. The presence of a fortunate soldier, however disinterested he may be, is dangerous to newly established States."

San Martín retired to his beloved Mendoza, but soon saw that he could not remain detached from the civil wars. Determined to have no part in them, he passed through Buenos Aires virtually unnoticed and embarked for France, where he lived alone and in poverty for twenty-five years until he died in Boulogne-sur-Mer on August 17, 1850, at the age of seventy-two. During the quarter-century of his exile he had only one close friend, Alejandro Aguado, a Spanish nobleman who had served in the same regiment with him in Spain. Aguado provided San Martín with funds and willed him all his money when he died. San Martín wrote to friends in Buenos Aires that if it had not been for Aguado he would have died of starvation and illness.

San Martín had attempted to return to Buenos Aires in February 1829, arriving on the *Chichester*, but the government had refused to allow him to disembark. At that time his name was the vortex of a wild storm of calumny and abuse that was raging in Buenos Aires because of jealousy aroused by his victorious wars against the Spaniards in Chile and Peru and hatred over his stubborn refusal to become involved in the civil wars. During the six days that the vessel was moored to two buoys off shore, San Martín had to be content with what he could see of the city from the rail. When the *Chichester* arrived at Montevideo on February 13, San Martín was taken ashore and entertained lavishly as a national hero. He remained in Montevideo until the middle of April and then, like so many other prominent Argentines of those times, sailed into the exile in which he was to spend the rest of his life.

When San Martín died, only seven people accompanied his remains to a crypt in the Church of Our Lady in Boulogne-sur-Mer and the newspapers made no mention of his death until a week after. Thirty years later, on May 24, 1880, the steamer *Villarino* delivered his ashes at Buenos Aires, where they now rest in a beautiful marble tomb in the Cathedral, with a permanent guard of honor of San Martín Mounted Grenadiers.

San Martín undoubtedly was one of the greatest men who ever lived. Had his lifework been accomplished in Europe or the United States, he would be a world-famed figure. At one time he held the destiny of three nations in his hands and could easily have made himself king of any one. But he renounced all personal honors, even refusing to accept the commission of brigadier-general of the Buenos Aires army which was offered to him after the liberation of Chile. He placed his life at the service of liberty, with the determination not to become involved in the internal strife of his own country or to accept any personal glory for what he did. History records few examples of self-denial and greatness of soul to compare with his retirement to poverty and lonely ostracism when he was at the very height of his career.

It has been said of San Martín that rather than a man he was a mission.

10. ANARCHY

WHILE San Martín and the other military leaders were trying to insure the safety of the independence movement by keeping the Spanish forces beyond the boundaries of the Viceroyalty of the River Plate, the people of the city of Buenos Aires undertook to set up a system of government based on French precedents—juntas, triumvirates, directors, and, finally, a constituent assembly. From the very first there was a violent clash between the city and the interior which quickly brought about the complete collapse of government and inaugurated a reign of anarchy.

At the time of the revolution there were three parties in the Viceroyalty: (a) those who believed that the South American colonies were bound to share the fate of Spain and who were therefore disposed to yield to the dominant power of France; (b) those who were resolved not to submit to the French dynasty but who acknowledged the existing loyal authorities in Spain; and (c) those who, though loyal to Ferdinand, denied the right of the local authorities in Spain to rule outside the limits of the Peninsula and who wished to be governed by juntas of their own election.

This third party included all the native-born and was therefore by far the most numerous. But as none of its partisans had been admitted to high office during the colonial regime, it had not previously been able to make itself felt. Now it was predominant. The other two parties, which until now had displayed the most violent animosity toward each other, forgot their own quarrel and joined forces to resist the common foe—the native-born people of the country, whom they described as the rabble.

The revolutionary government in Buenos Aires went through many vicissitudes and its form was changed frequently in an effort to compromise with the conflicting political opinions in the country. But never once was it supplanted by Spanish authority, as were the revolutionary governments in all the other South American colonies. To begin with there was the First Junta, of nine members, which governed from May 25 to December 18, 1810; then the Second Junta, of twenty-one members, which was in power from December 18, 1810, to September 23, 1811; followed by the First Triumvirate, which governed from September 23, 1811, to October 8 of the following year; and the Second Triumvirate, which lasted only four months, from October 8, 1812, to

February 20, 1813. From 1814 to 1820 there were seven Supreme
Directors, four of whom served a few months each in the year 1815.

The revolution was not completed by a declaration of independence
until July 9, 1816, the six years since 1810 having been spent in a futile
attempt to find a prince to head a monarchy. During those six years, as
it became increasingly apparent that a monarchy could not be established and that some form of republican government would have to be
set up, the rivalry between the city of Buenos Aires and the interior
grew more and more intense. This soon divided the country into two
political camps—the Unitarians and the Federalists.

The Unitarians were made up mostly of the great patrician *hidalgo*
families, *hidalgo* meaning *hijo de algo,* or son of somebody. These
families lived mostly in Buenos Aires and were descendants of nobles,
adelantados, governors, viceroys, and other civil or military authorities.
They wanted a strong centralized or unitarian form of government,
since they could not conceive of any system that would put the governing power into the hands of the rabble. They insisted on a constitutional
government with the governing power in the hands of a ruling class,
accustomed to governing by tradition and education, similar to the ruling class in England.

The Federalists were "the rabble"—the provincials, the masses of
gauchos and mestizos of the pampas. These people hated Buenos Aires
as a self-styled Queen City trying to lord it over the rest of the country
and they refused to submit to the dictates of an aristocratic oligarchy.

The Unitarians sought the centralization of the French Republic; the
Federalists wanted a federal system such as was being constituted in
the United States of America. Above everything else the provinces demanded autonomy and it was this demand that led to the civil wars. The
civil strife, which caused general dissatisfaction among the property
owners of the interior, led to the organization of a Federalist Party
which eventually brought about the formation of the Federation, and
out of the Federation grew the Republic.

All these difficulties were a natural heritage from the Spanish system
of colonization. The whole colonial structure had been designed to keep
the native population in subjugation to the Spaniards who were sent
out to govern them. This system finally collided with sociological and
psychological factors which it could not control. Under the adelantazgo
system the continent had been colonized without cost to the Spanish
Crown, and the rapidity and success of the Conquest were traceable to
the fact that this system left the Spanish adventurers who were financing

the colonization free to do as they pleased, with virtually no regulation of their personal aspirations and ambitions. Each conquistador became a force unto himself, restricted only by his personal limitations. This gave rise to a spirit of individualism which was passed on to his descendants. By the time of the revolution, these descendants of the original adventurers had become a class in revolt against the absolutism of Spanish government, a class whose inborn individualism found itself in conflict with the very feudalism from which it had sprung.

Another factor which operated against the union of the country was the political structure of the colony. The Viceroyalty had been made up of a dozen municipalities which were something like city-states, the authority of each extending as far as the city authorities could make themselves obeyed. (At one time the municipality of Buenos Aires extended across the 35-mile River Plate and far into the territory that is now Uruguay.) These cities were separated by vast distances inhabited by raiding Indians and nomad gauchos, and there was almost no communication between them. This naturally led to strongly centralized local governments in each city, where the power of government was exercised by a governor ruling over a community of rugged individualists and born rebels against outside authority.

The jealousy of the superior influence of Buenos Aires was typical of the spirit of provincialism which pervaded every part of South America. The people of each district or province, grouped around the central city, insisted on governing themselves. They seemed to think that by uniting with others they would impair their own dignity. This feeling is still dominant in Argentine character and explains the difficulty of enlisting Argentina's co-operation in any group undertaking unless she is recognized as the leader of the movement. By the formation of separate States the general vanity was gratified and each man, having a more intimate connection with the rulers, became of more consequence in his own eyes and could more plausibly flatter his own personal ambitions. In a large State most of the people could think of themselves only as citizens of the State, with no hope of holding the reins of government or tasting the pleasure of power; but in a small State every man could be either one of the government officials or closely related to those who were, and everyone could flatter himself with dreams of future authority while enjoying the present satisfaction of exerting some control over those in power.

It is only fair to say that these narrow views had been fostered by the ignorance in which the people were kept under Spanish dominion, which led each small group of men to consider themselves as the criterion of excellence and to despise as imperfect everything that differed from them.

This natural provincialism of the interior was antagonized by the city of Buenos Aires from the very beginning. In 1811 the First Triumvirate organized a unitarian form of government, abolished the provincial juntas that had been set up as local authorities to co-operate with the central government, and sent men from Buenos Aires to act as governors of the provinces. The caudillos of the interior saw their power threatened by Buenos Aires and declared war rather than accept the new governors.

The Spaniards of Buenos Aires, who were doing everything possible to hold onto the power they had enjoyed under the colonial system, argued that the reconstruction of the North American colonies into a political entity capable of governing itself could not serve as an example for the South American colonies because the North American colonials were all Europeans, unmixed with Indian blood; that the great majority of them were Anglo-Saxons, accustomed to the ideal of self-government and to the idea that there could be no liberty without self-discipline; that they were, in a word, a homogeneous and self-respecting population. It was argued that the people of the Argentine interior were almost all of mixed blood and roaming gauchos with no fixed place of abode, and that such people should be governed by their betters.

Nearly all the leaders of the revolutionary secret society, including Moreno, Rivadavia, Rodriguez Peña, and Belgrano, were ardent monarchists, as were General San Martín and Cornelio Saavedra, president of the First Junta. In 1811 Moreno was sent on a secret diplomatic mission to Brazil and England to sound out, first, Princess Carlota and, second, the English government on the matter of taking over the protectorate of the River Plate provinces. Carlota's consort was already the Portuguese regent and she was most eager to establish herself as the Spanish regent in the River Plate and Chilean colonies. As already noted, her intrigue failed because she insisted on continuing the absolutist form of monarchy over which her brother Ferdinand ruled in Spain. But there was a moment immediately after the May revolution when she no doubt could have been crowned in Buenos Aires if she had had the courage to go there. Moreno was unable to fulfill his mission because he died at sea.

Mariano Moreno had been the leading spirit of the revolution. He gave Buenos Aires its first uncensored newspaper, *La Gaceta*, and opened it to all shades of opinion. And in many other ways he became entirely worthy of the reverent esteem in which he has been held ever since in Argentine history.

In 1815 Manuel Belgrano and Bernardino Rivadavia were sent to Brazil and Europe in search of a prince to accept the crown of the River Plate provinces. Their mission in Rio de Janeiro had nothing to do with Carlota this time, however, but was confined to soliciting the co-operation of the British ambassador in the plan to set up a constitutional monarchy under the protection of England. They were unable to find either an English or a Spanish prince for their proposed monarchy, and Belgrano returned with a scheme to put an Inca on the throne. The search for a European prince had been supported on the argument that the establishment of such a monarchy would remove European opposi-tion to the revolutionary movement, which was believed to be due en-tirely to the fear that the Spanish colonies were to become republics. Belgrano maintained that the crowning of an Inca would pacify the Indians and permit their incorporation into the new State. But this scheme also fell through, and the constituent assembly which had finally met at Tucumán went ahead, rather reluctantly, with plans for setting up a republic.

San Martín could easily have had the presidency of the Congress of Tucumán but he felt that he could not leave his work of organizing the Army of the Andes. However, he exercised considerable influence on the Congress through Tomás Godoy Cruz, the delegate from Mendoza, and through his close friend Manuel Belgrano. When this Congress met in March 1816, the cause of independence in South America seemed lost. All the colonies had been recovered by Spain except Buenos Aires. The Argentine army in Upper Peru had been routed and dispersed at Sipe-Sipe and Bolivia was definitely lost. Nevertheless, San Martín, through Godoy Cruz and Belgrano, kept insisting that the Congress should issue a declaration of independence. Most of the delegates were of the opinion that such a declaration should not be made until the form of government had been decided upon. In addition to the movement for setting up a monarchy, there was the wide divergence of opinion be-tween Buenos Aires and the provinces regarding national authority and provincial rights.

San Martín wrote to Godoy Cruz, "I die every time I hear federation mentioned. If in a government already constituted and in a country edu-cated, inhabited, artistic, agricultural and commercial (I speak of North America) difficulties in the conduct of the last war with England (War of 1812) arose from the Federation, what would happen to us who lack these advantages? If with all the provinces and their united resources we are weak, what would happen if each one was separated from the rest?"

The Congress had been in session more than three months and still no decision had been reached. "Is it not ridiculous," again wrote San Martín to Godoy Cruz, "that we coin money, have our national flag and shield, and even make war on the sovereign to whom it is said we belong, and do not declare our independence? The enemy treats us as insurgents and with much reason." On July 6 Belgrano made a long and important speech and three days later, July 9, 1816, the Declaration of Independence was finally sworn to. "Truly," wrote Bartoliné Mitre, author of the most famous biographies of both San Martín and Belgrano, "San Martín and Belgraño were the real founders of Argentine independence."

But still the Congress of Tucumán went ahead with its plans for establishing a monarchy, in the belief that loyalty to an Argentine Crown would unify the divergent elements and end the civil strife that had been raging since the May revolution and for which no other end was in sight. Fantastic as it seems at this late day, Belgrano's plan to crown an Inca had considerable backing. San Martín approved it, as he would have approved anything that promised internal quiet and peace.

But the people of the country would have nothing to do with this scheme of the urban bourgeois. There was no class of nobles in the River Plate as in the other colonies, especially Peru. There was not even a real aristocracy, or a military class, or a tradition—nothing on which a monarchy could live. Furthermore, the colony had only a pastoral economy and was too poor to support a monarchy. Also, the participation of the masses in the May revolution had been inspired by social reasons—the desire to overthrow the ruling class—rather than by the political purpose of merely changing the form of government.

So the monarchical plan fell through and the Congress of Tucumán turned its attention to drawing up a Constitution that would establish a democratic form of government. This Constitution was finally concluded in 1819 and set up "The United Provinces of South America" with a unitarian form of government.

In drawing up this Constitution the Congress of Tucumán had deliberately acted contrary to the majority opinion of the country, with the result that it produced more evils than it was intended to cure. The provinces refused to accept the Constitution and for the next six years

there was no pretense of maintaining a national government. During
the ten years that had passed since the revolution of May, there had
been a long series of revolts, mutinies, and other disturbances throughout the country, all inspired by one clearly defined underlying sentiment in favor of federalism and contrary to a centralized government at
Buenos Aires. Nevertheless, the Congress of Tucumán undertook to set
up the very form of government that was opposed everywhere except in
Buenos Aires.

On February 2, 1820, the Congress adjourned and the Supreme Director at Buenos Aires resigned. The national government thus disappeared, and the ten years of effort to unite the country were in vain.
The Province of Buenos Aires undertook to hold the nation together,
but its own anarchy was so chaotic that it had three governors on a
single day in 1820 (June 20), besides several others who stayed in office
only a matter of days or weeks. The provinces seceded one by one and
set about establishing their own constitutions as independent autonomous States. Tucumán even set itself up as a separate republic. Certain
of the provinces signed treaties of alliance among themselves.

Yet it was from this crisis of 1820, rather than from the revolution of
1810, that Argentina's social and institutional life began to take form,
even though it still was destined to go through much suffering and hard-
ship and to spill a great deal of blood. Also, it was from 1820 that the
caudillo began to be an important factor in Argentine history as the
voice and representative of the masses in the interior. Ten years of foreign trade, especially with England, had resulted in such wholesale and
indiscriminate slaughter of cattle that the roving gauchos began to find
themselves without food and so tended to group themselves around certain leading estancieros who provided them with the means of livelihood.
The *patrón* was looked upon with great admiration, bordering on worship, by the simple-minded men he gathered around him and this tended
to feed his vanity and desire for command and authority.

Ever since the revolution of May, the outstanding Federalist in the
River Plate colony had been José G. Artigas, the patriotic leader of the
Banda Oriental del Uruguay. When the Congress of Tucumán met,
Artigas sent delegates from Uruguay with instructions to vote for the
establishment of a federal union of autonomous States or provinces similar to the United States of America. This was so contrary to what the
leaders of the Tucumán Congress were trying to do that they very
stupidly refused to seat the delegates from the Banda Oriental, and Uruguay was lost to Argentina. Any chance that might have existed for

reconciliation was destroyed when the Congress of Tucumán abandoned Artigas and Uruguay to their fate at the time the Portuguese invaded the Banda Oriental and annexed it to Brazil. Artigas finally was defeated by the Portuguese and crossed the river into the Province of Entre Rios, where he formerly had led a civil war against Buenos Aires. But the caudillo of Entre Rios, Rodriguez, rebelled against his authority and in two battles defeated him beyond any chance of recovery. This also was in 1820. Artigas fled to Paraguay. His strong championship of democracy during the years of monarchical scheming in Argentina had so impressed the United States government that it invited Artigas to spend his exile in the United States, offering him a life salary as general, a distinction that had been offered before only to Lafayette. But Artigas declined the offer and spent the rest of his life in Paraguay, finally dying with only an old Negro servant at his bedside.

In 1820 there was signed a treaty of peace between the provinces of Santa Fé and Buenos Aires in which Santa Fé stipulated the payment of an indemnity in cattle with which to repopulate its plains. There was only one man in all the Province of Buenos Aires who could fulfill that obligation for the province and he was a caudillo named Juan Manuel de Rosas. He gathered the leading estancieros together and the required number of cattle was collected and sent to Santa Fé. But with the payment of that indemnity Rosas decided that there had been enough of civil war and disorder in the country and that he was the man chosen by Heaven to bring order and discipline out of chaos.

11. ROSAS AND TYRANNY

J UAN MANUEL DE ROSAS was one of twenty children born to his
mother. Five died at birth, five before they were grown, and only ten
outlived their parents. Of these ten, Juan Manuel was the oldest. His
parents were among the richest and most prominent people in the
country, and the blue blood of Spain ran in their veins. His father, León
Ortiz de Rozas had been an officer in the Spanish garrison at Buenos
Aires. Juan Manuel was born on March 30, 1793, so was only thirteen
at the time of the English invasion, yet he assembled a group of his
chums and they presented themselves to Liniers. Rosas was assigned to
help serve one of the guns during the reconquest and was complimented
by the officer in charge when the fighting was over. But, he and his
parents being ardent royalists, he took no part in the May revolution.

Rosas had some schooling in one of the best of the few schools of
Buenos Aires, but the happiest days of his boyhood were spent at his
father's estancia at Rincón de Lopez at the mouth of the River Salado,
near the present town of Dolores in the Province of Buenos Aires. There
his early, impressionable years were spent in close contact with Nature,
with the gauchos and the Indians. His first rebellion against authority
occurred when he was still a small boy. After having received some
elementary schooling, he was hired out as a clerk in a general store to
learn the business, with a view to some day becoming an administrator
of an estancia. One of the recognized duties of a new clerk was to wash
the dishes after meals had been served. When Rosas was told to wash
the dishes, he haughtily retorted, "I didn't come here to learn to wash
dishes"—whereupon he was sent home.

On hearing the story, his mother took him by the ear and ordered him
to go back to the store and apologize. When he refused, his mother led
him by the ear to a room and locked him in, saying, "Here you stay on
bread and water until you obey me." Juan Manuel remained in the room
all day and had his bread and water. With the falling of twilight, he
began to reflect on the day's events and the longer he reflected the more
rebellious he became. Finally he undressed, penciled a few words on a
scrap of paper, forced the lock, and made his way naked into the street
and to the home of relatives, the Anchorenas.

On the following morning, when Juan Manuel's bread and water were
taken to his room, the servants found the scrap of paper with these
words: "I have left behind me everything that is not mine. Juan Manuel

de Rosas," with the name spelled with "s." This was his first rebellion against every authority against his own will, and thereafter he always signed his name Rosas instead of Rozas.

Shortly after his marriage, when he was twenty years old, Rosas's mother began to lose confidence in his management of the estancia, believing that he was not handling it honestly. One day he overheard her in an adjoining room urging his father to relieve him of the management, whereupon he walked into the room and surrendered his post. He then took off his coat and the poncho which his mother had presented to him, put them on the floor behind the door of her room, and walked out of the house, never to return. In vain his father begged him to come back. He refused to live in the house where his honor was doubted.

From the very beginning there was something of the mystic about Rosas. The long days on the open plains as a task-master over the gauchos and as a trainer of wild horses made him well aware of the physical power of his outer man, but he spent long hours in the solitude of the night on the pampas meditating and communing with the inner man. So intimate did the man become with his soul that there came a day in his career when Rosas was convinced, never to doubt again for even a moment, that there was no difficulty he could not overcome, no goal he could not reach. Unfortunately, he lived too much within himself to think of others except as they might serve as his instruments. He devoted his will power exclusively to furthering his own selfish ambitions. One of his biographers, Lucio V. Mansilla, says that Rosas had all the energy of a mother, but lacked the affection and pity of a mother. He loved things, but was indifferent to souls. He would weep over a dog, but keep back his tears at the funeral of a friend for fear someone might think him weak. And just as he rebelled against the conventional graveside tear, so he rebelled against every other rule of society, humanity, or the Church. He refused to be subject to any person or to any thing, idea, or sentiment except as directed by his own will.

Such was the man who was growing up and developing on the wild pampas during those years when the great civil war was gathering and preparing to engulf the country. When the time came, Juan Manuel de Rosas plunged into the storm of that civil war guided by his conviction that there was nothing he could not do, and he kept plunging through it until he finally conquered the storm itself and used it to sweep himself into power. For seventeen years he ruled as a dictator and a tyrant, and when at last he fled in exile to England he left behind him a country that was so glad to be released from the government of a blood-soaked iron hand that it was ready to accept without question a more lenient government.

After Rosas left the home of his parents he spent a couple of years in business for himself and then went again to his relatives the Anchorenas, to whom he had fled that night of his first boyhood rebellion. They appointed him administrator of their estates in the southern part of the Province of Buenos Aires. The country's big problem in those days was the same that it is today—population—and Rosas began populating the estancias with deserters from the army, with escaped convicts and other fugitives from justice, arming them with rifles which he obtained from the government for defense against the Indians. Rosas protected these men from the law, but ruled over them like a despot, his word being a law they dared not disobey because the withdrawal of Rosa's protection meant a return to jail or the army.

In this way Rosas organized a series of feudal establishments which lived independent of the national authorities. Order reigned on these estancias and the peons gave their absolute obedience and allegiance to Rosas, while on the outside there was nothing but disorder and a weak government toward which Rosas paid little heed and for which he felt and expressed only contempt. Having organized his outlaws into orderly communities, Rosas, impelled by that instinct which had guided him from youth, gradually became imbued with the idea that he was the only man capable of arranging the affairs of the nation and of establishing order.

Everything seems to have conspired to favor his ambition, no matter whether he plotted the events or merely waited for them to occur. And as the historian Vicente Fidel López says, "Rosas had the gift of imperturbable patience." The breaking down of government in 1820 made it possible for Rosas to rise to power. With the dissolution of the union in that year there began a wild outbreak of anarchy of the worst sort. Each province refused to recognize any authority except its own and there began a constant civil war between Buenos Aires and the provinces, each provincial governor trying to seize control of Buenos Aires and set up his own government there.

The more Rosas watched these events, the more he became ambitious for power, but he saw that he could play no important part until the country overcame the city, so he began planning accordingly. He was already prepared, therefore, when the governor of the Province of Buenos Aires, Dorrego, sent him an urgent appeal for aid in raising militia to protect the city of Buenos Aires. Rosas immediately rode to

Dorrego's assistance with 600 well-armed and well-mounted men from his estancias. These men were ready to obey Rosas to the death but they recognized no other authority. They restored order in Buenos Aires and Rosas was commissioned to organize a regiment of cavalry in the south.

Almost immediately there was another change in the governorship and the new governor, Rodriguez, called Rosas into Buenos Aires to put down a mutiny of municipal troops. It must have been a proud moment for Rosas when he rode into Buenos Aires at the head of his own regiment, every man uniformed in red. Again Rosas and his troops restored order and when they left the city after completing their task, Rosas issued an unusual proclamation to the people of Buenos Aires reviewing the victories of his troops and so cleverly worded that the people, tired of civil war, could never again dream of peace without thinking of Rosas as the logical man to establish that peace, as he had just finished doing for the second time.

Rosas then began a long series of intrigues in the provinces, stirring up civil war and using the leading military men of the day for his pawns, rising a little further in power himself as he pushed each one of them in turn into power, but never falling with them in their defeat. As each of them went down in the face of his more recent intrigue, Rosas became more and more recognized as the one really powerful man and, finally, in December 1828, the legislature proclaimed him governor of the Province of Buenos Aires for three years with extraordinary powers to restore the laws, giving him the rank of brigadier-general of the armies and the title of Restorer of the Laws.

In the meantime another attempt to set up a centralized, unitarian national government had failed. There had been no national structure from 1820 to 1826, but the successive governors of the Province of Buenos Aires had worked constantly to bring the provinces together again and call a constituent assembly. Finally, such an assembly met in 1824 and in spite of all previous experience drew up another unitarian Constitution in 1826 and elected Bernardino Rivadavia first President of the Argentine Republic without consulting the provinces or waiting for their action on the Constitution. This Constitution of 1826 established the form of government as a republican, representative government "consolidated in a unitarian regime." The autonomy of the provinces was to be destroyed by the provision that the locally elected governors were to be replaced by governors "immediately responsible to the President."

This Constitution, too, was rejected by the provinces and there was a new outbreak of civil war. When the country also became involved in a war with Brazil, President Rivadavia, faced by war at home and abroad, made an unfavorable peace with Brazil which aroused so much indignation among the people that he refused to sign the treaty his agent had negotiated and resigned the presidency on June 27, 1827, after having been in office a year and a half. He went to Europe and when he returned in 1834 was not permitted to land. Like so many of the other patriotic leaders of the country, he spent the last years of his life in exile and died in Cádiz in 1845. His ashes eventually were returned to Buenos Aires, where they now rest in a somber modernistic tomb in the Plaza Once in front of the Once railroad station.

Rivadavia was one of the most brilliant men of the revolutionary period. He had been a member of the secret society and secretary of the Triumvirate, and in 1814 was sent to Europe to seek diplomatic recognition of Argentine independence and a prince with whom to establish a monarchy. As minister of government under Supreme Director Martín Rodriguez and later during his short term as President he inaugurated some of the country's wisest laws and best institutions. Among other things, he established the first national bank, negotiated the first foreign loan, and founded the national charitable organization known as the Sociedad de Beneficencia, which still exists and accomplishes magnificent humanitarian work. His name is commemorated in the Calle Rivadavia, said to be the longest street in the world, running from the Plaza de Mayo to the town of Lujan, 42 miles from Buenos Aires.

After Rivadavia's resignation the Federalists and Unitarians agreed to keep the union together under an acting President until another constituent assembly could meet. Congress chose Vicente Lopez to be the acting President, but the situation was so hopeless that he resigned after a few days and the Congress dissolved itself after again charging the governor of the Province of Buenos Aires with the duty of carrying on the war with Brazil "and other foreign relations" until such time as the concourse of the other provinces could be obtained.

Manuel Dorrego was proclaimed governor of the province and set about the task of bringing the provinces together. He made an unpopular peace with Brazil and the first troops who returned in 1828, under the command of General Juan Lavalle, mutinied against Dorrego and demanded that he be ousted from office. Surprised at this attack, Dorrego called upon Rosas for help and with 2000 men set out to quell the rebellion. He was defeated and taken prisoner, and Lavalle, without any pretense of complying with either legal or military formality, ordered him shot. This high-handed act not only robbed the country of a sincere and widely admired governor, but opened the door for Rosas's entrance onto the national stage.

The execution of Dorrego was considered by most of the provinces to be an assassination, and with the exception of Tucumán and Salta they formed a block to make war on the Province of Buenos Aires. As already mentioned, the legislature of Buenos Aires proclaimed Rosas governor in 1828 with dictatorial powers. At the end of his three-year term he surrendered the dictatorial powers with which he had been invested, refused to accept re-election, and retired to his estancia.

The civil wars continued. Rival bands of gauchos armed with lances and knives rode at each other with all the ferocity of wild Indians. Prisoners were executed by having their throats slashed from ear to ear in the same manner that wild cattle had been slaughtered on the plains for more than a century. When the executed prisoner happened to be a caudillo, his head was sent to the nearest town to be stuck up on a pole in the plaza. The entire country was in a state of savagery only slightly if any better than when the pampas were the hunting grounds of the Indians.

In 1835 the legislature of Buenos Aires again sent for Rosas to restore law and order and invested him with unlimited dictatorial powers by passing the following unusual measure:

LAW
Sanctioned by the
Honorable House of Representatives
on the 7th of March 1835

The Honorable House of Representatives, exercising the sovereignty, both ordinary and extraordinary, which rests in it, has this day sanctioned with the validity and force of law the following:

Article 1. Brigadier-General Juan Manuel de Rosas is hereby nominated Governor and Captain-General of the Province for a period of five years.

Article 2. The entire public power of this Province is deposited in the person of Brigadier-General Juan Manuel de Rosas, without restrictions except the following:

1st. He must preserve, defend, and protect the Apostolic Roman Catholic religion.

2nd. He must defend and maintain the national cause of Federation, which has been proclaimed by all the people of the Republic.

Article 3. The exercise of this extraordinary power shall continue for such time as in the judgment of the Governor-elect may be necessary.

Article 4. A copy of this resolution shall be transcribed and sent to the aforementioned Brigadier-General in order that he may appear in this House on Wednesday at noon to take possession of the power confided in him, taking the oath to exercise it faithfully and in the manner which he believes best for the welfare of this Province and the Republic in general.

Article 5. The corresponding diploma shall be issued, signed by the Vice-President of the House, counter-signed by the Secretary, and sealed with the seal of the Legislature.

Article 6. The Executive Power shall be informed in the usual manner.

Eduardo Lahitte   Manuel G. Pinto
        Secretary   Vice-President

The audacity and cynicism of Rosas were never shown more conspicuously than in his manner of accepting that appointment. He insisted that the law be submitted to a plebiscite of the people. The voting was almost unanimously in favor of the question, and whatever may be said against Rosas and his government after that, it is an historical fact that his appointment as dictator with unlimited powers was confirmed by the vote of the great majority of the people over whom he was to rule. It is said that when Rosas stepped onto a British warship seventeen years later to spend the rest of his life in exile, someone asked him how he could have treated his own countrymen with such cruelty, and he replied: "Bah, they didn't deserve anything else."

At the end of his five-year term Rosas resigned, knowing undoubtedly that his resignation would not be accepted. At any rate, he was re-elected with even more powers. During the first five years he had made a pretense of keeping within the sane limits of constitutional power, but in 1840 there began that reign of terror which forms such a black page in Argentine history. Thousands of people were put to death after trials that were a mockery of justice, and Rosas laid down strict rules for every phase of daily life, even as to how mustaches must be worn. No one dared appear on the streets of Buenos Aires unless he wore a red ribbon, and everyone was in daily dread of the wrath of Rosas or the knife of his organized band of spies and assassins, known as the Mazorca.

There are many who contend that Rosas was crazy, and certainly his rule after 1840 was that of a madman, yet there is no trace of insanity either before or after his dictatorship. During all the time he was in power Rosas worked hard fifteen hours a day handling the affairs of government without the aid of ministers, dividing his time between the government office and his home in that part of Palermo which is now called Tres de Febrero Park in commemoration of the date of his down-fall.

In 1851 General Justo José de Urquiza, governor of the Province of Entre Rios, began a military campaign against Rosas, assisted by the Province of Corrientes and by Brazil and Uruguay. Brazil sent 3000 infantrymen, a regiment of cavalry, two batteries of artillery, and a naval squadron. The emperor of Brazil, Pedro II, contributed 100,000 pesos a month toward the upkeep of the Brazilian forces, on the understanding that the money would be repaid by whatever government succeeded Rosas.

On February 3, 1852 Urquiza, at the head of 24,000 men, defeated Rosas and his 22,000 men at Caseros, near the city of Buenos Aires, in a battle that lasted only four hours and a half. Rosas fled from the field, wrote his resignation with a pencil, and sought refuge in the British legation, whence he was taken on board a British warship in the river. Four days later he left Argentina forever, bound for Southampton.

Rosas remained in exile for twenty-six years. For many years after he became too old to earn his own living he lived on contributions that were sent to him by friends in Argentina. He seems to have been a fine-looking old gentleman, living the quiet life of an English country squire, with a large number of friends and with no traces of the cruel despot who had spread terror in the land of his birth. He was eighty-four when he died.

One might be tempted to make excuses for Rosas if there were any evidence that he was trying to establish a stable government, but there is no such evidence. He appears to have been only a cruel, selfish tyrant, ambitious for personal power. He was the classic type of patrician despot, without scruples of any kind, fighting foreigners and Argentines alike to make a historic place for himself and secure his own tyrannic power. He watched his enemies and former friends with feline cunning until the opportune moment arrived to pounce on them, usually from behind their backs, and destroy them. He spent many years of his life plotting the revolutions and counter-revolutions that paved the way to his dictatorship, and once in power he heartlessly ordered the death of everyone who opposed him, including many who were merely suspected of opposition.

Rosas has been described as the reincarnation in America of the very worst type of Spanish governor. He killed or exiled all the liberals who raised him to power. He was the idol of the masses, yet he closed their schools, burned their books, and reduced them to the level of vassals.

His motto was federalism, with death to the Unitarians, yet he sub-
jected the Province of Buenos Aires to the worst possible form of unitarian rule. He professed to be a faithful Catholic and had taken an oath
as governor to protect the Church, yet he continually fought and humili-
ated it. Pretending to be the ally of the caudillos, he destroyed them one
by one.

It was the great contribution of Rosas to the republic, however, that
he destroyed the power of the numerous gaucho caudillos who in-
fested the country and who for so many years effectively prevented
the establishment of any centralized government. Until the time Rosas
became dictator, the country was put above the city, anarchy above
law, barbaric force above civilized society. Rosas either exterminated or
tamed the gaucho caudillos, and when he was forced to give up the reins
of government, the gaucho for the first time in his life had become accustomed to submitting to authority and Argentina was ready to begin
its life as a nation.

12. FEDERATION

O N the day after the defeat of Rosas at Caseros, General Urquiza issued a proclamation declaring that all past grievances were to be forgotten for the sake of national peace. Then he set about organizing a nation out of the fourteen provinces which for forty years had been only loosely held together by a tacit association from which any one of them could and did withdraw whenever it felt that such secession suited its own local interests. One of Urquiza's first official acts was to appoint the president of the supreme court, Dr. Vicente Lopez y Planes, to be provisional governor of the Province of Buenos Aires to replace Rosas. Three months later the legislature elected Lopez governor. In 1813 he had written the very stirring national anthem, which was the first official document in which the word *Argentina* was used as the name of the country.

On February 20, less than three weeks after the battle of Caseros, Urquiza made the very serious but perhaps natural mistake of riding into the proud city of Buenos Aires at the head of his conquering troops. He wore a flowing white poncho and a plush hat and this attire seems to have enraged the people of Buenos Aires as bitterly as did the presence of Brazilian and Uruguayan troops, with their respective flags, in Urquiza's victory parade. The campaign against Rosas had been largely financed by the emperor of Brazil and both Brazil and Uruguay, at Urquiza's request, had sent soldiers for his army.

Regardless of their hatred of Rosas and his tyranny, the people of Buenos Aires were very proud of the fact that their governor had successfully defied both the English and the French navies which had been sent to blockade the port of Buenos Aires in an effort to bring about the overthrow of the dictator. Also, they remembered with pride that on two previous occasions they had defeated invading English troops and taken their battle flags away from them. And now here was Urquiza, an Argentine, leading 3000 Brazilian and 2000 Uruguayan soldiers through Calle Florida with their foreign flags flying in triumph over the city of Buenos Aires. The city that was logically destined to be the capital of any nation which Urquiza might establish became his sworn enemy.

Urquiza led his troops out to Palermo and established himself on the estancia that had belonged to Rosas. Two roads were open to him in his work of organizing the nation. One was to make a clean sweep of everything that had existed during Rosas's tyranny—there were both mili-

tary and political motives to justify such a step—but Urquiza knew that
such procedure would reawaken the civil strife he was so eager to avoid.
He therefore chose the other alternative, which was to confirm in their
posts all the provincial governors who had been in office during Rosas's
regime and appeal to their patriotism for co-operation in organizing the
Argentine Nation. Rosas had thoroughly suppressed both anarchy and
civil war, but in doing so had left the provinces prostrated. The governors as well as the people welcomed co-operation with any plan that
promised peace.

The governors of Buenos Aires, Entre Rios, Corrientes, and Santa Fé
met with Urquiza in Palermo and delegated to him the management of
foreign affairs during the reconstruction period. As a result of this meeting, the governors of ten provinces assembled at San Nicolás, in the
Province of Buenos Aires, in May 1852 and drew up an agreement which
became the cornerstone of the new national structure. The fact that this
meeting took place within two months of the meeting at Palermo speaks
well for Urquiza's energy and organizing ability, as there were neither
railroads nor telegraphs in the country.

The San Nicolás agreement renewed the Federal Pact of January
1831 by which the provinces had attempted to set up a federation. It
convoked a Federative Congress to arrange the general administration
of the country under the federal system. The agreement, consisting of
nineteen articles, repeatedly specified that the country was to be organized as a federation, thus leaving no doubt as to the political aspirations of the interior and forestalling any scheming by the Unitarians of
Buenos Aires to draw up another unitarian Constitution. The general
welfare of the nation was to be considered more important than the interests of the provinces, and the deputies to Congress were to be elected
as representatives of the country at large rather than of the provinces.
Urquiza was appointed Provisional Director of the Confederation pending presidential elections, was empowered to take whatever measures
might be necessary for restoring order, and was invested with the command of all the provincial militias, which in the future were to be considered as parts of the national army.

The city and Province of Buenos Aires, seeing in all this an attempt
by Urquiza to set himself up as a dictator with all the powers that Rosas
had exercised, refused to have anything to do with the San Nicolás agreement. Urquiza left Buenos Aires and went to Santa Fé to attend the sessions of the Constituent Assembly which met there on September 8. On
September 11 Buenos Aires rose in revolt against Urquiza, reserving the

right to accept or reject any Constitution which might be drawn up by
the Assembly. Urquiza rejected these pretensions, saying, "It is neither
just nor rational to admit that the Province of Buenos Aires has the right
of arbitrary veto by which it can prevent national organization just because this organization was not begun under its exclusive direction. But
neither is it politic nor practical to leave that large province as a disturbing element outside the Confederation." Urquiza offered to resign as
Director of the Confederation, believing that his person stood in the
way of union. But the provinces refused to accept his resignation.

While the Constituent Assembly at Santa Fé was drawing up a federal
Constitution for the Argentine Confederation, the legislature of the
Province of Buenos Aires was framing a unitarian Constitution for the
province. On May 1, 1853, the Assembly voted the Constitution of the
Argentine Confederation.[1] On May 25, the forty-third anniversary of
the revolution, Urquiza declared this Constitution to be the fundamental
law of the nation, and so, with a few alterations, it has continued ever
since.

The Constitution provided for a representative, republican, federal
form of government. It sought to conciliate the unitarian and federalist
camps by recognizing the autonomy of the provinces, but under a
strongly consolidated central government. It is one of the most liberal
constitutions in the world and, among other things, invites all men, regardless of nationality, to live in Argentina and guarantees them all the
civil rights enjoyed by Argentine citizens.

The Province of Buenos Aires refused to accept this Constitution and
set itself up as an autonomous State. Thus, as a climax to forty years of
strife and civil war, a situation was created in which for eight years
the city and Province of Buenos Aires did not belong to Argentina.

The Constituent Assembly had provided that the city of Buenos Aires
was to be the capital of the Confederation, but when Buenos Aires refused to join the Confederation, the national capital was established at
Paraná, capital of the Province of Entre Rios. Urquiza, as Director of
the Confederation, made his headquarters on his estancia at San José de
Flores, in the Province of Entre Rios, and it was there on July 27, 1853,
that the treaty of friendship, trade, and navigation was signed with the
United States.[2] This pact was the basis of the diplomatic and economic
relations between Argentina and the United States until the signing of
the reciprocal trade treaty at Buenos Aires on October 14, 1941.

---

[1] For text of the Argentine Constitution see Appendix VII.
[2] For text of this treaty see Appendix VI.

On July 10 Urquiza had signed treaties with England, France, and the United States guaranteeing freedom of navigation to all foreign vessels on the Paraná and Uruguay rivers, which had been closed to navigation during Rosas's regime. The underlying motive for Urquiza's action was to establish Rosario as the port of the Confederation instead of Buenos Aires.

Elections were held on November 20, and Urquiza was chosen first constitutional President of the Argentine Confederation, with Salvador María del Carril as Vice-President. Urquiza appointed José B. Gorostiaga as minister of foreign affairs. Del Carril and Gorostiaga had been the two plenipotentiaries of the Confederation during the negotiation of the trade treaty with the United States. Treaties of peace and commerce were also signed with Belgium, Prussia, Naples, and Sardinia. Peace was established in South America by the signing of treaties with Bolivia, Brazil, Chile, and Paraguay. But the position of the Confederation was impossible so long as Buenos Aires refused to join it. Rosario could not compete with the port of Buenos Aires, and the steps which Urquiza took in favor of the former led to a tariff war between the Confederation and the Province of Buenos Aires which soon developed into a military war.

After six years of conflict the Congress of the Confederation, sitting at Paraná in April 1859, authorized Urquiza to induce the Province of Buenos Aires to join the Confederation or to subdue it, "by force if necessary." The province put its minister of war, General Bartolomé Mitre, at the head of its army and prepared to resist Urquiza. But Mitre was routed at the battle of Cepeda, and Urquiza stipulated as a condition of peace the resignation of the governor of Buenos Aires, who along with Mitre was a bitter personal enemy of the President of the Confederation.

The governor resigned and on November 11, 1859, a treaty of peace was signed between the Confederation and the Province of Buenos Aires by which the province agreed to join the Confederation on condition that a provincial convention should meet to study the National Constitution of 1853 and that any modifications proposed by the province should be submitted to a General Constituent Congress to be elected for that purpose. The customs house at Buenos Aires was to pass to the Confederation, but the territorial integrity of the province was to be guaranteed and no division in that territory made without the consent of the provincial legislature. Urquiza's troops were to be removed from the city and Province of Buenos Aires within two weeks.

The Buenos Aires convention met on January 5, 1860, and was in session until May 12. It proposed twenty-two alterations in the text of the Constitution, the principal one of which was to change the name of the country from the Argentine Confederation to the United Provinces of the River Plate, as it had formerly been known. The entire session of May 11, the day before adjournment, was devoted to debating what the name of the country should be after Buenos Aires joined it. The word *Confederación* reminded the people of Buenos Aires too much of Rosas and his tyranny in the name of federation. Domingo Sarmiento and others argued that the restoration of the "legitimate and honorable name of the United Provinces of the River Plate" would be a balm for the passions that for twenty years had divided the country. Also, Sarmiento said, it would be a flag of peace and fraternity that would unite all parties; confederation represented a scandal that should not be immortalized by adopting it as the name of the country. The session adjourned with all the delegates on their feet cheering for the United Provinces of the River Plate.

The new National Constituent Congress met at Santa Fé in September to study the changes proposed by the Province of Buenos Aires. This Congress, representing all the provinces of the interior as well as Buenos Aires, refused to accept the name of United Provinces of the River Plate, but its attitude toward Buenos Aires was one of conciliation rather than contention. It compromised by substituting the word "nation" for "confederation" wherever it appeared in the Constitution and left only the word "provinces" when the Constitution referred to confederated provinces. It established in Article 35 that the various names by which the country had been known in the past were to continue as official names, but that in framing the laws the country would be known as the Argentine Nation, and that has been its official name ever since. The Argentine Confederation and the United Provinces are now merely historic names and the country is known at home and abroad as the Argentine Republic.

The Constitution of 1853 provided that the city of Buenos Aires should be the federal capital. The provincial convention proposed that this clause be altered to provide that the National Congress, when elected, should designate the capital city and that this city should then be ceded to the nation by the province to which it belonged. This suggestion was approved by the National Constituent Congress, but the question was not definitely settled until 1880, when the city of Buenos Aires was designated as the federal capital.

The National Constitution, as amended, was sworn to at Buenos Aires on October 21, 1860, and on that day the Argentine Republic became a united nation for the first time in its history.

Meanwhile, the Confederation in 1859 had elected Santiago Derqui, who had been Urquiza's minister of the interior, to succeed him as President. At about the same time General Bartolomé Mitre was elected governor of the Province of Buenos Aires. Both Derqui and Mitre announced themselves dedicated to the unifying of the nation and Derqui convoked the National Constituent Congress which accepted the changes proposed by Buenos Aires. As a public manifestation of reconciliation between the province and the Confederation, Mitre invited Derqui and Urquiza to Buenos Aires for the celebration of the anniversary of the declaration of independence on July 9. The presence of Derqui, Mitre, and Urquiza in the Plaza de Mayo evoked tremendous public demonstrations of jubilee and everything indicated that at long last the internal peace of the country had been definitely achieved.

But peace did not continue long. The Province of Buenos Aires insisted on electing its deputies to Congress in accordance with its own provincial election laws instead of as provided in the general election law which the Congress of the Confederation had passed in 1857 in compliance with the Constitution. The Chamber of Deputies, exercising its constitutional prerogative to be sole judge of the election of its members, refused to seat the deputies from Buenos Aires on the ground that they had not been legally elected and ordered the province to hold new elections in accordance with the general election law. Buenos Aires refused to call new elections, even though its stand might mean war, whereupon Congress nullified the peace pact of November 11 and decreed intervention in the province, as provided for in the Constitution. The Province of Buenos Aires was again at war with the Argentine Nation.

Mitre, at the head of 22,000 men, defeated the troops of Derqui and Urquiza on the plains of Pavon, in the Province of Santa Fé, on September 17, 1861. Urquiza retreated and Mitre occupied Rosario. Derqui found that as President he had little popular backing, so resigned the presidency and went to Montevideo. On November 12 the Vice-President, Esteban Pedernara, issued a decree declaring that the national government renounced its authority, which was tantamount to the resignation of the national government.

Mitre held Argentina's fate in his hands. A smaller man would have plunged the country back into civil war. The people of Buenos Aires wanted to carry on their victory to its ultimate goal, annihilate Urquiza and the other federalist leaders, and set up a new national organization under the unitarian authority of Buenos Aires. Mitre proved himself to be a great statesman and a great man by refusing to be blinded by his military triumph. With a coolness and dignity that have made him a noble figure in Argentine history, he refused to heed the counsel of the fanatical porteños and entered into negotiations with Urquiza, accepting the federal form of government and agreeing to respect the National Constitution and the autonomy of Urquiza's province, Entre Rios. Mitre thus undertook to respect and uphold the very political system which he himself had overthrown at Pavon.

Mitre was appointed Provisional President and immediately called elections for a new Congress, which was inaugurated on May 25, 1862, at Buenos Aires, where the national authorities had installed themselves. Congress passed a law calling elections for President and Vice-President and Mitre was chosen President by the unanimous vote of the Electoral College. Bartolomé Mitre thus became the first constitutional President of the Argentine Nation.

No other South American country experienced so many difficulties as Argentina in getting established as an independent nation and no other one has been known by so many different names.

Nevertheless, as early as 1813 the country and the people were being referred to as Argentina and Argentinos, respectively, in official documents. In 1815 and 1816 two periodicals were established with the names *Prensa Argentina* and *Crónica Argentina*, and in 1817 Buchardo gave the name *La Argentina* to the frigate which was to carry that name around the world for the first time. The first merchant vessel which the country sent abroad after its independence was *La Rosa Argentina*, which sailed for the Guianas in 1819. Vicente Lopez y Planes had used the word *Argentinos* in the national anthem, which the soldiers of San Martín's liberating army sang lustily in Chile and Peru.

In October 1826 the General Constituent Congress of the United Provinces of the River Plate framed "The Constitution of the Argentine Republic." From that time on the noun *Argentina* and the adjective *Argentine* came into general use throughout the country, which continued to be referred to as the Argentine Republic even though the Constitution of 1826 never was adopted and both Rivadavia and the Congress set up by that Constitution were overthrown.

Through the long years of anarchy, when the city of Buenos Aires was handling foreign affairs, the country and government became known in Europe as Buenos Aires and there are still in existence etchings of that period referring to the city of Buenos Aires as the capital of Buenos Aires.

During all this time, however, the federalist caudillos of the interior were calling the country the Argentine Confederation or the Argentine Federation. During the tyranny of Rosas the battle cry was *"Viva la Confederación Argentina!"* and by the time he was overthrown it had become obvious that whether the country was to be called a republic or a confederation its name was Argentina.

Argentina's efforts to set up a constitutional form of government had consumed and wasted fifty tragic years. The country's phenomenal growth and progress since 1862 justify the conviction that if those first fifty years could have been spent constructively the outbreak of the Second World War would have found Argentina one of the greatest nations on earth. Few countries, however, have begun their independent life under such unfavorable geographical, political, social, and economic conditions as those which the people of the Argentine Republic had to fight and overcome before they could set themselves up as a united nation.

The revolution of May 25, 1810, found the people completely unprepared for self-government. For more than two hundred years the River Plate country had been a colony of the Spanish Empire, one of the rottenest systems of government the world has ever seen. The colonial regime itself was designed and so operated as to keep the colonists subjugated, both legally and socially, to the Spaniards who were sent out to rule them. The colonists were permitted no voice whatsoever in the management of their own affairs. Every question of any importance had to be referred to Spain for decision and all the important government officials were sent out by the Crown to enforce the laws that were made in Spain.

Unlike the English colonies in North America, the Spanish colonies in South America did not contain within themselves the elements of growth. In 1818, nearly three hundred years after the arrival of the first colonists, there were only 1,300,000 whites and mestizos in the 1,305,000 square miles which comprised the present territories of Argentina, Bolivia, Paraguay, and Uruguay, according to the note handed to Rodney and Graham in that year by Gregorio Tagle, secretary of government and foreign affairs of the United Provinces of South America, as the former Viceroyalty of the River Plate was called at that time. Buenos Aires, two hundred and thirty-eight years after its founding by

Garay, had only 50,000 inhabitants. There was virtually no communication between the capital and the far-distant cities except the arrival once a year of a train of carretas. There were no fixed limits to the jurisdiction of the separate provinces. The gaucho who rode away from an adobe hut an hour before dawn knew that it was the last hut in that province and that if he galloped all day he might, with luck, reach the first hut in the next province by nightfall. The stubborn insistence of Buenos Aires that it should continue to exercise over these lonely, distant cities the same dictatorial authority and the same selfish trade monopoly that it had enjoyed under the colonial system injected serious political difficulties into an already almost impossible geographical situation.

Yet the Argentine Constitution, as finally adopted, provides the finest example to be found anywhere of the application of English law under Spanish administration. For the Constitution of 1853 was inspired by and largely copied from the Constitution of the United States of America. Ricardo Levene recounts in his *History of Argentina* that the secretariat of the Constituent Assembly which met at Santa Fé in 1853 had procured a copy of Alexander Hamilton's *Federalist*, which was to have served as a guide for the delegates, who had already determined on a federal Constitution similar to that of the United States. Just as the Assembly was to begin its sessions, this copy of the *Federalist* disappeared. But at the same time the delegates received copies of a book written in Chile by the Argentine exile Juan Bautista Alberdi and called *Bases and Starting Points for the Political Organization of the Argentine Republic*.

Alberdi, who was one of the greatest thinkers and writers of his age, had been forced to leave the country because of his opposition to Rosas. He had spent much time studying and thinking about the constitutional organization of his country and when Urquiza overthrew Rosas, Alberdi hurriedly put his thoughts into his book *Bases*, had it printed by the great Chilean newspaper *El Mercurio* of Valparaiso, and sent it to Urquiza for the use of the delegates to the Constituent Assembly. Throughout his book Alberdi cites the Constitution of the United States as the model for organizing Argentina as a federal republic.

At the convention which met in the Province of Buenos Aires in 1860 to amend the Constitution, the chairman of the committee on amendments said in his report:

The committee has been guided in its recommendations by the provisions of a similar constitution, recognized as the most perfect, i.e., that of the United States. The provisions of this Constitution are most readily applicable to Argentine conditions, having served as the basis for the formation of the Argentine Confederation. . . . The democratic government of the United States represents the last word of human logic, for the Constitution of the United States is the only one that has been made for and by the people. . . .

Seventeen years later, on August 21, 1877, the Argentine Supreme Court in deciding a habeas corpus case declared in its decision:

The system of government under which we are living was not of our creation. We found it in operation, tested by the experience of many years, and adopted it for our system.

The Argentine Constitution is built on the fundamental principles of personal liberty and representative government and is decidedly more advanced than was the United States Constitution as originally framed, since it contains the Bill of Rights in its introductory paragraphs. The United States Constitution set up a system of government by which the people were to handle their public affairs, but it was not until Virginia ratified the first ten amendments in 1791 that the Bill of Rights, establishing the individual freedoms upon which the government could not infringe, became law.

The Constitution framed at Santa Fé in 1853 prohibited further executions by the lance or the knife, a provision that was suppressed by Buenos Aires in the amended version on the ground that charity for one's fellow-beings could be included among the rights of man that need not be specified. A clause was inserted providing that any slave who managed to enter Argentine territory was automatically to become a free man. As far back as 1812, children born of slaves were born free, and the Constitution of 1853 provided that if there were still any slaves in the country they were to be free from the moment the Constitution was adopted.

The reformed Constitution adopted the principle of *jus soli*, in accordance with which citizenship is established by the place of birth rather than by the citizenship of the parents (*jus sanguinis*). As the Constitution specifically authorized the national government to stimulate European immigration there was the very obvious danger that within a few years most of the children born in the country would be foreigners if the European principle of *jus sanguinis* were recognized. The contrary was established by adding the words "subject to the principle of natural citizenship" to paragraph 11 of Article 67, which authorizes Congress to pass general laws for the whole nation regarding naturalization and citizenship. Under this principle Argentina considers and claims as native-born citizens all persons born in Argentina, and boys born there are subject to conscription for military service regardless of the nationality of their parents.

Although patterned very closely on the Constitution of the United States, the Argentine Constitution sets up one attribute of the national government which differs widely from the American principle of states' rights. This is the right of the national government to intervene in the provinces, overthrow the elected governor, legislature, and other authorities, and put the province under the rule of a federal commissioner who is known as the Federal Interventor. This power was given to the national government to enable it to restore order when necessary and prevent further secession of the provinces. But in practice it has proved a powerful political weapon which has enabled the Unitarians of Buenos Aires to continue to rule the country as a unitarian organization in spite of its federalist Constitution. The Interventor usually manages things so that the elections held under his supervision put the central government's party into office. When it is fairly obvious beforehand, as frequently happens, that popular opinion in the province is so overwhelmingly contrary to the government at Buenos Aires that this cannot be arranged without making the steal so scandalous as to discredit the national government beyond the limits it is willing to risk, the elections are postponed indefinitely and the province continues to be ruled by the Federal Interventor, occupying the position and exercising the functions of the presidentially appointed governors who were always provided for in the unitarian form of constitution which Buenos Aires tried so often to impose upon the country.

But the most interesting difference between the Argentine and United States structures, from the viewpoint of constitutional law, is that Argentina has set up a presidential form of government in contrast to the legislative form of the United States. As Alexander W. Weddell, former American ambassador to Argentina, pointed out in an extremely interesting address before the College of William and Mary at Williamsburg, Virginia, in 1937, the Anglo-Saxon mind is essentially legislative and the Latin mind essentially executive, and Argentina inherited from Spain traditions of a vigorous executive accustomed to act without consulting any other authority and overriding the legislative authority whenever brought into conflict with it. The idea of an executive who should be subordinate to the legislature was completely foreign to Spanish ideas in the eighteenth century, and during all Argentine history the supremacy of the executive over the legislative authority has been the outstanding characteristic of the political development of the country, in both the provincial and the federal governments.

The clauses of the Argentine Constitution which establish the powers of the President go far beyond those of the American Constitution because it was the frank desire and intention of the framers of the Argentine Constitution to grant far greater power to the executive than is granted under the United States system in order that he might be able to maintain national unity. The Argentine President, for example, takes a very active part in formulating the laws, in addition to approving and promulgating them. He is empowered by the Constitution to frame and introduce bills in Congress, instead of merely making suggestions to friendly Congressmen to prepare measures which he favors. The Argentine President also has far more liberty in the appointment of public officials than has the American President, very few of his appointments requiring the approval of the Senate. He also has exclusive power to appoint and remove the ministers of his cabinet without consulting the Senate. The Argentine Constitution adopted the precaution embodied in the French Constitution of 1791 which requires that executive orders and decrees of the President be counter-signed by the cabinet minister having jurisdiction over the subject treated in the decree. Cabinet ministers in Argentina occupy a recognized constitutional position, a subject on which the United States Constitution is silent. They represent the executive branch of the government in the Senate and Chamber and take part in the debate on proposed legislation, but have no vote. They can be called before either house of Congress at any time to explain points which the legislators want cleared up and they play a very important part in the passing of the laws by defending and explaining bills which have been sent to Congress by the President, instead of leaving this defense and explanation to members of Congress.

The Argentine President also has the authority, under certain circumstances, to suspend constitutional guarantees by declaring a state of siege. This is a modified form of martial law which suspends the personal liberties guaranteed by the Bill of Rights, enables the President to rule the country as a dictator by means of presidential decrees in place of legislation, and, in practice, overthrows the whole machinery of democracy except the civil courts, and these are not permitted to pass judgment on any of the President's actions. Naturally this is a power which is much abused, although Argentine Presidents abuse it less than do those of some of the other South American countries.

Having endowed the President with these extraordinary powers for a six-year term, the Constitution very wisely prohibits re-election of the President until at least one six-year term has been served by another. Only two Presidents, Julio A. Roca and Hipólito Irigoyen, have been elected for a second term.

13. THE NATION GROWS UP

THE people of Argentina have not extended to Urquiza the gratitude and veneration that are rightly due his memory for the patriotic manner in which he conducted the country's affairs during the short time he was in power. He was honest in government and honest in his private life. But Buenos Aires never has forgiven him for that victory parade through Calle Florida. Urquiza could easily have set himself up as a dictator to succeed Rosas but, instead, he united the country and organized it as a nation. After the battle of Pavon he retired to private life and lived quietly on his estancia in Entre Rios until he was assassinated at the instigation of Lopez Jordan, one of the last of the semi-savage caudillos who had ruled the interior for half a century.

General Bartolomé Mitre assumed the presidency of the new Argentine nation under very difficult circumstances aggravated by the keen and bitter rivalry which still existed between the porteños of Buenos Aires and the people of the provinces. Mitre adopted the policy of allowing each of the provinces to settle its own affairs as best it could while he devoted his thought and energies to the bigger problem of the long-neglected national interests. This was in complete accord, of course, with the new federal system of government but in sharp contrast with the policy which Buenos Aires had followed up to that time and which it has followed most of the time since. Mitre very wisely chose to allow the new statesmen of the provinces to experiment with and, in most cases, to explode their pet theories of autonomous government; taking care, of course, that none of them should attempt to emulate the famous caudillos whom Rosas had so effectually suppressed.

It was during this period that Urquiza proved his political honesty, because if he had been ambitious for power he could easily have organized another strong coalition of the provinces and led them against the porteños of Buenos Aires. Instead, until his tragic death he kept the peace he had agreed upon with Mitre.

Mitre again demonstrated his statesmanship by appointing one of the greatest cabinets the country ever has had. All five of its members were men of prestige and ability, and Mitre's administration is notable for its work of constructive organization and progress, in spite of almost insurmountable difficulties both at home and abroad. These difficulties included a war forced upon the country by the dictator of Paraguay, Solano Lopez. Mitre, as the pre-eminent military leader of the day, was compelled to spend much of his time at the front, but his very able cabinet carried on the work of the administration during his absence.

One of Mitre's early acts was to sign a contract with an American engineer, William Wheelwright, for the construction of a railroad from Rosario to Córdoba, a line which now forms part of the great Central Argentine Railroad's system. Wheelwright had built the first South American railroad, from Caldera to Copiapó, in Chile, and was the originator of the project for the Transandine Railroad. He had obtained the concession to build the Rosario–Córdoba line in 1855 but had been unable to raise the necessary capital in the United States. He finally succeeded in interesting English capitalists in the venture and the line from Rosario to Córdoba was the beginning of the great network of British-owned railroads which has done so much to make Argentina the wealthy and progressive country that it is.

President Mitre nationalized the Buenos Aires customs house, as provided for in the new Constitution; encouraged immigration, foreign trade, and foreign investments; began the construction of several railroad lines; started the building of schools; organized a national system of posts and telegraphs; and in 1863 signed a treaty of peace and friendship with Spain by which the former mother country finally recognized the independence of the wayward daughter.

Mitre was relieved of many of his internal troubles when Paraguay declared war on Argentina in 1865 and invaded the northern Province of Corrientes. This war united Argentina quicker and more solidly than could have been accomplished by many years of internal governmental effort and definitely consolidated the republic, at the same time completely ruining Paraguay. It was at the end of this war that Argentina declared its justly famous doctrine: Victory gives no rights. In accordance with this doctrine, Argentina submitted its still pending frontier differences with Paraguay to the arbitration of President Rutherford B. Hayes of the United States and loyally abided by the arbitral award, which was in favor of Paraguay.

But more important than anything else in Mitre's administration was the beginning of the sound immigration policy that was to make a civilized and prosperous nation out of the wilderness that had seen so much bloodshed. Alberdi, in his *Bases and Starting Points for the Political Organization of the Argentine Republic*, had explained that the greatest need of the country was a civilized, educated European population, such as had been attracted to the United States. "In order to civilize by means of population," he had written, "the population itself must be a civilized one. To educate our America to liberty and industry it is necessary to people it with those European populations which are most advanced in liberty and industry, as has been done in the United States."

The Constitution which had been framed on Alberdi's *Bases* welcomed in its Preamble "all people in the world who wish to inhabit Argentine soil." Article 25 provided: the Federal Government shall encourage European immigration; and it shall not restrict, limit, or impose taxation of any kind upon the entry into Argentine territory of aliens coming to it for the purpose of tilling the soil, improving industries, or introducing and teaching sciences and arts.

Mitre and the Presidents who followed him devoted much of their administrations to attracting European immigrants. Mitre granted colonization concessions to agents who went to Europe in search of settlers. The government built a large Immigrants' Hotel in the port of Buenos Aires where the newcomers were lodged and fed at government expense until they could be sent into the interior. Several agricultural colonies were founded during Mitre's administration, and 100,000 immigrants entered the country. The first British bank was established.

Mitre was succeeded in the presidency by Domingo Faustino Sarmiento,[1] one of the greatest men that Argentina has produced. Sarmiento built railroads and telegraph lines; organized the first national census, which showed a population of 1,830,000 in 1869; increased the foreign trade from 72,000,000 to 103,000,000 pesos a year; opened new ports, and dredged the rivers. Immigration increased from 34,000 in 1868 to 80,000 in 1873 and totaled 280,000 for the six years.

But Sarmiento is best known as the schoolmaster President because of his work in organizing education throughout the country. His government built more than a thousand primary schools and took a score of young American schoolteachers to Argentina to organize the normal schools and train a corps of teachers for the new schools. Sarmiento, while minister to the United States, had been a close friend and great admirer of Horace Mann, as well as a friend of Emerson and Longfellow, and he returned to Argentina determined that the greatest service he could render to his country was to educate its people. It has been said that Sarmiento's life was dominated by three ruling passions—to learn, to teach, and to serve his country.

Sarmiento's administration had to face many calamities, including several uprisings in the provinces, innumerable and ghastly Indian raids

---

[1] For list of Argentine Presidents see Appendix IX.

against the cities, disastrous floods in four provinces, and a drought which killed 2,000,000 head of cattle. But the worst of all was the great yellow fever epidemic which raged in the city of Buenos Aires for forty-five days in 1871, killing 13,500 people, or 7½ per cent of the total population of 180,000.

Nicolás Avellaneda, who had been Sarmiento's minister of justice, religion, and public instruction, defeated Mitre in the elections to choose Sarmiento's successor. Mitre was so enraged by his defeat that he started a revolution to prevent Avellaneda's inauguration, on the ground that there had been undue official pressure by the national government in favor of Avellaneda during the campaign. Mitre's revolt was suppressed and Avellaneda was inaugurated on October 12, 1874. He sought principally to continue the work of education which he had directed during Sarmiento's administration, but his presidency is best remembered for its campaign against the Indians.

Rosas had pushed the troublesome Indians back of the Colorado River in 1833, clearing the Province of Buenos Aires as far southward as Bahia Blanca. But the Indians had returned and were overrunning the country again, burning villages and stealing white women as the early conquistadors had stolen their women. As long as the Indians were at large it was useless for the government to undertake any general plan for settling European immigrants on the pampas. Avellaneda's minister of war, General Julio A. Roca, in 1879 finally led the provincial gaucho militias, which had been amalgamated into a national army, on the last great campaign against the Indians. For the gauchos it was the last glorious riot of bloodshed, hard riding, boleador-throwing, shooting, and throat-cutting. But it was the end of the gaucho as well as of the Indian: the Indians were exterminated; the gauchos rode slowly back to their barracks to be civilized by army discipline.

General Roca not only added the great expanse of Patagonia to the national domain; he solved for all time the troublesome racial problem by putting a definite and dramatic end to the mixing of white and Indian blood, through the simple process of removing the Indian blood. Subsequent governments have done little to colonize and develop Patagonia or to make it a living part of the nation, and its development and nationalization remains one of the important problems that must be solved by future governments.

President Avellaneda carried on the good work of constructive administration that had been begun by Mitre and continued by Sarmiento. During his term of office (1874–80), immigrants entered the country at the rate of 47,250 a year, bringing the total for the six-year period to 283,-500. By 1879, foreign trade had reached a total of 92,625,000 pesos, with a balance of 3,000,000 pesos in favor of Argentina's export trade.

In 1880 General Roca's election to succeed Avellaneda gave rise to the last revolutionary conflict between the people of Buenos Aires and those of the provinces. Subsequent revolutions were to be animated by the class conflict between the masses and the conservative landowners rather than by geographical considerations.

Roca's opponent in the presidential campaign was the governor of the Province of Buenos Aires, Carlos Tejedor, and he forced Avellaneda and the national government to leave the city of Buenos Aires, on the argument that it had been given only a five-year permission to use the city as its capital. For a short time the suburb of Belgrano was the national capital. When the revolution was suppressed, Congress passed the law provided for in the Constitution of 1860, federalizing the city of Buenos Aires as the national capital. In the interests of peace Tejedor resigned as governor of the province, and the provincial legislature ceded the city of Buenos Aires to the nation. A new city, La Plata, was laid out as the capital of the Province of Buenos Aires and since then the national capital has been neutral ground, politically, on which porteños and provincials meet as Argentines and nothing else.

When Roca assumed the presidency in 1880, he initiated a policy of his own which was very different from the one Avellaneda had followed. The latter was a strict observer of the Constitution, but Roca covered his steel hand with a velvet glove and applied just as much of the Constitution as he found useful in keeping law and order and in promoting the progress of the country. Argentina never had known so much peace, order, and general satisfaction as it enjoyed during the two administrations of General Roca, who with the exception of Hipólito Irigoyen was the country's most reserved and silent President.

Roca accomplished his purposes by lining up all the provincial governors and making them walk or trot as he ordered. Theoretically they were doing so autonomously, but in reality at the President's behest. When any of them had too much to say about his autonomy and his provincial rights, something always happened which sent him quietly back to private life. For those who toed the line there were subsidies for paying provincial salaries, grants for waterworks and inland ports, or other manifestations of good will on the part of the executive branch of the national government, which meant to say on the part of Julio A. Roca.

Roca's theory of provincial autonomy was to get the governor on his side and then look on quietly while he won over the rest of the citizens. Of course, there was much talk about Roca's methods, but he ignored all criticism and both the Conservatives and the working classes were pleased with his government. During his second term he reduced taxes, a government action which never has been repeated.

The country having been pacified, it developed rapidly after 1880. Foreign trade increased from 103,000,000 pesos in 1880 to 165,000,000 in 1886, and the national income increased during the same period from 20,000,000 to 42,000,000 pesos. Railroad mileage grew from 1250 in 1880 to 3750 in 1886, and 500,000 immigrants entered the country during the six-year period of Roca's presidency. Roca was able to say in his message to Congress in 1883: "No President of the Republic until now has had the satisfaction of opening the Argentine Congress in a period of such prosperity as the present."

In 1881 Roca negotiated a treaty by which Chile recognized Argentina's title to Patagonia, thus settling a conflict that had nearly led the two countries to war in the last year of Avellaneda's term when Chile protested against Argentina's first steps to extend its jurisdiction southward to the Magellan Strait. In 1885 Roca settled another troublesome frontier dispute, this time with Brazil, and in the treaty Brazil recognized Argentina's title to the Territory of Misiones. Roca sponsored the national education law, created the National Board of Education, organized the courts, drew up the penal and mining codes, founded the National Mortgage Bank, organized the police force in Buenos Aires, and signed the contract for the construction of the port of Buenos Aires.

Miguel Juarez Celman succeeded to the presidency in 1886 in the midst of Argentina's first great economic boom. Foreign trade rose to 254,715,000 pesos in 1889, in which year 260,000 immigrants arrived, bringing the total to 535,000 for the three-year period 1886–89. Railroad mileage increased to 5785 in 1889, by which time nearly all the provincial capitals had been connected with Buenos Aires by rail. The national capital was enlarged by taking in the suburbs of Belgrano and Flores, which augmented the city's population by 433,000; a great building boom started; work was begun on cutting the Avenida de Mayo through the heart of the city; Government House was enlarged, and many government buildings constructed.

Unfortunately, Juarez Celman was not a big enough man to handle a situation so fraught with danger. As José Astolfi and Raúl C. Migone describe it in their *Historia Argentina*, the country at large, and more especially the city of Buenos Aires, became almost hysterical as a result of the fever of wealth and dizzy progress. The most fantastic projects were launched, banks and corporations were organized without capital, and everybody plunged into a frenzy of speculation, confident of being able to pay obligations out of future profits.

Instead of trying to stem the current, the government let itself be carried along on its crest. Foreign trade in 1889 produced an unfavorable balance against Argentina of 74,355,000 pesos; the government was spending 18,000,000 pesos more a year than it was receiving; and the national debt grew from 117,000,000 in 1886 to 295,000,000 in 1889. Graft and incompetence ran riot in the national administration and the government eventually resorted to the good old remedy of printing paper money as fast as it could be spent.

Of course, the bubble burst, as all such bubbles must. The year 1890 found the country in a serious economic, political, and social crisis which came to a head in a rebellion against Juarez Celman. The rebellion was crushed, but the government had been so completely repudiated by the people that Juarez Celman resigned. Congress accepted the resignation without a dissenting vote, and the Vice-President, Carlos Pellegrini, became President. This event had produced a remarkable example of the new state of the national mind: Juarez Celman's home province, Córdoba, had joined in forcing him to resign, notwithstanding that Pellegrini, who was to succeed him, was a porteño.

Pellegrini was an honest man of great capability, energy, and patriotism and in the two years that remained of the presidential term he reestablished a normal political and economic situation, put the national finances and credit on a sound basis, and restored public confidence. He appointed Julio A. Roca to be minister of the interior, thus guaranteeing the maintenance of public order, which was constantly being threatened by a people which still was inclined to believe that economic, political, and social problems could be solved by revolution. The greatest single event of Pellegrini's administration was the founding of the Bank of the Argentine Nation, which did more than any other institution to restore faith in the government's credit.

During the thirty-eight years between the overthrow of Rosas and the overthrow of Juarez Celman, Argentina had grown up and entered into active relationship with the outside world. The port of Bahia Blanca, opened in 1856, was destined to become one of the world's greatest wheat-shipping ports. In 1874 Buenos Aires had been connected with

PLOWING ON THE PAMPAS

HARBOR VIEW OF BUENOS AIRES

CUTTING SUGAR CANE IN THE NORTHERN PROVINCE OF TUCUMÁN

MULE TEAM HAULING AMERICAN OIL DRILLING MACHINERY
UP A DRY RIVER BED IN NORTHERN ARGENTINA

Europe by transatlantic cable. In 1881 the Riachuelo River was dredged and widened at a cost of $6,300,000 and the shipping arriving at Buenos Aires increased from 827,072 tons in that year to 2,408,323 tons in 1886. Sarmiento's census of 1869 had shown a population of 1,737,076. By 1880 it had increased to 2,492,866. Sarmiento's census had shown also that in 1869 there were only 262,433 houses in the republic, of which 54,760 had tile roofs, the remaining 207,673 being roofed with wood, cane, or straw. The first railroad had been built in 1857 from the Plaza Lavalle in front of where the Colon Theater now stands to the suburb of Floresta, a distance of six and a half miles. By 1890 the pampas had been crossed and recrossed by railroads, the great port of Buenos Aires had been opened, and Argentina was ready to begin its career as one of the world's largest exporters of grains and meats.

But more important than anything else, there had been a complete transformation of the population: order had been established in the interior, the Indians had been eliminated, and life had been made safe at last on the pampas for the white man and his family. Beginning with Mitre, the successive national governments had devoted their energies to making Argentina a country where people could live in peace, earn a living from the soil, and educate their children. The number of schools in the republic had been increased from 205 in 1850, with 241 teachers and 12,000 pupils, to 1912 in 1884, with 4080 teachers and 164,600 pupils. In 1884, 38½ per cent of the children of school age were being educated, as compared with 6½ per cent in 1850. Many writers and poets had achieved national fame; the legend of the gaucho was being immortalized in verse and music; and in 1869 and 1870, respectively, the two great newspapers *La Prensa* and *La Nación* had been founded by Dr. José C. Paz and Bartolomé Mitre. Twenty river ports had been opened to foreign ships, a navy had been organized, and the army had been reorganized along scientific military lines.

On January 18, 1889, the docks and basins which form the port of Buenos Aires were opened, and Argentina's position in world markets dates from that event. Until that time access to Buenos Aires had been extremely difficult. Vessels anchored far out in the river, which is very shallow on the Argentine side, and passengers and cargo were taken off in rowboats and barges and then transferred to high-wheeled carts which transported them to the mole extending a mile out from the shore. With the opening of the port and the dredging of an entrance channel, vessels from overseas were able to enter the docks and land their passengers and cargoes directly. Shipping increased so rapidly that the port was soon inadequate and had to be enlarged, being finally completed in 1898, after eleven years' work, at a total cost of $35,624,000.

By 1890, railroad trackage had been increased from the 6½ miles of 1857 to 5895 miles, with a total invested capital of $531,000,000. This railroad construction was the most important single economic development that had taken place, for it united the far-scattered cities of Argentina's vast, lonely distances; did away with the long, dangerous journeys on horseback or by diligence or carreta; caused new cities to spring up everywhere; stimulated immigration; and made possible the colonization of the interior and its transformation from a wild cattle range to a wealthy agricultural zone.

The transformation in the population which took place in Argentina between the establishment of constitutional government and the outbreak of the First World War was one of the most striking social phenomena ever to occur anywhere. During the two hundred years of the colonial period Spain had prohibited the entry of foreigners through the port of Buenos Aires and strictly limited that of Spaniards. Until the revolution in 1810 the increase in population had been almost entirely the result of the relations between white men and Indian women. At the termination of Rosas's tyranny, the white population, including both foreign-born and locally born, was less than 3 per cent of the population. According to José Ingenieros, in his *Sociología Argentina*, there were 800,000 inhabitants in the Argentine Federation in 1852, of whom 553,000 were mestizos (white and Indian blood), 110,000 mulattoes (white and Negro blood), 100,000 Indians, 15,000 Negroes, 15,000 native-born whites, and 7000 European whites. The city of Buenos Aires, with a population of 76,000, had 33,000 mestizos, 26,000 Indians, Negroes, and mulattoes, and only 17,000 whites, of whom 5000 were Europeans.

After the establishment of law and order the population grew so rapidly that it doubled every twenty years, and by 1914, when the second census was taken, it was nearly ten times as large as in 1852. The 402,000 mestizos in 1914 constituted only 5 per cent of the total. Sixty-five per cent of the population was made up of Argentines who were descended from Europeans, and 30 per cent were foreigners. There were 200,000 mulattoes and 20,000 Indians in the country. By 1941 it was estimated that out of the total population of more than 13,000,000 only 1,000,000 were non-white. Many of the whites in the interior, however, are of that same *sui generis* species described in the chapter on the gaucho.

In the relatively short period of sixty years the population was changed from a mestizo mass such as still exists throughout most of Latin America, and among which there were very few whites, to an almost pure-white population in which European blood predominates. This remarkable transformation was effected by admitting 2,000,000 European immigrants between 1857 and 1900, of whom 1,116,000 remained in the country. Among those who remained there were 660,392 Italians, 250,135 Spaniards, 106,334 Frenchmen, 18,240 Austro-Hungarians, 18,095 Britons, 15,521 Swiss, 14,862 Russian Jews, and 14,737 Belgians. There were only 17,989 Germans. Most of the German population entered the country after 1890 and consisted largely of professional and business men who settled in the cities. It was not until after the First World War that Germany began sending agricultural colonists to Argentina and settling them in the Territory of Misiones as part of the Nazi political plans in South America.

The heavy immigration during the latter half of the nineteenth century and the first two decades of the twentieth was the successful outcome of the intelligent policy which the national government had based on Alberdi's principle that "to govern is to populate." The Spanish and Italian farmers and farm laborers were attracted by the government's offer of extraordinarily fertile land at very low prices, with the prospects of large profits in a new country. Most of the tenant farmers and sharecroppers originally entered the country as *golondrina* harvest hands, drifting back and forth between Argentina and their homelands with the change of seasons. They were men who did not have sufficient capital to buy land in the agricultural colonies that were established in the late 1850's, but after two or three seasons as harvest hands decided to try their luck at working the soil on a share basis. Good farmland in both Italy and Spain was scarce and expensive. Argentina promised economic independence. The promise was well kept and many of the immigrants became rich and established large families which were to become prominent in the Social Register and unbearably arrogant in their wealth and position.

Although many of the Spaniards who entered the country after 1900 settled in the cities as artisans, merchants, and clerks instead of going onto the land, the immigration over the seventy years was made up for the most part of hard-working farm labor which was distributed over the entire region of the fertile pampas. This naturally produced a striking change in the country's social, cultural, political, and economic life and enabled Argentina to assume that leading position among the nations of South America of which she has been so jealous and touchy since the close of the First World War.

The gaucho was replaced by the farmer. The two-wheeled carreta and the diligence were replaced by the the railroads. Revolutions became more and more difficult, because the European immigrants had little interest in which side governed the country as long as order was maintained by governments which were more or less honest. The provinces began to prosper for the first time in their history, and even the native population became interested in other things than fighting. Justice became a function of the courts instead of the personal whim of the caudillos. And although there still remained a great deal of corruption in the provincial governments, the newcomers enjoyed personal liberty to do and think as they pleased and a freedom from political persecution which made their new homes seem far more attractive than the lands they had left. The new settlers had fixed abodes, in contrast to the nomad gauchos. Many of them had financial investments in their farms. Consequently, they wanted good government, and in time they became important as one of the forces behind Argentina's brief experiment in democracy.

Most of today's political, economic, and social development can be traced from the year 1890, a significant milestone in Argentine history. Among the many historically important events which took place in that year probably the most important was the founding of the Unión Cívica Radical, or Radical Party, which was to bring onto the Argentine stage and eventually put into the presidency one of the most mysterious and interesting men produced in any of the American republics—Hipólito Irigoyen.

14. IRIGOYEN AND DEMOCRACY

HIPÓLITO IRIGOYEN, reticent, mysterious recluse and unseen but revered idol of the masses, was the spiritual and political inspiration of the Radical Party during the twenty-six years of its wanderings in the wilderness of Argentina's Conservative oligarchy before he finally was able to lead it into the Promised Land of the country's brief fourteen-year experiment with democratic government. When in 1916 he was elected fourteenth constitutional President of the Argentine Nation, he was the most fanatically loved and the most bitterly hated man in the country. In the meantime he had built around his personal leadership a great and highly efficient election machine that responded instantly to his slightest wish. Yet he never had made a speech, posed for a photograph, or written a personal letter. But he had devoted his entire life to a fight for universal suffrage and the secret ballot.

Although it is customary for American newspaper headline writers to refer to Argentine Radicals as "Reds," there is nothing radical about the party except its name. It is a centrist liberal party which fulfills perfectly the political definition of the word "liberal": one who opposes the abridgment of the civil rights of any group. But that was a very radical idea in the reactionary Conservative Argentina of 1890 and it still was a radical idea to the reactionary Conservative government that was in power in 1942, twelve years after Irigoyen had been ousted from the presidency by a revolution and followed to his grave by 250,000 bareheaded admirers.

Irigoyen was born into a family of tragedy in the year that Rosas was overthrown. His mother's father, Leandro Alén, was shot and his body hung for four hours in one of the plazas of Buenos Aires on the charge that he had been a member of Rosas's dreaded secret police, the Mazorca. His mother's mother, an attractive *china* with Indian blood in her veins, was believed to be an illegitimate relative of the Rosas family, according to Irigoyen's biographer Manuel Galvez. Irigoyen's mother had a fair education for her day, but married an illiterate Basque who had been one of Rosas's stable boys. This man was Irigoyen's father.

Irigoyen was born five months after Rosas was overthrown and he often referred to the tragedy, the worry, and the sorrow his mother lived through in the months just before his birth. He was a sad, moody child, which is hardly to be wondered at, since his mother and his grandmother were sad by nature and spent most of their time weeping over their troubles and especially at the ostracism they were forced to suffer after the public execution and disgrace of the head of the family. In Irigoyen's fifth year, tragedy again visited the family when his mother's elder sister left home to give birth to the child of a priest—the worst, the unpardonable form of illicit love in a Catholic country. The birth of a second child under the same shadow alienated the aunt from the family for the rest of her life.

Another source of unfavorable psychological influences during Irigoyen's childhood was his inseparable and admired companion, Leandro Além, an uncle ten years older than himself, who as a ten-year-old boy had gone to the plaza and stood there watching his father's corpse dangling at the end of a rope while the mob jeered at it. The boys were outcasts in their neighborhood and learned early in life to keep to themselves and to express their thoughts only to each other. It is hardly surprising that by the time they were grown they both were somewhat queer.

Leandro Além spelled his name with an *m* instead of the *n* used by his namesake, Irigoyen's maternal grandfather, and it has come down in Argentine history in that form as the founder and first leader of the Radical Party. His bronze statute stands at the corner of Calle Maipu and Avenida Leandro Além, near the Retiro railroad station.

Irigoyen was twelve years old when the Paraguayan war began and Além departed for the front. The boy left school and went to work as a clerk in a store, just as Rosas had done. And, like Rosas, he could not stand an inferior post in a retail store and soon left it. When Além returned from the war he insisted that Irigoyen return to school, and got him a job in a lawyer's office copying documents to improve his handwriting.

Irigoyen finished his schooling when he was seventeen and for three years worked for short periods at various jobs, leaving them all because he wanted to boss others instead of being bossed himself. Finally, when he was twenty years old, Leandro Além's influence got him an appointment as *comisario* of police, a position corresponding to that of an American precinct captain. Here, for the first time, he felt himself in a position of authority in keeping with his ambitions.

As Irigoyen's biographer remarks, next to the confessional the police force offers the best possible observatory for the study of life. In Argentina the post of comisario is one of the most influential positions to which a man can aspire, and many governors, legislators, and cabinet ministers have begun their political careers as comisarios. One of the most popular sayings in Argentina is: "The comisario's horse always wins." This saying is true throughout the country and is just as true in politics, gambling, and love as it is in racing. In Irigoyen's youth the post was even more powerful than it is today. The young comisario of police studied the virtues, the vices, and the secrets of the people in his district; learned to keep his eyes and ears open and his mouth closed; and became an adept in political intrigue.

As comisario, young Irigoyen bore himself like a much older man. He had a soft voice and courteous manner, along with a natural gift for making his authority felt. He appears to have been very attractive to women and to have had innumerable love affairs. One of the very first, with a servant of one of his aunts, resulted in the birth of a girl. Irigoyen gave the baby his name, educated her well, took her into his uncle's family, and kept her always close to him as his acknowledged daughter. He appears to have forgotten the mother almost immediately.

While still a comisario of police, Irigoyen got himself admitted to the law school of the university by devious and mysterious methods. Whether he ever completed the course is only one of many questions which remain unanswered in the continual mystery with which he seems purposely to have surrounded himself all through life.

After five years of police service, Irigoyen was removed from his post on the same day that Além was removed from his military command: they had both been on the losing side of one of the frequent provincial revolutions. Irigoyen had an innate capacity for politics and forty years later, when he was President, he told a friend that it was almost unbelievable what he had learned as a young police comisario. Some time after losing the latter post he was elected a deputy to the legislature of the Province of Buenos Aires and served until Roca was elected to the presidency. Roca appointed legislatures as well as governors, and as Além and Irigoyen were not of his party they again found themselves in private life.

In December 1880 Irigoyen was appointed professor of philosophy, history, and civics in the provincial normal school. With that appointment there began ten years of study, meditation, and communion with his inner consciousness which made him what he was to be all the rest of his life. For it was while studying and teaching philosophy to the young ladies of his classes that Hipólito Irigoyen became a disciple of the German philosopher Krause, whose teachings and ideals were to be his constant guide and inspiration.

Karl Christian Friedrich Krause (1781-1832) was the founder of a philosophy in which he tried to reconcile the idea of God, as made known to man by his faith and inner conscience, with the idea of the world, as known to man through his physical senses. He argued that God, as known intuitively through conscience, is not a personality, which would imply limitations, but an infinite, all-inclusive essence which embraces the universe within itself. His theory of the world and of humanity is universal and idealistic, the world and mankind being integral parts of the universe, which is a divine organism. The process of development is through the formation of ever-higher unities until the ultimate stage is reached in the identification of the world with God. The form which this development takes, according to Krause, is Right, or the perfect, divine law.

Most of Krause's works were translated into Spanish and were much in vogue in Spain and South America at the time that Irigoyen was teaching philosophy. The best-known English version of his philosophy is *The Ideal of Humanity and Universal Federation*. Krause taught that the individual mind is part of the Universal Mind; that the inner self is the source of all knowledge, being in contact with God; that the objective of religion is to unite one's life with the life of God; and that the ultimate goal of ethics is to do good for good's sake alone. Under these principles, self-realization will lead eventually to the realization of God.

The spirit of Krause's thought is highly metaphysical and mystical and difficult to follow. This difficulty is increased, even for German readers, by the use of abstract, artificial terminology and Germanized foreign words which are unintelligible to the ordinary man.

Irigoyen made a practice of using this same artificial, unintelligible terminology in his messages to Congress and other State papers after he became President, and was especially fond of the use of abstract plurals and meaningless words which he made up himself. The message which he read to President Hoover in inaugurating the wireless telephone service between Buenos Aires and the United States was so hopeless that the official interpreters in Washington could make nothing of it, nor could the newspaper editors in Buenos Aires.

Krause's theory that God manifests Himself on the human plane through all mankind leads necessarily to the concept of democratic equality among men and nations; of universal law and right; of perpetual peace; and the grouping of countries and peoples until the day when all nations shall be united in one brotherhood of man. This philosophy is plainly manifest in all Irigoyen's public and private life after

1884. He believed in absolute justice for all, in the equality of all men and all nations, and in universal peace. These principles were to inspire him as President a quarter of a century later to take a strong pacifist stand during the First World War, even to defying Congress and public opinion in keeping Argentina out of the war; in his policy of the equality of nations, which caused him to withdraw Argentina from the League of Nations when at the first assembly the victorious Allies refused to admit defeated Germany and its associated nations into the League as equals of the victors; and in his benevolent attitude toward labor.

In his private life, also, Irigoyen was a perfect follower of Krause except, as Galvez points out, in his weakness for women. He wore the somber clothes affected by Krause and his followers, never laughed, bore himself solemnly, and spoke always in a high moral tone, even though much of what he said was not intelligible. Men and women, especially of the poorer classes, left his presence transfixed, their faces gleaming as they exclaimed breathlessly, "He's a saint!" His political enemies cursed him with equal fervor as a devil.

Between 1880 and 1884 Irigoyen's philosophical studies and his constant meditation on that ever-pressing question "Who am I and why am I here?" resulted in a spiritual conversion which led him to believe that he was in direct touch with God and that God was guiding him. After he was elected President, the newspapers reported that he heard voices and compared him, somewhat sarcastically, with Joan of Arc. He had always been generous and as a result of his spiritual experience he decided in the middle of 1884 to give his normal school salary to charity, which he did by turning it over to the country's oldest charitable institution, the Sociedad de Beneficencia, for its Children's Hospital. During the eight years he was President all his salary and expense moneys were drawn by this same organization on a deed which he signed over to it before taking the oath of office.

Irigoyen was thirty-seven years old and Além forty-seven in 1890, when the people rose against President Juarez Celman. The leading young men of Buenos Aires met in April and organized the Young Men's Civic Union to oppose the President. Leandro Além was elected president of the organization and in that capacity led the revolution three months later. The Civic Union's slogan was free elections. It condemned the practice of government intervention in the elections and also promised the provinces to guarantee their enjoyment of complete autonomy. General Mitre and many other well-known men of the day were among the organizers. Later the name was changed to Unión Cívica Radical, by which it has been known ever since. The revolution broke out on July 26 and after two days of fierce fighting the revolutionists laid down their arms, but Juarez Celman was forced to resign the presidency. For the next twenty-five years the Radical Party was a revolutionary party with which every President had to contend until President Roque Saenz Peña in 1912 finally gave the country the secret-ballot law which put the Radicals into power.

When Além shot himself in 1896, Irigoyen, who had shared with him the leadership of the party, became the sole leader. He immediately assumed an intransigent position, demanding all or nothing. The Radical Party, as the majority, people's party, had the sacred right to govern the country, he argued. Various attempts were made to conciliate him by offering him a place in the cabinet, the governorship of the Province of Buenos Aires, a senatorship, and other positions in the government. He rejected all, saying always that he sought no office for himself. But he made the Radical Party and the principle of honest elections an idealistic crusade to which he devoted his whole life. Exile and persecution only spurred him on to greater efforts. He refused to allow the party to enter into any agreements, trades, or compromises with the government or with other parties, because he considered such transactions to be immoral. He argued that the party which could win an honest, open election had the right to rule, and he stubbornly fought for the establishment of such elections, knowing that the Radical Party would win them.

Irigoyen had been an able conspirator since the days of his boyhood, when he could not show himself on the streets of his neighborhood. He now became the greatest conspirator since Rosas. But, unlike Rosas, he conspired for the ideal of democracy rather than for personal position or power. He began guiding the party secretly and with much mystery from behind closed doors. In plotting the frequent revolutions with which he harassed the government, he never talked to more than one accomplice at a time. This gave them complete confidence in his leadership and flattered them with the personal confidence he placed in them. Having been a police officer, he knew how to fool the police and took great delight in doing so. At the party conventions he refused to appear on the platform, but ruled the proceedings from some small, closed room in the convention hall, from which he sent his orders to the leaders and delegations. His modest residence became the Mecca of the party and he its Prophet. He received hundreds of his followers, but always one at a time, surrounding the meeting with mystery and talking in a quiet persuasive tone of higher, spiritual ideals which were mostly unintelligible to the listener. Irigoyen exercised a hypnotic fascination over all those who came into this personal contact with him and all his callers became fervent disciples of his political creed. The party eventually developed into something of a cult, with his followers almost worshiping him. His mysterious master-to-disciple lessons in politics, ethics, and conspiracy were exact copies of the methods used by one of the greatest of the Krause masters in Spain.

The last revolution in 1905 was a failure and the party was dispersed and discouraged. Only Irigoyen's tenacious faith in his own leadership and his strong, personal influence over his party disciples held the Radicals together, as he had held them together and reorganized them after earlier crises. He retired to the privacy of his tightly shuttered, half-lighted house and spent the days teaching his political ideals to hundreds of young men, who went out over the country spreading these teachings.

In the meantime the continuance of rotten government was increasing Irigoyen's prestige and even the people who had denounced his frequent revolutions began to concede that probably they had been justified. It was becoming apparent that the people of Argentina, particularly the new generations of European Argentines, were tired of the old oligarchy, which Irigoyen and the Radicals branded as the Regime.

The historian Ricardo Levene says that, after the anarchy of 1820, elections had been dominated by violence and fraud; that every election resolved itself into an armed contest for possession of the voting booths or to seize the ballot boxes, and then into another one to wrest the victory away from the adversary. Galvez says that elections were such a farce as would arouse the indignation of any decent man, to say nothing of a moralist and idealist such as Irigoyen. Ex-President Carlos Pellegrini, who had been one of the creators of this system, described it in a letter written in the United States in 1905:

In our country the political power rests in the government, which does not permit the existence of any committees or parties which might limit this power, suppressing them in defense of what it calls the integrity of its authority. Senators and deputies are not representatives of the people of the provinces but of the governors, to whom they owe obedience. Those who do not obey are not re-elected, so lose their posts and their pay. If a few senators meet privately to discuss political questions, the meeting is denounced as a conspiracy and the guilty senators are called before their respective governors and severely reprimanded. If they make the proper excuses and express their repentance they can leave the governor's presence with some hope of being re-elected. The outgoing governor appoints his successor, as though he were a political heir. This is indispensable to guarantee the continuance of his politics. The governor appoints the senators and deputies to Congress and for this reason refers to them as my senators and my deputies. He trades their votes freely when carrying out any political combinations with other governors.

But, rotten as this system may have been from a political viewpoint, it had governed the country well and carried it to the leading position in South America during the comparatively few years of constitutional government. Railroads had been built, ports opened, agriculture established, and schools and universities founded. The country was progressing rapidly and prospering. The government graft that had accompanied all this business was no worse, perhaps, than that which has accompanied government business in all countries, including the United States.

The leaders of the Regime argued that universal suffrage and unrestricted elections would throw the governing power into the hands of the ignorant riff-raff and illiterate peon class. But it had taken good care to keep this class ignorant and illiterate, in spite of all that had been spent for schools. The country had always been ruled by the social elite—lawyers, doctors, professors, and army officers—and this class was certain that any other arrangement would result in the ruin of the country.

The Radical Party, under Irigoyen's guidance, had consolidated the masses for the first time in Argentine history and awakened a new class-consciousness which pitted them against this ruling class. It was the first really national party in the country and has remained the only party organized throughout the country as are the Democratic and Republican parties in the United States. After the failure of the 1905 revolution, Irigoyen designed a new political weapon which proved to be even more effective than armed revolt. The party stubbornly abstained from participating in elections, refusing to present candidates or to permit its members to vote for the candidates of other parties. And on the occasion of every election the party announced throughout the country that it was refusing to participate in the elections in protest against the fraudulent and violent manner in which they were being conducted. This branded each new incoming government, whether national, provincial, or municipal, as a dishonest government, fraudulently elected. Obviously such a condition could not continue indefinitely in a country pretending to be a democracy.

Roque Saenz Peña was the government candidate for the presidency in 1910, so won the elections. He had been a prominent member of Congress and had represented Argentina at several international conferences, but had no political following and was elected only because the outgoing President, Figueroa Alcorta, had chosen him as his successor. Saenz Peña was something of an idealist and shortly before his inauguration he sent for Irigoyen and complained, "The people don't vote." To which Irigoyen replied, "Give them honest elections and you'll see how they vote."

Saenz Peña offered the Radical Party four ministries in his cabinet, promised to institute the secret ballot and honest elections, and said that at the end of his term he would go to Europe, feeling that he had accomplished a life's work by leaving the government in the hands of Irigoyen and the Radical Party. Irigoyen accepted all the promises but refused to co-operate in the administration by accepting the proffered cabinet posts.

Saenz Peña made electoral reform the chief work of his administration, and in 1912 Congress passed his universal suffrage law, which is known as the Saenz Peña Law. This law not only provides the secret ballot and extends the right of voting to all citizens over the age of eighteen, but makes the exercise of the duty compulsory, with a fine of 20 pesos for each failure to vote. Voting is closely linked with military service as the two fundamental duties of every Argentine citizen. All young men are required to register for military service when they reach the age of eighteen. When they register they are given a pocket-sized enrollment book which they carry with them all the rest of their lives as their most important personal document. It establishes the identity and citizenship of the bearer, with his photograph, fingerprints, and detailed description; shows whether he was called up for military service or excused; and gives his rating in the reserves. This book has to be presented at the voting booth on election day and has several pages in the back for recording where the bearer voted at each election.

In the year after this law was passed, Saenz Peña had to turn the administration over to the Vice-President because of ill health, and he died in August 1914. His name has been given to the beautiful new diagonal avenue that has been cut through the downtown section of Buenos Aires from the Plaza de Mayo to Plaza Lavalle, and he has been further honored by a most atrocious modernistic monument at the city's busiest corner, Calle Florida and Avenida Roque Saenz Peña.

Irigoyen has no monument yet, but the ugly, unaesthetic obelisk in

the Plaza de la República, where the Avenida Roque Saenz Peña crosses
the Avenida 9 de Julio, is a monument to the hatred which the Conservatives still feel toward his memory. When the government learned
that the Radical majority in Congress was going to pass a law to set
up a monument to Irigoyen at this spot, the President and the mayor of
Buenos Aires ordered the obelisk built. Large crews of men worked
twenty-four hours a day building it, so that it might be completed before Congress could stop it. It was made so big that its destruction to
make way for Irigoyen's monument would be prohibitive. Although its
construction violated three specific laws, it stopped the plans for a
monument to Irigoyen, and the government has been careful since to
prevent the Radicals from getting another majority in the Senate.

With the passage of the Saenz Peña Law, Irigoyen undoubtedly medi-
tated again on that passage from Krause which had been a sort of golden
text to him during a quarter of a century: "When the time arrives to
execute some enterprise and when all the external conditions are set,
Providence sends a genius to carry out the dictates of the Supreme Will
in accordance with the laws of history."

The time had arrived in Argentina for the liberating of the masses,
for the establishment of equality among all men, and for the end of the
oppression of the many by the few. The transformation had occurred
in accordance with the laws of history. Is it surprising that Irigoyen
should have felt himself to be the one chosen by Providence for carrying out the Divine Will? There were many other big men in Argentina
at the time, some of them much better known than Irigoyen. But there
was no one in the country who had devoted his life to the ideal of
political morality as Irigoyen had. Ever since 1884 Irigoyen had felt
that he was charged with a divine mission, although he had not been
certain at first just what that mission was. But now he felt sure that he
had been called by Providence to awaken the Argentine masses from
their indifference, to destroy the evil forces which had been oppressing
them, and to give them liberty. Irigoyen believed devoutly in Divine
Providence and the Supreme Will, and in the future was to mention
them frequently in State papers. He now threw himself into what he
believed was the mission for which Providence had selected him—the
convincing of the masses that they could free themselves by using their
new-found right to vote.

Galvez calls Irigoyen the Don Quixote of democracy and points out
what is undoubtedly true: that if it had not been for Irigoyen, Argentina never would have known democracy. He also points out something

which Irigoyen's political enemies are not likely to admit: that his long crusade was impelled by no desire for power, but by the belief that he was carrying out the Divine Will.

Providence does seem to have stacked the cards for Irigoyen, because when Saenz Peña died the Vice-Presidency was occupied by Victorino de la Plaza, who had lived many years in England, was a great admirer of the English, and had become imbued with the English respect for the law. Whereas another might have found ways of circumventing the Saenz Peña Law, as others have since succeeded in doing, de la Plaza put it into effect and the Radical Party began winning all the provincial elections.

When the time arrived for the presidential elections, the national convention of the Radical Party nominated Irigoyen by acclamation in the most exciting and emotional political gathering since the Declaration of Independence. The delegates who jammed the theater rose to their feet and cheered themselves hoarse, waving hats and handkerchiefs, and with tears of emotion in many eyes. The crowds which packed the street in front of the theater took up the cheer and then, bareheaded, sang the national anthem. Irigoyen had remained at home. When the convention met next day to receive his acceptance of the nomination, the notifying committee reported his refusal instead. Irigoyen wrote that he had never desired office and did not desire it now; that his creed had been the restoration of political morality, which had now been accomplished. He referred to his lifework as an apostleship and expressed satisfaction that the apostleship had achieved its purpose, which was all the reward he wanted. He declined the nomination.

The convention refused to accept his declination and that night the chairmen of the provincial delegations visited Irigoyen at his home to inform him that the convention would have no other candidate. Irigoyen steadfastly declined the honor. The delegates were dumfounded and dejected. Finally they told Irigoyen that if he would not accept the nomination, they would disband the party and return to their provinces without nominating a candidate. Irigoyen was checkmated. He pondered the situation for a while: the disbanding of the party would mean the end of all he had worked for; his apostleship would have been in vain. With a gesture of surrender and his voice trembling with emotion, he said, "Do with me what you will." He took no part in the campaign, but retired to his estancia until the Electoral College had met and elected him President, all the while refusing to receive callers or open letters.

Irigoyen's inauguration on October 12, 1916, was an event that never will be forgotten by those who saw it. Nothing even approaching it ever had been seen in Buenos Aires. Diplomats said it outclassed the coronations they had witnessed in Europe. The police estimated that there were half a million people in the streets and plazas between Government House and the Congressional Palace, a mile distant. Irigoyen had remained in seclusion since his election and had made no statement as to what he expected to do as President. It was supposed, therefore, that he would make some statement to Congress when he appeared before it to take the oath of office. But he merely placed his hand on the Gospels and the crucifix that lay on the desk of the president of the Chamber of Deputies, repeated the oath of office after the president *pro tem* of the Senate, turned and stepped through the portieres behind the rostrum, and was gone.

When the President stepped into the State coach, the crowd unhitched the horses and men and boys fought to take their places. This was too much for the idealist who fanatically believed in the dignity and equality of man, and Irigoyen tried to get out of the coach, but the crowd would not let him. In a few minutes the first President of Argentina ever to be elected by the people was being hauled down the famous Avenida de Mayo by several hundred of those people. Women and girls threw flowers from the balconies until the coach was full of them. Irigoyen, standing in the coach, in deference to the men who were pulling it, waved and bowed to the crowds as though these people, rather than the ones he had almost snubbed in the Chamber of Deputies, were the people whose President he had become. After nearly an hour the strange cavalcade reached its destination and Hipólito Irigoyen stepped into Government House to receive from the hands of the outgoing incumbent the blue and white sash and the gold-headed ebony cane which are the insignia of the President of the Argentine Nation.

15. FROM VICTORY TO REVOLUTION

Hipólito Irigoyen, as President, made the great mistake of trying to run the country as he had run the Radical Party for twenty-five years—as an unquestioning, disciplined machine instantly responsive to his will. Of course it did not work, and the man who had made for himself the opportunity to become the greatest President in Argentine history failed in that opportunity, brought crushing tragedy down upon his own head in his old age, and made it possible for the Conservatives to return to power and undo his life's work. In his second administration Irigoyen was caught in the world-wide economic crash of 1928–29 and so was blamed for many things that were not his fault. But his faults were so many, and the faults of his government so disastrous, that it is doubtful if the country would have put up with him until the end of his term, even if the depression had not hastened his tragedy.

In spite of his lifelong "apostleship" in the cause of democracy, Irigoyen insisted on defying Congress and ruling as a dictator. He informed Congress in his message of October 1921 that he was not an ordinary executive, and on another occasion he declared, "I am the supreme leader of the nation." He spoke frequently and sententiously of his apostleship. While such statements had served to inspire his party followers to blind faith in his leadership, they sounded a bit ridiculous when spoken by the head of the State in defense of his refusal to practice the democracy which he had preached for so many years.

Irigoyen was sixty-four years old when he became President and was already being referred to affectionately in the Radical Party as *el Viejo*, the Old Man. He was a tall, heavy man with a large head set solidly above broad shoulders. He had long arms and legs and walked firmly, but slowly and sedately. On national holidays when he and his cabinet walked shoulder to shoulder to the Cathedral to attend the Te Deum, Irigoyen seemed to tower above all his ministers and made them appear as small and insignificant in real life as they were in his government. He enjoyed vigorous health, was apparently impervious to cold, and did not have a single gray hair. His teeth were still perfect, as they were when he died seventeen years later at the age of eighty-one. He had several suits made each year but gave them all to the poor while they were still new and always appeared to be carelessly and poorly dressed

139

because all his suits were made in the style of 1880 and never were pressed. Throughout his presidency, Irigoyen continued to live in the modest, almost shabby house in Calle Brasil which he had occupied for many years with his daughter and secretary. When his landlord called on him after his inauguration to offer him a palace that would be in keeping with his position as head of the State, Irigoyen asked that the rent be reduced on the house he already had, because "his duties as President made it impossible for him to continue looking after his own interests."

Irigoyen reached the presidency with the greatest moral prestige. But that was about all the prestige he had, aside from what attached to such personal qualities his great kindness and charity. While no one ever credited him with talents, education, or wisdom, everyone respected his absolute honesty. He had no taste for literature or any of the fine arts; never went to the theater; and his biographer reports that he read only one novel in his life. After becoming President he had to make an appearance at the gala performances at the Colon Theater on the two national independence days, but he always departed at the end of the first act.

It is completely incredible that after living through what he had seen and experienced Irigoyen should have been so naïve as to believe that all Radicals were as honest as himself, yet that appears to have been so. He seems to have believed that suffering made a man honorable and also that all Radicals had suffered as deeply as he had and so must be as honorable as himself. But by the time Irigoyen reached the presidency, the majority of the party was made up of men who had never known Leandro Além, nor taken part in the revolutions of the '90's, nor fought or suffered for the party. Thousands of them were government employees from former administrations who, seeing which way the wind was blowing, had joined the party to keep their jobs. Irigoyen appointed as bureau chiefs and other ranking functionaries hundreds of those young disciples whom he had taught so earnestly behind the closed doors of his half-lighted office. Having appointed them, he trusted them implicitly. And they betrayed him. The whole administration plunged into a wild carnival of graft in which even some of the trusted cabinet ministers joined.

Irigoyen had dreamed for twenty-five years of giving his country a perfect government, but when the time came to fit his Utopian dreams into the reality of practical politics in one of the most materialistic nations on the globe he found himself beyond his depth. He was not a man of ideas. The few he had were concerned with metaphysical abstractions. A cabinet of practical, intelligent ministers could have saved him, but he appointed as ministers men who had never occupied public office and who were completely unknown to the Argentine public, so he received no help from them. Since neither he nor his ministers knew what to do, now that they were in office, they held long cabinet meetings every day, at which they discussed at great length the most trivial details. In order to give the appearance that the government was hard at work, they issued numerous decrees every day, many of which ordered the adoption of measures and departmental routine that were already in use.

The President wanted, first of all, to improve the living and working conditions of the laboring class, but he had no program for social reform. In fact, the Radical Party had no platform or program on any subject. It was organized around the personal leadership of Irigoyen. After his inauguration, those who demanded a program of government were expelled from the party and it began to disintegrate almost as soon as it came to power. The working class very soon took the program into its own hands. Knowing that because of Irigoyen's great sympathy for them he would not send the mounted police to cut them down with their sabers as the Conservative governments had done, the workers began striking for what they wanted and Irigoyen's whole first administration was attended by violent strikes throughout the land. The strikes generally terminated with the President's issuing an arbitrary order to the employers to give the workmen what they demanded and take them all back to work.

By 1918 Irigoyen had studied the problems of the working class and began issuing decrees or sponsoring laws to solve them. He established a minimum wage law and an eight-hour day, increased government salaries that were less than 300 pesos a month, prohibited the raising of house rents, appropriated 50,000,000 pesos for the construction of workmen's houses, required that all workmen be paid in currency instead of the company scrip that was used on the big timber and sugar estates, and established compulsory arbitration for the settlement of disputes between capital and labor. These reforms represented tremendous social progress in a country where the laboring class had always been treated as social outcasts having no rights that need be respected.

When Irigoyen was inaugurated, the First World War had been in progress for two years. The preceding government had declared Argentina's neutrality and done nothing about either the German shooting of an Argentine consul in Belgium or the seizure of an Argentine vessel by the British navy in Argentine waters. Irigoyen's stubborn insistence on keeping Argentina out of the war caused him to be denounced, then and since, as pro-German, but his biographer Galvez probably is correct in denying the accusation. Irigoyen believed in peace at any price. He never had been to Europe, had no interest in Europe, and probably did not have more than a vague notion of where Germany is. He was equally uninterested in England, France, and the United States. He was interested only in Argentina and its internal problems. When the pressure from the interventionists became too strong, he threatened to resign the presidency rather than sever diplomatic relations with Germany or take any other step which might endanger Argentina's peace.

But he took a surprisingly energetic attitude against Germany six months after his inauguration when a German submarine sank the Argentine schooner *Monte Protegido*. His instructions to the Argentine minister at Berlin must have astounded that gentleman. Argentina declared the sinking to be a violation of international law, of Argentina's neutrality, and of the friendly relations existing between the two countries, constituting a serious offense against Argentina's sovereignty. Irigoyen demanded an explanation from the German government, the payment of an indemnity, and a salute to the Argentine flag. Germany conceded to Argentina what it had denied to the United States: its government apologized for the sinking of the *Monte Protegido*, paid an indemnity, and promised that the ceremony of saluting the Argentine flag would take place when the war terminated. It was held on the flagship *Hanover* at Kiel in September 1921, in the presence of the Argentine minister, and the German minister of foreign affairs delivered an address in which he said Germany was repaying a debt to Argentina which it had acquired in the war.

Until the armistice was signed, Irigoyen was equally prompt and energetic in calling the American and British ambassadors and the German minister to his presence and demanding explanations from them when he thought that things they had said were disrespectful of Argentina. His dislike for the United States arose from one of his fundamental tenets—that all nations are equal, regardless of their size. Consequently, he was opposed to the imperialistic policy which the United States was following at that time. When there seemed to be danger of an invasion of Uruguay by the German colonists in southern Brazil, Irigoyen promised Uruguay that Argentina would help expel the invaders. It is very probable that this firm stand prevented the invasion, which was to have punished Uruguay for following the United States into the war.

One of the first official acts of the moralist who was oppressed by all human suffering and degradation was to abolish licensed prostitution. For years Buenos Aires had been ranked as one of the three largest white-slave markets in the world and had acquired world-wide notoriety with the publication of *The Road to Buenos Aires,* by the French writer Albert Londres. Not even the President could make a port city as large as Buenos Aires pure, but at least he drove vice under cover and made it drab and shabby instead of the luxurious institution it had been for so many years.

Another moralist reform was the prohibition of mid-week horse-racing in the city of Buenos Aires, which kept employees' minds off their work for two days in the middle of the week, besides absorbing a large slice of their salaries. The Sunday races attracted the well-to-do; the Thursday races were the poor man's vice. Irigoyen took no measures against the Sunday meetings, but removed the expensive temptation from the poor man. He also abolished other forms of gambling.

For the first time in a twenty-year campaign, a bill to establish divorce in Argentina seemed likely to be passed by a Congress that had a large majority of anti-Catholic Radicals and Socialists. Irigoyen, who never had married but who acknowledged his fatherhood of several illegitimate children whom he had supported until they were adults, brought about the defeat of the project by sending a special message to Congress condemning it. His arguments were strong Catholic arguments against divorce as a social cancer threatening the sanctity of matrimony and the sacred institution of the family.

By January 1919 the labor situation had got clear out of hand and there was a Communist-inspired outburst which produced a general strike, accompanied by furious violence and the complete collapse of law and order. This week has come down in Argentine history as the Tragic Week, or the Week of Blood. More than a thousand people were killed and several thousand wounded. Buenos Aires took on the aspect of a besieged city, as in fact it was. Transportation was paralyzed; car tracks and manholes were covered with rust; streets were littered with garbage; private automobiles appearing in the streets were burned; and milkmen, icemen, and servants who attempted to go about their daily work were murdered with impunity. The strikers raided arms and ammunition shops and then captured several police stations.

Irigoyen probably suffered more that week than he ever had suffered before. It was simply beyond his power to understand that the workmen should have risen against the government of the only President who ever had tried to do anything for them. The strike and violence were directed by professional agitators belonging to the Argentine Regional Labor Federation, a Communist organization supported by Moscow. The word "regional" in the name identified the federation as part of the world-wide revolutionary machinery which the Communists were trying to organize at that time, and the outbreak had every appearance of being the beginning of a Communist-supported social revolution; but Irigoyen was reluctant to use armed force against the workmen. At the end of the week, however, he finally agreed that there was no other alternative. He put all the armed forces in the capital, including the police and city firemen, under the supreme command of General Dellepiane and the outbreak was suppressed.

The restoration of order gave the youth of Buenos Aires its first opportunity for a pogrom. Argentines consider all Russians to be Jews and all Jews Russians, so in reprisal for the Communist leadership of the uprising the Jewish sections of the city were invaded and many innocent people killed. In fact, most of the week's casualties were the Jews killed during the last two days while order was being restored.

In 1922 Irigoyen appointed as his successor Dr. Marcelo T. de Alvear, who as a youth just out of law school had been one of the group of well-to-do young men whom Irigoyen organized around Leandro Além in 1890. Alvear had taken part in the revolutions of 1890, 1893, and 1905 and had been particularly prominent in the one of 1893. Later he had lived a great deal in Paris as a member of the large group of lavish spenders who had first made the name Argentine known abroad. He was ambassador to France at the time of the elections of 1922, but it was necessary for Irigoyen to merely nominate him and the Radical Party elected him. Irigoyen expected to continue as the governing power, using Alvear as a puppet, and at the end of the six-year term Alvear was to hand the presidency back to Irigoyen. Thus Irigoyen was following the exact method of the Regime, which he had criticized so vigorously all his life and against which he and Além had led so many revolutions.

Once in office, Alvear refused to be a puppet and he gave the country one of its best governments. He was a strict constitutionalist and refused to quarrel with Congress or to try to dominate it. He conscientiously studied the country's problems and framed a brilliant series of measures designed to solve them, including a project for reforming the currency and another for establishing a Central Bank. When the legislative branch of the government failed to co-operate with the executive branch, Alvear maintained that he had complied with his constitutional duties and that it was up to Congress to do likewise.

Alvear appointed an unusually able cabinet and during his term the country enjoyed prosperity and order, with governmental respect for the rights of all men. The minister of agriculture, Tomás Le Breton, improved agriculture, set up experimental stations for plant breeding and seed selection, promoted cotton raising in the north, put the dairy industry on a prosperous footing that established it eventually as an important export producer, and then he was appointed ambassador to the United States. The minister of war, Colonel Agustín P. Justo, reorganized the army, enlarged the air force, built an airplane factory in the Province of Córdoba, constructed modern barracks throughout the country, and put a rearmament program into effect. Later he became President of the nation. The autonomy of the provinces was respected, in marked contrast to Irigoyen's policy of intervening in provincial affairs. Special attention was given to education. All in all, it was an exceptionally good government. Also, it was greatly favored by destiny, which allowed it to function during "those good old days" of the postwar boom when the country probably would have prospered under any kind of government.

Very soon after his inauguration, Alvear's refusal to accept dictation from Irigoyen led to a break between the two old friends and a split in the Radical Party, which, as already noted, had begun to disintegrate as soon as it got into power. All the discontented members of the party, including many of its better elements, organized an *anti-personalista* wing under the leadership of Alvear. This wing set itself up as a national party with a political platform, its policies and actions to be determined by the majority vote of its members instead of by the *personalista* direction of a leader, as in the case of the old Radical Party. The two parties have since been known as Personalista Radicals and Anti-Personalista Radicals.

Despite this split, Irigoyen had no trouble in being elected for his second term in 1928 and this time there was no doubt about his seeking the office. The Personalista Party was still a compact and obedient election machine and most of the government employees felt that they owed their positions to Irigoyen instead of to Alvear. And, anyway, the Constitution made it impossible for Alvear to run for re-election. Leopoldo Melo, candidate of the Anti-Personalistas, had no political strength, and Irigoyen was elected by an avalanche.

Irigoyen was seventy-six years old when inaugurated for his second term and there were many evidences that the years had done their work. He was no longer the strong, healthy man of his first term. Also, his friends noted with sorrow and anxiety that his mind as well as his body was getting old. He allowed his sentimentalism to come to the surface on all occasions and made no effort to hide the fact that he was suffering deeply at the loss of Alvear's friendship. Completely disillusioned by the betrayals of his first administration, the President refused to trust anyone, even his private secretaries, and would not sign anything until he had read it through carefully from beginning to end. The result was a paralysis of government, because not even a strong, young man could get through the detail which Irigoyen insisted on handling himself. The executive offices soon became piled high with documents awaiting the President's signature.

The government was faced with critical problems and Irigoyen obviously was unable to solve them. The budget had tripled since his first term and totaled 1,043,000,000 pesos in 1930, compared with 377,000,-000 in 1916. The Great Depression had set in all over the world and Argentina was not spared. Budget deficits were piling up, the 1930 deficit amounting to 34 per cent. Irigoyen closed the Conversion Office to prevent the exportation of gold, and the exchange value of the peso began to drop.

The President still insisted on being the court of last resort in all disputes between labor and capital, and by 1930 he had lost the support of labor as well as of capital. Workmen blamed him for the increased cost of living and the rapid rise in unemployment. Business men resented the higher costs which resulted from Irigoyen's efforts to help labor. The President continued his policy of isolation in foreign affairs: Argentina was not represented at international conferences, and a month after the inauguration Irigoyen recalled the ambassador from Washington and left the post vacant during the two years he was in office. Argentina was losing prestige abroad, and this added considerably to the opposition to the President which was becoming general in all classes of society.

By the middle of 1930 it was painfully apparent that Irigoyen's administration was crumbling. The President had become a tired, ill, pathetic old man. His remarks frequently had no relation to the subject under discussion or to the question he was supposed to be answering.

Since the beginning of the year there had been a conspiracy among his secretaries and his few close friends to prevent his being seen by people of responsibility who might spread the bad news. But even worse news was spread by the hundreds who were kept waiting in anterooms every afternoon, day after day. Many of these were government contractors and other creditors who for months could not collect their accounts because the President did not sign their invoices and would not let others do so. Even cabinet ministers were kept waiting for hours after their arrival had been announced, only to be told at six o'clock that the President would receive no more callers. One minister stated for publication that he had been unable to see the Chief Executive from February until the end of August. While generals, admirals, and State officials were denied admittance, the President was spending most of the afternoons talking nonsense to the women and girls whom the secretaries admitted for the old man's amusement. He seldom signed more than two or three State papers a day and it required substantial bribes to get one of these papers presented to him for signature.

In an effort to cut down expenses, 10,000 government employees had been discharged. They immediately joined the opposition, which had been swelled by thousands of unpaid creditors, disgruntled workmen, and dissatisfied business men. Finally the students declared themselves with the opposition. On all sides there was a disrespect toward the government. The newspapers used uncouth nicknames in referring to the President and one went so far as to call the eighty-five Radical deputies in Congress the eighty-five Irigoyen boot-lickers. By August it was widely known that General José F. Uriburu was lining up the army for a revolution. When a Socialist deputy declared in congressional debate that only a revolution could save the country from ruin, some of the opposition newspapers took up the cry. In the first days of September it was obvious that a revolution was about to break, but the government had collapsed so completely that it was unable to take any steps to defend itself.

On September 5 Irigoyen delegated the governing power to the Vice-President, on the grounds of ill health. The Vice-President immediately declared a state of siege, which suspended the Constitution, but it was too late to ward off the catastrophe. The orders he issued to the armed forces for the defense of the government were ignored, and on September 6, 1930, General Uriburu led the troops from army headquarters at Campo de Mayo into Buenos Aires and took over Government House. The Vice-President resigned. The revolution was a popular one and thousands of civilians marched along with the troops, shouting insults at the President, whose coach they had hauled down the Avenida de Mayo only fourteen years before in the most jubilant demonstration any man had ever received in Argentina. At daybreak the leaders of the opposition political parties had gone to Campo de Mayo at Uriburu's request and accompanied him on the march into the capital, in order to make the revolution look like a civilian uprising instead of a military one. Although Uriburu had been plotting the revolt for weeks, he always maintained the fiction that his march on Buenos Aires was in response to the urgent request of the leaders of the political parties who had gone to Campo de Mayo and asked the co-operation of the army.

At dusk that night two automobiles drew up in front of the tightly shuttered residence of the governor of the Province of Buenos Aires in La Plata. Several men assisted to alight from one of them a feeble, trembling, sick old man whom the sergeant of the guard immediately recognized as the President of the republic. He was helped into the house and wrapped up in blankets on a sofa. A friend had gone to his modest home in the afternoon and found the old man sitting there almost alone, deserted by friends and party in the hour of his trial. The revolutionary troops had already entered the city and the President was in grave personal danger. Despite the warning of his physician, who said the hour-and-a-half automobile trip to La Plata probably would kill him, his friends took him to the provincial capital for safety. A few hours later the mob sacked the house where Irigoyen had lived for so many years. All the furniture and all the President's books, papers, and other personal belongings were thrown out of the windows and burned in the street.

The governor of the province telephoned to the commander of the Seventh Infantry, whom he believed to be still loyal to the President, only to be told that if Irigoyen presented himself at the barracks he would be arrested. After a consultation between Irigoyen and his friends, it was decided that he would be safer in the barracks than anywhere else, so late that night he was taken there and handed his resignation of the presidency to the officer of the day, who in the name of Uriburu and the *de facto* government declared him a prisoner.

Thus Irigoyen became a martyr to his lifelong belief in the fundamental principles of the Bill of Rights. Because he believed in freedom of expression he had taken no steps to prevent the opposition newspapers from creating public opinion in favor of the revolution that was to overthrow him. Because he believed all men are equal he had not, like Ar-

gentine rulers before and since, imprisoned or exiled the political foes
who were openly working to undermine him. On the 10th, Irigoyen was
imprisoned incommunicado on a warship anchored in the river and Uriburu sent him a warning that he would be shot if anyone attempted a
counter-revolution. Nearly three months later, on November 29, he was
removed from the warship to the island of Martín Garcia in the River
Plate and kept a prisoner there for fifteen months, until the termination
of Uriburu's *de facto* government. His daughter and secretary were
permitted to live there with him and did what they could to alleviate his
sorrow and suffering.

All three returned to Buenos Aires on the morning of February 20,
1932. In December the government discovered a revolutionary plot,
led by Alvear and certain Radical army officers. Irigoyen was taken back
to Martín Garcia. In January he became seriously ill and the physicians
who examined him recommended to the government that he be taken
back to Buenos Aires, where he could have proper medical attention.
He became somewhat better and spent the last months of his life in lone-
liness except for the two women who had been his faithful companions
through all his troubles. He received no visitors and did not read. He
merely sat, doing nothing, and taking only a melancholy interest in what
his daughter and secretary told him about what was going on in the outside world. He died on July 3, 1933, at the age of eighty-one, in a cheap
iron bed in a little upstairs flat where he had lived since his return from
prison.

The government refused to allow the body of the ex-President to lie
in state in the Cathedral or any other public place, and the little flat with
its narrow staircase was far too small to accommodate the many thousands who, now that he was dead, wanted to pay their last respects. Since
the revolution of September 6, the people of Argentina had had a year
and a half of military dictatorship and the country was again being ruled
by the Regime with its fraudulent elections and suppression of personal
liberties and other constitutional rights. Now that Irigoyen was gone,
the masses to whom he had devoted his life grew aware of what they
had lost. Thousands of them jammed the street in front of the house
and stood for hours, bareheaded, in silent mourning. The trains from
the provinces were crowded with simple folk who had sat up all night
on hard wooden benches in second-class coaches that they might be
present at the funeral. A hundred thousand provincials hurried to Buenos
Aires, and most of those who did not have friends or relatives in the
capital had to sleep in the parks and plazas, because every hotel was

crowded, with two or three in a room. For three nights and two and a half days this great crowd kept up its vigil in front of the house where the remains of the former President lay dressed in the white robes of the Dominican Order, of which he had been a liberal supporter. On the last two nights the crowd stood in the rain holding torches till dawn. Men who never had seen Irigoyen in life stood and wept as though for a beloved member of their family. Thousands climbed the narrow stairs and filed past the coffin, weeping. Buenos Aires never had known a similar occasion of public mourning.

On the day of the funeral the government sent a cavalry escort but the crowd refused to have it and it was forced to retire. The coffin, carried on the shoulders of men who had fought violently for the honor, was followed by a quarter-million mourners while another quarter-million packed the balconies, windows, roofs, and trees along the line of march, as on that memorable afternoon of Irigoyen's first inauguration. It took the procession four hours to reach the Recoleta cemetery, less than two miles from the starting point. As the coffin passed, the people sang the national anthem with its thrice-repeated shout of *"Libertad!"* Directly behind the coffin, struggling hard to hold his position as chief mourner, walked Marcelo T. de Alvear, crying like a child.

Several generations will have to come and go before Irigoyen is accorded his rightful place in Argentine history. His life and work engendered so much hate that it will be a long time before it can burn itself out. But eventually Irigoyen will be recognized as one of the greatest men Argentina has produced. He devoted his whole life to the fight for democracy and universal suffrage. Argentina was a wealthy and prosperous country during the two decades between the First and Second World Wars because Irigoyen kept the country out of the first one and made it the granary and grazing ground for the Allies. By closing the Conversion Office in his second term and so preventing the draining of Argentina's gold reserve by the international bankers, he made possible the subsequent establishment of the Central Bank, the conversion of the public debt, and the other financial measures carried out during the administration of President Justo. By saving the gold reserve, Irigoyen left something for Justo's two finance ministers, Hueyo and Pinedo, to work with. And that was why Great Britain, France, and Germany were so eager to do business with Argentina during the 1930's.

16. THE PSYCHOLOGY OF REVOLUTION

THE revolution which overthrew Irigoyen was typically South American. It is almost impossible for North Americans to understand the psychology of these South American revolutions. They bear the same vital relation to practical democracy on the southern continent that the ballot box does in the United States. They are tragic, but we write comic operas about them because, tragic as they are, there really seems to be something comical about them to a non-Latin mind. It seems so funny that anyone should actually expect them to produce constructive results. Their tragedy lies not only in the blood and hunger, the death and suffering, but also in the cruel disillusionment which invariably follows them.

On September 6, 1930, Argentina exchanged a hopelessly inefficient democratic administration for a ruthless, cynical military dictatorship. But the great tragedy of the September revolt was that it wiped out democracy altogether, turned Argentina's political clock back forty years, and restored to power the regime of fraudulent elections and political oppression by which the country had been ruled prior to 1890.

What the North American does not understand, does not see, is the idealistic concept of revolution. The South American, and especially the Argentine, pretends to abhor revolution as an institution. He readily admits that all the South American revolutions of the past have been disappointing failures, even when they were successful in the sense of overthrowing the government. He usually explains that someone "sold out." Yet always he is enthusiastic about the new revolution that is being plotted. This one is going to be different from all the others. After this one there will be no more, because this one is going to remove the underlying causes of discontent; it is going to solve all the problems. That is why he is so eager to help win it.

South American revolutions are idealistic because uneducated people believe that life can be changed by one man. Getting rid of Irigoyen and putting in Uriburu was going to solve all Argentina's problems at one blow. Every revolution has its own set of highly idealistic objectives, of which the overthrow of the existing government is the least important. That will merely open the road to the higher objectives. Consequently, the people who support the revolution (such as the political leaders who met Uriburu at daylight and accompanied him into Buenos Aires) and those who fight in it go into it in an ecstasy of enthusiastic idealism that is almost religious in its intensity.

It is this idealistic enthusiasm which is difficult for Anglo-Saxons to understand. It carries the revolutionary armies through all kinds of hardships on empty stomachs. Eventually they win the revolution or they lose it, and only a tiny *if* determines whether they are patriots or traitors. If they win, they are feted for a week or two as patriots and heroes and then forgotten. If they lose, their leaders are deported and the rebel soldiers are not paid. Execution of the leaders would be a violation of the Latin gentlemen's code and just as unethical as wounding the opponent in a duel.

The main pillar of the whole structure of South American international law is the principle of the right of asylum, which protects the flight of escaping revolutionists. The great Congress of Montevideo which in 1889 took the first steps in the codification of South American international law spent much of its time and thought on the careful drafting of the treaty which made this principle a recognized institution. At the time of the civil war in Spain, Argentina sent its newest battleship to Spanish waters to force both sides of the conflict to recognize the right of asylum. Shorn of its legal and technical verbiage, this principle provides that if the fleeing leader of an abortive revolt can manage to get to some Latin American legation or embassy he is safe. The neighborly diplomat beds and boards him for a few days, pending the outcome of the very formal diplomatic conversations with the rebel's home government, and then escorts him to the frontier under the protection of the legation's flag. The United States always has refused to recognize the right of asylum, but in those few exceptional cases where the escaping rebel has not been well up on his international law or could not get farther than the American legation, the American diplomat usually has generously allowed him to hide for an hour or two until a Latin American colleague could come and get him.

But whether the leaders of the revolution have to flee or whether they take over the government, the public effect is the same: quick disillusionment. The disillusionment usually is strongest when the revolution has been a success, and this is so because the revolution almost invariably turns out to be merely a change of men, never of methods. Once in power, the leaders forget all about the idealistic objectives they promised to attain.

Of all the revolutions which swept over South America in 1930 and 1931, the Argentine revolt was the poorest in ideals and objectives. Its declared purpose was only to eliminate Irigoyen and the Radicals. Irigoyen could have been eliminated constitutionally by persuading him to resign or by impeaching him if he refused. There was nothing in the situation in Argentina in 1930 that could not have been cured by the ballot. In fact, the solution had already begun, as the Personalistas were losing elections in the provinces and Irigoyen soon would have lost his control in Congress. But the Conservatives who were backing Uriburu's revolt were determined to throw out the whole Radical government, provincial as well as national, and this could be accomplished only by revolution. A year after the revolution, there was not a more disillusioned people in all South America than the Argentine masses to whom Irigoyen had devoted his life.

This revolutionary cycle—idealistic concept, realization, deception—has been going on ever since the southern republics won their independence, yet no one can convince a South American that the next revolution will be no different.

Occasionally the leaders of a revolution are honest and sincere in their aims. Usually they are not. But even when they are, they become poisoned by power as soon as they attain it. They suddenly find themselves in control of the government and with all the national resources at their command. It would take supermen to remain honest and honorable, and South American politicians are no closer to being supermen than are the politicians of other countries. Once in power, they become convinced that they are there by some kind of divine dispensation. So they are perfectly willing to sacrifice the entire country, and often do sacrifice it, in order to retain the power. Uriburu was no exception. He had assured his military and civilian backers that he would occupy the provisional presidency only long enough to organize elections, the understanding being that the period would be about six months. But as soon as he was in power he began digging in, with the idea of remaining, and did not issue the call for elections until a counter-revolution was about to break and popular opposition to his remaining in office had become so active that he did not dare resist it any longer.

Revolution is the oldest institution in South America. It was deep-rooted in the territory that was destined to become the Argentine Republic more than two hundred years before the republic was founded. It began in the conflict between the white and half-breed races and later developed into the still existing conflict between the capital and the interior. As early as 1570 the conquistadors of the River Plate were founding new towns with the young mestizos they had fathered with their

Indian concubines. These young mestizos, in turn, took to themselves Indian mistresses. The mestizos inherited a morose, vindictive disposition from their Indian mothers and a quarrelsome nature from their hard-fighting Spanish fathers. Suffering from the sense of inferiority that is the dominant trait of the half-breed, they early began demanding the right to govern themselves, and there were serious revolts against white authority two centuries before anyone had even dreamed of revolting against Spain. Later, as the colonies prospered, professional and business men went out in large numbers from Spain, taking their families with them, and settled in the capital. They looked down with disdain on the mixed race in the interior and insisted on the white man's divine right to govern, a right which the mestizos stubbornly refused to recognize.

This disdain of the European-born Spaniard for the mestizo extended also to the criollo. The criollos were oppressed and despised by the Spaniards, and only Spaniards born in Spain could hold high office in the colonies. No matter how low, poor, or ignorant a man born in Spain might be, he looked down on the criollo, no matter how rich or well-educated he might be. The quarrel of the criollos for the right to participate in the government led to revolutions in Santa Fé as early as 1580 and to a serious one in Buenos Aires in 1583, when the criollos forced the Spaniards to accept their choice for governor, despite the fact that the government at Asunción had sent sixty soldiers to suppress them.

Democracy as it is understood in the United States never has existed in the South American republics, with the exception of Colombia and Uruguay, in Argentina for those few brief years before the revolution of 1930, and in Chile during the four years 1920–24 and after 1938. The governments either are oligarchies of the wealthy landlords or they are military dictatorships. At any given time, from four to six of the ten republics are likely to be under military rule, although this often is disguised by having a civilian figure-head who occupies the presidency only so long as he accepts orders from the army clique. There are only two great national parties in all South America: the Radical Party in Argentina and the Aprista Party in Peru. Both are parties of the masses and both are striving to wrest the governing power away from the wealthy conservative class. With the exception of these two parties and the unimportant Socialist Party in Argentina, all other political groupings are organized around the personal leadership of caudillos, or bosses, who hold out the promise of government jobs in exchange for loyalty to their personal leadership instead of to a party platform or political principle.

In most of the South American countries, including Argentina, new political parties are organized before each election, following certain trades and agreements among the strongest caudillos. The President then is elected as a result of an agreement among these leaders, and since he seldom has a clear majority he is faced with the alternative of governing with a coalition cabinet representing all the parties which supported him or of taking things into his own hands and setting up a dictatorship. Very often the latter alternative is forced upon him by his inability to muster a majority in Congress, in which case the only way he can get anything done is to dispense with Congress and govern by means of presidential decrees.

The governing power has been in the hands of the wealthy families ever since colonial times and it has been to their interest to keep the masses oppressed economically and suppressed politically. The peons and other workers vote as they are told to do by their employers. Under the Conservative regime in Argentina, the country stores which finance the tenant farmers require each heavily indebted farmer to bring in his army enrollment book and surrender it on the eve of elections. These books are then turned over to the local boss, who sees to it that they are voted "properly" by his repeaters. Later they are returned to their owners with the necessary stamp showing that they participated in the elections. Provincial police comisarios also manage to get possession of many voting books so that they may be used for the "cause."

When commodity prices fell throughout the world and produced the Depression, the reaction in the United States was economic—the erection of new and higher tariff walls. The reaction in South America was political—the wave of revolutions which swept over the continent in 1930 and 1931. Even the larger and wealthier countries, such as Argentina, which object so strenuously to being included in the general grouping of "South America," were unable to find a better solution for their economic troubles than a change in authority through revolution.

The 1930 revolutions halted the march of democracy in those few republics where it was making some progress, and between 1931 and 1941 there was a definite trend in Argentina and elsewhere toward pseudo-Fascist dictatorships to prevent the vote-conscious masses from overthrowing the Conservative minorities which were in power. The Argentine ruling class has improved its own condition steadily during the past hundred years by exploiting the masses until it has become at last an aristocracy of wealth, but not of birth. Little of the wealth has been passed on to the producers, and the landowners have arranged things nicely so that the taxes are paid by the tenant farmers and share-croppers while the big estates pay almost nothing in comparison. In the 1930's this ruling class saw its control being threatened by democracy and so welcomed fascism as a means of retaining its position. But this fascism, if it arrives, will be a South American brand of fascism. European fascism admits no class distinctions, while South American fascism, in Argentina and elsewhere, is designed purely to keep one class in power at the expense of the other class. By 1941 the most dangerous feature of this new development was that it was conditioning public opinion for the acceptance of totalitarian ideology. Thousands of young university students in Argentina, for instance, and the recent graduates who with them make up the nationalistic youth movement, were frank and loud in their contention that they would rather see Argentina under a Fascist government than permit the return of the Radicals to power.

After the establishment of constitutional government in 1853, the consolidation of the power of authority tended to restrict the freedom of suffrage and this created the widespread revolutionary spirit in the masses that was prominent up to the time of Irigoyen's election. There were serious national revolutionary outbreaks in 1874, 1880, 1890, 1893, and 1905, in addition to innumerable ones in the provinces. The passage of the Saenz Peña Election Law in 1912 put an end to these revolts, and Argentines were congratulating themselves that revolution was a thing of the past in their history. The revolution of September 6, 1930, not only dispelled that illusion but restored the political situation which had generated the revolutionary spirit among the masses originally.

The masses in Argentina and other South American countries want popular, representative government. Before they can get it, they must overthrow the oligarchies of wealthy landowners which control the governments. It is not the democratic institutions of representative government that are being threatened; the threat is directed against the unpopular governments which have set themselves up in violation of those very constitutions which they pretend to defend. The establishment of regimes such as these in countries which call themselves republics and where the people labor under the impression that they are guaranteed representative government by their constitutions naturally arouses widespread and more or less violent opposition. But even when the opposition is merely latent, the governments usually find some way to stir it into activity, and then South America's most typical institution —the state of siege—takes the stage.

South American constitutions provide that the country may be declared to be under a state of siege whenever internal disorders or foreign invasion endangers the constitutional form of government or the authorities set up under it. The constitutional form of government never is threatened, but the existing authorities frequently are, so the state of siege is usually in force in one or more of the republics. Argentina was put under a state of siege several times after the revolution of 1930. In December 1941 Acting President Ramón Castillo, who for some time had been looking for an excuse to declare a state of siege, seized upon the entrance of the United States into the war as a pretext for suspending the constitutional guarantees in Argentina.

The state of siege is a modified form of martial law which suspends all constitutional guarantees and gives the President dictatorial powers. It differs from strict martial law by the fact that the civil courts continue to function, although in most of the republics they may not revise any act of the President until after the termination of the state of siege. A strict censorship is established over the newspapers in an effort to control public opinion, and over foreign correspondents to keep the outside world from learning what is going on. The President's political opponents are rounded up and jailed or sent into exile. If elections are scheduled for some time in the near future, the President and his minions use the state of siege to prevent the opposition party from conducting political meetings or carrying on an electoral campaign. Castillo used it on the eve of the elections of March 1, 1942, to prevent the opposition from discussing his refusal to line up with the other American republics against the Axis, which was the most important point at issue in the elections.

When the state of siege, or dictatorship, is prolonged over an extended period, it often tempts the opposition to look to revolution for the overthrow of the dictatorship, and then the whole vicious cycle begins over again.

17. NATIONALISM

THE first thing General Uriburu did on seizing power was to declare a state of siege, and, as Ricardo Levene points out, his regime was inspired by a prejudice against democracy. He openly spoke depreciatively of democracy soon after assuming office. He immediately abolished Congress and intervened in twelve of the fourteen provinces, overthrowing the elected Radical governments and putting the provinces under the rule of federal commissioners taking their orders from him. Censorship was established and several newspapers suppressed, including *Crítica* of Buenos Aires. The publisher of *Crítica*, who had done more than anyone else to create public opinion in support of the revolution, was given his choice of leaving the country or being imprisoned. He chose exile. Many prominent citizens were arrested.

In addition to the serious political complications naturally arising from such a regime of force, Uriburu was confronted with the same urgent and critical economic and financial problems that had challenged Irigoyen. By the time Uriburu had got the political situation sufficiently under control to give his attention to the economic problems, they had become much more aggravated than they had been for his predecessor. After a study of two months, his minister of finance estimated that government revenues for 1931 would amount to only 650,000,000 pesos, compared with 718,000,000 in 1929. Of this estimated income, 239,000,-000 pesos would be absorbed by the service payments on the public debt and 36,000,000 would be required for paying pensions, leaving only 375,000,000 pesos for government expenses in 1931, as compared with nearly 600,000,000 available for this purpose in 1930.

Government expenditures were curtailed, mostly by suspending the bulk of the public works program. While this move saved money, it increased unemployment and left a new problem for Uriburu's successor. As approximately half of all government income is derived from customs duties, the duties were increased. This step was designed to decrease imports and balance foreign trade without decreasing the government's income. The desired objective was attained, and by June 1931 there was a favorable trade balance of 22,000,000 pesos. But there had been a decline of 17 per cent in the total foreign trade for the first five months of the year, as compared with the first five months of 1930.

In spite of his success in establishing a favorable trade balance, Uriburu was not able to alleviate the strain on the currency. The exchange value of the peso continued to fall and this became the most unfavorable factor in the country's economic situation. Uriburu began shipping gold to meet the service charges on the foreign debt. But instead of calling in the equivalent amount of paper currency, as the law required, he ordered the Conversion Office to issue currency against bank paper. When a so-called patriotic loan which he tried to float was a failure, he deposited the unsold bonds with the Conversion Office and issued money against them. At the end of his first year in office the reserve ratio of gold to paper had dropped to 62 per cent, as compared with 84¼ per cent in August 1928. The exchange value of the peso had dropped to 21.93 American cents (its par value is 42.45 cents). With the exception of a sharp spurt in the last six months of 1933 the exchange value of the peso in the free market never since has reached 30 cents. During 1941 and the first half of 1942 the rate was fairly stabilized at between 24 and 25 cents.

Uriburu immediately reversed the isolationist foreign policy of Irigoyen, and Argentina again took its place in the councils of nations. Uriburu appointed an Argentine member to the economic committee of the League of Nations, appointed three jurists to serve on the Hague Court of Arbitration, and sent an ambassador to Washington. He offered Argentina's good offices to Bolivia and Paraguay in an attempt to prevent the Chaco War and to Colombia and Ecuador for the settlement of their boundary dispute.

The permanent effects of the Uriburu regime on Argentina were in the political rather than the economic field and they were all negative, as far as democracy was concerned. The backbone of his civilian support came from the youth of the distinguished families. There was at least one *niño bien* and sometimes two or three in most of these families of *distinguidos*—young men between the ages of sixteen and twenty-five who had had Fascist ideas drilled into them by their college and university professors. These young men knew virtually nothing about Irigoyen or his government, but they hated him with a bitter class hatred. Their opposition was inspired not by a desire for power or office for themselves but by patriotism and what they were pleased to call decency. Uriburu organized these young men into a uniformed civilian militia known as the Legión Cívica Argentina, or Argentine Civic Legion, which was the beginning of the strong nationalistic youth movement.

In April 1931 the Radicals won the elections for governor and legislators in the Province of Buenos Aires. Uriburu canceled the elections and exiled to the prison colony at Ushuaia the new leader of the Radical

Party, former President Marcelo T. de Alvear, and the victorious candidate for the governorship of the province, Honorio Pueyrredon, former ambassador to Washington. That was Argentina's last honest election until 1938. The minister of the interior committed political hara-kiri by resigning from the cabinet because he had so mismanaged the elections that the opposition had been able to win them. Uriburu ordered the suspension of all other provincial elections and set about making it impossible for the Radicals to win any more elections. This he did by the very simple but obviously illegal method of issuing a decree declaring that no member of the Personalista wing of the Radical Party could run for any office in any election. He based this edict on what he called the sacred duty of the revolution to insure the country against the return to power of the regime which the revolution had overthrown. The Personalista Radicals countered with the weapon which Irigoyen had invented: they abstained from voting and loudly denounced each successive election as an illegal farce.

In an effort to make his edict permanent and at the same time legal, Uriburu proposed to amend the Constitution and revise the Saenz Peña Election Law. He advanced the novel theory that the masses were not yet prepared for democratic government and that the country should be governed by its *select minority*—in other words, by the Conservative elite which always had ruled until Irigoyen appeared on the scene. Here he ran up against the serious opposition of many of the army officers who had been backing him. They reminded him that he had taken an oath to uphold the Constitution and respect the laws. They assured him that public opinion would not permit the changes he advocated and suggested that it was time that the *de facto* government handed over the reins of office to an elected government. Uriburu made two conditions for terminating the provisional government: first, the reorganization of all political parties in accordance with his own personal views and especially in such a way as to prevent the Irigoyen Radicals from getting back into office; second, the amendment of the Constitution in accordance with his suggestions.

Uriburu was a strong believer in the Fascist concept of the State and the relationship of the individual to the State. He favored the abolishment of political parties and the organization of citizens in accordance with their professional, trade, or business activities. Then the citizen would be permitted to vote as a member of his guild rather than as a member of a political party. The right to vote, therefore, would not be inherent in citizenship but in the citizen's social activity within the

State. And since the State and the ruling party would have been amal-gamated, there never would be any question of a political change as a result of such guild voting. This theory was much too advanced for the Argentina of 1930, and Uriburu never seriously pushed it, but by 1940 there was a large body of public opinion among the Conservatives which held that this Fascist concept of the State offered the only satis-factory solution to the problem of how to destroy the political power of the masses in Argentina and insure the country's being ruled by the educated and cultured class.

By May 1931 the opposition to Uriburu had become so strong and or-ganized that a counter-revolution was being plotted against him. This plot had considerable backing from the younger set of army officers. Uriburu very effectively foiled the plot by signing a secret and highly ingenious decree providing that the government would pay all the outstanding private debts of army officers. All the officers had to do was to tell their colonel that they owed a specified amount; no details were required and no questions asked. It was one of the cleverest wholesale bribery schemes ever invented in South America. The officers appar-ently did fairly well by themselves, for the newspapers published, a long while after, that the decree had cost the government more than 7,000,000 pesos.

Following this the plot against Uriburu limped along without mili-tary support and finally broke under civilian leadership in July in the provinces of Santa Fé and Corrientes but was quickly suppressed.

On the same day that Uriburu signed the decree paying the debts of the army officers he also surrendered to public opinion and issued the long-awaited call for general elections, but fixing the date six months hence, on November 8, 1931. During the intervening six months, the Provisional President was unable to make any important headway with his electoral reforms, but he refused to allow Alvear to run for the presidency and prohibited the Personalista Radicals from putting up any other candidate. Whereupon they announced that they would not vote. This was just what Uriburu wanted. General Agustín P. Justo was elected by a combination of Conservatives, Anti-Personalista Radicals, and Independent Socialists, and was inaugurated on February 20, 1932. His Vice-President was Dr. Julio A. Roca, son of the former president. Uriburu went to Paris, where he died a few months before Irigoyen.

Justo devoted his early efforts to healing, as far as he could, the wounds left by the revolution, to restoring constitutional government, to establishing peace among Argentines at home, and to initiating a pacific policy abroad, especially among the neighboring republics. He abolished the state of siege, released all political prisoners, and reinstated the university professors whom Uriburu had dismissed. The greatest achievement of his administration was the initiation of the National Recovery Plan and directed economy, which are discussed in a separate chapter.

Despite his election as an Anti-Personalista Radical, Justo from the first allied himself closely with the Conservative oligarchy which had been returned to power by Uriburu's revolt, and the worst feature of his administration, from the viewpoint of democracy, was the intrusion of the army into politics. For many years the Argentine army had refrained from political activity, but Justo, while minister of war in Alvear's cabinet, had paved the way for its return to politics. It was during his administration as minister of war that there rose in the army the two strong political factions which later were to become known as the Uriburistas and Justistas because they looked for political leadership to Generals Uriburu and Justo. It was the existence of these two political cliques in the army that made possible Uriburu's revolution against Irigoyen, with all its disastrous aftermath.

While Justo was President, the Province of Buenos Aires became a hotbed of corruption and Fascist propaganda under a provincial government which made no attempt to disguise its totalitarian sympathies. Provincial elections were a farce of violence, intimidation, and illegality designed to keep the Conservatives in power and the Radicals out. In the meantime the Conservatives, the least democratic of all Argentine parties, had changed their name to National Democrats.

The first four years of Justo's administration were devoted to constructive government, even though his actions did not always conform with his public utterances in praise of democracy. Besides keeping up the payments on the foreign debt, in spite of the economic and financial difficulties which faced the administration during its first two years, Justo also paid off 196,000,000 pesos of the floating debt, of which 165,-000,000 had been inherited from previous administrations. When he left office all the government's accounts had been paid up to date, and the last year of his term was one of the most prosperous in the country's history. His foreign policy was notable for its close co-operation with the United States, which constituted a complete about-face in Argentine policy. After the Pan-American Conference at Montevideo in 1933 at which Secretary of State Hull so successfully launched the good-neighbor policy, the Argentine ministry of foreign affairs and the

American State Department were in almost daily contact with each other on questions of policy.

The last two years of Justo's administration were devoted largely to politics and the "organization" of the elections which were to designate the next President. Justo "appointed" as the government candidate Dr. Roberto M. Ortiz, who was elected eighteenth constitutional President of Argentina on September 5, 1937, by the most fraudulent elections the country had seen in many years.

Immediately upon his inauguration President Ortiz repudiated election frauds, including those which had won him the presidency, and pledged himself to restore democratic government and honest elections. Since this spelled doom for the anti-democratic Conservatives, they became his implacable enemies. Ortiz also refused to accept dictation from his predecessor and insisted on exercising the presidency in his own independent way. This made a powerful enemy of Justo, who considered Ortiz ungrateful to him who had made him politically.

Ortiz was born in the city of Buenos Aires on September 24, 1886, the son of a wealthy Basque wholesale grocer. He joined the Radical Party just before the revolution of 1905, while he was a medical student. When the medical college was closed along with other university faculties because of the revolt, Ortiz was one of many imprisoned for their participation in the student disturbances which were a part of the revolution. When he was released from jail, Ortiz decided that he preferred law to medicine and entered the law school, from which he was graduated in 1909. He immediately became an attorney for British-owned railroads and other foreign corporations and later admitted to friends that between 1910 and 1918 he made "considerable" money practicing law.

After 1918 Ortiz let his legal practice decline and devoted more and more time to politics and to the pleasure of living. He delighted in spending hours at tremendous meals, accompanied by rich wines and fine cigars, and had made enough money to enjoy life without having to continue working. He also was collecting large profits from several businesses which his father had founded. He had been appointed secretary of the Radical Party's national committee and in that capacity was the principal collaborator with Dr. Tomás Le Breton, the committee's chairman, during the presidential campaign which put Irigoyen into office in 1916. When in 1918 a law was passed creating a city council for the federal capital, Ortiz was elected by the Radicals as a member of the first council. Several years later he told an Argentine reporter that in that first city council to be elected by universal suffrage, Radicals, Socialists, Communists, and independents forgot their political differences and co-operated sincerely and enthusiastically in solving the city's problems.

In 1920 Ortiz was elected to the Chamber of Deputies and immediately began to specialize in laws concerning finance and economics. He introduced thirty-four bills during his four years in the Chamber, many of which became law.

Ortiz was a close personal friend of President Alvear and when Alvear split with Irigoyen, as Ortiz later was to split with Justo, Ortiz abandoned the Irigoyen wing of the party and became one of the most enthusiastic members of the Anti-Personalista Party that was organized under Alvear's leadership. In 1924 Alvear appointed Ortiz to his first public office by making him collector of internal revenue in the ministry of finance. In February 1925 he became Alvear's minister of public works, in which position he resumed construction on the long-paralyzed new port works at Buenos Aires and also built or improved the ports at Mar del Plata, Quequén, Deseado, and La Plata. He directed the expenditure of 340,000,000 pesos on the magnificent new port of Buenos Aires and of 200,000,000 on the new waterworks of the federal capital. After the revolution of 1930 and while Irigoyen was imprisoned on Martín Garcia Island, Ortiz joined Alvear in the vain attempt to bring together the Personalistas and Anti-Personalistas so that the Radical Party could be reorganized as a strong national unit.

In 1932 President Justo offered Ortiz the portfolio of finance in his first cabinet. Ortiz refused the offer, but his hitherto strong allegiance to the Radical Party appeared to decline from that time onward and when the same ministry was offered to him again in 1935 he accepted it. By this time his love for a richly laden table had given him diabetes, and a year after becoming minister of finance he was so ill that he had to remain away from his duties for two months. When Justo selected him as the government's candidate for the presidency, Ortiz resigned from the cabinet to carry on his electoral campaign.

The inauguration of Roberto M. Ortiz as President of Argentina on February 20, 1938, was made the occasion for the greatest demonstration of United States progress in military aviation that ever had been staged in any foreign country. More than 100 American-built fighting planes were flown by Argentine army and navy pilots and the United States sent six Flying Fortresses under the command of Colonel Robert S. Olds, who later, as brigadier-general, organized the United States Army Air Corps Ferrying Command.

A few minutes after Ortiz took the oath of office, Ramón S. Castillo was sworn in as Vice-President. He was destined to take over the reigns of government from Ortiz and to occupy a much more prominent place in Argentine history than Ortiz, whose ill health had unfitted him physically to carry out the responsible duties of President during the critical times that were ahead.

During his first year in the presidency Ortiz guaranteed unrestricted legal elections, and those held in the provinces of Tucumán, Entre Rios, La Rioja, and Mendoza were honest. But in spite of the President's instructions, the Conservative governors of Buenos Aires, Catamarca, and San Juan permitted fraudulent elections in their provinces, whereupon Ortiz canceled the elections and intervened in the provinces. The intervention in the Province of Buenos Aires put an end, for the time being at least, to the scandalous situation that had existed there ever since the revolution of 1930, but it spelled the political doom of Ortiz.

When President Roosevelt sent his famous message to Hitler and Mussolini in 1938, urging them not to plunge the world into another war, President Ortiz was the first head of a State to express hearty approval of the American President's action. A few days later, in addressing the annual banquet of army and navy officers, President Ortiz pointed out the gravity of the world situation and declared that Argentina and the United States must be on the alert and prepared to face any eventuality.

The Conservatives were becoming increasingly bitter against the man they had placed in the presidency and who had betrayed them by putting an end to election frauds. His pro-American speech to the army and navy further aroused the ire of the large and powerful Fascist-minded element among the Conservatives. But his strong stand for democracy had made him the idol of the common people, who presented a great popular resistance to the various Conservative intrigues against him. For the first time since Irigoyen had been overthrown, the President of Argentina was cheered by the people wherever he went, and there was no more of the whistling and silence that so often had annoyed Uriburu and Justo when they appeared in public.

Ortiz had the support of that considerable portion of the army which was strongly loyal to General Marquez, his minister of war. It was a faction that was not loyal to Justo. Marquez also had been "made" by Justo but, like Ortiz, had rebelled against the former President's insistence on running the Ortiz administration. So the Conservatives set out to destroy Marquez. They made a great scandal out of some land frauds in connection with the army's purchase of the new site for the military academy and forced Marquez to resign from the cabinet, although he was not personally involved. Then they started out to undo Ortiz.

The Conservative plot against the President was greatly aided by the fact that Ortiz's health was steadily growing worse, the diabetes having also nearly destroyed his sight. In May 1940 he had to turn the government over to the Vice-President for a month and take a complete rest, under medical attention. He had tried to resume his duties, but his health was so bad that on July 3, 1940, he again delegated the executive power to Vice-President Castillo. This time the Vice-President laid down the condition that he was to be Acting President, carrying out his own policies rather than continuing those of the President, and that he would reorganize the cabinet with men he could trust to execute his policies. Ortiz had no choice but to accept.

Castillo immediately launched an anti-democratic program along the lines favored by the Conservatives, and there was a return to fraudulent elections in favor of Conservative candidates. Castillo told the newspapers that fraudulent and violent elections always had been a part of Argentine political life and that their correction was a matter for legislation and education rather than for presidential action.

Castillo is a perfect example of the provincial criollo—clever, sharp, and cynical in politics, but exceedingly attractive and *simpático* in his personal contacts. He proudly calls himself a *criollo de pura cepa* (criollo of pure stock) and is given to sucking yerba-maté, or Paraguayan tea, through a silver tube from the traditional gourd cup, an old criollo custom that the porteños are beginning to abandon because they no longer have the quiet leisure so necessary for its enjoyment. Castillo has always said that his only diversion in life has been his six children—four sons and two daughters, who are all grown now. He is very proud of his honorary degree from Heidelberg, Germany's oldest university, and of his membership in the Spanish Academy.

In public life Castillo gives the impression of being a country judge or professor who has no idea of what is going on in the world of reality, but he has been nicknamed the Fox, which takes care of that appearance. Newspapermen like him and he apparently likes them. It is easier for them to get to him than it was to any of his recent predecessors, and he always tries to have something interesting to say that will make news. When he does not wish to talk, he says so pleasantly and sends the reporters away in a good humor.

Chance played a greater part in putting Castillo into the presidency than it usually does in such cases. He was born in one of the poorest and remotest of the provinces—Catamarca. According to his own state-ments, he was born on November 20, 1873, which made him sixty-seven years old when he assumed the presidency. But many who know him say that he carries several more winters on his shoulders and that in 1940 he was closer to seventy-four than to sixty-seven. As with most criollos, his early retiring and early rising have kept him so well preserved that he does not show his age.

When Castillo's parents sent him to Buenos Aires to study law he got a clerical job in one of the courts, where he could study its practical ap-plication at the same time that he was studying its theory. As his studies advanced, his position in the court also advanced, and by 1895 he was legal secretary to the judge, which under the Napoleonic Code made him assistant judge. In 1896 he was admitted to practice and with rare good judgment left the capital, where competition was keen, and went to the Province of Buenos Aires, where he almost immediately got him-self appointed county judge. In that position he soon became well known for his energy and severity. When a provincial legislator was taken *in flagrante* in the commission of a crime, Castillo sent him to prison in spite of his legislative immunities. When the president of the legislature issued an order on the judge to release the prisoner, Castillo ignored the order. This action brought him promotion to the provincial criminal bench, a position which he later resigned to accept a judgeship in the commercial court of the federal capital. In 1910 he was appointed pro-fessor of commercial law at the University of La Plata. Later he became chief justice of the commercial court. In 1915 he was appointed profes-sor of commercial law in the University of Buenos Aires. By 1921 Cas-tillo had become a recognized authority on commercial law and was appointed councilor on the law faculty of the University of Buenos Aires. Two years later he was elected dean of the faculty. Castillo was perfectly frank in admitting subsequently that he had voted for himself.

As dean of the law faculty, Castillo immediately became unpopular with those students who held democratic ideas. During the sessions of the faculty, over which he presided as dean, he would sit unmoved, play-ing with his watch chain, while students made the most violent accusa-tions against him because of his undemocratic attitude. When the debate was exhausted, Castillo would adjourn the session without announcing any decision and as though nothing out of the ordinary had taken place.

While dean of the law faculty, Castillo associated himself with the re-actionary Conservatives in politics and took an active part in the prepa-ration for Uriburu's revolt against the democratic government headed by Irigoyen. When Uriburu, as Provisional President, intervened in the provinces where the Radical Party was in power, he appointed Castillo Interventor, or federal commissioner, for the Province of Tucumán. Upon his arrival at Tucumán, he gave an interesting interview to the local newspapers in which he traced his life's career in the courts and the law faculty, boasting that when he retired as a judge he was not given a single banquet—probably the only time in Argentine history that a retiring judge had not been feted by his friends and associates. Castillo explained that his failure to be so honored was proof that he had been so severe a judge that he had never granted anyone a single favor, but had always applied the law as written. He expressed the following interesting opinion of justice in Argentina and the other Latin American countries: "Justice is one of the greatest conquests in the Americas, where it is one of the governing powers, while in Europe it is merely a judicial administration."

In Tucumán, Castillo "organized" the elections so the Conservatives could win them and was then elected to the national Senate in 1932 by the Conservatives of his home province, Catamarca. In an interview two years later, Castillo declared that he was a bad politician because he always said what was on his mind.

On January 4, 1936, President Justo appointed Castillo minister of justice and public instruction and in August he became minister of the interior, which in Argentina is the minister of government, the key position in the cabinet. As minister of the interior, it became Castillo's duty to suppress the democratic forces which were trying to regain their former position in the government. It was Castillo, the severe and unrelenting judge, who ordered the exiling of Radical leaders to the Antarctic prison colony at Ushuaia in an effort to halt democratic agitation against the Justo regime.

As the time approached for the presidential elections at the end of 1937, Justo, as already mentioned, selected Ortiz, of the Anti-Personalista Radicals, to be the government's candidate for President. Political tradition in Argentina requires that when the presidential candidate is a porteño the vice-presidential candidate must be a provincial. Justo therefore selected Miguel Angel Cárcano, of the Conservatives, for Vice-President. Cárcano who had been minister of agriculture and ambassador to France, was very popular with the younger Conservatives, but the older, and reactionary, Conservatives vetoed his candidacy. Justo remembered that Castillo was from the Province of Catamarca, although he had not lived there since he was a boy, and appointed him vice-presidential candidate to run with Ortiz. As Vice-President, Castillo became president of the Conservative Senate, which set itself up to oppose everything that Ortiz tried to do after it became apparent that he meant to restore a democratic form of government in spite of the pressure to the contrary from Justo and the Conservatives.

When Castillo took over the presidency the second time, in 1940, Virginio Gayda's *Giornale d'Italia*, in Rome, jubilantly announced that this meant the establishment of a pro-Fascist government in Argentina and gave the names of several well-known Fascist sympathizers who were to serve in Castillo's reorganized cabinet. This report agreed with the rumors that had circulated in Argentina as to what would occur in case of the death of President Ortiz. But since Ortiz was still alive and threatening to resume the presidency, the men mentioned by the *Giornale d'Italia* were not appointed to the cabinet, although their names still continued to be mentioned as potential ministers.

Castillo kept up the appearance of being on good terms with Ortiz by visiting him once a week. But Ortiz continued to insist that he was still President of Argentina and in that capacity he issued several statements repudiating the anti-democratic policy of the Acting President as concerned both elections and the attitude of the government toward the European war. Inasmuch as Ortiz kept telling the newspapers that he would return to office and put things right again, the Conservative Senate appointed a committee to visit him and certify that his health and sight were such that he was permanently disabled from acting as President. When Castillo made his next visit to Ortiz, on February 1, 1941, Ortiz refused to see him. After that there was no more pretense of keeping up appearances, and Argentina had two Presidents whose policies were diametrically opposed to each other: the elected President was pledged to democracy and friendship with the United States; the Acting President had devoted his whole public career to those political forces which were opposed to everything that Ortiz stood for.

The elections in the Province of Santa Fé, after Castillo became Acting President, were so fraudulent that they aroused public protest throughout the country. The democratic Chamber of Deputies wanted to annul them. The Conservative Senate approved them. Castillo said he was a strong believer in the autonomy of the provinces and would take no steps to interfere in provincial affairs. This respect for the autonomy of the provinces did not extend, however, to the federal capital, and Castillo's most flagrant anti-democratic act in 1941 was to dissolve the elected city council of Buenos Aires. He based his action on Article

86, paragraph 3, of the Constitution, which says that the President "is the local and immediate Head of the Capital of the Nation." Democratically inclined Argentines saw in Castillo's interpretation of this clause a dangerous precedent for the interpretation of the first paragraph of the same article, which provides that "the President is the supreme Head of the Nation."

In March 1941, when the Senate's campaign of opposition against Ortiz was at its height, a member of the Chamber of Deputies declared that it was the duty of the Chamber to impeach Castillo. No steps were taken in that direction, but the threat caused the Senate to ease its anti-Ortiz activities.

On December 7, 1941, elections were held in the Province of Buenos Aires to put an end to the intervention decreed by Ortiz. So scandalously fraudulent were they that the great Buenos Aires newspaper *La Prensa* since then has always put the words *elections, ballots, voting*, etc., in quotation marks when referring to the elections in Buenos Aires. The elections, of course, put the Conservatives back in power in the Queen Province.

At the end of 1941 there seemed little likelihood that Ortiz ever would be able to resume the presidency, which still had two years to run. There was nothing to indicate that the Acting President contemplated any drastic change in the anti-democratic policy that had characterized his whole public career.

18. CONFUSION

WHEN the Conference of American Ministers of Foreign Affairs met at Rio de Janeiro in January 1942, the political situation in the Argentine Republic was one of general confusion, a confusion that reigned both in home affairs and in the average Argentine's attitude toward world affairs. The democratic forces of the country were demoralized by the serious illness of President Ortiz and ex-President Alvear, the two recognized democratic leaders, and by the brutality with which the election frauds of the 1880's had been revived to keep the majority party out of power. The government was back in the hands of a clique of professional office holders and that upper crust of Argentine wealth and society which controls the country's economy —the elite which had controlled the country before Irigoyen forced democracy upon it. Many influential people, especially in government circles and in the army, were convinced that Germany was going to win the war in spite of the entrance of the United States and so were loath to take any steps which might adversely affect Argentina's future relations with the victor. Many of these people, in fact, were fervently wishing for the defeat of the United States in the belief that the downfall of the United States would remove the only obstacle in the way of Argentina's achieving its destiny as the political leader of Latin America.

Ever since the outbreak of the war, Germany, Italy, and Japan had utilized their diplomatic power to keep Argentina neutral so that they could continue using the country as the propaganda and espionage base for South American operations. The diplomatic agents of the totalitarian powers had done their work well and efficiently, not only as regarded the official attitude of the Argentine government toward the war, but also in spreading that doubt and confusion which is such an important weapon in the war of nerves. Furthermore, the Argentine army had been German-trained for many years and many of its top-ranking officers had taken war college or other special courses in Germany or had served on the large armament-purchasing commissions which the Argentine government had maintained in Germany since the First World War. These officers were frank admirers of the efficiency of the German war machine and had been deeply impressed by the rapidity with which it had swept over Europe and almost to Moscow. They were convinced that Germany could not be defeated. They were convinced that Hitler would force the victory before the United States could throw effective assistance onto the side of Great Britain and Russia. Since these officers had all been taking an active part in politics since the revolution of 1930, their opinion carried weight with the government.

The United States had attempted to counteract this impression by inviting the Argentine chief-of-staff, along with other South American chiefs-of-staff, to tour the United States and see what the American army had to throw into the balance. He returned to Buenos Aires enthusiastic over what he had seen, made two speeches predicting the victory of democracy, and was retired from active service.

In addition to this military influence on official opinion, the German residents themselves were exercising a very strong influence on unofficial public opinion. The Germans always have been the best liked of all the non-Latin foreigners in Argentina. They adopt the local customs, intermarry with Argentines, and become absorbed into Argentine life to a far greater extent than either the British or the Americans. They spend more time than do the British and Americans on those cultural activities which appeal to Latins. And, perhaps most important, they treat the Argentines as their equals, instead of assuming the superior, patronizing attitude usually adopted by both Americans and British. Also, the Argentines like German business methods. Consequently, the average German has much more influence on Argentine public opinion than has either the Briton or the American. The American's influence is practically nil and the Briton's is not much more, except in commercial matters.

At the Nuremberg conference of the Nazi Party in 1938 it was announced that there were 236,000 German residents in Argentina, including German-born and those of German descent, and that 43,624 of these were citizens of the Reich. At that time there were only 3000 Americans in Argentina. Under the efficient regime by which these Germans had been organized by the Nazi Party, nearly all had become active instruments of Nazi propaganda and their opinions had considerable influence on their Argentine friends. Also, the German ambassador had succeeded in making himself very popular in Argentine society, and especially among army officers and government officials. As a result, there was little sympathy in government, army, and social circles for the investigation of Nazi activities that was undertaken by a committee appointed by the Chamber of Deputies.

In 1937 there were 203 German schools in Argentina, of which 22 were in the city of Buenos Aires. Many Argentines sent their children to these schools because of their efficient manner of teaching and because the discipline was much better than in Argentine schools. These schools were part of a well-organized and disciplined Volksbund which had 102 branches in all parts of the country. In the Territory of the Chaco there were 1800 German families, with a total of 11,000 persons, while the Territory of Misiones was virtually in the hands of German settlers. A film exhibited in Berlin described the German settlers in Misiones as missionaries of the Third Reich. Argentina was the first American country in which storm troop units were organized under the guise of sports clubs.

The intensive propaganda activities of the German embassy in Buenos Aires were first reported to the Argentine ministry of foreign affairs in 1936 by the Argentine ambassador at Berlin, Eduardo Labougle, but no steps were taken to curb these activities. In 1938 Ambassador Labougle sent to the Argentine government a map published by the Nazi Party showing how Argentina was to be deprived of Patagonia, the Territory of Misiones, and parts of the provinces of Corrientes and Santa Fé when the Nazis got around to redrawing the whole map of South America. Yet Argentine government officials and army officers laughed superciliously at the idea that Argentina might have anything to fear in the way of Nazi invasion or interference with its political and economic *status quo*. Labougle was transferred to Rio de Janeiro.

Many people in Argentina believed early in 1942 that the fact that President Ortiz was still alive was the only thing preventing a more open demonstration of the government's sympathy for the totalitarian powers. Ortiz was reported to be toying with the idea of resuming the presidency and appointing a minister of the interior in whom he had absolute confidence, then letting the minister indicate to him the papers that should be signed. Such a move on the part of Ortiz would have had tremendous popular backing, which might have embarrassed the government seriously if it had taken steps to prevent the President from returning to office. Therefore, Castillo was believed to be refraining from steps that might cause Ortiz to make the last supreme effort to save Argentina's democracy. The President had confided to his closest friends his intense desire to return to the presidency in time to prevent frauds in the election of his successor in 1943.

At the time of his retirement in 1940 President Ortiz was supported by all the democratic forces of the country but had been deserted by the rightist, conservative, and reactionary forces. The Unión Cívica Radical, whose national chairman, former President Alvear, had run against Ortiz in the elections of 1931, threw its support to Ortiz as soon as it became clear that he was determined to have honest elections and re-establish the democratic institutions set up by the Constitution of 1853. The President also had the support of the Socialist Party, organized labor, and the great democratic newspapers which constituted the bulk of the Argentine press. Vice-President Castillo, on the other hand, was being supported by the anti-democratic forces that had rallied around the reactionary National Democratic Party, which had nothing democratic about it except the name which the Conservatives had adopted when they reorganized under the Uriburu regime to add weight to the Provisional President's insistence that all political parties should reorganize. The anti-democratic forces supporting the Vice-President included the Fascist and Nazi sympathizers, among both the Argentine population and the foreign-born residents.

In spite of President Ortiz and those who believed as he did, Argentine democracy appeared to be decaying in the early months of 1942. So often had the Argentine people been disillusioned that they appeared to be losing faith in democracy. Also, they seemed to feel that democracy was inferior to the totalitarian systems in the matter of ideology. It was painfully obvious that there was nothing in democracy that appealed to Argentine youth as did the ideology of the Fascists and Nazis. The Bill of Rights did not appeal to a great many Argentines as anything worth fighting for. Furthermore, dictatorship *per se* is not abhorrent to the great mass of Argentines. Through most of their history they have lived under dictatorships in one form or another, and the main question which dictatorship awakens in their minds is whether it is a good or a bad dictatorship rather than whether dictatorship itself is good or bad.

By the time the United States entered the war the general confusion in Argentina's thinking was being aggravated by the very efficient manner in which the totalitarian agents and the Fascist-sympathizing Argentines were playing up the United States as an undesirable example. While the democratic people of the world were looking to the United States as the outstanding leader of democracy, propaganda agents in Argentina were painting the Yankees as the foremost example of the inefficiency of democracy and of the imperialism that has always been held up as a threat against South American democracy. This bugbear of Yankee imperialism is a theme that always makes a strong appeal to uninformed and unthinking Argentines in spite of the good-neighbor policy and everything that was done by Washington after 1933 to prove to South Americans that the policy of imperialism and intervention had been abandoned. Propaganda agents had capitalized the American congressional filibusters against the government's defense program, the strikes and other labor troubles, and all the other delays in getting ready for participation in the war. These had been compared unfavorably with the apparent promptness and efficiency of the totalitarian way of doing things until many Argentines appeared to be honestly convinced that their country could be governed better by the totalitarian system than by the seemingly inefficient democratic way. While distrust of the United States was being sown widely on the grounds of alleged imperialism, there appeared to be no fear of the totalitarian penetration which already had begun on a large and active scale.

Fascist and Nazi penetration in Argentina has been greatly facilitated by the fact that there is much more fear of leftist extremism than rightist. Consequently, Communist organizations are outlawed but Fascist and Nazi groups are not molested. When a court investigation disclosed Nazi Party activities of such alarming proportions that they could no longer be ignored, the government decreed that all foreign organizations must have Spanish names and conduct their meetings in the Spanish language. The decree was made all-embracing in order to preserve Argentina's neutrality and avoid giving the Nazis any cause for offense. So the American Club, the American Society, the Ladies' Aid Society, and various other social and church groups adopted Spanish names and struggled through their meetings with the aid of the few members who could speak Spanish. A new Gauleiter or little Führer was appointed for the country and the Nazi Party in Argentina, under the guise of a charitable and welfare organization, continued with its subversive and anti-democratic operations as before.

Rightist penetration has been confined to the activities of the large German and Italian communities, there being virtually no Japanese population or influence. About one-third of Argentina's population is Italian or of Italian descent, Italy and Spain having provided nearly equal numbers of immigrants. There is, therefore, a strong natural sympathy with Italian ideas. Although the German population is much smaller, the Germans are much more methodical than the Italians and have been much more aggressive in their propaganda. As a result, the German community is almost 100 per cent Nazi, while there are many thousands of Italians who are avowedly anti-Fascist. Soon after the Nazi regime was established in Germany, all German institutions in Argentina were "purged," first by the elimination of non-Aryans and then by the elimination of the few Germans who still were not ready to accept Nazism.

The Germans have been very active in creating and then fostering an anti-Semitic movement which has been featured by Jew-baiting on every possible occasion. This anti-Semitic sentiment received a temporary setback when the Argentine courts imposed long prison sentences on a group of young Argentine nationalists who, under the direction of a German Nazi agent, defaced the Buenos Aires synagogue with tar bombs and annoyed Jewish business men. The group was arrested while entering a Jewish theater and the police found in its possession a large quantity of small bombs and inflammable materials with which the prisoners had planned, according to their confessions, to start a fire during the performance.

Argentine sympathy for the Fascist and Nazi regimes is the result of a strong fear, either real or pretended, of Russian communism. In the early 1940's Argentina still had the fear of Soviet Russia that Western Europe and the United States had in the 1920's. But there is less communism in Argentina than in probably any other South American republic. What little Communist sympathy exists is confined to the self-styled intellectuals and to a few members of the laboring class in Buenos Aires and two or three of the other cities.

The Germans in Argentina belong to a higher social class than do the Italians, and the influence of the Germans in the upper classes is shown by the large number of German names in the society columns of the Buenos Aires newspapers. As a rule, Argentines of German descent have more sympathy with the land of their ancestors and its Nazi regime than have Argentines of Italian stock. Unlike the bulk of the Italian population, the Germans in Argentina generally do not work as peons or day laborers. Most Germans are artisans or professional and business men. German professors always have been popular in Argentine universities. There are many German physicians, surgeons, dentists, and oculists, and before the outbreak of the war Argentine doctors usually studied in Germany or Austria before settling down to practice.

German propaganda before the war was devoted largely to attracting Argentine tourists to Germany and to selling German goods in the Argentine market. The fastest and finest steamer on the South Atlantic run was a German vessel, and the Germans also made good propaganda use of their efficient airmail service between Buenos Aires and Berlin.

The Italians, on the other hand, were engaged in an intelligent and well-managed campaign of propaganda which had greatly enhanced Italy's prestige, not only in Argentina but throughout South America. This propaganda was political, cultural, and commercial in character, and was succeeding in all three phases. It had completely wiped out the antipathy which had been aroused against Italy by the invasion of Ethiopia. Immediately after the Ethiopian campaign, Italy set out deliberately to increase its popularity throughout South America, and especially in Argentina, and had succeeded better than any other country in winning Argentine and other South American interest. The Italian propaganda included free news service to all the newspapers that would print it, as well as a daily news broadcast from Rome. This was supplemented by the frequent visits of Italian lecturers who explained Italian policies and stressed Italian successes, whether of a political or an economic nature. Prominent Argentines were invited to visit Italy as official guests of the State and were flattered by being received in private audience by Mussolini and feted by the State.

Italy literally "stole" the Pan-American Aviation Conference at Lima, Peru, in 1937 by sending a large squadron of brilliant and reckless stunt fliers to Lima while the conference was in session. After the conference adjourned, the Italians flew to Chile, Argentina, and Brazil and won tremendous popularity wherever they went. With the exception of a few short dispatches in the larger newspapers, the rest of South America outside of Peru heard nothing about the Pan-American Aviation Conference, but the whole continent heard a great deal about the Italian fliers, Italian airplanes, and Italian aviation in general. The Italians planned to repeat this feat the next year at the inauguration of President Ortiz, but when they arrived in Brazil on their way to Buenos Aires they learned that the United States was sending six Flying Fortresses to the inauguration, so they returned to Italy.

The Italians have never overlooked any opportunity to spread their propaganda. When Marconi died, a huge memorial service was conducted in Buenos Aires. It began with the singing of the Fascist anthem, after which the Italian speakers made it appear that Marconi's genius was the outcome of Fascist rule in Italy and it was intimated that he was an everyday example of the class of men being produced by Fascism.

The distribution of free telegraphic news service to Argentine and other South American newspapers by the Italian official press service was the most ambitious propaganda of this kind ever undertaken by any European country. As a general rule, the larger newspapers were not influenced by this propaganda under the guise of news, but one important afternoon paper in the city of Buenos Aires was openly under its domination. On the other hand, hundreds of smaller newspapers outside of the capital eagerly use everything they can get free and print it as news from their special correspondents. In none of these papers was there anything to indicate that the so-called news came from Italian sources.

There was a noticeable falling off in Fascist enthusiasm after the inauguration of President Ortiz. Under President Justo the various Fascist movements had flourished until they had assumed threatening proportions. The visit of the American Flying Fortresses at the inauguration of Ortiz revived enthusiasm for the United States. A few months before the inauguration, President Vargas of Brazil had set up a totalitarian State. Argentines saw how easily the Brazilians had lost their civic rights and pondered the outlook of their own country. President Ortiz, in his inaugural address and later in his first message to Congress, emphatically affirmed his faith in democracy, as opposed to all the new European ideologies, and promised an early abolishment of all the restrictions which the Justo administration had put on democratic institutions. When illness forced Ortiz to delegate the executive power to Vice-President Castillo, there was a recurrence of Fascist activity and all the Justo restrictions on democracy were restored by the action of Castillo in putting the country under a state of siege in December 1941.

In the early months of 1942, while the democratic nations of the world were lining up for a battle to the death against the totalitarian powers, democracy in Argentina was being seriously menaced by the activities of a large, well-organized, and disciplined nationalistic youth movement. Having sprung from the revolution of 1930, this movement was deliberately undermining democracy, identifying itself with intolerance, and working energetically for the establishment of a government of force along Fascist lines. Known as the Federación Patriótica Argentina, this movement embraced the Argentine Civic Legion which Uriburu organized as a civilian militia and a dozen other nationalistic, pro-Fascist leagues and legions. The Patriotic Federation, organized on national lines, is reputed to have more than half a million members, and has shock troop brigades in every important city and town in the country. Many army and navy officers belong to the Federation or one of its several affiliated groups and the movement is organized for effective action. Whenever the time seems to be ripe for an attempt to set up a Fascist government in Argentina, the Federación Patriótica expects to play the same role *vis-à-vis* the State that the Fascists played in Italy. The confidential booklet issued to members contains a 22-point minimum program of action to be put into operation in taking over the State.

Point No. 1 of the program is the cessation of the democratic form of government. Political parties are to be abolished and a corporate State set up, with a one-chamber parliament of 260 members who are to be elected as representatives of guilds rather than of political parties. Foreign-owned industries and properties are to be expropriated, and Jews and Communists are to be "handled with a maximum of energy," an Argentine euphemism for "liquidated." Argentine nationalists have adopted the Nazi creed that all Jews are Communists and supporters of the Communist cause and so must be eliminated.

Only native-born Argentines are to occupy positions in the new State and they will be designated instead of elected, according to the program of action. The police are to be organized as a federal force and put on a military basis. The army and navy are to be enlarged and strengthened. Point No. 13 provides that "the care, development, and education of children throughout the country shall be the most fundamental pre-occupation of the central government." Thus the State will take over the children and train them to devote their lives to the State, as in Germany and Italy. All labor is to be put under collective contracts, which means the establishment of State-protected labor unions and syndicates. Capital and labor are to be put on an equal footing as regards rights and obliga-tions, and all disputes between them are to be settled by courts of com-pulsory arbitration. Trusts and monopolies are to be abolished and foreign-owned public services turned over to the State.

In keeping with the typical Argentine trait of never calling things by their right names, the confidential booklet of the Federación Patriótica is careful to point out that all this should not be confused with fascism, since "the only form of government that can live is a healthy and loyal democracy."

With this anti-democratic nationalistic youth movement rapidly gain-ing strength and with the democratic forces confused and demoralized, what Argentina needed more than anything else at the beginning of 1942 was intelligent leadership. Unfortunately, there was little prospect that the democratic forces would be able to supply such leadership. There were three nationally recognized democratic leaders. One of them, President Ortiz, was almost completely blind; the second, former Presi-dent Alvear, was seriously ill with tuberculosis; the leadership of the third, Senator Alfredo L. Palacios, was circumscribed by his member-ship in the Socialist Party.

Alvear died on March 23, 1942, and his funeral was made the occasion for one of the greatest popular demonstrations in favor of democracy ever seen in Buenos Aires. In sharp contrast with the Justo government's attitude toward Irigoyen's death, Alvear was accorded all the State and military honors due him as a former President. His body lay in state in the Cathedral and left there on a gun caisson, escorted by 5000 troops. The streets were packed, as they were when Irigoyen was buried, and the multitude, shouting *"Viva la democracia!"* broke through the police lines and the military escort, took the casket from the caisson, and carried it to the cemetery.

Senator Palacios undoubtedly would make a really great Argentine President if he operated in another party. But the Socialist Party, in which the Senator has become internationally famous, is not important outside the city of Buenos Aires, and because of that there is little likelihood of his reaching the presidency—which is Argentina's misfortune.

In the confused panorama of Argentine politics at the time the United States entered the European war, Dr. Alfredo L. Palacios stood out as a figure of the first magnitude. He was more typically an Argentine than most of the men in public life, who prided themselves on their European veneer, and he was tremendously admired by true Argentines in all parts of the country and in all walks of life, whether they were Radicals or Conservatives, Catholics or independents, army officers or workers.

Palacios was the first Socialist to be elected to Congress anywhere in Latin America. He was born on August 10, 1880, and lived in the Boca, a thickly populated neighborhood of poor working people. He was an unusually bright pupil in the primary and secondary schools and was graduated from the university with high honors as a lawyer. Before he was twenty-four years old, the Boca district elected him to Congress as the youngest man ever to sit in the Argentine Chamber of Deputies. He returned to private life in 1908 and spent the next four years as a close collaborator with the famous Juan B. Justo in reorganizing and strengthening the Socialist Party. When the Saenz Peña Election Law became effective, Palacios and Justo were elected to the Chamber of Deputies. In 1915 Palacios became involved in one of those questions of honor which in Latin America can be cleared up only by a duel, and as the Socialist Party prohibited dueling, the young Congressman resigned from the party and from Congress.

Palacios attempted to organize a new Socialist Party in which he hoped to adapt the Socialist doctrine to Argentine realities. But Argentine socialism always has insisted on clinging to European principles as formulated by the Second International. This is one of the basic reasons that the party never has become important outside of the city of Buenos Aires, which is dominated by European rather than criollo influence. The failure of his project kept Palacios out of Congress but resulted in a much greater achievement than anything he could have done in Congress. Always one of the most popular university professors in the country, Palacios spent the years of the First World War leading the great educational reform which swept through all Argentine universities and later spread throughout Latin America, having especially strong influence on university life in Peru and Uruguay. This reform provided for student participation in the administration of the universities and insured their autonomy. It also brought about a radical change in teaching methods and the appointment of professors as the result of competitive examinations. The most striking innovation was academic freedom and the liberty of attending classes or staying away. Formerly, the professor was nothing more than a glorified reader and students were required to sit and listen to all his so-called lectures. As a result of the reform, professors were forced to study and make their lectures interesting, otherwise they had no students. The students could stay away from the lectures, learn the subjects from books, and pass the final examinations. In 1919 Palacios went to Peru and collaborated with Raúl Haya de la Torre in establishing the university reform there.

After the revolution of 1930, Uriburu removed Palacios from his post as dean of the law school of the University of Buenos Aires because of his democratic activities. The professor rejoined the Socialist Party and in 1931 was elected to the Senate from the city of Buenos Aires, the Socialists having won both of the capital's seats by a landslide, much to Uriburu's chagrin. Senator Palacios has been one of the strongest democratic forces in the Senate, which ever since the revolution of 1930 has been strongly Conservative and reactionary. He has stoutly maintained that democracy in Argentina must be strengthened and perfected, not by means of governments of force or by the action of the "select minority" but by governmental respect for individual rights and the unrestricted use of the ballot. One of his bills, which the Senate did not pass, would require political parties to publish the sources of their campaign funds and the manner of their disbursement. He would prohibit political parties from accepting financial support from foreign corporations. He has the most biting contempt for Argentine lawyers who "sell out," as he expresses it, by becoming attorneys for foreign corporations. He insists that in order to keep their jobs and draw their fees, these Argentine attorneys must work against Argentine interests, otherwise there would be no object in the foreign corporations' keeping them.

At sixty-one, Senator Palacios is one of the most attractive men in

Argentine public life. He is recognized as one of the best swordsmen in the country, and always wins his duels. He wears a great flowing black mustache turned up pirate fashion, and affects large black felt hats turned up on one side and down on the other. Women openly admire him wherever he goes, but he has managed to remain a bachelor and lives alone in a big house that is filled with books and attended by an aged housekeeper and an old criolla cook. Working women and girls owe to Senator Palacios nearly all the social reforms for their benefit. Argentina is far behind both Chile and Uruguay in social legislation, and the progress that has been attained is due almost exclusively to Palacios's lifelong efforts on behalf of the poor and oppressed. He is the author of the laws which provide for Sunday rest, chairs for women workers, the suppression of white slavery, the protection of working women and children, minimum wages and accident insurance, the care of poor women before and after childbirth, State support for the war against tuberculosis, and many other measures of a similar nature.

Senator Palacios has refused all offers of decorations on the ground that they have no place in a democratic community. He has written a score of books on such subjects as the social consequences of fatigue; the university and democracy; women and children who work; the right of asylum; and the Falkland Islands. He is one of the most energetic leaders of the movement to recover the Falkland Islands from British occupation and the most persistent critic of the unfortunate part played by the United States in taking the islands away from Argentina and turning them over to Great Britain. Although he is a great admirer of President Roosevelt and the good-neighbor policy, he is opposed to Argentina's making any permanent commitments on the basis of that policy because he does not believe it will outlast the Roosevelt administration. He vigorously opposed acceptance of the loans which the United States offered Argentina in 1941 because he felt they would tend to limit Argentina's sovereignty and freedom of action.

Dr. Palacios is one of the most fervent and sincere democrats in Argentine public life and one of the very few who all through their public career have been willing to subordinate their own position and their own profits to their democratic principles. Because of his widespread popularity among university students, he appeared to be the only man in 1942 who might be able to lead Argentine youth away from the pro-Fascist nationalist movement and organize it for the support of democracy.

19. THE PRESS AND CENSORSHIP

THE confusion and demoralization of the democratic forces in Argentina in 1942 had been aggravated by the repeated efforts of the Conservatives since the revolution of 1930 to curb the freedom of the press and establish permanent censorship. Argentine newspapers are far ahead of those of any other South American country and always have been a strong force in favor of democracy. By their maintenance of constant vigilance and their refusal to surrender an inch of ground, they had achieved a very high degree of freedom of expression, in spite of persistent government efforts to control them. As soon as the Conservatives seized the government in 1930, they began a determined fight against the freedom of the press, one of democracy's most alert guardians.

The Argentine public is not a book-reading public, but it devours news, and especially foreign news, in much greater volume than do the people of the United States in time of peace. Argentina is one of the world's largest consumers of newsprint per capita and uses more of it than all the rest of South America combined. Argentina always has been noted for the independence and unusually high quality of its leading newspapers. *La Prensa* and *La Nación* would be great newspapers anywhere and invariably are included in any listing of the world's principal journals. The afternoon daily, *Crítica*, is one of the foremost champions of democracy and a continual thorn in the flesh of the country's reactionaries. *El Mundo* has risen rapidly to a leading position, in both circulation and influence, by publishing a high-grade, conservative daily in tabloid form, but having none of the accepted characteristics of the tabloid except its format. The oldest newspaper in the country is the English-language *Standard*, founded in the early 1800's. The Buenos Aires *Herald*, long the chief English-language newspaper in South America, circulates throughout the continent and in several of the British dominions.

La Prensa publishes more foreign news than any other paper in the world. But even more important than this, it is unquestionably the world's most independent newspaper. This is due mainly to its success in building up such a large volume of classified advertising that it has been able to achieve that ideal goal of every editor—independence of "the advertiser," whose opinion still has to be considered by the most independent newspapers in the rest of the world, including the United

183

States. *La Prensa* still sticks to the old Victorian custom of printing its want ads ahead of the news, and well it may, considering that it owes its highly enviable independence to these ads. So *La Prensa* appears every morning with from seven to ten of its first pages printed solidly with classified advertising. Then there are from six to nine pages more of such ads at the back of the paper. *La Prensa* thus publishes from 104 to 152 columns of classified advertising every day that has been paid for in cash across the counter before the paper is published. Consequently, it can tell industry and commerce, as well as governments, what it thinks of them. Its editorials lean over backward in their insistence that the government live up to the Constitution. They argue that if laws have proved themselves unworkable or otherwise undesirable they should be repealed, but that as long as they are on the books they must be respected.

After the revolution of 1930, when Provisional President Uriburu was closing newspapers which would not accept his dictation on editorial and news policy, Señor Ezequiel Paz, publisher of *La Prensa*, sent word to Uriburu that if he carried out his threat to close *La Prensa* the paper would be published every morning in Paris with a line across the front page explaining that Uriburu's dictatorship made it impossible to publish in Buenos Aires. *La Prensa* has made Señor Paz one of the wealthiest men in the country and Uriburu knew that he could and would do what he said. So *La Prensa* continued attacking the unconstitutionality of the Uriburu regime and did much to create the public opinion that finally forced Uriburu to relinquish his dictatorship and call elections.

Outside of Buenos Aires there are several newspapers which maintain unusually high standards for news and editing. *La Capital*, of Rosario, belonging to the Lagos family, is the oldest Spanish-language newspaper in the country and can stand up against any paper in the world published in a city of equal size and importance. *La Capital* has a four-hour advantage over the Buenos Aires newspapers in competing for circulation in the west and north and thus has a large volume of readers throughout the provinces of Santa Fé, Córdoba, and Tucumán. *Los Andes*, of Mendoza, belonging to the Calle family, looks like an American paper in make-up, publishes a large volume of foreign news, and would be a highly creditable newspaper anywhere.

One of the most powerful champions of the freedom of the press is the Círculo de la Prensa, of Buenos Aires, Argentina's great national press club. Every newspaper editor of any importance in the republic is a member, as are hundreds of reporters, editorial writers, and copy-readers throughout the country. The Círculo maintains free medical, dental, hospital, and legal service for its members and their families and pays the funeral expenses of members. It demands and usually obtains the immediate release of newspapermen who are arrested by provincial authorities whom they have offended, and protests vigorously, and usually effectively, to the national as well as provincial governments against every effort they make to curtail the freedom of the press.

The Constitution specifically prohibits Congress from passing any law which might restrict the liberty of the newspapers or put them under federal jurisdiction. Article 32 provides: "The Federal Congress shall not dictate laws which restrict the liberty of the press or which establish federal jurisdiction over it." Consequently, the Círculo de la Prensa and the leading newspapers usually succeed, except when the country is under a state of siege, in forcing the government to grant the Argentine newspapers a freedom that is far beyond that allowed anywhere else in South America except in Colombia and Uruguay. But the Constitution says nothing about foreign correspondents, so the censorship of outgoing news has become a permanent government institution, just as it is in almost all the other South American countries.

Without Congress having passed any law on the subject, and despite the absence of any legal grounds for doing so, the Director of Posts and Telegraphs has set up the principle that no news that is "alarming or sensational" may be sent out of the country at any time. There are no official censors and the censorship is secret, but it is none the less effective. The government makes the managers of the cable and radio companies act as censors under the threat of heavily fining them or closing the companies down altogether for several months if "anything sensational or alarming" is allowed to leave the country over their lines. The managers pass this threat along to the counter clerks, who are warned that they will lose their jobs if they pass anything that gets the company into trouble. This sets up a very effective censorship and enables the government at the same time to deny, as it does, that there is censorship in Argentina.

"Anything sensational or alarming" is a broad order. Also, it is largely a matter of individual opinion. Cable clerks in Buenos Aires have been known to use this order to make correspondents rewrite financial and market dispatches because the clerks considered the wording "sensational." Almost any attempt to follow the American method of reporting by putting the news into the opening paragraph is considered "sensational" even when the context of the dispatch is not "alarming."

This censorship, as exercised by counter clerks of the cable companies, is applied throughout the year and regardless of the news sent. Whenever anything happens in Argentina which the government thinks might cause an unfavorable impression abroad, the postoffice instructs the cable companies to send to it for revision all dispatches relating to that particular event. On one occasion when the government became alarmed over the violence accompanying a general strike and sent federal troops to assist the police of Buenos Aires, putting an army officer in supreme power as chief of police, the cable companies were warned specifically not to permit any dispatch to leave the country which referred in any way to the co-operation of the army in suppressing the disturbance.

President Justo became a stanch champion of censorship as soon as he took over the revolutionary government from Uriburu. Early in 1935 he established the precedent that a foreign correspondent who sends out any news which the government does not like, even though not sensational or alarming, can be deported without trial under the *Ley de Residencia* (Alien Residence Law)[1] which up to that time had been used only for deporting white-slavers, Communist agitators, and similar undesirables. Argentina's already efficient censorship has thus been strengthened by the constant threat of deportation.

Under the Justo administration two determined attempts were made to establish strict control over the newspapers and correspondents in spite of the constitutional guarantee of the liberty of the press. In June 1934 a bill was introduced in the Senate to establish one of the most drastic laws for government control of newspapers ever drawn up on the American continent. Senator Matías Sanchez Sorondo, in introducing the bill, stated that it had the full support of President Justo and his cabinet. The bill was supported by the government throughout the debate and finally was passed by the Senate. It was not passed by the democratic Chamber of Deputies, but there always was the danger that the government would force the bill through the Chamber at any time that it obtained a majority. There is no time limit for a bill's passage through both houses.

This proposed press control law goes so far as to provide that in certain cases a newspaper can be permanently closed on the petition of a single citizen. Most of its provisions are mandatory, requiring that the courts enforce sentences of fines and imprisonment, as scheduled in the

---

[1] For text of this law see Appendix VIII.

law, on the request of government authorities or of persons who consider themselves to have been libeled.

Senator Sanchez Sorondo, a wealthy landowner and one of the most reactionary of the Conservatives, was minister of the interior in Uriburu's *de facto* government. In that position he ordered the closing of newspapers all over the country. Although his bill is called a "Project of Law for the Protection of the Press," there is little in it that protects the press but much about threat of fines, imprisonment, and closure for violation of any of its many extremely strict regulations.

After this bill was sidetracked in the Chamber, President Justo issued a decree putting all newspaper correspondents, both domestic and foreign, under heavy bonds and providing for a strict censorship of news. This censorship, however, was to be exercised after the news had been published, and correspondents could be fined two years after writing something that later turned out to have caused unfavorable impressions abroad. This decree aroused unanimous and vigorous protest throughout the country and never was enforced. But it was still on the law books in 1942 and could be used by any government that cared to put it into effect.

Justo ordered the deportation of an American correspondent on the charge that he had sent from Buenos Aires a dispatch which offended President Vargas of Brazil. Newspapers throughout the country made such a violent protest against what they called the governing of Argentina by the President of Brazil that Justo canceled the deportation order. It transpired later that Brazil never had made the complaint cited by Justo. Castillo went even further in his intimidation of foreign correspondents almost immediately after assuming the presidency by ordering the deportation of an American correspondent who had gone to Montevideo and sent from there a dispatch about a purely Uruguayan matter that did not even concern Argentina. Castillo was persuaded to cancel this order, but soon after declaring a state of siege in December 1941 he publicly threatened to deport American correspondents who criticized his government. Significantly enough, he chose the most notorious Nazi-subsidized newspaper in Buenos Aires as the medium for announcing this threat.

A census of the publishing business in 1938 showed that there were 2881 publications in the country, of which 383 were daily newspapers, 1282 newspapers other than dailies, and 1216 reviews and magazines. These publications had a total circulation of 1,000,000,000 a year. Seventy-five of the newspapers and 1204 of the other publications were published in the city of Buenos Aires and accounted for 800,000,000 of the total circulation. Twenty-three of the Buenos Aires periodicals were published in foreign languages. The Province of Buenos Aires had 546 newspapers and other publications with a total circulation of 75,000,000, leaving 1047 publications with a total circulation of 125,000,000 a year in the rest of the country.

The people of Argentina provide a market for a tremendous number of cheap weekly reviews, most of which are issued on newsprint and sell for 10 to 20 centavos (2½ to 5 cents). Several attempts to establish higher-grade magazines to sell at 50 centavos (12 cents) have failed. Most of the reading matter in these reviews, and also in the majority of the technical journals, is translated without acknowledgment from United States magazines and newspapers. At a South American conference for the codification of international law at Montevideo in 1939, Argentina took the lead in opposing the international recognition of copyright laws on the ground that this pirating of magazine material tended to spread culture. Most of the pictures in the popular reviews are provided by American photo services or Hollywood press-agencies or copied from American picture magazines.

During 1939 the publishing houses of the country issued 1090 original books by Argentine writers and 1040 translations of foreign works. This large production is partly due to the fact that several Spanish publishing houses have moved to Buenos Aires and are producing Spanish editions of foreign works that formerly were published in Spain. Argentine commentators complain that the quality of most of the books produced is not of as high a level as might be desired and that only 15 per cent of the 1939 production could be considered of high cultural value. Eighty per cent of the original Argentine works came under four headings—social sciences, applied sciences, literature, and geography and history. There were 31 books on philosophy, 16 on religious subjects, and 38 on the fine arts. Of the 182 books classified as applied science, 118 were on medical subjects.

Authors of books usually have to finance the publication of their own work and consider themselves fortunate if they get back their investment. They write books for the prestige it gives them rather than with the idea of making money from their work. Most books are published with paper covers and limited to editions of 2000 or 3000 copies.

There were 1450 public libraries in the country in 1940 with a total of 4,141,576 volumes on their shelves. They reported an attendance of 4,000,000 readers during the year.

20. ARGENTINA'S BEEF

EVERY year, in August, the Argentine government and the cream of Argentine society turn out in their best attire to pay annual homage to a bull. The opening day of the livestock show of the Argentine Rural Society in Palermo Park vies with the Independence Day gala performance at the opera as the important official and social event of the year. The President attends in state, accompanied by the entire cabinet and escorted by the magnificent San Martín Mounted Grenadiers. A formal-dress "must" for the diplomatic corps, the occasion provides the same lucrative source for furriers, dress designers, and milliners that Easter Sunday does in the United States. Mr. Bull, who is the hero of this elaborate spectacle, is the much beribboned grand champion Shorthorn of the year, and it is he who receives, with blinking, bovine unconcern, Argentina's cheering tribute to all the Ferdinands of the pampas, of whom he has just been crowned king.

Among the early arrivals are the American ambassador and his wife. They might stay away from the gala performance at the Colon Theater and not be missed, but the meat question between Argentina and the United States being what it is they would not dare be absent from this homage to the father of Argentina's beef industry. For the United States turns up its nose and refuses to eat the richly succulent beef produced on the Argentine pampas, and one of the major failures of Washington diplomacy has been its inability to explain the United States position to Argentines in a manner sufficiently satisfactory to permit at least the pretense of friendship on the part of Argentina toward the United States. Great Britain can take the Falkland Islands away from Argentina and continue to occupy them on Argentina's very doorstep and still be considered Argentina's best friend; but Great Britain buys Argentine beef and we do not.

The opening of the annual livestock exposition is really a great show. It would be a great show in any country. The President sits among his cabinet ministers, surrounded by the silk hats of the diplomatic corps, with flags flying and military bands playing. Beautiful debutantes, whose names will appear at the top of the society column next day as "among those present," gasp their excited ah's and oh's as the grand champion Shorthorn and all the lesser prize bulls of the season are solemnly led back and forth in front of the admiring thousands, in what the newspapers and the official records call the Grand Parade. It is perfectly fitting that

189

Argentina's *nouveau riche* aristocracy should thus pay its respects each year to the love-life of the pampa bulls, because most of the great fortunes of the country have been piled up by these bulls and their lady friends while their owners lived in Paris and tried, usually in vain, to spend the money as fast as the bulls produced it.

No king's mistress ever was pampered as are these pedigreed bulls in Argentina. Two or three peons spend all their time looking after the comfort and love-affairs of each bull—a far different type of bull from the personification of masculine fury that fights for its life in the bull-ring. These big, fat, lazy Argentine fellows are gigolo bulls. They are carefully escorted to their comfortable barns every afternoon and fed warm mash while their coats are washed, combed, brushed, and curled, if you please, and their hoofs manicured. Never weaned, each bull finishes his day by nursing at the dugs of two young cows.

Mexican aristocracy was chased into hiding, Porfirio Diaz deposed, and Mexico has been in a revolution ever since because a poor, ignorant Indian named Emiliano Zapata suddenly observed one day that the race-horses for which he was caring had better food, housing, and attention than his mother and sisters. One shudders to think what might have happened in Argentina if the cattle-chasing Indians of the pampas had not been killed off before they had an opportunity to see the care and attention that are bestowed on the pedigreed bulls of today.

Shortly after the opening of the livestock show in Palermo there is another big event which the President usually tries to attend. It is the auctioning of the grand champion Shorthorn. The greatest event of this kind that ever took place in Argentina, or anywhere else for that matter, was in 1925 when a bull named "Faithful 20" was auctioned in the presence of the President, the Prince of Wales, the Maharaja of Kapurthala, and the diplomatic representatives of nearly every land on earth at the all-time record price of 152,000 pesos, which was equivalent at that time to $62,320. Higher prices have been paid in other countries for champions in the dairy class, but no such price ever was paid before or since for a Shorthorn. A few months after the sale, the grand champion died of foot-and-mouth disease, which he had at the time of the exposition, and the purchaser got his money back, that having been one of the conditions of the sale.

Since the beginning of the century, Argentina has become one of the greatest beef-producing countries and there is no indication anywhere of a prospective rival capable of producing as good quality beef at such low prices. As has been related in an earlier chapter, cattle ran wild on the Argentine plains for three hundred years and were hunted only for their hides and tallow. But the growth of the population in Western Europe and the introduction of artificial refrigeration awakened a new interest in the production of livestock in Argentina. By 1875 England was producing only one steer for every seven people of its population, whereas a century earlier it had produced one steer for every two people. To meet this deficiency in British supplies, the United States began shipping its excess beef to the Smithfield market in refrigerated vessels. The first successful experiments in this business had been made in 1874, and although the methods of refrigeration were very crude, subsequent improvements definitely assured the permanency of an international trade in meat and directed the attention of foreign capitalists to the immense possibilities of Argentina as a source of meat supplies for Europe.

The first *frigorífico*, or freezing plant, was established in Argentina in 1883 at Campana and was known as the River Plate Fresh Meat Company. This company began exporting frozen beef to Europe and by 1900 had perfected a system for chilling beef which soon led to large exports of that type of meat. Another plant was built in 1883 by Argentine interests in Avellaneda, across the Riachuelo River from Buenos Aires. A third frigorífico was built at Las Palmas in 1886 by the British firm of James Nelson and Sons, Ltd., which after 1892 was operated by an Argentine company known as Las Palmas Produce Co., Ltd. These three companies had the South American beef export trade to themselves for twenty years and during the Boer War their business was so profitable that new capital was attracted to the industry. Shortly after 1902 four new frigoríficos were built.

In response to the increasing demand from Europe for imported beef, repeated attempts were made to export live cattle from Argentina. But these efforts were not successful. Argentina soon learned, as every other meat-producing country has learned, that the shipment of cattle "on the hoof" is uneconomical as compared with the shipment of beef under refrigeration.

Before the building of the freezing works, salted and dried meats were in general use in Argentina and small quantities were being exported to Europe. This meat, which is known as "jerked meat," is called *tasajo* in Argentina and is still used in some parts of South America, Cuba, and other regions where the climate makes it almost impossible to keep fresh meat. Since the meat-drying plants could use inferior cattle and since there was very little demand for the product in Europe, there had been no incentive for improving the quality of the native criollo cattle. The introduction of refrigeration and the construction of the freezing plants after 1883 did much to improve the Argentine cattle industry. The freezing plants paid better prices for higher-grade animals, and the cattle-raisers found it to their advantage to improve their breeds. They began importing the best British bulls obtainable, regardless of price, and the inferior native cattle gradually were replaced by highly bred beef-producing animals.

Moreover, Argentina was especially well fitted by nature for an active livestock industry. The conditions of production were similar to, but usually better than, those which had existed on the frontiers of the United States in the old days of the Wild West. There was an abundant supply of native grass pasturelands, and in some of the provinces the soil was peculiarly adapted to the production of alfalfa and other fodder.

By 1900 the cost of producing prime-quality beef in Argentina was far less than in any other part of the Western Hemisphere, and with the development of regular South American shipping facilities the cost of transporting meats from the River Plate ports to England was scarcely greater than the cost for the much shorter haul from the United States to England. These conditions gave rise to keen competition between the United States and Argentine plants for supremacy in the British market. But the growth of the population in the United States after 1900 and the per capita decline in cattle-production in North America finally settled the issue in favor of Argentina.

This threatened serious consequences for the United States companies that had been exporting meat to England. Some of the larger companies had established their own selling organizations in England and on the Continent to insure the proper care and distribution of their meats and they had succeeded in developing their European business on a profitable basis only after the expenditure of a great deal of money. When it became apparent that the United States could no longer produce a large surplus of beef for export and that in the future the British imports would come chiefly from Argentina, the United States trading and selling organizations in Europe were threatened with destruction. These facilities could not be sold to the South American companies because they already had developed their own selling organizations. Rather than scrap these organizations, sacrifice their good will, and withdraw from the field, the United States companies decided to establish themselves in Argentina.

One of the largest United States packing companies purchased a plant in Argentina in 1907 and began shipping beef to England. Within a short time three other American companies entered the field by purchasing plants already in existence. The advent of these American companies with long experience in the national meat trade and the enlargement and extension of other existing plants to meet the increased demands from Europe for imported meats were the means of developing the industry to a high standard of efficiency. In 1941 there were sixteen packing plants in the country, employing 30,500 persons at an annual payroll of more than 50,000,000 pesos. One of the Chicago-owned plants had the largest killing floor in the world.

When the Second World War began, the cattle population of Argentina was 33,000,000 head, having declined 4,000,000 since 1922. Half of this population was made up of the Shorthorn breed, which is the favorite type for the export trade. Nearly all the cattle slaughtered for export are raised on alfalfa or are taken off the native grass pastures and finished on alfalfa. The enormous use of alfalfa for fattening is one of the factors responsible for the rapid development of Argentina's beef trade. As the climate is mild, the animals are left outdoors winter and summer and are turned loose to graze in growing alfalfa, a procedure which in the United States invariably causes death from colic.

The monthly trade publication of the cattle industry, *La Res*, prints in every issue this answer to the question as to why Argentine meat is the best in the world: "Because the soil of the vast area of the central part of the Republic is composed of earth and sand mixed with a high vegetable mold content with deep and permeable subsoils covered with alfalfa fields, the roots of which penetrate to a depth of 20 meters [64 feet] and bring up to the surface the necessary mineral and organic elements for rapidly building up an animal of tender organism with a well-balanced weight of bone, meat, and fat."

The type of meat for which Argentina has become particularly famous is chilled beef. This is beef that is carried to the British market at a temperature of 29° to 30° Fahrenheit, arriving soft and ready for immediate consumption. Frozen beef, which goes mostly to the Continent, is shipped at a much lower temperature, arriving hard and requiring to be thawed out before it can be used. In normal times two-thirds of Argentina's shipments of beef consist of the chilled type and one-third is frozen.

The high standing which is accorded to chilled beef in the English market is due to two factors: (a) the excellent manner in which the beef is prepared and handled, (b) the excellent quality of the cattle from which it comes. The packing companies are directly responsible for the first of these factors as well as indirectly responsible for the second.

After chilled beef has been prepared in the packing house, it is inspected by an Argentine government inspector who makes certain that it is in a thoroughly sound condition, free from all traces of disease. It is then washed with clean water, graded according to quality, and sent to the cooling room, where it remains for at least twenty-four hours, or until all the animal heat has been dispelled. Next it is removed to a chilling room, where it remains for forty-eight hours, or until it is loaded into a meat boat. But it must be shipped within seven days after the steer has been slaughtered. Chilled beef is a highly perishable product, subject to rapid deterioration unless it is handled expeditiously.

When a side of beef is ready to be loaded, it is divided into two equal parts, producing a hindquarter and a forequarter. These quarters are then wrapped in cheesecloth and again in Hessian cloth as a protection against dirt and damage in transit to England. They are then lowered into the insulated chambers of a meat boat, hung on hooks arranged for the purpose, and exposed to a temperature of two or three degrees (Fahrenheit) below freezing. This temperature must be kept constant through the voyage. If the vessel is delayed a week or more in reaching the English port, the captain of the vessel is instructed to lower the temperature in the chambers and freeze the meat hard to prevent deterioration. Once frozen, it cannot be thawed out and sold as chilled, so has to be marketed at the lower prices which prevail for the frozen product.

When the beef arrives in England, it is promptly taken from the boat and sent to the large distributing centers, where it is unwrapped, exhibited, and sold. As a rule, chilled beef arrives in such excellent condition, clean and bright in appearance, that the layman cannot distinguish it from fresh beef produced in the United Kingdom. This remarkable result is achieved only because of the attention given to every detail in the preparation, transportation, and final sale of the product.

Frozen beef is not subject to rapid deterioration and therefore does not require such careful handling. As a meat product, it is just as wholesome as chilled or fresh beef, but since it is readily distinguishable from the latter in appearance, it sells at a discount.

Only the very best cattle are converted into chilled beef, hence the necessity of maintaining the best breeds of animals. Much of the trouble in the Argentine livestock industry in recent years, however, and the refusal of breeders to adjust themselves to falling prices have been due to the ridiculously high prices which the packers have paid for prize-winning animals in order to stimulate production of the best types of beef cattle. Regardless of the uneconomically high prices which the packers bid against one another, the animals so purchased were slaughtered and exported as ordinary range cattle. In 1917 one company paid 78,000 pesos for three prize-winning steers and then converted them into chilled beef and sold them on the London market at the quotation of the day.

Argentina's exports of chilled beef during the five normal years just previous to the Second World War were: 1935, 348,351 tons; 1936, 357,473 tons; 1937, 349,481 tons; 1938, 342,426 tons; 1939, 353,527. The exports of frozen beef were: 1935, 30,651 tons; 1936, 39,651; 1937, 92,113; 1938, 102,731; 1939, 110,546.

That Argentina's meat exports were increasing, rather than decreasing, despite the wartime difficulties of shipping, was made apparent by the minister of agriculture in opening the seventy-fifth annual livestock show on August 16, 1941, when he stated that the total shipments of meat during the twelve months from September 1940 through August 1941 amounted to 730,000 tons, which was 30,000 tons more than in the previous year and 70,000 tons more than the last five-year average.

During the calendar year 1940, the United States bought 27,058,800 pounds of Argentine canned beef, valued (F.O.B. Buenos Aires) at $3,137,326. This was a decline of more than $1,000,000 from the 1939 purchases, which had totaled 38,607,912 pounds valued at $4,257,126.

But the United States steadfastly refuses to import Argentine chilled beef and this is at the bottom of all the ill will that Argentina harbors against the United States. The United States charges that Argentine cattle suffer from foot-and-mouth disease. So they do, many of them. But Argentina counters with the inescapable fact that Great Britain continues to spend several million pounds year after year for Argentine beef and builds vessels especially designed for the shallow depth of the River Plate to carry this beef to England. These vessels carry a few passengers, but they are fast luxury liners and only first-class passengers are carried on most of them. Their main objective is to get the chilled beef home to England quickly and in good condition.

The root of the controversy is that neither Argentina nor the United States is being honest with the other. Every time anyone mentions foot-and-mouth disease (which is called *aftosa* in Argentina), a great howl goes up from Argentine officials and newspapers that there is no foot-and-mouth disease in the country. Yet in 1940 the government appointed a commission to study what measures, if any, could be taken toward wiping out this plague. On the other hand, the Argentines know perfectly well that the so-called sanitary embargo against Argentine beef on the ground that it is diseased is merely a subterfuge to keep high-quality but low-priced Argentine meat out of the American market, where the American product could not compete with it.

But it also is true that if the American public were ever allowed to eat the delicious fillet steaks which can be had at the best hotels in Buenos Aires for 30 or 35 cents they probably would stop eating Chicago beef, in which case the American cattle industry would be ruined, and the next time the United States found itself involved in a war it would be dependent on Argentina for its meat supplies and be forced to divert a large portion of the navy to patrol the 6300-mile shipping lane over which the meat would have to move from Buenos Aires to New York.

It is a complicated and delicate problem, yet diplomacy is supposed to exist for the solution of just such problems in international relations. If we were half as intelligent in getting our viewpoint and our problems across to the people of South America as are the British and the Germans, this problem never would have been allowed to reach its present importance. In Argentina it has become a phobia, and nothing the United States tries to do to pacify the Argentines is accepted at its face value, but always in some relation to the meat problem.

When Tony Muto, of Movietone News, took a camera crew into Argentina after the Pan-American Conference at Lima to make some news-reels of Argentina and give the country some of the favorable publicity it is always complaining that it does not get in the United States, he encountered the meat phobia among the customs officials at the airport when he arrived at Buenos Aires. Tony had a free-entry permit for all his photographic equipment, but the customs authorities seized his portable typewriter and insisted that he pay duty on it or leave it in their possession until he left the country. Tony explained that the typewriter was just as much part of his working equipment as the movie camera, but the customs men were adamant. Finally, after much argument, the chief customs officer puffed up red as a turkey-gobbler and burst out, "You won't buy our meat. Why shouldn't you pay duty on your typewriter?" And to all the other Argentines within hearing that was a perfectly logical argument for an Argentine official to make.

Foot-and-mouth disease is endemic in Argentina, but as the cattle always are outdoors they have become almost immune to it and when the disease does strike them it is in a very mild form. It does not affect the quality of the meat, but the germ is carried in the bone marrow, and once it gets started among the herds of the United States it wipes them out as rapidly and efficiently as cholera does human beings. Surely the perfectly justified fear of American cattle-breeders against another repetition of one of these plagues could have been explained to the Argentine government and people in a manner to make them understand it.

On the other hand, the Argentine beef business was built up exclusively to satisfy the needs of the British market, and now that the British have put a quota on meat imports to protect Empire trade and the business in Argentina has outgrown the needs of the British market, there really is no logical reason why Argentina should expect the United States to absorb what the British refuse to take. Yet merely from the viewpoint of astute international policy the United States ought to admit a small quantity of Argentine chilled beef, putting it on a quota as the British do and distributing in the Southeast and other regions where the discarded bones would not come into contact with American herds. It is often argued that if the Argentine quota were only 1 per cent of the American consumption it would not affect prices, yet the quantity would so increase Argentina's exports as to add very substantially to its annual income.

Meat really does not occupy the vitally preponderant place in Argentina's national economy that the Argentines would like to have us believe. But the cattle business is the best-organized business in the country and the breeders are just as vociferous and politically important as are our own cattlemen of the Southwest. When prices are good and the cattle-breeders have money, the socially elite of Argentina's ruling class are contented—and the government is safe.

21. "BUY FROM THOSE WHO
BUY FROM US"

ARGENTINA'S foreign policy, including her divergent attitudes toward Great Britain and the United States and her efforts during 1940–41 not to offend Germany, is dictated and controlled by the cold, inescapable economic fact that practically 100 per cent of the country's exports consist of raw materials, of which 60 per cent are agricultural and 34 per cent livestock products. By 1941 the production of wealth by industry, which has been developed largely since the First World War, exceeded that of agriculture and livestock combined, but did not yet enter into export trade in any appreciable quantity. Difficulties in disposing of the crops at good prices, whether due to crop failure, frost, drought, locusts, war and blockade, or to decline in world prices, cause immediate difficulties in the general economy, in the currency, in the bank situation, and in the financial condition of the State. The resulting decrease in the purchasing power of the rural population produces a corresponding decline in the purchasing power of all other sections of the population, and this is reflected immediately in the volume of imports, to the prejudice of those countries which produce manufactured goods.

Because of her heavy dependence on other countries for the disposal of her production, Argentina suffered acutely from the Great Depression. But by means of a National Recovery Plan that was based largely on several lessons learned from the New Deal in the United States, the government put its financial affairs in order and greatly strengthened the country's economic position. The recovery plan had for its slogan, "Buy from those who buy from us," and for nearly a decade the United States was looked upon as a major enemy, being falsely represented as not belonging within the charmed circle covered by the slogan. At least a superficial understanding of Argentina's financial and economic problems during that decade is essential to any attempt to understand her political attitude toward the United States both before and after the Rio de Janeiro Conference of Ministers of Foreign Affairs in January 1942.

Argentina's urgent and constant problem is to keep her export products moving and so maintain the country's income. Otherwise she cannot continue to import the innumerable materials, products, equipment, and machinery needed for the maintenance of local industries. These industries, in spite of the great advance of recent years, are far from being able to satisfy home consumption, and except in a very few lines, such as shoes, sugar, wine, cement, etc., manufactured goods must be imported, either partially or totally. In addition, Argentine industries are dependent on foreign countries for many of their raw materials, such as iron, rubber, copper, coal, etc.

Foreign capital has been invested abundantly in Argentina, and the country's economic development has been linked intimately with the entry of foreign capital, in the form of permanent investments and as loans. Nearly all the public services and most of the great industries are foreign-owned, requiring heavy remittances abroad to cover dividend earnings. These remittances of dividends on private capital during the five-year period 1933–37 reached an annual average of 277,000,000 pesos.[1] The exportation of capital during the same period in payment of imports, interest on the foreign debt,[2] and other charges averaged 1,773,-000,000 pesos, and the total remittances, including extraordinary items, reached 1,918,000,000 pesos a year. The interest payments on foreign capital thus represented 14.4 per cent of all the foreign remittances. Services on the foreign debt during the five-year period averaged 185,000,000 pesos, or 9.6 per cent of the total. The only means Argentina has for meeting these payments is to export her raw products or contract foreign loans.

All these factors combine to keep Juan Pueblo as keenly aware of foreign exchange as he is of the day's football scores, whereas John Citizen in the United States knows virtually nothing about foreign exchange except that it is an unfamiliar term used by bankers. Before the government's control measures put an end to the daily fluctuations in the value of the peso in terms of other currencies, it was usual for bootblacks and elevator boys to greet their patrons each morning with some remark about foreign exchange instead of commenting on the weather. In the score of city blocks which comprise the heart of the downtown district of Buenos Aires, along Calles San Martín, Reconquista, and 25 de Mayo, from Corrientes to Rivadavia, there are more than twenty-five foreign exchange shops which buy and sell foreign currencies, often in connection with a cigarette business or a bootblack stand. These shops post the day's quotations in the window, and when there are no restrictions on exchange the passers-by consult these quotations every day in the same way that they glance at the news bulletins in front of the newspaper offices. Foreign exchange and its highly nervous response to events in the

[1] For Argentina's balance of payments see Appendix XIII.
[2] For Argentina's public debt see Appendix IV.

farthest corners of the world have the same place in the life and interest of the average Argentine as the Stock Exchange and its quotations had in the life of the average New Yorker in the great boom days before the crash.

In 1927 Argentina, along with the rest of the world, was in a flourishing economic condition. A large crop had been sold at good prices and there had been a heavy exportation of chilled and frozen meats valued at 2,294,000,000 pesos, the highest total since 1920. Foreign trade reached a total of 3,962,000,000 pesos and left a favorable trade balance of 626,-000,000. Foreign capital was entering the country in large volume and the peso was close to par. In August 1927 Argentina returned to the gold standard after being off it for fourteen years. But a year later the tightness of the international money market put an end to the flow of foreign capital into the country and in September 1928 Argentina began to export gold in response to the high interest rates that were being paid on short-term loans. This caused a decline in the gold holdings of the Caja de Conversión (Gold Conversion Office) [3] and, later, of the banks. The exchange value of the peso began to decline and has been quoted below par ever since July 1928.

In July 1929, exports declined by 229,000,000 pesos, but imports continued to increase, even though slightly, owing to the liberal loan policy of the banks in spite of their reduced cash balances. The favorable trade balance dropped to only 209,000,000 pesos, or approximately an eighth of the country's requirements for remittances abroad. Government expenditures exceeded revenue and there was a budget deficit of 215,-000,000 pesos, or 22 per cent of a budget which reached 988,200,000 pesos. In Argentina a budget deficit usually tends to increase the import trade because when government expenditures are held down to the level of receipts, credit has to be restricted, with a consequent restriction of imports.

Gold shipments continued in such volume during 1929 that the government closed the Caja de Conversión in December and Argentina was again off the gold standard. Until the establishment of the Central Bank the Caja had been the issuing agency for currency, but the issuance or retirement of currency was strictly automatic, the Caja issuing or receiving paper in exchange for gold at the fixed rate of $0.44, gold, for each paper peso.

---

[3] The Caja de Conversión was abolished in 1934 when the Central Bank was created.

These events in Argentina were taking place during an epoch in which the whole world was dropping rapidly into the Great Depression and the trend toward autarchy was developing.

In 1930 the passage of the Smoot-Hawley Tariff in the United States dealt a terrific blow to Argentina's economy by closing the profitable American market to many of Argentina's farm products. Argentina's troubles were aggravated by a bad crop failure, so that the export trade totaled only 1,396,000,000 pesos, or 772,000,000 less than the previous year. The industrial crisis throughout the world had decreased the purchasing power of consuming markets and there were large surpluses of unsold wheat in other producing countries, with the result that Argentina received low prices for the reduced volume it had for shipment. Since imports did not decline as rapidly as exports, there was an unfavorable trade balance of 284,000,000 pesos. And as a debtor country, Argentina always requires a large favorable balance to meet its international payments.

Despite the closing of the Caja de Conversión, gold shipments continued, with the private banks drawing on their own reserves. Argentina's balance of payments left an unfavorable balance of 262,000,000 pesos for 1930, and the peso was quoted at 22 per cent below par. The provisional government which had overthrown President Irigoyen decided to pay the service charges on the foreign debt in gold, in an effort to relieve the pressure on the exchange market. But despite all these unfavorable conditions, the *de facto* government continued to increase instead of decreasing its expenditures. The year closed with a budget deficit of 357,000,000 pesos, or 34 per cent, with total expenditures at 1,043,000,000 pesos. The floating debt on December 31, 1930, totaled 1,181,000,000 pesos, or more than the entire annual budget, with the consequent difficulties for creditors of the State as well as for the banks.

The acuteness of this economic depression, added to by the urgent necessity for the adjustment of the balance of payments and the improvement of the State's finances, obliged the government to seek the reduction of expenditures and measures for increasing revenue. Since 50 per cent of the government's revenue is collected from customs duties, the duties were increased by 10 per cent and there was a general increase in the arbitrary ad valorem assessments on which the duties are levied. The consequent increase in the cost of imported articles, coupled with the decreased purchasing power of the masses, caused a 30 per cent decline in imports during 1931. These measures did not succeed, however, in eliminating the budget deficit and the unfavorable balance in the international payments, and at the end of 1931 the floating debt was 1,342,-000,000 pesos.

Although the government's internal credit was exhausted, it did not suspend payments on the foreign debt, despite the continued decline in the value of the currency. Argentina was the only South American country which religiously kept up its payments on its foreign debt, no matter how serious the financial situation became at home from time to time.

The sharp decline in exports, especially grains, had deprived the exchange market of balances abroad, and the situation was aggravated by Great Britain's abandonment of the gold standard. This exchange problem presented a serious obstacle to any recovery projects, so Provisional President Uriburu in October 1931 set up an Exchange Control Commission with authority to fix the rates of exchange daily.[4] Export permits for the shipment of goods could not be obtained until the shippers had proved that they had sold their drafts through some bank in the city of Buenos Aires. As the country's requirements in foreign exchange were heavily in excess of receipts, this control caused the "freezing" of huge sums which could not be sent out of the country. It was officially estimated that these blocked funds amounted to approximately 1,000,000 pesos a day. The Bank of the Nation estimated in 1933 that the exchange requirements were 1,347,000,000 pesos; since only 1,092,000,000 were available, there remained a "frozen" deficit for that year of 255,000,000 pesos.

These blocked funds represented the cost of imported merchandise and the profits of foreign-owned corporations which could not be remitted abroad because the necessary exchange was unavailable. As long as this mass of funds was awaiting transfer abroad it weighed heavily on the exchange market and made the future of the Argentine peso uncertain. In 1933 the government began to seek means of relieving this pressure. A "thawing" loan to release the sterling funds was included in the Roca-Runciman Trade Treaty which was signed with Great Britain on May 2, 1933, and that treaty became the cornerstone of Argentina's National Recovery Plan and also of its foreign economic policy.

---

[4] For distribution of exchange allotments see Appendix XIV.

THE ROCA-RUNCIMAN TREATY[5]

The Roca-Runciman Treaty "implemented," as the diplomats express it, the slogan "Buy from those who buy from us," which had been coined by the British ambassador at Buenos Aires, Sir Malcolm Robertson, and "sold" to the Argentine Rural Society, the official organization of the cattle barons. It was aimed directly against the United States, which is an advocate of "triangular" or multilateral trade, as opposed to bilateral and barter arrangements. The treaty guaranteed Argentina against any reduction in the British importation of Argentine meat as a result of the Ottawa Agreement which had set up dominion preference as the basis of Britain's foreign trade policy. But in exchange for this security the treaty obligated Argentina to abandon triangular trade and adopt bilateral trade, which is a first cousin of barter. Thus it was Great Britain, not Germany, which forced Argentina into its disastrous experiment with bilateral trade and barter. The treaty provided:

(a). The United Kingdom would not reduce its imports of Argentine chilled beef in any quarter below the quantity imported in the corresponding quarter of the fiscal year ended June 30, 1932, with the exception that if the United Kingdom considered it necessary to reduce imports in order to keep prices at a remunerative level at home, Argentina would be consulted in the matter. In other words, Argentina was not to suffer as a result of the Ottawa Agreement. But, for the first time in history, quotas were set up for the importation of Argentine meat into the United Kingdom.

(b). The full amount of sterling exchange arising from Argentine exports to the United Kingdom was to be made available for remittances from Argentina to the United Kingdom, after deducting a "reasonable sum" for payments on Argentina's foreign debt in countries other than Great Britain. In other words, money which Argentina received from its sales to Great Britain could not be spent anywhere except in Great Britain. No more of this triangular trade the Americans were talking so much about.

(c). The British funds which had been blocked prior to May 1 were to be converted into a 4 per cent sterling loan, repayable in twenty years. Argentina pledged herself not to extend to importers of any other nationality more favorable terms and conditions than those extended to the British. Nor were the owners of blocked funds in other

---

[5] For text of this treaty see Appendix XI.

currencies to receive better terms on their "thawing" loans than those fixed in the treaty.

(d). A supplementary agreement was to be concluded regarding duties and other charges on British goods entering Argentina and Argentine goods entering the United Kingdom.

(e). In a protocol, Argentina promised benevolent treatment of British capital invested in Argentina. The United Kingdom promised to co-operate in a joint inquiry of the meat trade "with particular reference to the means to be adopted to insure a reasonable return to cattle-producers." Argentina promised to keep coal and other duty-free goods on the free list and to restore the lower duties in effect before 1930 for goods purchased principally from England. In return, the United Kingdom promised not to levy new duties on meat, bacon, hams, wheat, linseed, corn, and quebracho extract imported from Argentina.

The treaty made a gesture of relieving Argentine livestock growers from the monopoly of the American and British-owned packing houses by providing that 15 per cent of the meat quotas were to be filled by the Argentine government from Argentine-owned co-operatives. This did not work out in practice because the American and British packers' pool controlled the shipping and no refrigerated vessels were available except for meat shipped by members of the pool.

DIRECTED ECONOMY

With the Roca-Runciman Treaty as its Bible, Argentina set out to put into effect a National Recovery Plan of directed economy along lines similar to the New Deal in the United States. Until its operation was disturbed by the outbreak of war in Europe, the Argentine recovery plan had been a success almost from the moment of its inception, in both its material and its psychological objectives. From the very beginning it supplied the national government with funds and reduced the public debt. In its broad scope, the plan provided for depreciated currency, controlled grain prices, restriction of imports through government control of exchange rates, increase of exports by means of new trade treaties, and the solution of the unemployment problem by means of a vast program of public works.

By October 1933, just before directed economy was instituted, the problems of the economic crisis in Argentina had become almost identical with those which faced the United States on March 4 of that year. The most urgent problems were low prices for agricultural products, penniless farmers threatened with the foreclosure of their mortgages, unemployment, an unbalanced budget, and declining government revenue. Grain prices were the lowest in thirty-four years. Bank clearings had declined 40 per cent since 1928. The most important indexes of the country's economic activities reached an all-time low in 1933, the Bank of the Nation's indexes, for example, standing at 56, compared with 100 in 1926. Foreign trade was down 19 per cent from the previous year. The favorable trade balance had dropped from $136,000,000 to $48,000,000. It was estimated officially that there were 335,000 unemployed. Only the industrial factor was lacking to make a perfect parallel with the situation in the United States.

By the end of October, farmers throughout the country were threatening not to harvest their grain unless the government established a minimum price or other relief measures. It was estimated that farmers would lose 800,000,000 pesos between the cost of production and the sale price and that in the preceding four years they already had lost 4,000,000,000. A succession of several years of low prices made it impossible for the country stores to continue financing the farmers. These stores, up until that time, had been the backbone of the nation's agricultural financial structure. When they cut off the farmers' credit and refused to finance the forthcoming harvest, they made it impossible for the small farmers to harvest their crops, even if they had wanted to, unless they received financial assistance elsewhere.

The regime of directed economy designed to solve these problems was launched by President Justo on November 28, 1933, by a decree which depreciated the peso by 20 per cent, fixed minimum prices for grains, and established an import license system through the control of all operations in foreign exchange. A National Grain Board was created and authorized to purchase at the prices fixed by the government all grains offered to it, and to sell them exclusively for export at the prices fixed by the international markets. Later the flour mills were required to purchase their wheat from the Grain Board. In the meantime the government had insured the harvesting of the crop by authorizing the Bank of the Nation to finance it through loans to farmers under the Agrarian Pledge Law.

In less than a year after the issuance of this decree all the economic indexes showed rapid progress toward definite recovery. Cereal prices were the highest in several years. Export trade had increased by more than 27 per cent. The favorable trade balance was 35 per cent higher than in 1933. Bank clearings showed an increase of 20 per cent in business. The Bank of the Nation's indexes rose to 67.9, compared with the 56 of the previous year. There had been a slow, steady increase in the exchange value of the peso. Conversion operations in both the foreign and the internal debt had reduced the interest and service charges on the public debt by one-fifth, with an annual saving of $18,000,000.

Good fortune had favored Argentina, as it so often does, in the form of higher world prices for agricultural and pastoral products. The country is dependent on the prices that are fixed in world consuming markets and these cannot be raised by government measures. But the government measures had caused a good share of the price increase to be passed along to the producer instead of remaining in the hands of the exporters and speculators as formerly.

All this was accomplished without putting any new burdens on the taxpayer. In accordance with the narrow nationalistic policy which accompanied the recovery plan, importation was deemed anti-patriotic, so the cost of the economic recovery was put on the shoulders of those who purchased imported goods. The depreciation of the peso added 20 per cent to the cost of imports, and later there was a further increase by the manner in which exchange control was manipulated.

The government's plan for economic recovery had four principal objectives:

(a). To solve the unfavorable situation regarding foreign exchange.
(b). To re-establish a favorable balance in foreign trade.
(c). To find new export markets for Argentine products.
(d). To raise the home prices for agricultural products.

The Roca-Runciman Treaty, it will be remembered, had provided for the thawing of frozen sterling credits by lending them to the Argentine government for twenty years at 4 per cent interest. Argentina then offered the owners of other blocked funds the choice between lending them to the government on equal terms or freezing them in the country indefinitely. Loan agreements were signed with Belgium, France, Italy, Holland, Switzerland, and the United States, the agreements being negotiated not with the governments, as in the case of Great Britain, but with the business men and companies of those nationalities. The American owners of frozen dollar credits took 60,000,000 pesos' worth of Argentine government fifteen-year Treasury notes, paying 2 per cent interest. The owners of dollars thus got their money back sooner, but by accepting 2 instead of 4 per cent interest did not violate the provision of the British treaty prohibiting more favorable terms than those arranged for unblocking the sterling funds.

These various thawing loans totaled 329,900,000 pesos, distributed as follows: sterling, 184,600,000 pesos; dollars, 60,100,000 pesos; Swiss francs, 75,600,000 pesos; and lire, 9,600,000 pesos. With this large sum on hand, the minister of finance was able to undertake the market manipulations by which he converted the internal bonded debt from a 6 and 5½ per cent basis to 5 per cent, thus effecting an annual saving of 53,500,000 pesos in interest charges. Although sprung upon the public without warning and without discussion and put through in a ruthless manner, these financial operations were sound and the public eventually recognized their wisdom. Some of the funds from the thawing loans were used for paying part of the floating debt, which at that time was established at 852,000,000 pesos.

The foreign debt services (interest and sinking fund) have always weighed heavily on Argentina's balance of payments. In 1933 the government began a series of operations designed to reduce the cost of these services and also to contract the foreign debt into a smaller number of loans. Eight 5 per cent sterling loans totaling £15,300,000 were converted into three new 4½ per cent loans. The annual saving in service charges was 21,800,000 pesos. In 1936 the government converted its dollar loans, on which it was making annual payments of $20,200,000. Of the $234,000,000 outstanding, only $112,900,000 were reissued in dollar bonds, the remaining $121,100,000 being converted into an internal peso loan. These conversion operations reduced the annual service charges from $20,200,000 to $7,200,000, effecting a saving of $13,000,000.

At the same time that the government was strengthening its own financial situation by these conversion operations it was also strengthening the economic situation of the country at large by the various measures decreed for carrying out the recovery program.

Later, the government tightened the import license regulations by refusing entry to all merchandise unless the importer had applied for an exchange permit before ordering the goods. This decree represented the government's most advanced spearhead into private business, since it authorized the Exchange Control Commission to refuse permits to importers who failed to supply the government with all the information requested regarding their business.

The Japanese presented an interesting sideshow at this time by continuing to order merchandise from Japan as though they never had heard of these import licenses and other exchange restrictions. When the merchandise arrived and was forbidden entrance, they shrugged their shoulders resignedly, smiled and bowed, and permitted the goods to be sent to the customs warehouses for storage. After several months of this, the Japanese government offered to sign a "compensated" trade agreement by which it would buy large quantities of wool, hides, canned meats, and other army supplies if Argentina would purchase an equal amount of Japanese products. When the agreement was signed, it carried a clause releasing from custody all the Japanese merchandise in the customs warehouses.

Exchange control proved a bountiful source of revenue to the government, which made a profit of two pesos on every pound sterling bought and sold, and an equivalent profit on dollars and other currencies. Between 1933 and 1938 the government used 12,200,000 pesos of these profits for the construction of grain elevators and another 4,000,000 to finance the operation of the National Cotton Board. Profits from exchange operations also were used to guarantee minimum prices to cattle-growers on four occasions—in 1935, 1936, 1938, and 1940. The government also drew on these profits for 257,200,000 pesos up to the end of 1938 for payments on the foreign debt; another 106,400,000 pesos went toward financing public works; and 44,700,000 pesos were used for the operations of the National Wine Board.

The Exchange Control Commission manipulated its purchases and sales of exchange at all times in such a way as to restrict imports and increase exports. Meanwhile there was a notable recovery in trade and industry as a result of the operations of the National Grain Board, and bankruptcies in 1934 were 50 per cent fewer than in 1933. An interesting indication of improved conditions in the interior was that the consumption of wine increased by one-third and the price doubled.

During the first year of its operation, the Grain Board purchased 4,012,129 tons of cereals, or 75 per cent of the exportable surplus, at a loss of nearly 9,000,000 pesos. It also lent 304,000,000 pesos to farmers. The board reported a loss of 1,488,417 pesos in 1935 and a profit of 2,650,799 pesos in 1936.

Eventually the government set up nearly a score of boards and commissions to regulate virtually every line of production in the country, as well as boards to study other problems, such as unemployment, transportation, and public works, and to suggest remedies.[6] Eight of these boards,

---

[6] For complete list of these boards and their duties see Appendix II.

or juntas, protected the principal sources of production. There were the National Meat Board, the National Grain Board, the Board to Promote the Exportation of Meat, the Dairy Industry Board, the National Wine Board, the National Cotton Board, the Yerba-Maté Board, and the National Grain and Elevators Board. Only three of these boards intervened in international trade, the functions of the others being confined within the country.

One of the most important permanent results of this vast recovery plan was the establishment of the Central Bank in 1934 to act as a bank of issue as well as a controller of credit operations by discounting the paper of the private banks. The value of the country's exports, which, as has been mentioned, are practically 100 per cent agrarian, fluctuates violently according to the size of the crops and the prices at which they can be sold and has a direct influence on the country's financial policy. As an example, the value of the exports in 1933 was only half the value of the 1928 exports, a drop from 2,400,000,000 pesos to 1,100,000,000. This produced complicated monetary and credit problems which the country was not in a position to handle satisfactorily, because of the inelasticity of its banking and currency organization.

The old Caja de Conversión, the main function of which was to exchange gold for paper and vice versa, was not organized to handle extreme expansion or restriction of credit. Also, in actual practice, the Caja had found that it could not function in the face of a long-continued flight of gold. In such circumstances the Caja had to be closed, which took Argentina off the gold standard.

The creation of the Central Bank was made the occasion for revaluing the gold reserves of the Caja, another lesson which Argentina had learned from the New Deal in Washington. This reserve figured on the books of the Caja at 561,006,035 pesos. It was revalued at 1,224,417,645 pesos, giving the government, at the stroke of a pen, the tidy profit of 663,411,-610 pesos, to which were added 37,649,156 pesos in nickel and copper coins taken over by the Central Bank from the government, making a total profit of 701,060,766 pesos. The government used this profit to pay off some of its debts to the Bank of the Nation and private banks, and to buy up and liquidate three unsound private banks.

The existence of the Central Bank in 1939 enabled Argentina to withstand the shock of the outbreak of war a great deal better than it had met the war of 1914. The war accentuated the restrictive effects of bilateral compensation in Argentina's international trade by interrupting what little fluidity had still remained in several important sectors of the international monetary mechanism. Imports were costing 36 per cent more than formerly, while the country was receiving only 18 per cent more for its exports.

As in 1914, the first psychological effect of the war manifested itself in a wave of selling on the Stock Exchange. In 1914 the government had been forced to close the Exchange in order to curb the panic. In 1939 the government announced through the Central Bank that it would purchase all government securities offered for sale on the Exchange, and the Central Bank purchased 33,000,000 pesos' worth of such securities before calm finally was restored. The whole banking system had been so strengthened since the creation of the Central Bank that the bank was called upon to discount only 5,000,000 pesos' worth of bank paper during the few days of uneasiness that followed the outbreak of war.

BILATERAL TRADE TREATIES

Since the Roca-Runciman Treaty had provided that none of the money which Argentina received from Great Britain could be spent anywhere except in Great Britain, Argentina was compelled to revise its trade treaties with other countries to put them on a bilateral basis designed to channelize all Argentina's foreign trade into two-way exchanges which should balance themselves. In some cases entirely new treaties were signed.[7] In others the desired bilateral arrangement was achieved by agreements regarding "compensated" exchange operations.[8]

Great Britain's contention in negotiating the Roca-Runciman Treaty was that as Argentina's best customer she was entitled to special, preferential treatment. In 1933 the British purchases of Argentine products amounted to 388,636,000 pesos, or 34.8 per cent of Argentina's total exports. The next best customer was Belgium, which bought 9.3 per cent of the total, or 104,112,000 pesos. Great Britain thus was able to support with figures her contention that she was buying almost four times as much as Argentina's second-best customer.

Third on the list were the Netherlands, taking 8.2 per cent of the total exports. The United States was fourth, with 85,978,000 pesos, or 7.7 per cent of the total. Then followed Germany with 7.3 per cent, France 6 per cent, Brazil 4.2 per cent, and Italy 3.9 per cent.

Great Britain also was first on the list of countries selling to Argentina, but the percentage was only 21.4 and the total value 208,269,000 pesos,

[7] For a list of new treaties and agreements see Appendix III.
[8] For a typical bilateral exchange agreement see Appendix X.

which gave Great Britain an unfavorable balance of 180,367,000 pesos in its trading with Argentina. This cash balance formerly had been an important item to Argentina's credit in her international balance of payments.

The United States was second on the list of countries from which Argentina imported in 1933 and supplied 12.7 per cent of the total imports, to a value of 123,260,000 pesos, which produced an unfavorable balance against Argentina of 37,282,000 pesos.

The other principal suppliers of Argentina's imports were Germany 10.8 per cent, Italy 9 per cent, Brazil 5.5 per cent, India 5.4 per cent, France 5.1 per cent, Belgium 3.8 per cent, and Spain 2.5 per cent.

Since the constitutional organization of the country in 1853, Argentina had negotiated commercial treaties with the principal countries with which she trades. These treaties had been modeled after the Treaty of Friendship, Commerce, and Navigation signed with Great Britain in 1825, Argentina's first treaty. The first commercial treaty signed after the constitutional organization of the Confederation was the one with the United States.

All Argentina's treaties had contained the most-favored-nation clause in everything relating to customs duties, the navigation of rivers, and the freedom of trade. In some cases this clause was unconditional; in others it was granted in the form of reciprocal concessions. The most-favored-nation clause tends to develop and expand international trade by guaranteeing a system of free competition and equality of opportunity in which those countries which can produce particular goods at the lowest prices are able to compete freely for the trade of consuming markets. It was the basis of trade among nations under the old liberal economy which ruled in the world up to the 1920's, but in recent years, under the policy of economic self-sufficiency, there has been an ever-growing tendency to restrict the application of the clause by surrounding it with interpretations which narrow its scope. Since the principle upon which the clause is based is that of absolute equality and impartiality, these restrictive interpretations have had the effect of nullifying the clause. The restrictive interpretations have become more and more general since the Great Depression and usually have been designed to mask protective policies which are contrary to the very principle of equality of opportunity.

Argentine economists point to the Smoot-Hawley Tariff and the United States sanitary embargo against Argentine meat as two outstanding examples of restrictive measures designed to nullify the operation of the most-favored-nation clause, since they deny to Argentine exporters that equality of opportunity in American markets which is the underlying principle of the clause.

When protective tariffs failed to kill the foreign competition which the most-favored-nation clause fosters, some nations began setting up import quotas. These quotas constituted the most flagrant of all the violations of the most-favored-nation principle because they eliminate free competition altogether. While they are designed to protect local industry, they offer an arbitrary means for putting an end to the competition of countries which can produce certain goods at low prices. In the 1930's some of the European countries began using quotas as a means of extending trade concessions to certain other nations for political and military purposes. The reciprocal exchanging of such concessions tended to put international trade on a bilateral basis and by the time the Second World War began, the most-favored-nation clause virtually had ceased to function in the traditional form in which it was known during the nineteenth century and the first quarter of the twentieth.

Although Argentina continued to use the most-favored-nation clause as regards customs treatment in most of its new trade treaties, the clause was abolished effectively in practice by the arbitrary manner in which exchange control was used to favor those nations which Argentina wished to favor and to discriminate against those it did not wish to favor.

The new agreement with Germany provided for a bilateral balancing interchange of exports and imports very similar to that provided for in the British treaty. In the case of Germany the export and import trade consisted almost exclusively of merchandise. In the case of Great Britain a very important factor consisted of the "invisible imports" for which Argentina had to pay just as though they had been merchandise. These "invisible imports" comprised ocean freights, insurance, earnings of British-owned railroads, and dividends of other British companies in Argentina. But whether the imports were visible merchandise or invisible services, the principle was the same under the new bilateral arrangement—Argentina must balance its exports and its imports.

Germany and Argentina extended most-favored-nation treatment to each other regarding exchange control and it was agreed that the entire proceeds from Argentine exports to Germany would be used for the purchase of German imports, after the deduction of a reasonable sum for payments on Argentina's foreign debt. The amount of this "reasonable sum" never was published but was understood in banking circles to be approximately 10 per cent in all cases. Germany promised to extend to Argentine merchandise "the most favorable treatment possible, taking into consideration the volume of the ordinary interchange between the two countries and the quotas that might be set up for each product." A list of products was included on which Germany promised Argentina equitable quotas. After the outbreak of the war the Central Bank reported that the exchange compensations between Argentina and Germany from October 20, 1934, to December 31, 1939, had reached a volume of 1,597,300,000 pesos.

New trade treaties containing some form of bilateral or compensated arrangement were signed with Chile, Italy, Belgium, the Netherlands, Brazil, France, Spain, Uruguay, Finland, Rumania, Austria, Peru, Czechoslovakia, Hungary, and others. The unsuccessful negotiations between Argentina and the United States looking to the framing of a new trade treaty in 1939, and the eventual signing of such a treaty on October 14, 1941, are discussed in another chapter.

In all these new trade treaties the specific provision was made that Argentina might deduct a reasonable amount from the exchange created by its exports and use this exchange for payments on its foreign debt before granting permits for remittances to the country with which the treaty was signed. Thus, while signing a whole series of new treaties designed to put all her international trade on a bilateral basis, Argentina at the same time was carefully taking measures in each treaty to protect herself from the natural and inevitable consequence of bilateral trade, which seeks to have imports and exports cancel each other and so leave no cash balance at either end of the channel.

In drawing up these treaties Argentina did not always follow the formal diplomatic negotiations that previously had been usual in such cases. Because of the predominance of the economic questions and the complications which governed international trade in the years preceding the outbreak of the war, technical advisers and trade counselors had an important part in the negotiation of the treaties signed after 1933. For the negotiation of the Roca-Runciman Treaty, Argentina sent its dapper and very able, English-speaking Vice-President, Dr. Julio A. Roca, to London as ambassador extraordinary on special mission at the head of a large commission of economists, exchange experts, and other technical advisers. The German treaty was negotiated in Buenos Aires with a special mission headed by Otto Kiep which Germany sent around South America to arrange barter and compensated exchange agreements with the principal republics. Most of the other treaties were negotiated with the accredited diplomatic representatives in Buenos Aires.

In November 1938 the government set up a Permanent Inter-Ministerial Commission on Political Economy to insure unity of policy and action among the three ministries that are closely involved in the country's foreign economic policy. These are the ministries of foreign affairs, finance, and agriculture, the latter including industry and commerce. The Permanent Commission, which is composed of representatives of these three ministries, studies all treaty proposals made to Argentina, suggests the negotiation of new treaties and the renewal or modification of existing ones, and usually handles the Argentine end of the negotiations. This has tended to take the negotiation of trade treaties out of the hands of the ministry of foreign affairs and turn it over to the ministries of finance and agriculture.

Whatever may be the opinion of the government economists who have directed Argentina's experiments in bilateral trade and barter, the Central Bank's opinion is clearly stated in its report for 1939 (published in March 1940), which says:

By means of compensation agreements, which have developed since the world crisis, various countries have attempted to exploit their position as large purchasers of the products of other countries in order to assure their own sales there, either for commercial or exchange reasons or, as in the case of several European countries, because of motives of international policy. The experience with them is sufficient to lead to the conclusion that even if in some individual cases, country by country, this kind of compensation may promote an increase of trade, from the larger point of view its generalization seriously injures international trade by segregating it in a series of watertight compartments and forcing transactions into them in an endeavor to balance them bilaterally, with the inevitable complications that this system implies for the regular exercise of monetary activity.

Comparing Argentina's bilateral arrangements with Great Britain and Germany, the Central Bank's report says:

In the course of events we have reached in our economic and financial relations with Great Britain a system of compensation of payments (or of "clearing") similar to that which was in effect in our commerce with Germany before the war. It is true that after 1933 the transactions between our two countries had developed some of the fundamental characteristics of compensation agreements. The funds proceeding from our sales of merchandise to Great Britain had to be reserved, except for a reasonable amount for the payment of the public debt in other countries, for the payment of our imports, financial services, and other remittances to that country. But the temporary surplus amounts could be transferred in a form considered convenient. This availability of the excess exchange constituted the principal difference, certainly of some importance, between the system of payments which we had with Great Britain and that which we had concluded with Germany.[9]

After certain experiences, there was developed with Germany a system of compensation accounts which functioned satisfactorily within the complications and inconveniences which these expedients presented in comparison with the free functioning of the gold standard. Practice in this procedure corrected the initial evils. At one point it was necessary to take measures to limit the risk of holding a considerable quantity of Reichsmarks without cover against possible fluctuations and without convertibility into other currencies. Since Germany was not able to assure this free conversion, there was no other solution than to limit the exports to the amount of the imports. . . . It may be mentioned that, owing to the foresight with which this business was conducted, the agreement with Germany did not leave any balances on hand at the beginning of the war which might carry complications or losses for the interests of the country.

---

[9] Subsequent to this report, the British government froze all Argentine funds until the end of the war, permitting Argentina to convert them into gold bullion which was to remain in British vaults until hostilities ceased.

22. TRADE RELATIONS WITH THE UNITED STATES

FOR more than eight years, from the signing of the Roca-Runciman Treaty in May 1933 until the signing of the trade agreement with the United States in October 1941, Argentina's trade policy toward the United States was one of resentment and discrimination. Under the country's arbitrary and discriminatory policy, seventeen nations received most-favored-nation treatment in the matter of import licenses under the guise of "prior exchange permits," without which nothing could be imported. The United States received least-favored-nation treatment. The trade treaty negotiations between Argentina and the United States at Buenos Aires at the end of 1939 failed because Argentina proposed to continue this system by treaty.

Argentina's resentment against the United States is perfectly understandable, however, when it is remembered that her whole economic structure is based on her export trade in agricultural products and that the United States tariff endeavors to protect American farmers from the competition of these exports. Argentines have resented the protective tariff policy of the United States ever since 1867, when a prohibitive duty was put on wool for the specific purpose of keeping Argentine wool out of the American market. They looked upon the Smoot-Hawley Tariff of 1930 as also being aimed directly at Argentine products. While this was not entirely true, the effect on Argentina's trade with the United States was just as disastrous as though it had been true, for exports from Argentina to the United States dropped 87 per cent, from $117,000,000 in 1929 to only $16,000,000 in 1932. During the five-year period 1936–40 they averaged only $78,000,000, as compared with $95,000,000 in the 1926–30 period.

The exchange control system that was set up in 1931 was designed fundamentally to cut down imports from the United States in something like the proportion that the Smoot-Hawley Tariff had curtailed American imports from Argentina. But American specialties such as automobiles, radios, electric refrigerators, home and office equipment, and the other products of mass production which have become synonymous with home comfort, office efficiency, and a high standard of living, continued to enter the Argentine market in spite of all measures taken against them. Importers of many of these United States products were denied dollar exchange at the official rate and had to buy their dollars in the open market, which added considerably to the cost of their merchandise. When this failed to decrease sales, importers were forced to pay a surcharge of 20 per cent for their dollars, which of course added that much to the cost of the goods. But this, too, proved ineffectual and it became apparent that price was not a decisive factor in marketing these American specialties. As a last resort, the Exchange Control Commission established a black list and flatly refused to grant import licenses for many American products.

During these eight years Argentina's foreign economic policy was in the hands of a group of young economists who were completely convinced of the merits of the bilateral system of trade. After the signing of the Roca-Runciman Treaty they had dedicated themselves to an attempt to put all Argentine foreign trade on a bilateral basis that would fit into the frame that had been laid out by the British treaty. More than one of these young men was rabidly anti-American in his personal feelings, entirely aside from his economic theories, and they had been made the targets of intensive British and German propaganda which pictured the old Colossus of the North as an imperialistic villain intent on flooding the Argentine market with manufactured goods while refusing to buy Argentine raw materials.

At the time of the treaty negotiations in 1939, Argentina had been trying for several years to get a bilateral balancing agreement with the United States which would channelize all peso and dollar transactions and eliminate them from the free exchange markets of the world. Having tied herself up with seventeen barter and compensated trade agreements, Argentina was receiving virtually no free exchange from her foreign trade except from the United States, and these dollars were insufficient to pay for the traditional excess of imports from the United States.

In addition to the pure barter deals, there were compensated and other clearing agreements, payments agreements, and other trade arrangements containing in some form a clause providing for the setting aside of the exchange created by exports to the country in question to pay for the imports from that country or to take care of remittances to that country. These agreements had abolished effectively foreign exchange, which by definition means something that can be exchanged. In the agreements which Argentina had signed, the balances were not exchanged in the true sense of the word but were paid for in token money. As long as there were a few countries left which had relatively free exchange, such as the Netherlands, Belgium, Switzerland, and the Scandi-

navian countries, Argentina had balances of foreign exchange which
could be exchanged into dollars in the foreign exchange centers of the
world. But as soon as the free currency countries of Europe were overrun by the Nazis, Argentina was left trading only with compensated
currency countries and the United States. Argentina's young economists
therefore hoped to club the United States into signing some form of
compensated agreement which would limit imports from the United
States to the value of American purchases in Argentina, less the amount
which Argentina had to pay to the United States as interest and service
charges on its dollar debt.

The British had forced the Roca-Runciman Treaty upon Argentina
while she was in the depths of the economic depression and financial
crisis of 1933. The treaty was to run for three years. When the three
years expired and it was time to renew the pact, Argentina was at the
height of a boom, so did not feel the treaty's restrictive powers. But at
the time the treaty was originally signed, it was so bitterly attacked by
the Buenos Aires newspapers as an infringement of Argentina's sovereignty that Alberto Hueyo, the finance minister under whom it was
negotiated, was forced to resign from the cabinet. Federico Pinedo replaced Hueyo and by means of the various measures of directed economy
which he framed succeeded in obscuring the dependence on Great
Britain which the treaty forced on Argentina. But he did not succeed
in hiding the fact that Great Britain did not permit British importers to
pay for Argentine products in anything except blocked or *aski* sterling.

Argentina's discriminatory policy toward the United States was accompanied by constant misstatements in the newspapers to the effect
that the United States buys practically nothing from Argentina. Yet
the United States was, and had been for thirty years, with occasional exceptions as in 1933, Argentina's best customer after Great Britain and
had constantly been buying 60 per cent more than the third best customer, Germany. In the angry criticism of the United States for failure
to buy Argentine fresh beef, the importance of its other purchases was
passed over.

In 1937, for example, the United States bought Argentine linseed to
the value of 102,000,000 pesos, as compared with Great Britain's purchases of chilled beef amounting to 180,000,000 pesos. Yet Argentines
heard nothing of the linseed purchases. While it was true that the United
States did not buy any chilled beef from Argentina that year, it also was
true that no other country except Great Britain took more than $12,500
worth and that all countries, excluding Great Britain, bought only $44,-

ooo worth. The United States is criticized continually for not taking Argentine beef but seldom is any criticism directed against the many other non-purchasers. Nor is it ever mentioned that the United States is itself the largest beef-producing country in the world. Other countries restricted or prohibited imports of meat from Argentina without their action ever being made a political issue, as in the case of the United States. Norway prohibited it altogether, Holland restricted it by refusing to grant exchange, Austria had prohibitive restrictions, and quota limitations had been established in Belgium, France, Italy, and Germany.

On the other hand, Argentina cannot understand why the American cattlemen have such fear of competition from Argentina. It is pointed out that Argentina's entire export of meat, totaling 600,000 tons a year, is only 7½ per cent of the American consumption of 8,000,000 tons. From which it is argued that if the United States would permit the entry of Argentine meat up to only 2 per cent of the total consumption, or 160,000 tons, this step would increase Argentina's exports by 26 per cent.

In normal times, before defense purchases boomed imports from Argentina to their unprecedented 1941 level, the United States was a constant purchaser of 25 per cent of Argentina's linseed exports, 15 per cent of the wool shipments, 25 per cent of its hides and skins, 22 per cent of its animal by-products, 29 per cent of its quebracho, and 25 per cent of its canned meats. But these purchases were of no consequence in creating good will for the United States because no purchases of fresh beef were included, despite the fact that Argentina's own statistics had shown that the country had a favorable trade balance with the United States in 1935, 1936, and 1937. Argentina's official figures of American purchases were published constantly at 20 per cent under their declared valuation on United States consular invoices, in an effort to maintain the fiction of an unfavorable trade balance with the United States.

Some of the countries to which Argentina was extending most-favored-nation treatment while denying it to the United States did not even have recent trade treaties with Argentina.

Italy retaliated against Argentina's exchange restrictions immediately by refusing to buy from Argentina as long as the restrictions against Italy were in force. In the first year, Italian purchases dropped from 30,000,000 to 18,500,000 pesos. Japan likewise cut its purchases from 14,-000,000 to 5,500,000. The United States took no retaliatory measures, and Argentina misinterpreted this failure as weakness and increased its discrimination against American imports. At one time nearly 3000 American articles were embargoed absolutely or strictly limited. At a luncheon of the British Chamber of Commerce in Buenos Aires the British ambassador announced that the Argentine government was being supplied from time to time with lists of the products which Great Britain was in a position to export. Argentina then clamped an embargo on the importation of those articles from the United States. At one time, United States photographic cameras, moving picture cameras, and projectors were put on the black list and kept there for several weeks while the market was being flooded with British cameras. Importers who applied for licenses to bring in American goods often were told that they could not get exchange permits unless they bought the goods in Great Britain.

In a published report of the board of governors of the American Chamber of Commerce in Buenos Aires it was stated:

According to the published statement of the Exchange Control Office of the Ministry of Finance, the Argentine Government has followed a policy of charging all dollar debt services against the exchange created by American purchases of Argentine products, although these dollar loans were made for the benefit of the economy of the country. Furthermore, investigations show that over 45 per cent of all dollar loans are held by investors in Great Britain and Continental Europe. Nor was American trade credited with any of the 25 million dollar loan placed in the United States last November. A policy which penalizes a country for loaning money seems difficult to understand.

The present restrictions on the importation of automobiles from countries which do not have trade agreements with Argentina result in discrimination against the United States. The importation of automobiles into Argentina has always received more importance than was really due it in the matter of exchange consumption. It is not generally realized that American purchases of Argentine linseed more than offset the imports of automobiles. During the last three years, including 1938, according to the figures published by the United States Department of Commerce, the United States imported from Argentina linseed to the value of 67 million dollars and exported automobiles, trucks, and parts to Argentina valued at 65 million dollars.

The Board regrets that the Argentine Government has seen fit to direct the purchases of government departments to other sources in cases when American bidders have been lowest. The refusal of the government to accept bids for supplies of American merchandise at official exchange rates makes American companies unable to compete at free market rates with suppliers from countries accorded official exchange.

Such was the picture in November 1939, when Washington sent a staff of negotiators to Buenos Aires to arrange a trade treaty. The Argentine government had refused to let the negotiations take place in Washington on the ground that the members of the Permanent Inter-Ministerial Commission who were to be the Argentine negotiators could not be spared from Buenos Aires for the length of time the negotiations were likely to consume.

When the negotiations began, the United States had lost its markets for agricultural products in Great Britain and France under the escape clause in the trade treaties with those countries and then lost its market for manufactured goods in Argentina because Argentina was trading its agricultural products for European manufactured goods.

The negotiations brought into conflict two irreconcilable schools of thought in international trade—bilateralism and multilateralism—so no treaty could be drawn up until either Argentina or the United States changed its whole trade policy. Since the signing of the Roca-Runciman Treaty, Argentina had rebuilt her entire economic structure on bilateral compensated trade treaties that sought balanced trade with each of the nations with which she trades. Argentina obviously could not scrap seventeen treaties with European customers to sign a treaty with the United States. The young economists who were directing Argentina's trade policy apparently thought they could persuade the United States to abandon its insistence on most-favored-nation treatment.

Yet there had been a clear understanding that the treaty would be a most-favored-nation one, otherwise the State Department would not have undertaken the negotiations, since the keystone of Secretary Hull's whole international trade policy was equality of opportunity and free competition. In fact, it was officially announced when the negotiations began that the United States was to be given equality of treatment. But on the day before this announcement was made, Argentina put hundreds of United States articles on the black list to serve as trading weapons. After the negotiations began, Argentina refused to agree upon non-discriminatory treatment of the United States while insisting on more concessions from the United States, refusing at the same time to give any in exchange. Argentina refused to fix the duties on radio tubes at the existing rate, for example, because of the "local industry," and refused to grant any concessions on American lumber.

On January 16, 1940, two weeks after the negotiations had collapsed, Mr. Manuel Fox, of the United States Tariff Commission, told a hearing of the House Ways and Means Committee that the insistence of the United States on most-favored-nation treatment had led to the breakdown in the negotiations and that the State Department had protested to Great Britain and France against their efforts to gain discriminatory trade concessions in order to channelize Argentina's foreign trade in their favor.

During the negotiations the Argentine newspapers acted as though they never had heard of the most-favored-nation clause, although it had been the whole basis of Argentina's international trade up to the time that its economic brain trust became converted to the barter idea of international trade. It is quite possible that this conversion had been facilitated by the six decorations which Herr Hitler sent to the young Argentine economists who had sat in on the negotiation of the trade agreement with Germany in 1934. But up to the time the war broke out, Argentina was getting the benefit of the most-favored-nation clause throughout the world and was profiting not only from its own treaties but also from all the treaties made by the United States, without having to give anything in exchange. Argentina had obtained United States tariff reductions on at least two dozen articles by the automatic operation of the most-favored-nation clause. But when the United States wanted the proposed trade treaty to be based on most-favored-nation treatment, Washington was accused of insisting on extraordinary and singular economic theories and pretensions.

All the United States asked for was equality of treatment. Although this was a request for much less favorable treatment than Argentina already was getting in the United States market, the Buenos Aires newspapers insisted on making it appear that the United States was asking for special concessions. It was charged repeatedly that the United States was trying to insure for the future all the gains made in the Argentine market as a result of the European war. This was absolutely untrue.

There was a gentlemen's agreement not to discuss publicly the controversial details of the negotiations. The State Department and the United States negotiators apparently considered themselves bound to silence by this gentlemen's agreement, but for several weeks there were officially inspired articles in the Buenos Aires newspapers bitterly attacking the United States and its negotiators, and the articles contained details that could have come only from the Argentine negotiators because they had been discussed only in confidential memoranda.

Argentina reserved the right to fix arbitrary quotas on any and all American products but would not agree to a fair limit on only one or two of its agricultural products. It was a well-known fact in business circles of Buenos Aires that there were several commodities such as tinplate and coal, usually imported from Great Britain, on which Argentina was unwilling to give the United States even a minimum quota.

The traditional policy of the United States toward quotas has been that it be accorded a representative share in the allotment of quotas. That principle is incorporated in the American treaties with Great Britain, Canada, France, and others. The United States maintains that, if any quota limitations are put on imports, it shall get an equitable share, based on its past trade. Under this principle, Argentina would have had the right to limit any imports from the United States, based on imports in previous years, which in many cases would have meant very unfavorable handicapping of our trade. Nevertheless, under the equitable principle the United States would have had to accede to this, as in its other treaties. Theoretically, in a year of exchange stringency Argentina could limit the imports of automobiles, for example, to a negligible figure.

The United States offered tariff concessions on a long list of important items, including wool, hides and skins, animal by-products, and quebracho extract. The list was almost identical with the one on which tariff reductions eventually were granted in the agreement signed in October 1941. Argentina would have profited further by the concessions that were to have been made in a similar treaty with Uruguay. When the Argentine negotiations failed, Uruguay was denied a trade treaty with the United States because the concessions would have to be extended automatically to Argentina under the operation of the most-favored-nation clause in the treaty of 1853.

The tariff concessions which the United States offered to Argentina were substantial and tended to expand Argentina's trade. Those which Argentina offered to the United States were not important because they could be nullified by quotas. This was why it was so necessary to get into the agreement a statement as to how exchange permits were to be allocated, since the proposed tariff reductions would be useless if the United States was not to be accorded equality of treatment in the issuance of import licenses. But as a result of several years of arbitrary discriminatory treatment of imports under the exchange control system, Argentina insisted on avoiding any recognition of most-favored-nation treatment, which is the *sine qua non* of any United States treaty. Consequently the negotiations collapsed.

During the treaty negotiations, the United States had offered a substantial tariff reduction on linseed, with a quota limit on the amount that could be shipped to the United States at the lower duty. The quota was to have been fixed at 25 per cent above the average shipments to the United States in recent years, with no limitation on the amount that could be shipped at the old tariff rate. Yet it was charged in the Buenos Aires newspapers that this quota would radically reduce Argentina's exports of linseed to the United States and it was made to appear that the negotiations had failed because of this unjust discrimination by the United States against Argentine linseed.

On the day before the failure of the negotiations was announced, two of the Argentine negotiators who could not be spared long enough to go to Washington departed for Tokyo to participate in the negotiation of a new trade agreement with Japan, which the Japanese government had stipulated must be arranged in Tokyo, not Buenos Aires.

When a new attempt was made to negotiate a trade agreement in the latter part of 1941, Argentina was in a much different frame of mind than on the former occasion. The war had been in progress for two years and it was painfully apparent that it was not going to make Argentina rich, as had the First World War. Instead of being the granary for Great Britain and France, as in the 1914–18 conflict, Argentina had on hand an ever-growing stock of unsalable grains. At the end of 1941 the country's elevators and warehouses were overflowing with 4,592,537 tons of wheat and 1,225,697 tons of linseed, with the new harvest augmenting this surplus every day. At the end of 1940 the carryover had been only 1,349,416 tons of wheat and 262,689 tons of linseed.

The exports of wheat and linseed during 1941 were 3,253,000 tons less than in 1940, causing a decline of 34 per cent in the volume of the year's exports. Fortunately for Argentina's balance of international payments, the adverse effect of this decline in volume was compensated for by the higher prices received for the other products exported, so that the value of the year's shipments was 1,463,479,000 pesos, an increase of 2½ per cent over 1940. But the inability to dispose of the crops was causing a serious situation in government finances. The National Grain Board owed the Bank of the Nation 765,000,000 pesos on its operations for financing grain farmers and no serious attempt had been made to curtail acreage. Customs receipts were down 53,000,000 pesos from 1940 and there was a budget deficit of 186,000,000 pesos, or 17 per cent.

Furthermore, two years' operation of the Roca-Runciman agreement under war conditions had disillusioned Argentine economists regarding the benefits of bilaterally balanced trade. The country could not spend except in Great Britain the credits it received for the one-third of its export trade that was going to the British market, and as the war made it impossible for Great Britain to supply and ship the goods which Argentina needed urgently, these credits were being converted into gold bars and stored in the vaults of the Bank of England. Of the seventeen nations with which Argentina had bilateral trade agreements, five were at war—Great Britain, Germany, Italy, Hungary, and Rumania; ten were occupied by the Germans—Austria, Belgium, Czechoslovakia, Denmark, Finland, France, Greece, Lithuania, the Netherlands, and Poland; and shipping conditions had virtually ended all trade with the other two—Spain and Switzerland.

Argentina was clamoring for more American products than the United States could ship, and it was obvious that the Argentine market belonged to American exporters for the duration of the war, whether a trade treaty was signed or not. The importance of the agreement signed at Buenos Aires on October 14, 1941,[1] lay in its political significance rather than in its commercial provisions. Its signing was one of the greatest diplomatic victories achieved by the State Department in South America in recent years and was a tribute to the stubborn, uncompromising insistence of Secretary of State Hull on recognition of the principle of free competition and equality of opportunity in international trade. It was also another tribute to the negotiating talent of Ambassador Norman Armour at Buenos Aires, one of the most efficient and accomplished career men in the United States Foreign Service.

The agreement repudiated the bilateral system of trade set up by the Roca-Runciman Treaty and pledged Argentina to support the multilateral system favored by the United States, a fact that was completely overlooked by correspondents and editors when the signing was announced. The United States was guaranteed equal treatment as regards exchange control regulations and the issuance of import licenses, and also a proportional share of any quotas which Argentina might establish. The agreement put an end to the black list against American products by providing that no prohibition or restriction of any kind shall be imposed by the government of either country on the importation of any article from the other unless the importation from all third countries is similarly prohibited or restricted. (Article III, paragraph 1.) No restrictions of any kind shall be imposed on the importation of any article by means of import licenses, permits, or otherwise, unless the total quantity or value of such article permitted to be imported has been established and made public. (Article III, paragraph 2.) If quotas are established either by Argentina or by the United States, the other is to be allotted an equitable share of the quota, in accordance with its proportion of the

---

[1] For text of this agreement see Appendix XII.

total trade in the article under question during a previous representative period. (Article III, paragraph 3.) The United States is guaranteed unconditional most-favored-nation treatment in the administration of any rules for exchange control. (Article IV, paragraph 1.) No prohibition, restriction, or delay is to be imposed on remittances in payment of imports unless similar restrictions are imposed on similar remittances to all third countries, and such control is to be so administered as not to influence to the disadvantage of the other signatory country the competition of its products with those of third countries. (Article IV, paragraph 2.) The signatory governments agree to accord fair and equitable treatment to the commerce of the other in awarding contracts for public works and the purchase of supplies. (Article V, paragraph 2.) This last provision abolished the Argentine government's discrimination against American products in public works and governmental purchases against which the American Chamber of Commerce had formally protested in the already cited report of its board of governors.

In the purely commercial provisions of the agreement, Argentina granted customs reductions or guaranteed not to increase existing duties on 127 groups of articles which in 1940 accounted for 47 per cent of the American exports to Argentina, with a total value of $33,000,000. The reductions, however, were not to go into effect until such time as Argentine customs receipts from import duties exceeded 270,000,000 pesos in any calendar year. Once put into effect, the lower duties were to continue regardless of customs receipts. Since this provision meant that Argentina's customs receipts must increase about 17 per cent over the 1940 receipts, and as the 1941 receipts were 17 per cent below the 1940 figures, the tariff reductions on American imports were largely academic. But, as already noted, customs duties were not an important factor in the situation and the weakness of the agreement on that score should not have been allowed to obscure the political triumph that had been achieved in the guarantee of equal treatment for American imports for the first time in eight years.

The United States granted substantial tariff reductions or bound to the present level the duties on 84 groups of products which in 1940 accounted for 92 per cent of Argentina's exports to the United States and were valued at $54,000,000. The agreement also opened the American market to a dozen groups of wines, champagnes, brandies, vermouths, edible oils, canned fish, macaronis, cheeses, and tomato sauces which the United States formerly had imported from Italy and France. Argentine industry has made tremendous strides in the production of some of these products, especially the Italian-style cheeses, vermouths, and edible oils, and it is very probable that they will become firmly established in the American market.

Since the agreement did not provide for American imports of any grain except linseed and did not open the United States markets to chilled and frozen beef, it could not seem in Argentine eyes more than a beginning. But it did include substantial concessions on the highly controversial items of linseed and the important Argentine types of wool and on canned meats, and to that extent was a considerable advance against the protectionist opposition in the United States. Rearmament and the defense boom already had expanded to record-breaking volume American purchases of all Argentine products except grains and fresh meats, so as long as the war lasted the agreement was not expected to do much more than add to Argentine income through a reduction of the duties that Argentine shipments to the United States must bear. The question of whether the duty is paid by the producer or the consumer is an old controversy, of course, and the protectionists love to argue that it always is paid by the producer. In the case of Argentina the argument has stood up, because in the United States Argentina has been selling in a highly competitive market and the tariff has served to reduce Argentine income by forcing price reductions in order to "jump" the duty and meet domestic prices in the United States. The duty reduction, therefore, permitted Argentine exporters to continue selling in the United States at the necessary competitive price and at the same time receive larger peso returns.

The agreement contained a provision never before included in trade agreements made by the United States; consultation between the two governments regarding all matters affecting the operation of the agreement. This obviously was a good-neighbor agreement to talk over any difficulties or differences which might arise, rather than terminate the pact, as usually happens when difficulties arise.

Editorial writers were inclined to belittle the accomplishments of the agreement because an exchange of notes between Ambassador Armour and the Argentine minister of foreign affairs provided that some of these clauses could not be put into effect until the termination of hostilities. One commentator gibed that the pact was meaningless because it did not provide a fleet of merchant vessels to transport the products of Argentina and the United States. In so belittling the accomplishments of the agreement, the commentators completely overlooked the very important fact that the Argentine note put its government on record as

pledging non-discriminatory treatment of the United States and that it
definitely promised to put all the provisions of the agreement into full
effect just as soon as Argentina could convert its blocked sterling credit
balances into free currencies. The note constituted a complete about-
face in Argentina's economic policy toward the United States and said,
in effect, that that policy had been conditioned by circumstances which
had been forced upon Argentina and were, for the moment, beyond the
control of the Argentine government. The Foreign Minister's note to
Ambassador Armour said:

I have the honor to refer to the discussions during the course of the
negotiations of the Trade Agreement between our two Governments
signed this day regarding the provisions of the Agreement which provide for non-discriminatory treatment by each country of the trade of
the other.

During the negotiations of the Agreement, the representatives of the
United States Government have emphasized the great importance which
that Government attaches to these provisions. The representatives of the
Argentine Government have stated, on their part, that their Government likewise attaches great importance to these provisions and to the
principle of unconditional most-favored-nation treatment which under-
lies them. They have pointed out that this principle is the basis of Argentine commercial policy, which has for its objective the development of
Argentine foreign trade on a multilateral basis.

The representatives of the Argentine Government have also pointed
out that the ability of Argentina to give full effect to these principles
is dependent on circumstances beyond the control of Argentina. Recently, the Argentine trade and payments position has been aggravated
to a very important extent by the trade and financial controls which have
been adopted by the belligerents in the present European conflict, nota-
bly the United Kingdom, one of the principal markets for Argentine
export products. In particular, the inability of Argentina to convert
freely into dollars the proceeds of sales to the United Kingdom makes
it impossible for the Argentine Government to extend full non-
discriminatory treatment to the trade of the United States of America.

The representatives of the Argentine Government have accordingly
stated in the negotiations that the acceptance by the Argentine Government of the provisions of the Trade Agreement relating to non-
discriminatory treatment must be qualified by the practical limitations
which are imposed on the Argentine Government's freedom of action
by the circumstances to which I have referred. However, they have
assured the representatives of the United States Government that, subject to the practical limitations imposed by the existing payments arrangements in effect between Argentina and the United Kingdom, the
Argentine Government will at all times give the fullest possible effect
to the provisions under reference. They have further assured the repre-

sentatives of the United States Government that, as soon as it becomes possible for Argentina to convert its sterling balances into free currencies, the Argentine Government will give full effect to those provisions.

The representatives of the Argentine Government expressed the hope that the reconstruction of world economy after the war would create favorable conditions that would enable Argentina to participate in an active interchange with other nations within a liberal system in which the barriers which in recent years have handicapped its normal development have been eliminated.

The agreement was to remain in force until November 15, 1944, and unless one of the governments had notified the other in writing of its intention to terminate the agreement on that date it was to remain in force thereafter until the expiration of six months from the date on which such notice should have been given.

Having signed this agreement with the United States, Argentina was bound by treaty to both of the two conflicting and irreconcilable principles of international trade—the narrowly restricted bilateral system as represented by the Roca-Runciman Treaty and the other sixteen bilateral agreements which she had signed, and the liberal, democratic mutilateral system, as represented by the 1941 agreement with the United States. The Argentine market promised, therefore, to be the arena for some very interesting diplomatic sparring after the military battles of the World War were terminated.

ARGENTINA'S MERCHANT MARINE

Three months before signing the trade agreement with the United States, Argentina had taken steps to establish a merchant marine by purchasing from Italy sixteen steamers, including the passenger liner *Principessa Maria*, which had taken refuge in Argentine ports upon the outbreak of war. Several of these were immediately put on the Buenos Aires–New York run and with the others a drastic remapping of foreign shipping routes was undertaken in an attempt to create lasting trade intercourse with the other American nations that would tend to relieve the country of its dependence on Europe. Before the war began, attempts to establish trade with Colombia, Peru, Venezuela, and Cuba had failed for lack of shipping. It was hoped that the newly purchased steamers would permit the sale of the country's agricultural, pastoral, and industrial products among the 120,000,000 people of Chile, Peru, Ecuador, Colombia, Venezuela, and Mexico.

Despite an Atlantic coastline of 1565 miles, Argentina never had been a maritime nation and had no overseas merchant marine. Two or three old navy transports were used to send occasional cargoes to Europe, but in the main Argentina always had depended on the shipping of the nations which sent vessels to the River Plate to load grains and meats. But the war decreased this shipping so drastically that it became imperative for Argentina to establish her own shipping lines. In 1937, 12,000,000 tons of foreign shipping entered Argentine ports. Only 6,-700,000 tons entered during 1940 and there was a further sharp decline to only 2,300,000 tons during the first six months of 1941. Nine months after the war began, the few neutral ships still arriving at Argentine ports were charging freights exceeding the value of the cargo, which, of course, effectively stopped the exportation of many products.

In 1938, Argentine exports totaled 19,000,000 tons. Less than 3 per cent was carried in Argentine vessels, 62½ per cent by liners from those countries with which Argentina maintains regular trade, and 34½ per cent by tramp steamers. It was estimated that these tramps collected 130,000,000 pesos in freight. Argentina hoped eventually to replace much of this tramp business with its own vessels.

At the time the Italian steamers were purchased, freights were between 100 and 150 pesos a ton, compared with 15 and 20 pesos in normal times, and it was expected that if the newly purchased vessels made six round trips in a year they would pay for themselves in that time. The sixteen vessels totaled 88,528 tons, net, and the price agreed upon was 359,523,700 lire, equivalent to 63,541,939 pesos, which worked out at approximately $172 a ton. Half the purchase price was deposited in the Central Bank at 2½ per cent interest, to be paid to Italy at the termination of hostilities. The balance was to be paid in Argentine products after the war.

23. BRITISH INTERESTS AND INFLUENCE

> When with the passage of time the Argentine Nation is
> called upon to render to the world an account of its sovereignty,
> Great Britain will figure in the balance sheet as the principal
> factor in the country's political, social, and economic progress:
> her influence has been beneficial to Argentina's destiny at all
> times and should be so to still greater extent as time goes on.
> —BARTOLOMÉ MITRE

Long before they began to buy Argentine beef, the British were doing more than anyone else—far more than the Argentines themselves, in fact—to develop "the Argentine," as they call it, using
an adjective as a noun. The land which Spain had kept under the yoke
of colonial slavery became a rich, prosperous nation because British
capital spent hundreds of millions of pounds in building the railroads,
which did more than any other single factor to develop the country.
The dusty, miserable, unkempt towns which for nearly three hundred
years had been the isolated centers of colonial life, and later of the
bloody, throat-cutting gaucho revolutions, became clean, healthful, and
attractive cities to live in because British investors installed waterworks,
gas plants, electric lights, street cars, and telephones, and then sent out
as managers and "clarks" an army of those honest, unimaginative empire
builders who drank gin and bitters between ten-thirty and noon and
wore their dinner jackets when dining alone at night, that they might
not "go native."

There were English or Strangers' clubs in the interior towns of Argentina long before there were Argentine clubs, and the oldest corporation
of any kind in the country is the Strangers' Club of Buenos Aires which
was organized by a group of lonesome Englishmen a hundred years ago.
The Strangers' Clubs in Argentina and throughout South America are
further examples of what Hubert Herring calls the Englishman's in-
comparable gift of translating names into meaningless English. The *Club
de Extranjeros* (foreigners) became to its English members the Strangers'
Club, just as *el campo* (the country) became "the camp" and the Rio de
la Plata, the River Plate.

These Englishmen and Scotchmen and Irishmen with their fragrant
pipes and mellow whisky, their Pears soap and Lea & Perrins sauce, and,
above all, with their public school code of personal honor and honesty
created for the Empire an economic dominion out of the land that so

231

narrowly missed becoming a political dominion in 1807. (When the British government began taking measures to protect sterling just before the outbreak of the war in 1939, it extended dominion status to Argentina by granting it the same exemptions that were extended to the British dominions.) The hard-drinking, hard-working, unemotional Britons who built this economic dominion did not give a damn whether the Argentines liked them or not. They had a job to do and they did it. They still call the Argentines "natives," just as they do the black and brown people over whom they rule in various corners of the earth. But they won the respect, if not the love, of the Argentines to such an extent that the Englishman's word, *palabra inglés,* is the word of honor which an Argentine still gives today if he really intends to keep the promise he is making.

Having invested their millions in great public service enterprises, and having lived in the country and worked hard at developing it during the hundred years that the Americans were too busy with their own empire-building in the West even to care where Argentina was on the map, the British resentment against the newly arrived, loud-talking, braggart Americans is understandable, even though it is based on unsound economics and dangerous politics. The English see Argentina spending in the United States the good sovereigns it got from them for meat and wheat and immediately jump to the conclusion that the Americans are swindling them, forgetting that Brazil and other Latin American countries spend in Great Britain millions of the good dollars they get from the United States. In their resentment against the American competition which they cannot meet, the English have forced upon Argentina the bilaterally balanced system of trade which is the backbone of totalitarian economics and which, if it can be forced upon the rest of the world, will wipe out the multilateral or triangular system and so do much more than all the Stukas and U-boats toward destroying that democracy which Great Britain went to war to defend.

British influence in the River Plate dates as far back as 1713, when the Treaty of Utrecht gave England a 30-year grant on the South American slave trade. England put commercial agents in Buenos Aires and other South American ports on the pretext of introducing slaves and began a prosperous smuggling trade in many other articles. From Buenos Aires it was mainly hides and tallow. A census taken by the Spanish government in 1744 showed that there were seven English residents in Buenos Aires. It was English recognition of the great trade potentialities of Buenos Aires that led to their attempt to capture the country in 1807.

The British recognized the independence of the Argentine Republic on January 1, 1825, thirteen years after the arrival of the American vice-consul, William Gilchrist Miller, who was the first representative of any foreign government to be recognized by the Argentine government, and fourteen months after the arrival at Buenos Aires of the first United States minister, Caesar Augustus Rodney. But the English have been telling the Argentines for so long that they were the first to recognize Argentine independence that they now believe it themselves and the misstatement is the *pièce de résistance* of after-dinner oratory at every British celebration where prominent Argentine guests are present. The British did sign the first treaty of friendship and commerce with Argentina on February 2, 1825, and one of its clauses provided for the abolishment of the slave trade. The British also made the first foreign loan to Argentina, in November 1822. The loan was for £1,000,000 at an issue price of 70, the English bankers collecting their 30 per cent interest in advance. The Argentine government received 3,500,000 gold pesos, which it used for building a mole at Buenos Aires and for the installation of waterworks.

At the end of 1940 there was an aggregate of £417,307,804 of British capital invested in Argentina, compared with £408,518,172 at the end of 1939 and £435,128,482 at the end of 1930. The permanent investment in British-owned railroads was £263,745,180, which was yielding an average dividend of 1.5 per cent per annum, including £156,897,230 which for several years had been yielding no return. There were £92,712,644 in other Argentine enterprises, yielding an average dividend of 3.8 per cent and including £30,246,282 which was producing no interest. British investors also held £60,849,980 worth of Argentine government bonds which were yielding an average return of 4 per cent per annum.

After the Crimean War the British shipped to Buenos Aires a locomotive, several coaches, and six miles of track that had been intended for the use of the British forces in the siege of Sevastopol. An English engineer, William Bragge, took 160 workmen to Buenos Aires from England to lay the track. This was the beginning of the first British-owned railroad in Argentina, today known as the Buenos Aires Western. Its line from the Plaza Lavalle to the suburb of Floresta was inaugurated in August 1857. The queer little locomotive, which was christened *La Porteña*, is one of the chief attractions at the museum in Lujan. It was of the Russian wide gauge of five feet six inches, and from this accidental choice of gauge the wide-gauge lines have extended all over Argentina until today they account for approximately 15,000 of the total trackage of 26,800 miles.

As Argentina's new national army began pushing the marauding Indians farther and farther beyond the horizon, British engineers followed, laying rails across a country so flat and so abandoned that it might have been a desert. The Pacific Railroad, running from Buenos Aires to Mendoza, is said to have the longest stretch of right of way in the world without a curve or a grade.

Of the 26,800 miles of railroads in Argentina in 1941, 20,000 were British-owned. The earning capacity of the railroads has been falling steadily since 1929, owing largely to the competition of motor traffic on the rapidly expanding highways and to the necessity of making their remittances in a markedly depreciated curency. The official exchange rate for sterling in 1941 represented a depreciation of 40 per cent in the value of the peso since 1929.

The British also have heavy investments in the meat packing industry, in estancias, in manufacturing enterprises, and in the old British standbys of banking, shipping, and insurance.

These permanent British investments were the foundation of Argentine good will toward the British. They helped develop the country, whereas until very recently the bulk of American investments consisted of loans made to the government to cover deficits in unbalanced budgets, thereby putting a premium on reckless spending. In 1935, the annual charges on these foreign loans absorbed 20 per cent of the budget and constituted one of the main reasons for Argentine resentment against the United States, the traditional resentment of the debtor toward the man who has lent him money when he needed it.

Aside from building the railroads, Great Britain's greatest influence on Argentina's economic life has been in the livestock industry. As detailed in the chapter on Argentina's beef, the livestock industry and the meat packing business were established and developed solely to supply the British market. English methods are used on the great estancias; selected animals from the most famous herds of British thoroughbred cattle have been imported continuously into Argentina; and the Argentine estancieros have developed huge herds of cattle and sheep for the production of meat, wool, and other products of the types preferred by British tastes. Argentina, in fact, has developed its whole national economic system to meet the requirements of British tastes.

The British also were responsible for starting the raising of cotton in Argentina. When it became apparent in 1860 that there was likely to

A BUSY STREET IN BUENOS AIRES SHOWING TRAFFIC MOVING ON
THE LEFT-HAND SIDE OF THE STREET AS IN ENGLAND

AN AVENUE IN ROSARIO, SECOND LARGEST CITY OF ARGENTINA,
SHOWING ITS MODERN BUILDINGS AND CLEAN WIDE STREETS

A STADIUM CROWD WATCHING A SOCCER FOOTBALL GAME

GRAIN ELEVATOR IN THE PORT OF BUENOS AIRES

be war between the northern and southern States in the United States, the British cotton associations sent an expert to Argentina to help farmers in the selection of seed and the cultivation of the plant. The first bales of Argentine cotton reached England in 1863.

British trade supremacy in the Argentine Republic offers an enlightening lesson in foreign penetration, in contrast with the many mistakes the Americans have made. First and most important, the British took root in the country, as did the Germans. Young Englishmen by the hundreds went out to "the Argentine" with the intention of making their homes there. The American announces for all the world to hear as he walks down the gangplank that he's going back to God's own country in two years, and he usually does. In 1941 there were approximately 50,000 Britons in Argentina, compared with 3000 Americans. Second, the British followed their merchandise with investments, as already noted. Third, they never have tried to capitalize sentiment as the Americans do. They do not send "good will" missions to Argentina, which in itself would guarantee the admiration of the Argentines even if nothing else did. Americans are forever talking about the kinship set up by Pan-Americanism, of wanting to be good neighbors, and of wanting—oh, so earnestly—to help Argentina. The English learned ages ago that nations love one another only when it is profitable for them to do so and they have never pretended that their tie with Argentina is anything except frankly and purely material, the everyday, practical need of one country for another. Fourth, is the integrity of dealing, honesty of merchandise, and careful attention to the peculiar requirements of Argentine trade that have become symbolized in the palabra inglés.

British smugglers were the principal agents in the contraband trade in the port of Buenos Aires at the beginning of the nineteenth century. When the revolution of 1810 opened Buenos Aires to overseas shipping, the British immediately became the most active competitors of the Americans, who also began sending their barks and schooners to Buenos Aires. Argentina's import trade increased from 2,600,000 gold pesos at the beginning of the century to 11,000,000 in 1822, and of this latter figure the British supplied half, or 5,731,000 gold pesos. In the years immediately before the outbreak of the Second World War, Great Britain was supplying 80 per cent of Argentina's coal imports, 40 per cent of the cotton fabrics, 79 per cent of the woolen fabrics, 55 per cent of the sheet-iron, 40 per cent of the tinplate, 57 per cent of the cotton yarn, 34 per cent of the iron pipe, 62 per cent of the cotton thread, 67 per cent of the wire, 60 per cent of the silk yarn, and 50 per cent of the tea.

But Great Britain's share in Argentina's import trade had been declining steadily from around 25 per cent before the First World War to 19 per cent when the Second World War started, while the share of the United States had increased from around 10 per cent before the First World War to 17 per cent in 1938 and 1939, after touching 25 per cent in the late 1920's. Ever since the First World War the British in Argentina had been very bitter against their American trade rivals, making the persistent but completely false accusation that the Americans had stolen the Argentine market from the British while they were fighting the war. Had the British studied the detailed import statistics instead of merely looking at the annual totals, they would have found that the United States had increased its exports to Argentina, not by taking trade away from England, but by developing new lines of manufacture and production the products of which are purchased in large quantities by England herself and by the British dominions.

A thorough study of American and British competition in the Argentine market was made in 1931 by George J. Eder, of the American Bureau of Foreign and Domestic Commerce. His report showed that one-fourth of the American exports to Argentina were goods that are not and cannot be produced in England; one-half were goods that England's present industrial organization is manifestly not equipped to manufacture at competitive prices and in which England cannot compete unless she first completely revolutionizes her social and economic structure; while only from 14 to 28 per cent of the American trade could be considered in any way open to British rivalry. The report pointed out, for instance, that England cannot produce automobiles to compete with American cars in price and quality so long as the purchasing power of the bulk of the British population is inadequate to buy automobiles. At the time the survey was made, England led in sales of light, cheap motorcycles in Argentina because there is no appreciable market for that product in the United States, the typical American motorcycle being a heavy, high-powered machine for police or military use.

In the 1930's the British found that they could no longer compete with the Americans on a price and quality basis for that portion of the market which was competitive. American-made radios, cameras, electrical appliances, office equipment, and those other articles which are universally recognized as American specialties, and which the British themselves buy from the United States, were so much in demand that they continued to outsell the British products in spite of the 20 per cent discriminatory exchange surtax which the Argentine government put on the importation of these articles from the United States. It was not until the British induced Argentina to establish the system of import licenses that they were able to shut the American products out of the market by artificial means and so let their own products in.

It is very probable that American and British trade rivalry in Argentina eventually will become a question for negotiation in London or Washington rather than in Buenos Aires.

Entirely apart from trade, English influence is evident wherever one goes, especially in the city of Buenos Aires. Every second street corner has the round, red mail box which the English call a "pillar box." Street car conductors are "guards," as in England, and instead of ringing up the fare they give the passenger a small paper ticket which he must carefully hold onto until the end of his journey, because somewhere along the line an inspector will get on and want to punch it. Trains are started by the English bedlam of bell-ringing by the station master and shrill whistling by the "guard." Traffic moves on the left-hand side. Five o'clock tea is as much an institution in Argentina as it is in England, but rich French pastries are served in preference to English scones. Business houses have found that the late afternoon pick-up on the part of their employees is well worth the five or ten minutes that are lost in serving tea, and many American offices have adopted the custom.

But when the time comes to strike a balance, in accordance with the quotation from Mitre which appears at the head of this chapter, it probably will be found that Argentina's greatest debt to the British is not the £300,000,000 invested in the railroads or the waterworks or the banks nor any of the obvious influences. Britain's greatest gift to the Argentines was soccer football, or *fútbal* as they call it, because that game has completely changed the Argentine character. As recently as 1920, Argentine football players carried knives onto the field and stabbed their opponents when they could not win otherwise. But that phase has long since passed, and by playing fútbal Argentine youths have learned to become good losers and good winners. They have carried this spirit of sportsmanship over into their later professional and business life, with a tremendously marked difference in character. Football is the national game in Argentina and the big professional games pack the bleachers until they rival the big baseball games in the United States. And from Tierra del Fuego to the Bolivian border men and boys play football on vacant lots and use all the usual terms of the game in English because they have been absorbed into the Spanish language instead of translated.

Football and other English sports have contributed heavily to making the Argentine language a horrible conglomeration of Spanish and English. The Argentines are inordinately proud of the fact that they speak the worst Spanish in the world. They do not even pretend that it is Castilian, but call it the *idioma nacional*. Señoritas playing tennis call out "sorry" in true English style, although they never use the word, or any other English, off the courts. *Beisbal* is not played very extensively, but when it is the English terms are used instead of their Spanish equivalents. The latest English word to be added to the language, however, comes from the United States rather than England and was grafted onto the *idioma nacional* when automobile-racing became popular. It is *pareformáncay*, the Argentine pronunciation of "performance."

24. AMERICAN INTERESTS AND INFLUENCE

T HE thirty-five-year-old government of the United States of America did more than any other country to help the infant republic of the River Plate get its start in life. It sent the first diplomatic representative and the first consular officer accredited by any government to that at Buenos Aires, after having appointed an agent for seamen and commerce within three months of the Buenos Aires revolution of May 25, 1810. As it required from fifty to sixty days and sometimes longer for a sailing vessel to make the voyage from Buenos Aires to New York or Philadelphia, this meant that the American government took steps to recognize the newly independent River Plate government as soon as news of the revolution reached the United States.

For many years the relations between the two young democratic governments of the Western Hemisphere were the most cordial that could be imagined. Although the Argentine revolution had been inspired by the French Revolution rather than the American, the people of Buenos Aires soon began to look to the young United States instead of to France for an example of the practical working of democracy. Through all its early vicissitudes, the government of Buenos Aires looked to the United States for inspiration and material assistance, and received both in abundance. This was natural, of course, because the United States was eager to see democracy established in the Western Hemisphere and Buenos Aires had taken the lead in throwing off the Spanish yoke and not only setting itself up as an independent nation but in helping the neighboring countries to do likewise.

Commercial relations were mutually satisfactory and mutually profitable for more than half a century and the United States was a close business partner of Argentina until the invention of the steam engine drove the famous Yankee clippers from the seas and the United States lost to Great Britain its position as the leading maritime nation of the world.

The first official representative of the United States government at Buenos Aires was Joel Roberts Poinsett, whose name has been immortalized in the poinsettia. He was appointed by President Madison on August 27, 1810, only three months after the revolution, and arrived at his post on February 13, 1811. Learning that a vessel was sailing for the United States that same afternoon, he called immediately on the governing junta, was formally recognized as "agent for seamen and commerce of the United States," and got a report of his recognition on the departing vessel.

Nine months later, on November 22, 1811, the young Buenos Aires government recognized William Gilchrist Miller, of Philadelphia, as United States vice-consul. According to page 921 of the official *Catalogue of the Library and Archives of the Argentine Ministry of Foreign Affairs*, published in Buenos Aires in 1910,[1] Miller was the first representative of any government to be recognized by the Argentine government.

The first diplomatic representative to be accredited by any country to the government of Buenos Aires was the American minister, Caesar Augustus Rodney. He was appointed by President Monroe on May 19, 1823, and arrived at Buenos Aires in November. The speeches, newspapers, and official documents of Rodney's day show that he was held in unusually high esteem by the Argentine government and people, who looked upon him as the man directly responsible for their being recognized as an independent nation. There also are letters showing that the American consular representatives, as well as Rodney, were on extremely friendly relations with Rivadavia, General San Martín, and the other leaders of the day.

Transportation in those days was dependent on horses and sailing vessels. Communication usually was by word of mouth or by letters and dispatches carried by messengers. Under these circumstances international affairs, especially among the young countries of the Americas, were much more a matter of personal relations among individuals than they are today. The American government appears to have been much more fortunate in the selection of the representatives it sent to South America in those days than it has been on frequent occasions in more recent years. The old documents and chronicles contain repeated evidence that in the trying years when both the United States and Argentina were laboriously and painfully emerging from colonial bondage into republican independence the relationship between the two countries was friendly and cordial, to the point of becoming at times almost lyrical.

In December 1811 Poinsett went to Chile, where he remained until August 1814. His services there appear to have been helpful and interesting, judging by the enthusiastic compliments paid him by O'Higgins and the Chilean government. He passed through Buenos Aires in Sep-

---

[1] *Ministerio de Relaciones Exteriores y Culto—Catálogo de la Biblioteca, Mapoteca y Archivo.*

JAMES MONROE,

PRESIDENT OF THE UNITED STATES OF AMERICA.

TO HIS EXCELLENCY THE GOVERNOR

AND CAPTAIN-GENERAL OF THE PROVINCE OF BUENOS AYRES.

Great and Good Friend:

I have made choice of Caesar A. Rodney, one of our distinguished citizens, to reside near the Government of Buenos Aires in quality of Minister Plenipotentiary of the United States of America. He is well apprized of the friendship which we bear to your Government and of our desire to cultivate the harmony and good correspondence, so happily subsisting between us. From a knowledge of his fidelity, probity, and good conduct, I have entire confidence that he will render himself acceptable to you and give effect to our desire of preserving and advancing on all occasions the interest and happiness of the two nations. I beseech Your Excellency, therefore, to give full credence to whatever he shall say on the part of the United States and most of all when he shall assure you of their friendship and wish for the prosperity of your Nation; and I pray God to have you always in His safe and holy keeping.

Written at the City of Washington the nineteenth day of May, in the year of Our Lord 1823.

Your good Friend
James Monroe

BY THE PRESIDENT
JOHN QUINCY ADAMS
SECRETARY OF STATE

tember 1814, on his way back to the United States. In 1825 he was appointed United States Minister to Mexico and remained at that post until 1829. It was in Mexico that Poinsett discovered the magnificent flowering star which now bears his name. He took several plants back to the United States and the botanists named the new flower in his honor. In Argentina, however, the poinsettia is called *estrella federal,* or federal star, because its color is identical with the red which the federalist dictator Rosas forced everyone to wear during the years of his tyranny.

Thomas Lloyd Halsey, the first American consul at Buenos Aires, was born in Providence, Rhode Island, in 1775 and died there in 1855. He was engaged in the import and export business in Buenos Aires in 1810, went to the United States in 1812, and in May 1813 President Madison appointed him consul at Buenos Aires, a position which he held until 1818. Halsey was engaged in business throughout his consulship, as was customary in those days, and introduced several useful breeds of sheep into Argentina from the United States. On November 7, 1815, he wrote to James Monroe, then Secretary of State, urging that the United States lend money and arms to the Buenos Aires government. Without waiting for instructions, he guaranteed a loan of 2,000,000 pesos which was made to the government by General Devereux, a citizen of the United States. Halsey failed in his efforts to have the State Department confirm his guarantee, but nevertheless Devereux made the loan on Halsey's personal guarantee and this loan is credited with having saved the life of the young republic.

In 1820 John Murray Forbes arrived in Buenos Aires as special diplomatic agent of the United States. He had risen to the rank of colonel in the American army and then entered the foreign service and served under five Presidents. After serving in Haiti and Paris, he was sent to Copenhagen to counteract the influence which Napoleon's agents were exercising on trade relations from their base at Hamburg. After his arrival at Buenos Aires, Forbes became a great friend of Bernardino Rivadavia, who was minister of government and foreign affairs. When Rodney arrived and presented his credentials as American minister, he also presented a commission from President Monroe appointing Forbes secretary of legation. On Rodney's death in 1824, Forbes became the first American chargé d'affaires at Buenos Aires and later the second American minister. He died at Buenos Aires in 1831 at the age of sixty and was buried there. His funeral was a very impressive one and was attended by a great throng of admirers, among whom was John C. Zimmermann, grandfather of the highly esteemed gentleman of the same name who at about the time of the First World War began to be generally and affectionately recognized as the oldest American resident in Argentina.

Thirty American citizens celebrated the Fourth of July in Buenos Aires in 1823, at Mrs. Thorn's hotel. Forbes, who presided, announced that he had received a note from the Buenos Aires minister of state offering his felicitations to the United States on the glorious anniversary they were celebrating, and informing him that at that moment a preliminary treaty had been signed between the Spanish commissioners and the State of Buenos Aires.

Forbes then offered the following toasts:

1. "The honorable Mr. Rivadavia, Minister of Government and Foreign Affairs—the champion of moral influence; the enemy of prejudice; the enlightened and honest statesman; patriotism his motive and guide; his shield and reward the approbation of a pure and elevated conscience."

2. "The preliminary treaty between Buenos Aires and the King of Spain, this day signed—may it lead to a definitive treaty equally honorable and advantageous to both parties; may it open a new political millennium in agitated Europe, by strengthening right and tempering power."

Unfortunately, the gods were not listening when Forbes offered his toasts. Eleven months later Rivadavia was out of office and on his way to Europe, and the treaty of peace with Spain was not signed until 1863.

When those thirty Americans met at Mrs. Thorn's hotel on July 4, 1823, Argentina did not yet exist as a political division. Forbes had been accredited "to the Government of Buenos Ayres" and Rodney was to arrive a few months later accredited to that same government. In 1823 that government was enjoying a brief lull in the almost continuous civil wars which had followed the war of independence and preceded the formation of the Argentine Confederation. Buenos Aires was being ruled by an oligarchy of liberals who had suppressed the Triumvirate and assumed the sovereignty of the whole Viceroyalty. Although the people of Buenos Aires quarreled a great deal among themselves as to which individuals should exercise the supreme power, they were united in insisting that the capital should continue to enjoy the privileges and exclusive trading rights with which the Spanish system had endowed it. General Rodriguez was the head of the government at the moment with the title of Governor and Captain-General, and Bernardino Rivadavia was his minister of government and foreign affairs.

Several American business houses already had been established. One of the largest was Zimmermann, Frazier and Company. Zimmermann had gone to New York from Germany in 1802 and then to Buenos Aires in 1815 as supercargo on a vessel that sailed from Baltimore with arms for the Argentine patriots. Benjamin W. Frazier, the junior member of the firm, had gone to Buenos Aires from Philadelphia and married a daughter of Zimmermann. Another important American firm was that of Danna and Carman. Carman left several children, and his descendants are still living in Buenos Aires, although they long ago drifted away from the American community.

When in November, following the celebration at Mrs. Thorn's, Caesar A. Rodney arrived in Buenos Aires on the *Sally*, of Salem, as the first minister plenipotentiary of the United States of America, he already was well known to the government and people of the young republic. In 1818 President Monroe had sent him and John Graham to the River Plate in the frigate *Congress* to report on the state of the United Provinces of the River Plate and the advisability of diplomatic recognition. Buenos Aires at that time offered little promise of future greatness. The population was about 50,000 and the streets not only were unpaved but unclean. The houses of even the leading families had no floors and only bare whitewashed walls. Occasionally a fine carpet would partly cover the broken brick floor and a piano and costly imported furniture would adorn the rooms, but the many comforts and conveniences of the American colonial houses were unknown.

The unattractive town was the capital of a province seething with unrest and virtually in a state of anarchy. The several other provinces which were supposed to form the United Provinces of the River Plate were divided by political quarrels and engaged in open civil war. Graham can hardly be blamed, therefore, for sending back a pessimistic report. But Rodney, much more far-sighted in his study of the land and its people, saw the possibilities of the new republic. He sent back a favorable report recommending the formal recognition of the new government, and President Monroe presented this report to Congress on March 8, 1823, with his own personal proposal for the recognition of the River Plate Provinces.

Rodney's first mission to Buenos Aires had been the outcome of the action of the Congress of Tucumán in sending Don Manuel H. de Aguirre as diplomatic agent to the United States to request the official recognition of the American government. Monroe did not recognize Aguirre in his diplomatic capacity but permitted him to buy and arm two vessels for the use of San Martín against Peru. Buenos Aires had abolished slavery, and the slave States, through their representatives in

Congress, were vigorously opposed to recognizing the independence of a new South American country which had taken such a step. But the intense interest which President Monroe and his Secretary of State, John Quincy Adams, felt for the River Plate colonies and their earnest desire to bring them into the family of nations were shown by their selection of a man of Rodney's position to head the mission which was sent to Buenos Aires to study the situation of the new government.

Rodney was the son of Colonel Thomas Rodney, of Revolutionary fame, and a nephew of Caesar Thomas Rodney, who signed the Declaration of Independence. He had been Attorney-General in Jefferson's cabinet and had served two terms in the House of Representatives and one in the Senate. Because of his having been elected to Congress as an Anti-Federalist in 1805, Rodney has been called the first Democrat ever to sit in the American Congress. Rivadavia was so impressed by the fact that Rodney had given up his position and comfortable surroundings to go to live among the struggling patriots of the River Plate that he declared him to be the definition *par excellence* of "the hero of liberty and civilization."

In May 1824, six months after his arrival, Rodney was the guest of honor at the official banquet given by the government as part of the first celebration of the national fete day that Argentina observed as a recognized independent nation. Rodney appears to have been of considerable service to the Buenos Aires government in an advisory capacity because of the active part he had taken in the formation of the new United States government. Unfortunately, his career in Buenos Aires was very brief, as he died suddenly on June 10, 1824, seven months after his arrival. He was buried on June 12 with the full state and military honors due a Captain-General. The funeral served to inaugurate the first Protestant cemetery in the country and exceeded in magnificence anything of the kind previously seen in Buenos Aires. More than 10,000 people, or one-fifth of the entire population, were present. The cannon on the fortress boomed out a national salute as he was buried. Rivadavia had followed the coffin to the cemetery as chief mourner and made a stirring address at the graveside, praising Rodney's invaluable services to the country. The body was sent to the United States later, and a pedestal was erected to his memory in St. John's Anglican Pro-Cathedral in Buenos Aires, where members of the American community held a memorial service on the centennial of his death.

Six years after Rodney's death there arrived at Buenos Aires on a Boston vessel a young supercargo whose name was to become one of the most prominent and beloved in all the history of American relations in Argentina. He was Samuel B. Hale, who had been born in Boston in 1804 and educated at Harvard. Upon his arrival at Buenos Aires he saw with true Yankee foresight the possibilities which the new country offered and determined to make his home there and invest his capital. In 1833 he founded the export and import firm of Samuel B. Hale and Company, which for more than a century was to be one of the best known in the country. He married into a distinguished Argentine family and soon became affiliated with many great Argentine enterprises. He was among the leading spirits in the first great railroad undertaking, the Western; was a director of many banks and corporations, and a member of the city council of Buenos Aires. He died on September 21, 1888, and was buried on the same day and in the same cemetery as his old and very close friend, former President Domingo Sarmiento.

Several prominent Argentine families were founded by those ambitious young Americans who went to Buenos Aires a hundred years or more ago to seek their fortunes. The Hales, the Zimmermanns, the Cooks, the Pages, the Carmans, and several others, although pure Argentines today, are descended from American forefathers. Most of the present generation cannot speak English. As recently as the First World War the nucleus of the American community in Buenos Aires still was formed by a group of families that had been established in Argentina for a quarter of a century or more but had remained American foreigners instead of becoming absorbed into Argentine society. Most of these old-timers, however, have disappeared and are not being replaced. By the time the Second World War began, any American who had lived in Buenos Aires as long as eight years was considered an old-timer.

In May 1865 there took place in Buenos Aires another of those meetings which brought the American community and the Argentine government into close relationship. It was the memorial service for President Lincoln. News of the assassination did not reach Buenos Aires until May 27, five weeks after it occurred. On the following Monday there was a meeting of many American citizens at which a committee was appointed to draft suitable resolutions of regret and grief. One of the members of this committee was the American consul, Hinton Rowan Helper, who had been personally appointed consul at Buenos Aires by Lincoln in 1861. At a largely attended meeting at the American legation on May 31, 1865, it was resolved that all the Americans in Buenos Aires were to wear a badge of black crape on the left arm for thirty days and formal thanks were voted to President Mitre and his cabinet for causing all flags to be flown at half-mast on Sunday, May 28, the day after the arrival of the news. The constant loyalty of President Mitre and his cabinet to the cause of the North during the Civil War was favorably commented on.

Another resolution expressed thanks to Governor Saavedra and the legislature of the Province of Buenos Aires for the resolution they adopted on May 30, declaring that the next new town or city to be organized in the Province of Buenos Aires should be called Lincoln, in honor of the late President. When the town eventually was founded and ceremoniously inaugurated, Samuel B. Hale presented it with a bronze statue of the martyred President. Yet there are many people in Argentina who still pretend to believe that the town of Lincoln was named for the Lincoln breed of sheep.

Long before diplomatic and consular relations were established, the United States held a leading position in Buenos Aires shipping. The first American vessel to enter the River Plate appears to have been the *John*, of Philadelphia, which arrived at Montevideo in November 1798 and sailed for Philadelphia in March 1799 with a cargo of "the products of the country," which is now Uruguay. The *Liberty*, also of Philadelphia, arrived at Montevideo in March 1790 and sailed in June, carrying a shipment of tallow from Buenos Aires, which is the first shipment on record of any commodity carried by an American vessel from what is now the Argentine Republic. Ten years after the Civil War, when steam shipping had become well established, American sailing vessels still were prominent on the River Plate, and in 1873, 253 American ships entered the port of Buenos Aires, as compared with 243 British. But the day of sailers was drawing to a close and each year saw fewer in service. The American clippers were not being replaced by steamers under the American flag and in 1873 not a single American steamer arrived at Buenos Aires, although there were 141 British steamers. Although the United States had built up a flourishing trade with Argentina, which had not yet become an agricultural producer, by 1874 this trade was suffering many difficulties due mostly to lack of shipping. In 1865 the Argentine government had offered a bounty of $30,000 to any company that would establish a direct steamship service between Buenos Aires and New York, an offer that later was raised to $50,000, without any takers.

By the time the Argentine people finally got over their civil wars and organized as a nation in 1862, the United States was in the throes of its own Civil War. When that war ended in 1865, the people of the United States were too absorbed in their own problems to take any interest in

South America, and Argentina turned to Great Britain for the trade and other co-operation she formerly had received from the United States. In 1869 the first transcontinental railroad was completed in the United States by the driving of a golden spike to mark the junction of the Central Pacific and Union Pacific at Ogden, Utah. The conquest of the Far West began and Argentina was completely forgotten in the exciting activity of building a great empire in the wilderness of the Indian country. Trade with Argentina continued to dwindle and the Stars and Stripes virtually disappeared from the River Plate. In one period of more than three years, shortly before the outbreak of the First World War, only 2 steamers and 30 sailers flying the American flag entered Buenos Aires. In the same period, 28,303 vessels of other nationalities arrived. Only one-tenth of 1 per cent of the arrivals flew the American flag, while 21 per cent flew the British flag. When the war broke out in 1914, 210 British ships were entering Argentine ports to one American. Exports from the United States to Argentina were averaging $50,000,000 a year, but the shippers were clearly at the mercy of their trade rivals for the delivery of their merchandise and the carrying of their mail.

By this time both the diplomatic and commercial relations between Argentina and the United States had become so unsatisfactory, and the people of the United States had forgotten and neglected Argentina for so long, that no one remembered that Argentina once had looked to the United States for inspiration and leadership. Great Britain, by following a much more intelligent diplomatic policy and a much more realistic trade policy, had almost completely replaced the United States, in both the affections and the bank accounts of the Argentines.

During the World War the United States suddenly "discovered" Argentina and since that discovery American influence on the daily life of the Argentines has been out of all proportion to the American investments in the country and the small size of the American community in Buenos Aires. This is because most of the things which the United States sells to Argentina help to interpret American life, customs, and standards of living to the Argentines, so that they have a fairly accurate idea of the United States and how Americans live. The things which Argentina sells to the United States, on the other hand, are for the most part identical with the same class of raw materials wherever produced and do not interpret Argentine life to the American consumers.

Argentines strongly resent the fact that they and their country are so little known in the United States. Actually, though, Argentina is much better known in the United States than in Europe. While Argentines can say truthfully, and do say, that they know Americans better than the Argentines are known by the people of the United States, their knowledge is not traceable altogether to an interest on their part that is any more determined than the perfectly honest and sincere desire of Americans to know Argentina better than they do. But American exports interpret American life to the Argentine people better than theirs do to the people of the United States.

American automobiles, electric refrigerators, motion pictures, phonographs, radio sets, and jazz bands have done much to interpret American life to the Argentines. American office equipment makes the daily work less arduous and American home equipment makes life more comfortable and more pleasant. Thousands of Argentine señoritas use American tooth brushes and American tooth paste on their beautifully white teeth every morning and it would not be feminine nature if they did not compare what they see in the mirror with the pretty American girl in the advertisement which brought the brush and the dentifrice to their attention. When the Argentine youth climbs into a flashy American automobile at about eleven o'clock for his morning parade through Calle Florida, he usually is dressed like and acts like the American youth in the colored advertising which has so lavishly accompanied American sales efforts in the Argentine automobile market.

Argentina was one of the first countries to suffer the curse which Americans put on civilization when they began exporting jazz, and American jazz long ago replaced everything except the tango at Argentine dances. Radio later killed the musical profession in Argentina and those few restaurants and tea shops which still have orchestras are made nerve-racking bedlams by the blare and crash of young Argentine musicians trying to act as insanely as the orchestras they see in American motion pictures.

When the Argentine business man opens his morning newspaper, he finds that about 75 per cent of its contents have been delivered by the American news agencies and that most of the news of the world has been written and interpreted by American correspondents. And the haughty, arrogant Argentine matron who tries to flee from all this American influence by hiding behind shuttered windows absorbs it in large doses when she picks up an Argentine magazine, because most of them consist of little else than translations from American magazines. Even the American illustrations are stolen. There have been instances of the same stolen picture being used to illustrate two different advertisements in the same magazine.

Fashionable women's stores in Buenos Aires, Rosario, and other cities are stocked with the latest American novelties; American cigarettes are smoked in great quantities, by women as well as by men; and American-made goods of every description come into almost hourly contact with all classes of Argentine men, women, and children. They see the same articles in American motion pictures and see how Americans live surrounded by the same things that they are wearing, eating, drinking, smoking, and otherwise using every day. And the voice from the American-made phonograph disks coming over the radio makes the atmosphere complete. It has been estimated that at least 200,000 Argentines are learning English for no better purpose than to be able to understand the conversation in the movies.

What is the other side of the picture? The principal imports into the United States from Argentina are hides, wool, linseed, and corned beef; and these products look very much alike all over the world.[2] Furthermore, by the time these raw materials have been worked up in American factories there is nothing left to identify them as being from Argentina, even if they had looked any different when imported. So even when the American is using Argentine products he usually does not know it. About all he does know about Argentina is what he has read, and much of that is incorrect. It is natural in human relations to pick out the unusual as a peg on which to hang the relationship, so the American whose only contact with Argentina is through what he reads holds onto such words as gaucho and pampas with which to form the background of his mental picture of Argentina, unaware that the gaucho and the storied pampas belong to Argentina's past just as truly as powdered wigs and dueling belong to the American past.

Although for many years the British exports to Argentina were far in excess of the American, they consisted mostly of bulk goods which were shipped in cargo lots, such as coal, iron, cement, and railroad equipment which did not come into personal contact with the consumer and so did not have any direct personal influence on the Argentines. The rapid spread of American influence on Argentine life as a result of the export trade after the First World War undoubtedly was one of the causes of the intense British jealousy of the American position in Argentina, which they tried to combat by persuading the Argentines to "Buy from those who buy from us," which simply meant "Buy from the British."

---

[2] For value of Argentine exports to the United States see Appendix V.

GRAPE GATHERING IN THE PROVINCE OF MENDOZA

AERIAL VIEW OF AN AMERICAN OWNED PACKING PLANT, LA PLATA

AMERICAN OIL WELLS IN PATAGONIA

AMERICAN OWNED CEMENT FACTORY AT SIERRAS BAYAS

Much is being written and spoken about the value of travel in cementing international relations, and an Argentine never misses an opportunity to say that more Americans ought to go to Argentina—which is true But it also is true that the number of Americans who go to Argentina is greatly in excess of the number of Argentines who go to the United States. What has made Americans better known to them is the American-made goods they use. Until Argentina produces and exports something that will come into closer personal touch with the consumer than grains and hides and wool, the acquaintance is likely to remain very one-sided, much as the Argentines regret it and however many tourists the United States may send for week-end visits to Buenos Aires on their wild race down the Atlantic, across the Andes, and up the Pacific.

American investments in the Argentine Republic are of comparatively recent date, most of them having been made since the First World War. According to a report made to the Chamber of Deputies in September 1941, the United States investments in Argentina at that time totaled 1,771,254,000 pesos, which at the current rate of exchange (24 cents to the peso) was equivalent to $425,100,960. This was approximately one-fifth of the total foreign investment in the country and equaled the aggregate of all other foreign investments except the British. The American investments, however, amounted to only one-third of the total British investment and to only one-half of what the British have invested in railroads alone.

As a large volume of the American investments were made when the peso was at par or close to it, the number of dollars invested in the country is considerably larger than the 425,000,000 indicated by the report to the Chamber of Deputies. This report gave the British investments at 20 per cent less than the total fixed by official British sources, and the amount given for the American investments probably is incorrect by at least the same margin. Dudley M. Phelps, in his *Migration of Industry to South America*, estimated in 1936 that between $400,000,000 and $425,-000,000 had been invested in American branch factories, in merchandising enterprises, including automobile assembly plants, and in public utilities, not taking into account the dollar investment in Argentine government bonds. As the investment in bonds is approximately $182,-000,000, this would indicate a total American investment of between $580,000,000 and $610,000,000.

The report made to the Chamber of Deputies showed that 40½ per cent of the American investment is in government bonds, the total being given at 716,438,000 pesos ($171,945,120), while the British investment of 872,436,000 pesos in Argentine government loans represents only 16 per cent of the total British investment.

The heaviest American investment is in telephone and radio communication companies—338,336,000 pesos ($81,200,640). Another 198,898,-000 pesos ($47,735,520) is invested in power plants. These two items are made up largely of the investments of the American and Foreign Power Company and the International Telephone and Telegraph Corporation in buying up plants that were already established and operating.

The Argentine investment of the three big Chicago meat-packing companies was given at 145,621,000 pesos ($34,949,040). The American investment in other local industries was reported at 258,130,000 pesos ($61,951,200). This represents the investment in about fifty American branch factories that have been established in Argentina and is far below the actual amount invested in these enterprises. Phelps, in the work already cited, reported that $164,721,000 had been invested in thirty-one branch plant operations in 1936, of which $55,498,000 represented the investments of two oil companies and a mining company.

Americans have 30,622,000 pesos ($7,349,280) invested in one of the subway companies, an estimated 73,161,000 pesos ($17,558,640) in commercial undertakings, 8,513,000 pesos ($2,043,120) in two banks, 1,432,-000 pesos ($343,680) in insurance companies, and 2,101,000 pesos ($504,-240) in other enterprises.

These dollar investments have made Argentines familiar with American merchandising methods and American service. American automobiles dominate the Argentine market very largely because Ford and General Motors spare parts can be found at every crossroads store from La Quiaca to Ushuaia. After the First World War, one of the largest British companies in Buenos Aires put up an attractive building and announced that it had taken on the selling agency of some of the best automobiles made in England. The cars were high grade and attractive and sold well at very high prices to some of the wealthiest families in Buenos Aires. Everything went along beautifully until things began to happen to the cars, as they will to the best of cars. Then the owners found that they had to leave their cars in the garage for at least two months, while the representative sent to London for the necessary spare parts. When the owners complained because the agency did not stock spare parts as the Americans do, the agents replied rather haughtily that they would not dream of tying up a lot of good money in spare parts. After a few months they decided that the automobile business was no way to make money, and rented their building to the Argentine government.

Argentine estancieros curse what they call the poor quality of American farm machinery. But when a machine breaks, the estanciero can send a horseman to the village, have the necessary spare part charged on his monthly account, and have the machine operating again in a couple of hours. When he used British and Canadian machinery, he had to suspend his plowing, sowing, or harvesting for three or four days while he sent to Buenos Aires or Bahia Blanca for the required spare part.

Some years ago the president of a British company making a very well-known high-quality line of scales visited Buenos Aires. After looking around for a couple of days, he went in to see the manager of one of the British banks one morning, mad as a hornet, and demanding to know why it was that the damned Yanks had all the scale business in town. The banker asked him if his scales were carried in stock in Buenos Aires. "No," he replied, "but the So-and-So Company are our agents and would be glad to send anybody's order to London." When the banker asked him how long it would take to get delivery, the scale man thought he could have a scale in Buenos Aires three months after the order was given to the agent. The banker explained that when anyone wanted to open a grocery store, a butcher shop, or a delicatessen shop, in Buenos Aires, Rosario, Bahia Blanca, or any other large city, he could go to the American companies' show-rooms, pick out the scale he liked, pay 100 pesos on account, and the scale would be in his place of business the next morning. "Hell!" exclaimed the Londoner. "We wouldn't dream of doing business that way." So the Yanks still control the scale business in Argentina.

It has been this insistence of the British in clinging, like the Chinese, to business methods that were good enough for their fathers and grandfathers that has made it impossible for them to keep up with American competition in the Argentine market and to seek refuge in artificial measures as impracticable as the Roca-Runciman Treaty in an effort to force trade into channels from which it is escaping in accordance with economic laws that are as old and implacable as the law of gravity.

Although installment selling is considerably more complicated under Argentine law than in the United States, the American companies have succeeded in introducing this system of high-pressure salesmanship for such household articles as electric refrigerators, vacuum cleaners, radio sets, and the higher-priced phonographs.

American branch factories are now manufacturing locally most of the advertised brands of soaps, dentifrices, and other toilet articles. American cosmetics dominate the market. American advertising agencies moved in with the branch factories and have imposed American advertising methods, so that the weekly magazines and the Sunday newspapers are becoming more and more like Spanish editions of American publications. American advertising has made the Argentines conscious of their halitosis, their B.O., and other bodily conditions which were considered bathroom secrets until they became subjects for illustrated American advertising. The advertising agencies, however, have not been able to break down the resistance of refined Argentine ladies to airing their toilet preferences in print, so the testimonials used in Argentine advertising tend to feature titled ladies of Great Britain or wealthy society ladies of the United States, both designed to appeal to the Argentines' snobbish admiration of anything that is foreign.

When an American advertising agency with a rolled oats account ran up against the difficulty that Argentines do not eat American breakfasts, it launched a national advertising campaign directed to men and boys who play football and engage in other athletics. This particular brand of rolled oats—no other, of course—would make them stronger and healthier athletes and make them winners. Before long, young Argentine huskies were eating American breakfast food with their lunch. In 1939 the last bulwark of sales resistance was overcome by the persistent American offensive and Argentines began chewing gum.

American newspaper comics have become so popular that several newspapers publish them in the middle of the week as well as on Sundays. One Buenos Aires newspaper charges extra for its mid-week edition carrying a supplement of comics and still sells more papers that day than on any other day of the week.

The two organizations which are doing most to spread United States influence among Argentines along non-commercial, cultural lines are not American organizations, but Argentine. One is the Argentine-North American Cultural Institute, known locally as Icana from the initials of its official name, Instituto Cultural Argentino-Norte Americano. The Cultural Institute is an organization that is worthy of much more support from the American colony in Buenos Aires than it receives. It was organized originally by a group of Argentines and Americans. The Argentines were mostly men who had studied in the United States or spent some time there for business or professional reasons. They all were enthusiastic admirers of the United States, of American democratic institutions and American traditions, and believed that there were certain things which young Argentines could learn to their advantage from the United States. The Americans were mostly managers of local American business houses or other prominent members of the American community. Most of the Americans dropped out later, leaving the Argentines to finance the undertaking as well as do the actual work of operating it. Similar Argentine organizations working to strengthen the cultural ties between Argentina and other countries, including Japan, receive hearty financial support as well as personal co-operation from the local residents of the foreign country interested. The American residents of Buenos Aires do not even buy their American books from Icana's American bookshop.

Icana conducts 100 classes in English, with a total of 3500 students every year, taking in the whole field of English study, from the primary lessons for children to advanced classes in American literature. There is an annual program of lectures at which Argentines and visiting Americans speak on subjects connected with the cultural relations, either real or potential, between the two countries. The Institute has from twelve to fifteen scholarships under which it sends a group of young Argentine students to the United States every year for post-graduate work. In this branch of its activities the Institute has been accorded the co-operation of certain institutions in the United States. Two of the scholarships are financed by the Institute itself and are awarded to the two outstanding students of its English classes. An American steamship line and an American airline donate the round-trip passages and the Institute pays the expenses of a six-month sojourn in the United States. The experience with these scholarships indicates that one of the very best investments that the United States could make would be to take fifty or a hundred young Argentines to the United States every year on scholarships. At least five of them should be Argentine newspapermen selected by the Círculo de la Prensa, the great national press club. Another five should be young medical students.

The Institute has established another extremely valuable means of cultural relations between Argentina and the United States by organizing an exchange of letter-writing between Argentine and American students. It also gives motion picture shows relating to various aspects of cultural and intellectual life in the United States. The dramatic department, made up of teachers, students, and alumni of the English classes, gives performances in both English and Spanish of the outstanding American plays of the year. In the American bookstore operated by the

Institute all the American books are available shortly after publication. Most of its clientele is made up of Argentines, and one of its busiest activities is keeping Argentine doctors, engineers, and other professional men supplied with the latest American books on scientific subjects.

The other agency for creating interest in the United States is an Argentine public school. Most of the members of the American colony never have heard of it and probably not more than thirty of the oldest residents could tell a visitor where the school is. In most of the Latin American capitals, twenty of the public schools have been named after each one of the other twenty American republics. Consequently, there is one in Buenos Aires called the Estados Unidos de Norte America School. In addition to their regular studies, the pupils of this school study United States history, institutions, and the lives of leading Americans. A large American flag stands alongside the Argentine flag in the assembly hall, and throughout the school there are large framed pictures of Washington, Lincoln, the two Roosevelts and other American Presidents, and views of New York and Washington.

One of the most interesting features of the celebration of the Fourth of July in Buenos Aires is the program of patriotic exercises which takes place at this United States of America School. The entertainment is attended by United States government officials, the chairmen of the various American clubs and societies, and other prominent members of the American community. The American ambassador usually is accompanied by the military and naval attachés, in uniform and gold braid, which gives the children a thrill. The pupils wear freshly starched white smocks over their street clothes and on the smocks are rosettes or knots combining the Argentine and American colors. The exercises open with the pupils lustily singing "The Star-Spangled Banner" in English and without any of the tra-la-las which Americans so often substitute for the words. Then the Argentine anthem is sung in Spanish. The rest of the program is carried out in Spanish and consists of songs, recitations, and dramatic sketches featuring references to patriotic and historic events in the United States and Argentina.

The young lady principal of this school has succeeded in making all her pupils enthusiastic little admirers of the United States who take home to their parents and other relatives what they learn about the big country up north. The American community in Buenos Aires could do much worse than work out some arrangement for continuing the interest of these children in the United States after they leave the grade school in which the interest was first awakened.

25. WHY AMERICANS ARE DISLIKED

THE answer to the question as to why Argentines dislike Americans is a long, sad story of distrust and disillusionment that goes as far back as 1824, when Argentina was the first South American country to recognize the Monroe Doctrine and to seek to base its foreign policy on collaboration with the United States and that doctrine. It includes the unfortunate part played by the United States in depriving Argentina of the Falkland Islands and turning them over to England. It is kept alive today by the presence in Argentina of hundreds of American missionaries who have been sent "to save the heathen."

Argentines hate to face an issue or to call things by their right names and it is almost impossible to get one to discuss with an American the things they do not like about the Yankee. They prefer to deny that there is any such dislike. But occasionally one can be persuaded to admit the truth. Then it transpires that they have a long list of political and commercial grievances and an equally long list of personal dislikes and prejudices. Many of these dislikes are perfectly justified, when the subject is looked at from their viewpoint; others are merely prejudices due to differences in race, education, and customs.

Argentines distrust Americans as being materialistic, imperialistic, hypocritical, overbearing, and insincere, among other things They do not like the hard drinking and rowdy behavior of Americans in public places. They dislike being discovered by North Americans every ten or fifteen years and then being just as suddenly dropped and forgotten when the little boom which led to their discovery subsides. And above everything else they detest American "good will" junkets. If it were possible for the United States Congress to pass a law prohibiting the use of the words "good will" by anyone going to Argentina, a long step toward real friendship would have been made.

Argentines are inclined to be very conservative and they do not like the free and easy way of American life, and especially the liberty between the sexes as shown in American motion pictures. This is one of several prejudices about which nothing can be done, a prejudice which explains why Argentine men will entertain their American friends in their clubs but never at their homes. Argentines sometimes inquire of Americans in perfectly good faith as to how many wives a man can have in a year in the United States. Some of them actually fear to let their sons and daughters go to the United States to study lest they be shot in one of those hair-raising running fights between G-men and gangsters in Fifth Avenue.

It is complained that American business men often have taken advantage of the good faith of their Argentine customers who expected that Americans also based their trade ethics on the palabra inglés. It is also complained that American investments in Argentina have not been of a nature to help develop the country but that they have been only in guaranteed government bonds or in enterprises likely to pay quick profits to the American investor without leaving any lasting improvement in the country. In all these cases it is customary to compare American business and investments unfavorably with the British.

One of the bitterest complaints against Americans in Argentina and elsewhere in South America is that we treat them as Indians and "niggers," while the Europeans treat them as equals. Instead of maintaining an intelligent public relations service throughout South America, we appear to take the position that any people who are not of pure white blood are "spicks" and "greasers" and that it would be beneath our dignity to explain ourselves to them. In this attitude, we include Argentina along with the rest of South America. Then we stand by in dignified silence and permit ourselves to be pictured by European propaganda as the "Octopus of the North," waiting our opportunity to gobble up all the southern countries.

It never has seemed worth while, for example, to explain to Argentines why we do not want to import their fresh beef, with the result that many educated, well-read Argentines actually believe that it is because we fear the consumer will be poisoned by eating it. As a result of our superior and completely insincere attitude on this question, it has become an acute phobia with the Argentines and critically threatens continental defense at one of its most vital points. Argentines know that arrangements could be made between the United States and Argentine meat inspection services that would prevent diseased meat from being shipped to the United States. And they know that Americans know it. So they look upon the refusal of the United States Senate to ratify the Sanitary Convention between Argentina and the United States as further evidence of American bad faith and a protectionist subterfuge for keeping cheap Argentine meat out of the American market. The Sanitary Convention, signed in 1935, would permit the entry of Argentine meat from regions which had been certified free from foot-and-mouth disease.

One of the most serious political stumbling blocks on the path to better understanding is the Smoot-Hawley Tariff, which Argentines believe was aimed directly at them.

We have ignored Argentina and the other South American nations ever since our own Civil War because they have been difficult to get to and because they have not attained an economic status comparable to our own. It has required another world war and the threat of a Nazi invasion of South America to awaken us to the necessity of reviewing our economic and cultural relations with the twenty countries south of us, each one of which could have been made a strong pillar in the American democratic structure during the twenty years following the First World War. Argentina is the one country in South America with which we should have established a close and continuing friendship long ago. It would be difficult to find two other countries whose origins and whose social and economic development have been as closely parallel as those of Argentina and the United States or whose common interests offer greater opportunity for co-operation.

Although Argentina has chosen in recent years to assume a cantankerous attitude of non-co-operation and opposition to the United States, truth compels the confession that the fault is very largely our own. Argentina merely has been stubborn about accepting our sudden new bid for friendship after many years of neglect. Argentina is not yet convinced that this desire for friendship is not being inspired by our self-interest rather than by any real interest in Argentina and its problems.

Alberdi laid the basis for United States influence in Argentine politics and institutions nearly a hundred years ago when he caused the Argentine Constitution to be patterned on that of the United States. Sarmiento laid the foundation for American influence and co-operation in education by taking a large group of American schoolteachers to Argentina to organize the schools, especially the normal schools. But we were too busy with our own internal problems to take any interest in Argentina's. We were not yet ready to expand or to send our capital abroad. Great Britain profited by this preparation for American influence: it invested capital in Argentina, became a heavy purchaser of Argentine products, and assumed the role in Argentine affairs that the United States could have had.

Argentina fulfilled Europe's need for somewhere to send its excess population. It had excellent climate, fertile soil, and a white population. Italy and Spain had no colonies and the German colonies in Africa were unsuitable. So settlers were sent to Argentina by the hundreds of thousands and there was a convenient division of labor and industry. Argentina began producing foodstuffs for Europe, and Europe produced manufactured goods for Argentina. The Argentines found that they could get along very well without the United States and we did not care particularly.

Europe's economic influence led naturally to political and cultural influence. The thousands of Spaniards who went to Argentina after the war in Cuba spread anti-American ideas. Washington's policy in the Caribbean caused many refugees to flee to Buenos Aires. Most of them were writers and they were all anti-United States. When Argentines grew rich after 1900 they went to London and Paris and were deeply impressed by the British aristocracy. France made determined efforts to spread its cultural influence in Argentina and succeeded magnificently. The United States sent nothing, and it probably was natural that the Argentines should come to believe that the United States had nothing to offer.

During and after the First World War, Argentina turned in desperation to the United States for the goods which it could no longer get from Europe. The experience was unfortunate, to express it in the mildest possible terms. New York was full of so-called export firms that had sprung up overnight. They took orders for anything they could get, requiring the buyer to pay cash in advance because they had no financial backing or credit of their own. The goods they shipped to Argentina bore little resemblance to the samples on which they had obtained the orders. They paid no attention to the buyers' instructions regarding packing, shipping, and the consular and other documents required by Argentine customs regulations. One Buenos Aires firm, on opening its cases, found that it had paid in advance for a large shipment of second-hand silk stockings that had been mended and ironed.

Argentine business men were not interested in the American explanation that most of this trouble was not the fault of American business, since the orders had been given to fly-by-night concerns or individuals most of whom were not Americans at all. The Argentines knew only that they had paid good American dollars through American banks to concerns having American addresses and they considered that American trade ethics were at fault. The American Chamber of Commerce in Buenos Aires did magnificent work in arbitrating more than a thousand of these cases. But when the boom petered out and prices began to fall and the Argentine buyers refused to accept delivery on a falling market, Americans denounced them in obscene language as pikers and crooks and washed their hands of the Argentine market. When several of the South American republics which had been overloaded with American loans began to default on their annual payments, American bankers and business men abandoned South America to its fate. Argentina suffered along with the rest in spite of having religiously kept up its payments through all its political and economic troubles. Perhaps it is only natural that Argentina should remain cool toward a renewal of American overtures of friendship.

Argentines still remember that the United States sent a naval squadron of three cruisers to Buenos Aires in an effort to break Argentine neutrality after the United States entered World War I, and while the majority of Argentines were in favor of the objective sought by the squadron they looked upon its visit as a demonstration of American imperialism and big-stick politics.

For more than two years President Wilson had been sending notes to the South American governments explaining why it was imperative that all the American nations remain strictly neutral while Europe fought. This policy coincided with that of President Irigoyen and he strongly supported it. Then the United States entered the war and asked the South American republics to accompany her. Most of them did. Irigoyen refused, in spite of a congressional resolution asking the government to break off diplomatic relations with Germany and Austria. The United States sent a squadron on a propaganda tour to Brazil and the River Plate, under the command of Rear Admiral Caperton. Most of the sailors were young high school boys from Washington and Oregon. They were on their best behavior and made an excellent impression in Rio de Janeiro and Montevideo, where they were enthusiastically welcomed and lavishly entertained.

Irigoyen played dumb when the American embassy insinuated that it would be considered a friendly gesture if the Argentine government would invite the American warships to visit Buenos Aires. As the date approached for the departure of the squadron from Montevideo, the embassy again brought up the subject of an invitation to visit Buenos Aires. It had been announced that the squadron was on its way to the Pacific. Finally Irigoyen, with rather poor grace, sent Admiral Caperton a cablegram inviting him to call at Bahia Blanca on his way to the Pacific. Caperton could play dumb as well as Irigoyen. He sent a cablegram accepting with pleasure the President's kind invitation to visit Buenos Aires, weighed anchors, and started up the river. Under international law, the American warships could remain only twenty-four hours in the neutral port of Buenos Aires, so the reporters' first question to the admiral was how long he expected to stay. He replied that the squadron would remain ten days, and it did. Irigoyen was inclined to be anti-American after that and had a great deal to do with the anti-American stand taken by the Argentine delegation to the Pan-American Conference at Havana in 1928, even though he was not President at the time.

The underlying reason for Argentina's constant opposition to the United States at Pan-American conferences and its refusal to co-operate in the general Pan-American effort is the jealousy of Washington's leadership in continental affairs. Argentina is interested in co-operation only when the initiative arises in Buenos Aires. Her only field for economic and political expansion is Latin America, and the United States, not Argentina, dominates in Latin America. Argentines feel that if it were not for the United States the other countries of South America would look to the Argentine Republic for leadership. This is highly debatable, however, as all the other republics distrust Argentina's imperialistic designs in South America more than they distrust the United States. But that does not prevent Argentina from believing that it could be the leader if the United States did not stand in the way. Argentina lost whatever prestige it had as a leader in South American affairs as a result of the obstructionist attitude at the Lima, Havana, and Rio de Janeiro conferences, yet Argentines blame the United States rather than their own government for this situation.

Since the second Pan-American Conference at Mexico City in 1902, the American nations have signed eighty-four treaties and conventions. (None was signed at the first conference in Washington in 1890.) Of these eighty-four measures for Pan-American co-operation, Argentina had ratified only seven up to January 1, 1942. Bolivia had ratified eight. The average for the other nineteen governments was forty. It is interesting to note that Argentina lost no time in ratifying the convention providing for joint administration by the Pan-American governments of any European colonies or possessions in the Western Hemisphere which the United States might find it necessary or desirable to occupy. The Argentine delegation at the Havana conference of ministers of foreign affairs in 1940 stubbornly opposed this convention, but finally signed it when they became convinced that the United States was determined to be the sole judge of the military expediency involved in occupying European possessions for the sake of hemispheric defense. By hurriedly ratifying this convention, Argentina expected to qualify for a voice in the administration of any European possession which might be occupied by American troops. On January 1, 1942, Argentina had not ratified any of the eleven conventions drawn up at the Conference for the Maintenance of Peace which met at Buenos Aires in 1936 to lay the foundations for hemispheric defense.

Argentina has well-defined imperialistic aspirations in Bolivia, Paraguay, and Uruguay, and believes that the United States is preventing her from establishing her hegemony over these neighboring countries which at one time belonged to the Viceroyalty of the River Plate. There is a large school of thought in Argentina which favors the absorption into the Argentine domain of all the territory which formerly was ruled by the Spanish viceroy at Buenos Aires. United States predominance in Pan-American affairs is a serious barrier to the realization of this dream.

Argentina exercises an economic control over Paraguay that is much more inclusive than any control the United States ever has exercised in any of the Caribbean countries. Every pound of merchandise entering or leaving Paraguay has to pay tribute either to the Argentine government direct or to Argentine transportation companies. Argentines were furious when the Export-Import Bank made a loan to Paraguay for road construction and Paraguay began building its long-dreamed-of road toward Brazil, by which it hopes eventually to escape at least part of its economic dependence on Argentina. Paraguay previously had planned to buy two American steamboats to carry its produce and imports between Asunción and Buenos Aires, but had to abandon the project when the Argentine government ruled that the steamboats could not touch at any Argentine river ports because they would be competing with the two Argentine shipping companies which have a monopoly of the traffic on the Paraná and Paraguay rivers.

In Bolivia, Argentina has undertaken to finance the construction of a railroad from Yacuiba on the Argentine frontier to Santa Cruz de la Sierra and to let Bolivia repay the loan in petroleum. It also has lent Bolivia 500,000 pesos to finance the drilling of oil wells in the region to be traversed by the railroad. It is expected that the railroad will cost at least 100,000,000 pesos ($24,000,000). Argentina is lending the money at 3 per cent a year, which is considerably less than she has to pay for the money she borrows herself. This arrangement has been denounced by some of the leading Argentine newspapers, especially *La Prensa*, as a violation of Bolivian sovereignty that is filled with dangerous possibilities.

Ezequiel Ramos Mexía, who was Argentine minister of public works when a similar project was under discussion during Figueroa Alcorta's administration (1906–10), said in his *Memoirs*, published in 1936, that he knew of only one other case where one government had undertaken to build a railroad into the territory of a neighboring country and that was the Russian railroad into Manchuria which caused the subsequent war between Russia and Japan. "This project means," he wrote, the "dissimulated conquest of Bolivia or a subordination of Bolivia's sovereignty that is unworthy of Argentina."

But aside from Argentina's political jealousy of Washington's position in South America there are a large number of pernicious American influences constantly at work against a closer understanding with the Argentine people. Argentines have tried repeatedly to like Americans and American goods. We, not they, are responsible for the undercurrent of prejudice which they now feel toward us. Argentines charge that Americans do not deal with them on a man-to-man, face-to-face basis, but that we insist on regarding all South Americans as younger brothers who need our frequent advice and occasional chastisement. They strongly resent the popular American cartoons which show Uncle Sam as a big masculine personality and the South Americans as pygmies wearing Mexican hats. Often, Uncle Sam has two of them by the scruff of the neck, bumping their heads together. Argentines particularly resent the mental attitude of Americans which makes these cartoons popular. They argue that if we are the educated, cultured people we pretend to be, we should know that South American culture is equal to our own. In Argentina the general average of culture and good manners is considerably higher than the general average in the United States. Argentines also charge, probably correctly, that Americans are much too patronizing in their efforts to be friendly. And they insist, perhaps not unreasonably, that Americans who go to Argentina on business should learn to speak Spanish, just as we require people to speak English when they want to do business with us.

Argentines are a proud people with a rich heritage of tradition and culture. Friendship means more to them than anything else, but we never seem to have time to cultivate their friendship and it cannot be bought. They want no favors from us; they want only to be treated as equals. They want economic co-operation, but not to be put on "relief" by means of loans. Personality plays a very important part in business relations in Argentina and the average Argentine would much prefer to do business with a man who is *simpático*, even if his prices and conditions are not always the most attractive. The Germans have learned better than any other foreigners how to make themselves *simpático* to the Argentines. Americans all too frequently are inclined to be brusque and hurried and much too obviously intent on closing the deal rather than making a permanent friend of the customer.

Unlike most of the other foreigners who go to Argentina, the American does not look upon the country as a new home. To him it is a place to put over a business deal, make a profit, and get out. If he is sent to Buenos Aires as manager of a business, his principal interest usually is to outsell his competitors and use the Argentine post as a stepping stone to a higher one. As a rule, he lives in a tight community within the American colony and mixes even less than the Briton with the people of the country. Usually he is too busy making and spending money to give any time to learning Spanish. There are many Americans in Buenos Aires who have lived there for ten years or longer and still cannot speak Spanish. The Germans, on the other hand, trained young men to speak Spanish and Portuguese and sent them to Argentina and other South American countries to live among the people, marry South American girls, and learn South American politics and psychology. These German representatives catered to the Argentine market and complied with Argentine preferences and even idiosyncrasies in packaging, colors, etc. They put Spanish names and trade marks on their products, many of which were lower-priced imitations of American goods. The American selling policy all too often was "take it or leave it." The Argentines frequently left it, and bought the inferior German product offered by a salesman who had "sold" himself before showing his samples.

Argentines are inclined to resent the high salaries earned by Americans and the ostentation of their wealth. There are several American business men in Buenos Aires whose salaries equal that of the Argentine President, while most Americans in secondary positions earn more than the managers of Argentine businesses. These Americans undoubtedly earn their salaries and are worth to their firms all that they are paid. Their mistake lies in their tendency to lord it over the Argentines among whom they live and work, thus aggravating the Argentines' already existent inferiority complex.

There will have to be some kind of control, either voluntary or governmental, over the American motion picture films that are sent to Argentina before there can be any real friendship between the two countries. Every time Hollywood tries to depict Argentine life on the screen, the Argentine distributor either has to prevent the picture from being shown or there are riots in protest against the gross misrepresentation of everything Argentine that appears in the film. Argentina has a highly developed motion picture industry of its own and seems to be perfectly justified in its demand that Hollywood devote its activities to depicting life and customs in the United States and leave the interpretation of Argentine life to Buenos Aires.

But of all the pernicious American influences which are working permanently against a better understanding between the people of the United States and those of Argentina, the worst undoubtedly is the American missionary. A directory published by one of the missionary organizations in Buenos Aires shows that there are nearly 400 foreign missionaries and their wives in Argentina, not counting the Salvation Army. Most of these missionaries are Americans and are supported by the boards of foreign missions of religious sects in the United States. But they do not go into the hot Chaco to carry the gospel to the Indians, or into the cold wastes of Tierra del Fuego to preach to the rapidly disappearing Fuegians, or into the lonely, windswept regions of Patagonia. They settle down in the large cities of Argentina or their attractive suburbs and devote themselves exclusively to trying to persuade Christian communicants to renounce the sect they already are in and join the one represented by the missionary.

This is not missionary work; it is proselytizing in its worst form. Considered from a purely religious viewpoint, these so-called missionaries do more harm than good, because they take away from their "converts" the elaborate ritual of the faith in which they have been raised and give them no equivalent in return for it. Experience has shown that a very large number of these so-called converts, having had doubt sown in their hearts, soon begin to doubt the new faith as well, and wind up by becoming unbelievers altogether.

But there is a far more serious aspect of this question as far as our relations with Argentina are concerned, and that is that the activities of these American missionaries very naturally arouse the enmity of the Catholic Church, against which they are directed, with the result that it has become the most formidable single vehicle for anti-American propaganda and for sowing suspicion and dislike of everything American. The Catholic Church is one of the most efficient organizations in all South America; it is heavily subsidized by nearly all the South American governments, including the Argentine, and its ramifications extend into the tiniest villages and remotest towns. Both it and the Church of England carry on real missionary work in the less civilized districts of Argentina, in Patagonia and the Chaco district bordering on Bolivia and Paraguay. The proselytizing activities of the North Americans are viewed as unfair competition, and as long as it continues it will keep alive a highly efficient agency for opposing every American effort to get in closer touch with the Argentines.

Before these missionary organizations can operate in Argentina they must incorporate themselves, just like any other business, and have their statutes approved by the government. These statutes almost invariably set forth that the purpose of the organization is "to save the heathen and bring Christianity to them." (The phrase is copied from the papers filed by one of the newcomers "in the field.") The opinion of Americans that is thus engendered in the minds of Argentine government officials can best be judged by the opinion that would be engendered by the filing of such statutes in the Department of Justice at Washington by some organization of foreign missionaries setting themselves up in the United States.

One hundred and thirty-six of these American missionaries live and work in the city of Buenos Aires and its suburbs. One American board of foreign missions sent a mission to Argentina as recently as 1927 and soon had twenty-six American missionaries at work "in the field." Five other American missionary organizations have established themselves in Argentina since 1900, three having been incorporated in 1906, one in 1908, and one in 1918. The mere presence of these American missionaries is an insult to the Argentine people.

Another basic cause of misunderstanding is that Argentines and Americans do not know each other better. It is obviously difficult to understand people we have never met. The remedy, of course, lies in more personal contacts, and the best way to achieve this is through the wholesale exchange of students, professors, and newspapermen. China's close friendship for the United States is directly traceable to the influence of the hundreds of students who were taken to the United States after the Boxer Rebellion and to the fact that many of these former students now occupy important posts in the Chinese government or are married to men who do. Likewise, Argentina's leaning toward Europe is traceable to the fact that many of the men who are guiding the country's destinies spent their impressionable years as students in Europe, not in the United States.

The whole problem is big and complicated, largely because for so many years we were too busy to bother about Argentina. Yet there is nothing in our relationship with Argentina and the Argentine people which could not be put on a perfectly satisfactory basis if the proper thought and effort were devoted to it. But it is a matter for thought and effort by individual American citizens even more than by the Washington government. Because, whether he is aware of it or not, every American who goes to Argentina is an unofficial ambassador whose attitude and actions have far more effect on Argentine thought than do those of the official ambassador.

26. ARGENTINA
AND THE MONROE DOCTRINE

IN support of its claim to leadership in Latin American affairs, Argentina for many years has maintained a constant and belligerent refusal to recognize the Monroe Doctrine. Its persistent opposition to United States proposals at Pan-American conferences usually is framed to make the obstruction look like a noble stand against the legality of the Monroe Doctrine, taken on behalf of the other American republics to protect them from North American imperialism. Yet Argentina was the first of the South American governments to recognize the doctrine, adhere to its principles, and offer to base its foreign policy on collaboration with the United States in carrying out the doctrine. After so enthusiastically supporting President Monroe's initiative, Argentina soon found that it was to receive no help or comfort from the doctrine; and the doctrine's best friend became its most implacable enemy.

General Juan Gregorio de Las Heras, head of the Buenos Aires government, in formally receiving John Murray Forbes as United States chargé d'affaires on July 28, 1825, following the death of Rodney, said:

"The Government of the United Provinces realizes the importance of the two principles which the President of the United States has expressed in his message to Congress and, convinced of the utility of their adoption by all the States of the continent, will consider it to be its duty to support them and, accordingly, will take advantage of every opportunity to do so that presents itself."

A year earlier, Las Heras had proposed to the United States that the Monroe Doctrine be broadened in scope to preclude the recognition of territorial aggression on the part of any of the American nations themselves. In his message to the Fourth Legislature on May 3, 1824, five months after the enunciation of the Monroe Doctrine, Las Heras said:

"Peace has been maintained with the nations of the continent and every true American heart has thrilled with joy at the arrival in our city of the first minister plenipotentiary of the Republic of the United States. This honor has been reciprocated by sending a minister of equal rank, who already has departed for Washington. He has been instructed to insinuate to the Government of that Republic how desirable it is that in addition to the two great principles of the abolition of privateering and the non-colonization of American territory by Europe there be established the principle that none of the new governments of this continent alter by force their frontiers as recognized at the time of their emancipation. This would destroy the seed of war which, sprouting up with the new States, would have a lamentable influence on their civilization and their customs."

General Las Heras had been one of San Martín's closest collaborators in the glorious campaigns by which the great Argentine liberator had carried independence to Chile and Peru. He had commanded that column of San Martín's Army of the Andes which had made the famous march through the Uspallata Pass with the artillery and munitions. He had then commanded the right wing at the battle of Maipó which established Chile's independence, and had been San Martín's chief-of-staff in the subsequent campaign to Lima which freed Peru from Spain. Las Heras had thus become imbued with San Martín's noble ideal of a united America in which all the new nations were to stand together and defend one another from outside aggression, rather than become nationalistic, selfish aggressors themselves.

The raising of the Monroe Doctrine to the higher, unselfish plane proposed by Las Heras might have prevented many of the regrettable things that happened in inter-American relations during the next hundred years. It almost certainly would have bound the North and South American continents together in a more effective Pan-Americanism than it ever has been possible to achieve. But it might also have prevented the establishment of several of the South American republics which exist today. For when the Monroe Doctrine was set up, there were only five independent countries in South America—the United Provinces of the River Plate, Brazil, Chile, Colombia, and Peru. Paraguay and Uruguay were not yet independent of Buenos Aires; Bolivia was a part of Peru; and Ecuador and Venezuela still belonged to Colombia.

The failure of the American government to accept the Argentine proposal and its action twenty years later in annexing more than half of Mexico's national territory convinced Argentina and the other Latin American countries that the doctrine was a one-sided, selfish policy of the United States and that it was not designed to extend to them the protection and support which they originally had interpreted the doctrine to guarantee. Yet there is reason to believe that President Monroe's opportune enunciation of the doctrine which bears his name played an important part in protecting Argentina and the other newly created South American States from European invasion at a moment when they were not in a position to defend themselves.

The United States had declared its neutrality in the wars of independence between the Spanish colonies and the mother country, but lost no opportunity to express its sympathy toward the new governments. The American legations in Europe had instructions not to participate in any negotiations looking toward a reconciliation between Spain and the colonies. Russia, Austria, Prussia, and France had united in the so-called Holy Alliance to defend the divine right of monarchs against governments based on the sovereignty of the people, and at the Congress of Verona in 1822 had signed a secret treaty by which they pledged themselves to use all the power and resources at their command to terminate the system of popular, representative government wherever it might exist in Europe and prevent its introduction in those countries where it was not known.

With Napoleon defeated and Ferdinand VII restored to the throne in Spain, the Holy Alliance was planning in 1823 to call a conference to draw up measures for helping Spain get back its American colonies. France and Russia, in particular, were eager to rehabilitate Spain as a world power to counter-balance the rapidly growing power of England. This could be done only by restoring Spain's empire and its colonial trade monopoly. The plan was to seize Buenos Aires and then send a fleet to the Pacific to re-establish the Spanish viceroy at Lima. France had 50,000 men in Spanish ports ready for the expedition, and Russia had promised to send troops. Buenos Aires could not possibly have resisted a force of 60,000 or 70,000 French, Spanish, and Russian troops. Spain was to cede Buenos Aires and the River Plate provinces to France in return for France's help in re-establishing Spain's dominion over all the other Spanish colonies, as far north as and including Mexico.

England had helped Spain expel Napoleon, but was opposed to restoring Spain's trade monopoly in South America; and though willing to help bring about a reconciliation between Spain and the former colonies, England was opposed to the use of force against the new governments of South America. The Duke of Wellington, hero of Waterloo, who represented England at the Congress of Verona, withdrew from the conference when the powers agreed to use force to put down the republican form of government. This was in keeping with an earlier declaration by the English minister of foreign affairs, Castlereagh, that the Holy Alliance had been created to block the French Empire but not to dominate the world. At Verona, England rejected the exclusive trade privileges in South America which were offered in exchange for the use of its fleet in crushing the new South American nations.

Shortly before the Congress of Verona, George Canning succeeded Castlereagh in the Foreign Office and immediately tried to arrange an entente with the United States to oppose the intervention of the Holy Alliance in South American affairs. In a note handed to the American minister in London on August 20, 1823, Canning proposed a joint declaration by England and the United States to the effect that the independence of the new States would be recognized whenever it should become opportune, but that in the meantime the two English-speaking countries would not oppose the idea of a reconciliation with Spain. The joint declaration was to consist of the following five points:

1. We consider that there is no hope that Spain will recover its colonies.

2. We believe that the question of the recognition of the colonies as independent States is a question of time and circumstances.

3. Nevertheless, we are by no means disposed to put any obstacles in the way of an arrangement between them and the mother country through amicable negotiations.

4. We do not aspire, on our part, to the possession of any part of the aforesaid colonies.

5. We could not view with indifference the transfer of any part of them to any other power.

Canning was vitally interested in restoring the colonial balance that had been upset by England's loss of its American colonies. It suited England as a maritime nation that the South American countries should remain free so that England could trade with them. But because of its recent alliance with Spain, England was reluctant to take any step that would openly offend it. Kasson, in his *Evolution of the United States Constitution*, quotes a dispatch from the American minister at London, Rush, to the State Department, dated October 10, 1823, in which Rush reported that Canning's entire effort was inspired by the interests of England, as opposed to the ambitions of France and Russia, and that his love for the independence of the South American colonies was measured by England's commercial interests rather than the ideal of liberty. Canning declared with pride in one of his later writings, "I called the New World into existence to redress the balance of the Old." His negotiations with the United States for a joint declaration of policy toward the South American colonies are widely credited with having inspired the Monroe Doctrine.

In reply to the proposal for a joint declaration, Rush informed Canning that the United States was in favor of the immediate recognition of the new South American States. On September 26, 1823, Canning asked Rush if the United States would not be satisfied with a promise of recognition at some time in the future. Rush replied in the negative and the negotiations lapsed. President Monroe had already appointed Caesar Rodney as minister to Buenos Aires in May 1823. Two and a half months after the collapse of Canning's efforts for joint action, Monroe sent to the American Congress the annual message which was to become famous as setting up the Monroe Doctrine.

Dropping his conversations with the United States Canning opened negotiations with France for a joint policy toward the South American colonies, and succeeded in obtaining from France a formal declaration that it would not help Spain recover its colonies. England declared, on its part, that it would recognize the independence of the South American countries if France should attempt to subjugate them or if Spain attempted to re-establish its former trade monopoly or refused to recognize the rights acquired by England in the new States.

The statement of foreign policy which has become known as the Monroe Doctrine was contained in the seventh, forty-eighth, and forty-ninth paragraphs of the President's message to Congress on December 2, 1823. In these paragraphs, the President stated, in part:

"The occasion has been judged proper for asserting as a principle in which the rights and interests of the United States are involved, that the American continents, by the free and independent condition which they have assumed and maintain, are henceforth not to be considered as subjects for future colonization by any European powers. . . . In the wars of the European powers in matters relating to themselves we have never taken any part, nor does it comport with our policy so to do. . . . With the movements in this hemisphere we are, of necessity, more immediately connected. . . . The political system of the allied powers is essentially different in this respect from that of America. . . . We owe it, therefore, to candor and to the amicable relations existing between the United States and those powers to declare that we should consider any attempt on their part to extend their system to any portion of this hemisphere as dangerous to our peace and safety. With the existing colonies or dependencies of any European power we have not interfered and shall not interfere. But with the Governments who have declared their independence, and maintained it, and whose independence we have, on great consideration and on just principles, acknowledged, we could not view any interposition for the purpose of oppressing them or controlling in any other manner their destiny, by any European power, in other light than as the manifestation of an unfriendly disposition toward the United States."

Canning immediately denied the right of the United States or any other power to proclaim such a principle of non-colonization, much less to enforce it. But Buenos Aires and the other South American governments received Monroe's declarations with rejoicing. They interpreted the doctrine as meaning that the United States would defend their territorial integrity and their political independence against European aggression. Brazil and Colombia enthusiastically offered to enter into a defensive alliance with the United States, but their offers were declined politely.

Buenos Aires received its first disillusionment in 1825 when it became involved in war with Brazil over the province of Uruguay. President Rivadavia inquired of the American chargé d'affaires, Forbes, if the United States would send help to the United Provinces in case Portugal sent help to Brazil. Emperor Pedro of Brazil was a Braganza, related to the Hapsburgs of Austria, who were very powerful in the Holy Alliance. His wife was the sister of Ferdinand VII of Spain, who wanted his River Plate colonies back. Rivadavia tried to make it appear that Portuguese aid for Brazil against the United Provinces would be an intervention of the Holy Alliance in South America. Secretary of State Henry Clay replied that there was no occasion for the intervention of the United States, since the war between Brazil and the United Provinces was strictly American both in origin and in objectives.

Argentina's next disillusionment came in 1831, when the American 18-gun sloop *Lexington* destroyed the Argentine settlement in the Falklands and Washington declared that the islands belonged to England, which has occupied them ever since.

The Falkland Islands were claimed for the French king in 1764 by the famous French explorer Bougainville. There are two main islands —East Falkland and West Falkland—and a hundred smaller islands and rocks. They lie approximately 250 miles off the coast of Argentina in the latitude of the Strait of Magellan. Bougainville founded a settlement on East Falkland at Fort Louis on the north shore of Berkeley Sound, which he called French Bay. Port Stanley, the present capital of the islands and site of the British naval base, is situated on the south shore of Berkeley Sound near the site of Bougainville's original settlement.

On January 23, 1765, Commodore John Byron, grandfather of the famous poet, landed at Port Egmont on Saunders's Island, off the coast of West Falkland, and claimed the islands in the name of George III. Byron did not remain, however, and it was not until the following year that an English settlement was established by Captain McBride of the frigate *Jason*.

When the Spanish government heard of the French settlement on the islands it protested to the French king, contending that the islands belonged to Spain as geographical dependencies of the South American continent. France recognized Spain's sovereignty over the islands and ordered Bougainville to surrender his settlement to the Spaniards. The Spanish governor at Buenos Aires appointed Felipe Ruiz Puente governor of the Falklands, and Bougainville writes in his *Voyage autour du Monde* that he turned the settlement over to Puente on April 1, 1767. The Spanish flag was raised and saluted by twenty-one guns. After Bougainville returned to Paris, the Spanish government paid him £618,-108, the amount of the account he had rendered covering the costs of establishing the settlement at Fort Louis.

On February 25, 1768, the governor at Buenos Aires received instructions from the Spanish king to oust the English who were still at Port Egmont. The frigate *Santa Catalina* was sent to Port Egmont and its commander ordered the English to leave the islands. When they refused, the governor at Buenos Aires sent an expedition of five frigates and 1500 men and the English surrendered their settlement to the Spaniards from Buenos Aires on June 10, 1770. England was furious over the incident and nearly went to war with Spain, but hostilities were avoided by an apology from the Spanish king, who said he disapproved of the violent manner in which the English had been dispossessed of their settlement and promised that it should be returned with all due formalities, but with the clear provision that this was not to affect Spain's sovereignty over the islands. The English returned to Port Egmont in 1771 but abandoned the islands voluntarily in 1774. Senator Palacios in a long and learned exposition before the Argentine Senate in 1934 maintained that the abandonment of the islands was in accord with a secret agreement between Spain and England and that the failure of the English government to make any reservations regarding its sovereignty when Port Egmont was returned to the English was a legal recognition of Spain's sovereignty.

At any rate, the Falkland Islands, or Malvinas, were in possession of Spain at the time that the United Provinces of the River Plate declared their independence. In 1820, Colonel Daniel Jewit, commanding the Argentine frigate *Heroína,* took possession of the islands in the name

of the government at Buenos Aires. A witness to this ceremony was the
English explorer John Weddell, for whom the Weddell Sea is named
in the Antarctic. Weddell had stopped at the Falklands on his first
voyage to the Antarctic and describes the incident in his *Voyage towards
the South Pole*. When Jewit found more than fifty English and American vessels in Berkeley Sound engaged in seal-hunting and slaughtering
the cattle which the Spaniards had left on the islands, he informed the
commanders of all these vessels that the Falklands belonged to the
government of Buenos Aires and that they could no longer fish or hunt
there. In 1826 the Buenos Aires government granted exclusive fishing
and colonization rights in the Falklands to Louis Vernet, an English
naval officer who had been living at Buenos Aires for some time and
who was married to an Argentine lady. On June 10, 1829, Rosas appointed Vernet governor of the islands with full military authority to
enforce the orders of the Buenos Aires government against foreign seal-
hunters. The sealers, however, paid no attention to Vernet and in August
1831 he seized the American vessels *Harriet, Breakwater,* and *Superior*.
On December 7 Captain Silas Duncan of the American sloop *Lexington*
addressed a note to the Argentine minister of government charging that
Vernet had engaged in piracy in arresting the three American vessels
and demanding that he be turned over to the United States authorities
for trial. Duncan had already notified the government that he was taking the *Lexington* to the Falklands to protect American interests there.
The American consul, George W. Slacum, addressed several insolent
notes to the government, which finally refused to continue recognizing
him as the consul of the United States. In his correspondence, the American consul had denied the sovereignty of the Buenos Aires government
over the Falklands.

The *Lexington* proceeded to the Falklands, where Captain Duncan
destroyed the artillery, blew up the powder depot, arrested six Argentine citizens, and declared the islands free of all government. Later, the
United States chargé d'affaires informed the Buenos Aires government
that the United States recognized British sovereignty over the Falklands, and in 1833 the British took possession of them and have occupied
them ever since. Washington refused to hear Argentina's protests or
claims to indemnity on the ground that the islands were occupied by
Great Britain and that Argentina must first settle with the British government the question of possession. The *Lexington* incident led to prolonged claims on the part of Argentina, which the United States refused
to accept. When Argentina appealed to the Monroe Doctrine, the State

Department said the doctrine was not retroactive and that Great Britain had presented titles to sovereignty which antedated the doctrine.

One of the strong Nazi baits held out to Argentina as a reward for her neutrality during World War II was the promise that the Falklands would be returned to the Buenos Aires government when Herr Hitler dictated the terms of peace, after defeating Great Britain and her allies.

In 1885 President Cleveland, in his annual message to Congress, said that the government had refused to entertain Argentina's renewed claims for indemnity for the loss of the Falklands, since the *Lexington* had been fully justified in destroying "a piratical colony" in view of the "derelict condition in the islands" and their abandonment before and after the claimed occupation by Argentine colonists. The Argentine minister at Washington, Vicente Quesada, addressed a strong protest to the Secretary of State taking exception to the President's language and especially his statement that the American government considered the Argentine claims to be "wholly groundless." The Argentine minister reminded the American government that it had always refused to let Argentina present its titles to sovereignty, so was not in a position to say whether the claims were groundless or not.

Ever since the Cleveland administration Argentina has been a bitter enemy of the Monroe Doctrine.

27. ARGENTINE-AMERICAN COLLABORATION

THERE are many ways in which the United States and Argentina, as the two principal republics of the Western World, might collaborate to their advantage. They must collaborate if there is to be a solid unit of neutrality, independence, and economic strength in this hemisphere that can survive the endless struggle in Europe and serve as a pillar upon which exhausted nations may lean and from which they may draw new strength and encouragement.

If Argentina believes in democracy, it also believes in a high standard of living for its people. In order to achieve that standard a great deal of development is needed and this requires ample capital investment. The United States can help Argentina with its industries, its road-building, its housing, the modernization of its transportation facilities, its merchant marine, its irrigation and hydro-electric development, its exploitation of mineral resources, its air transport, and with its scientific and medical research, library science, improvement of fruit and poultry varieties, rural electrification, education, and many other fields where experience, combined with wise capital investment, could bring about a great amelioration in living conditions and a general advancement in civilization.

Obviously such a program would have to be based on the continued prosperity of Argentina, and as Argentine prosperity is founded on trade, it is in trade and in keeping open the world trade channels that the two countries should seek to co-operate. When the Second World War began, the United States trade agreement program was the greatest single force in the world working for the general expansion of trade. Argentina's trade policy was more limited, as its bilateral agreements were on a more precarious basis.

The countries of the American continent must develop their resources and production in a way that will make them as nearly independent as possible of the European nations, so that if those nations eventually are dragged down into an economic collapse they will not drag any of the Latin American countries with them. There usually is an abundance of capital in the United States seeking investment. The only factor delaying its investment on a large scale in Argentina and the other South American nations is that of confidence and the knowledge that stability and correct governmental policies have been established.

The chief trading principle advocated by the United States is equality of treatment for all products on an unconditional most-favored-nation basis. This would mean that any country having a trade agreement with Argentina could sell its products in the Argentine market on the same competitive footing as that of other selling countries. This should be sufficient for any producing country unless it is offering only inferior goods which require exclusive governmental privileges in the import market to promote their sale. Argentina does not need to ask any more than this equality of treatment in foreign markets because it knows that in reasonably free competition in the world markets its producers can compete on a price and quality basis with those of any other country. Its guarantee of equal treatment in its own market should be sufficient to insure it similar treatment in foreign markets and if it does not, the guarantee can always be withdrawn from the offending country.

Argentina has proved several times in recent years that it is strong enough economically to stand up under possible "reprisals." It must be remembered that the sales of the European countries to Argentina usually are more important to them than Argentina's sales to them are important to Argentina. This will be seen to be true when it is recalled that markets for manufactured goods are almost always built up laboriously and when abandoned are often lost without equivalent compensation elsewhere. But markets for primary products such as Argentina's (with the exception of chilled beef, which is "made to order" for England) are on a world scale and are readily transferable from one market to another without excessive or irreparable loss. In marketing primary products price, rather than salesmanship or terms, is the determining factor, and Argentina has a decided advantage when it comes to price.

Argentina benefits in nearly all the markets of the world from the principle of equality of treatment. Its whole prosperity and progress has been built on that principle. Exclusive arrangements between other countries by which Argentina would be prevented from selling its products freely in world markets on the basis of price, equality, marketability, and terms of sale would spell disaster for Argentine trade. For a debtor nation such as Argentina it is imperative that it be permitted to sell freely in order that it may build up adequate exchange balances to take care not only of debt service but also of amortization, redemption, dividend remittances, governmental and armament expenditures, and other necessary transfers abroad, and at the same time leave a margin to tide it over bad years.

When traders are allowed to buy and sell freely they will seek for themselves, and ultimately for the producers and wage-earners whom they benefit, the greatest possible advantage and profit. To sell in the highest market and buy in the lowest (which is effectively prevented by special exclusive arrangements between governments) is such an obvious business maxim that to dispute it, or conduct a national trading policy in violence of it, seems foolish.

The countries which in the years just preceding the Second World War were opposed to common sense trading methods were the totalitarian States, their satellites, and those countries which by reason of fear or weakness were not able to stand up against economic dictation and the stranglehold type of trade agreements imposed upon them by the totalitarian nations. They were the countries which had so dislocated their national economies by top-heavy armament expenditures that they could no longer produce consumer goods salable in world markets on a basis of free competition. Hence they could dispose of their inferior goods only by forcing them onto unwilling countries which were anxious to sell their surpluses or countries which were willing for opportunistic or other reasons to enter into exclusive arrangements that were damaging to the principle of equality of treatment.

The United States seeks no special privileges in the Argentine market. It asks only equality of treatment; that is, if Argentine imports must be restricted for reasons of currency protection, the United States maintains that the restriction should apply uniformly and equitably to all suppliers. Restricting imports only from certain countries does not save the exchange situation.

Argentina's fear of losing European markets is largely groundless. Argentines who foster this idea either are trying to deceive others or are deceiving themselves. Under a regime of equality of treatment Argentina, with its low-cost and high-quality production, has nothing to fear from competitors or from governmental restrictions in foreign countries. If Argentina were frankly to tell the European countries to which it sells its products that it considers most-favored-nation treatment—that is, equal treatment—to be a reciprocal matter and that its continuing to grant such treatment was contingent on their doing so also, the nightmare of the loss of markets would soon vanish. It is no less vital for those countries, and especially the ones which are desperately in need of foreign exchange, to sell their goods to Argentina than it is for Argentina to sell to them.

Suppose that one country, say, Italy, should drop completely out of the Argentine foreign trade picture for a whole calendar year, what would be the result? Would it mean disaster for Argentina? Not at all. Rather, it would mean a great loss to Italy. Italy would be forced to look elsewhere for its raw materials and foodstuffs and might not be able to find them. Or it might find them only in a country where it could not pay for them because it had no foreign exchange. Also, Italy's shipping would be seriously disrupted. Argentina, on the other hand, would sell its surplus products on the world market at the best prices it could get. This might involve some loss, but it would be nothing as compared with the irreparable loss to Italy of its outlet for manufactured products in Argentina. Meanwhile Argentina could obtain all the substitute manufactured products it needed in other countries.

The so-called unfavorable aspect of Argentina's trade with the United States, about which Argentines talk so much, is a purely academic idea. The excess of imports from the United States in normal times is easily overbalanced by the natural excess of exports over imports in Argentina's trade with other countries. No loss is involved in this. On the contrary, it shows that Argentina is successfully selling its products to countries that need and want them and is buying in markets which are equipped to supply its needs and wants. Statistics and experience over a long period of years demonstrate that there is nothing wrong with this and that there is nothing that need be remedied as regards trade in normal times. The truth of this situation is not altered by the desirability of our adopting emergency measures to help relieve Argentina of the effects of the loss of European markets during wartime.

Discussion of the balance of payments between individual countries for some given period is interesting from the viewpoint of theoretical economics, but practically it is meaningless. World trade accounts are constantly being balanced, just as banks balance their exchange commitments daily. Money transfers, capital movements, gold, and credits are the mechanism used. Accounts between pairs of countries are not balanced, and do not need to be balanced, unless there are special compensation agreements or similar arrangements. The foreign exchange, capital, and bullion markets of the world take care of all the balancing requirements with complete efficiency. A balance of payments between any pair of countries operating normally is a purely academic hypothesis.

Actually, it is important to note that when the Second World War broke out in 1939 Argentina's trade was not rigidly bilateral, except possibly to a certain extent with Great Britain, Italy, Spain, and Japan. Several of the most important countries with which Argentina traded, including the United States, Belgium, the Netherlands, Brazil, and Scandinavia, did not favor such a channelized system. The payments agreements with some were relatively harmless in practice, since they provided merely that exchange at the official rate would be made available to them up to the amount of their purchases in Argentina. This did not mean that the accounts had to balance. It left the road open to those countries to sell as much as they could, within certain limits, and did not obligate Argentina to buy that amount of goods. The burden was on the other countries to try to sell that much to Argentine importers. Frequently they did not do so, because they could not. The excess exchange then was available to Argentina to sell in either the official or the free market. That was as it should be.

The United States cannot accept the Roca-Runciman formula as being permanently applicable to American trade in Argentina because the United States knows, and informed Argentines know, that the natural Argentine market for American products is larger than the natural American market for Argentine products, just as the reverse is true of Argentine-British trade and Argentine-Brazilian trade, to cite only two examples.

It is often said that it is not proper for a rich creditor country such as the United States to "drain" funds from a smaller typical debtor country such as Argentina. Argentines and others who hold this view are laboring under a serious misconception of the whole nature and purpose of international finance. The capital transactions between the United States and Argentina are largely unrelated to trade. United States citizens are in the position of being stockholders in Argentina, Inc. They have bought its stocks and bonds because it has been reported to be a successful, going concern, and they expect a dividend on their investment. If no return is forthcoming, they will invest elsewhere. Their interests are entirely separate from and generally not associated with the interests of American exporters.

The American exporters have a completely different problem. They are supplying Argentina with needed merchandise at acceptable prices and under acceptable terms. Argentine citizens need these products. Argentine exporters are doing precisely the same thing wherever they can in countries abroad. They frequently sell to countries which are not capable of supplying Argentina with what it needs. No matter. Those countries in turn sell their products to other countries which need what they have to sell. The more widespread and general the system of equality of treatment becomes, the more smoothly these natural and profitable relationships operate. The United States is not draining Argentina any more than Brazil is draining the United States. American investors in Argentine business and in Argentine government are merely drawing their fair share in the profits of Argentina, Inc. If Argentina were not a going concern showing an attractive gross profit, Americans would not invest in it and Argentina would lose its credit standing and all the advantages for the development of its productive capacities which that implies.

It probably is no exaggeration to say that for every dollar that the United States has withdrawn from Argentina, anywhere from two to five dollars has accrued to Argentina in the form of trade profits. Is this draining Argentina? It would be just as proper for the directors of the United States Steel Corporation to complain that all the profits were not going into their own pockets because the stockholders were continuing to draw dividends. The fact that Argentina also happens to be a buyer of American goods is intrinsically unrelated to the finance question and should not be confused with it. Argentina's affairs balance themselves out in a larger arena.

Exchange balances created by certain European countries would certainly not be used to pay for imports from the United States if those countries were able to supply Argentina with what it needs. The idea that a country has a sacred right to such exchange is a pernicious one that has been successfully exploited by certain European countries but which has no basis in economic fact or common sense. The world contains realities and realities. There are the realities of the German barter system and such doubtful treaties as the Roca-Runciman pact, and there are the realities of normal international trade as still carried on by a large number of responsible countries. Who shall say that the former are more compelling than the latter and that the United States must therefore adjust itself to them?

It is not the responsibility of either the United States or Argentina to worry about balancing their merchandise account; it does not need to be balanced. The notion that it must be is at once a bugaboo, a red herring, and a publicist's weapon. Argentina, with its excellent productive capacity, is well able in most years to sell sufficient produce in world markets to pay for all its imports, with plenty to spare for all other cash transfers. If its imports begin getting out of hand over a long period it can increase the exchange rate or restrict certain classes of imports. But such restrictions obviously cannot be effective in the long run unless they are made applicable to all suppliers.

Once the country has its trade policy on a sound footing and the world's capital markets have confidence in its ultimate soundness and permanent credit-worthiness, loans and investments will flow into Argentina as a matter of course. No special agreements are necessary for this purpose. Clearly, it would be foolish in the long run for Argentina to buy from the United States with American loans what it could not pay for with its world trade. Money should be lent to Argentina to increase productive capacity or to tide it over temporary difficulties, but not to perpetuate a false economic doctrine and a system that is condemned by business, both large and small.

Argentina never could succeed in arranging for bilateral balancing with all the countries with which it trades. Therefore, it should not attempt it with any countries. Argentina's whole prosperity and credit position has been founded on its ability to sell more to the world than it buys, and in order for this to hold true there must be ample elasticity. The country could not possibly bind itself all around in such rigid bilateral arrangements as the type concluded with Italy on June 1, 1939. This agreement, apparently, was only an expedient which was forced upon Argentina by Italy's desperate necessities. Argentina should want to get away from this sort of thing and toward a free system such as is advocated by the United States trade agreements program.

American co-operation with Argentina is conditioned by the fact that Argentina's dual problem, in peace and war, is to keep its exports moving and maintain its income so that it can remain solvent. Therefore, any effort toward continental solidarity during wartime requires that the United States co-operate in the solution of this problem. But American co-operation, if it is to be successful and not create new problems as serious as the one it seeks to solve, must be in the realm of trade rather than in that of finance. In normal times, between 35 and 40 per cent of Argentina's exports go to Germany, Scandinavia, the Low Countries, and the Mediterranean countries, excluding Spain. At the outbreak of the Second World War, this trade was completely cut off by the British blockade, posing a problem that could not be solved by lending money to Argentina.

All Latin American governments, including Argentina's, look to foreign loans as quick and easy solutions of their economic difficulties. Such loans appeal to the Latin temperament because they postpone the final and disagreeable reckoning until *mañana*, which in this case is the next generation. Argentina has one of the highest gold reserves in the world, but since the scare of 1928–29, when the very existence of the reserve was threatened by the world crisis, Argentina considers its gold untouchable and would much rather borrow money abroad than allow any of the gold to leave the country. Not only do such loans fail to solve anything, but at least 50 per cent of Argentina's ill will toward the United States in the 1930's was traceable to the inevitable debtor vindictiveness toward the creditor.

When the Second World War began, the men at the head of the Argentine government were fully prepared to take full advantage of Uncle Sam's paternalistic attitude toward the countries of Latin America and his fear of totalitarian inroads in the Western Hemisphere. They were confident that the United States could be depended upon to make political loans. Their surmise proved correct, for political loans of $110,-000,000 were made to Argentina, but the Argentine Congress refused to ratify the contracts.

Instead of making political loans to South America, it would be much better economics and much better politics for the United States to suspend the tariff on most Argentine products during wartime. France has provided the world with an excellent example of the failure of the policy of lending money to countries to keep them in line politically. During the twenty years between the end of the First World War and the beginning of the second one the French government poured billions of francs of its people's savings into Poland, Rumania, Czechoslovakia, and Yugoslavia to maintain them as bulwarks against Germany. And what happened? These subsidized countries were the first to fall. A country must remain solvent by its own efforts and its own trade, otherwise it loses its self-respect, its strength, and its moral fiber. A subsidized Argentina would become corrupt and fall eventual prey to the totalitarian powers much more certainly than if the attempt to buy the country had never been made.

When United States industry is on a war footing it needs so many raw materials of all kinds that the domestic production has to be supplemented by imports. There is little possibility that under war conditions increased imports from Argentina and other Latin American countries would hurt United States raw commodity prices, even if all import duties were eliminated. The cue of the United States would therefore seem to be to suspend the tariff on all Latin American imports except cereals, fruits, fats, meat, and dairy products, of which the United States already has a surplus production. Such a step would, without affecting United States prices, put enormously increased income into the hands of the Latin American people, and this bolstering of their purchasing power would enable these countries to continue importing from the United States to keep their industries going and would help them (especially Argentina) to keep up their payments on their foreign loans.

Such a policy would be infinitely wiser than making loans that could not be repaid later except by sacrificing the interests of American trade or by the United States accepting compensated or barter European currencies, redeemable only in useless or worthless merchandise. If Argentine export commodities are allowed to be dammed up by war and blockade, the end of any war will mean a tremendous flow of Argentine exports to European countries which will be unable to pay for them except in barter currencies. This will force Argentina to exclude American products from the Argentine market because Argentina cannot absorb both American and European goods in large volume except during short periods of readjustment.

Temporary wartime suspension of the American tariff would cause an immediate increase in Argentina's exports to the United States of linseed, wool, hides, skin, canned meats, casein, quebracho (for tanning purposes), etc., without injuring American farmers and producers. The only Argentine commodities on which the tariff need be retained are wheat, corn, fruits, fats, and dairy products.

Argentina, like other Latin American countries, is tempted to ask for loans whenever any emergency arises because it is the easiest way out. But what Argentina really needs is every possible trade facility, including the suspension of the American tariff, plus shipping and transportation assistance. Also, it needs for its industries short-term credits, which are, of course, a completely different kind of loan from the long-term political loans made to governments. Argentina needs to build as rapidly as she can all kinds of industries, such as oil-seed crushing, wool and cotton spinning and weaving, tanning, chemicals, metal smelting and refining, canning, cosmetics, pharmaceuticals, perfumes, clothing, hats, shoes, etc. Some of these industries have already been considerably developed, but require expansion as rapidly as possible, and for this machinery and credits are needed. Also, the United States could co-operate very effectively by helping Argentina to stimulate the production of agricultural products that would not be competitive with those of the United States and which could therefore be exported to the American market.

Argentina has plentiful reserves to weather a financial storm. What it does not have is plentiful foreign exchange, and the only way the United States can help Argentina solve that problem is to open the

American market to Argentine products during any world war emergency which may arise. The market can always be closed again to protect American agricultural interests after the emergency is over, if actual experience shows that such a step is necessary.

Another way in which the United States could collaborate with Argentina to the advantage of both countries would be to encourage the formation of regional groups among the South American republics similar to the River Plate Regional Conference which met at Montevideo in 1940. This is a development in which Argentina is keenly interested and it offers one of the most practical means of strengthening the South American economy. During the negotiation of the Argentine-American trade agreement in October 1941, the Argentine representatives informed the United States negotiators that the Argentine government intends to promote the development of reciprocal trade among the American republics, especially with those which are contiguous, and to improve the internal economic conditions through the encouragement of domestic and foreign investments in new industries which would be adapted to the resources and possibilities of each country. The American representatives also were informed that Argentina plans to promote tariff reductions between itself and contiguous countries with a view to the gradual and ultimate achievement of a customs union among such countries.

Since there is an immense body of public opinion in Argentina in favor of the establishment of a customs union of the American nations, anything that is done in this direction is bound to be beneficial to all concerned. Helping such a move would be one of the best defense measures that the United States could take. The Argentine and Brazilian ministers of finance worked out the bases for such an arrangement in 1941 and submitted them for the consideration of their respective governments.

Membership in the regional groups would be determined by geographical factors, such as their situation in the same river basin or their separation from other countries by the same mountain range, etc. The River Plate Regional Conference at Montevideo proved that it is fairly simple for representatives of four or five adjacent countries having some common geographical relationship to sit around a conference table and solve their joint problems. These include tariffs, navigation and rail communications, uniform consular practices and fees, methods for increasing the flow of trade among members of the group, and the suppression of smuggling across their frontiers.

Experience has proved that it is practically impossible to work out continental solutions of such problems at Pan-American conferences of twenty-one nations, some of which have no contact with and no interest in some of the others. In order to hold the Pan-American Union together it is imperative to get unanimous consent on all really important projects. This means reducing them to the lowest common denominator acceptable to everyone. And this usually means that by the time the project is ready for signature everything that would have made it work has been removed.

As soon as the several regional groups in South America have worked out local solutions of their problems, it will be much easier to dovetail these groups and their group machinery into a strong continental union, especially as some of the countries will belong to more than one regional group. Bolivia, for example, will belong to the River Plate group, the Amazon group, and the Pacific group. Brazil will belong to both the River Plate group and the Amazon group.

Argentina believes that these regional groups offer the most practical means of carrying out the objectives of the Inter-American Financial and Economic Advisory Committee that was set up by the Panama Conference of Foreign Ministers. This committee proposes to develop and co-ordinate production among the South American countries, especially of raw materials, and to find capital for new industries. It will endeavor to persuade each country to produce what it can produce cheapest and to trade with its neighbors for what they can produce cheapest. One of the troubles in South America is that production is too highly specialized, thus making the economy weak. The successful operation of this project would strengthen South America economically by widening the range of products and increasing inter-American trade. The idea has been welcomed by Argentina and other South American countries because they see in a stronger union among themselves the best protective measure against economic and political absorption by the United States, which they fear more than they do invasion from Europe.

The United States should help Argentina and the other South American nations to become economically stronger, thus raising their standard of living. The whole problem of the South American relations of the United States, and more especially the relations with Argentina, is an economic one, and when it has been solved the political and cultural relations will take care of themselves. The very satisfactory relations which have always existed between Argentina and Great Britain, in spite of the British occupation of the Falkland Islands, proves that the satisfaction arising from profitable economic relations is strong enough to overcome the friction of unsettled political differences. In the case of the United States, Brazil offers the outstanding example in South America of the fact that the buying of goods creates closer friendship than the lending of money. Brazil always has had a large favorable trade balance with the United States and always has been free to spend that balance wherever it desires. It spends most of it in Argentina and Great Britain.

This problem of the trade relations between the United States and Argentina is not an easy one to solve. But it is a test of the ability of the United States to conduct itself as a world power and to handle the difficulties that arise from its foreign relationships. In nearly all the South American republics, and especially in Argentina, the solution lies in the willingness of the United States to help its southern neighbors develop new products which it can use or to increase the production of materials which it has been buying elsewhere. In Argentina, where the agricultural production competes directly with that of the United States, the indicated solution is to assist Argentina in developing its almost non-existent trade relations with other South American countries which can consume the goods which the United States cannot take.

Buenos Aires is the natural point of contact for any steps in this direction because the Argentine capital already is the seat of a permanent office set up by the River Plate Regional Conference to watch over the operation of regional agreements, conduct studies, and report on measures for keeping the regional group alive as a vital, functioning organization. The preamble of the convention establishing this permanent office sets forth that it is to co-ordinate its activities with those of the Pan-American Union, the International Labor Office, and the Inter-American Economic and Financial Advisory Committee. An Argentine spokesman explained at the time that the idea in setting up the regional office was to have it look after the regional interests in a more intensive manner than was possible on the part of the Pan-American Union, but to co-operate closely with the Union rather than set up an antagonistic organization.

The need for stimulating new currents of trade among the American nations has been making itself felt for several years. Those who favor such a move maintain that it would be a mistake to undertake to create such inter-American trade solely as a transitory measure for the duration of any war. They argue that the reasons which favor such a move would continue to exist after the war terminated and perhaps be even stronger than during hostilities. But, if the truth were told, it would not require war or other artificial stimulation for intracontinental trade to reach surprising proportions. It requires only the removal of the existing trade barriers, particularly the high protective tariffs which have been created in all the countries, including the United States, to satisfy certain private interests, without considering the great general damage which they cause.

Co-operation between the United States, Argentina, and the other South American countries should be undertaken with the idea of making that co-operation permanent. The facilities granted by any republic to another should be made available to all. The help of the United States in developing new industries should be extended with only one proviso —that the new industries must not be artificial ones which require protective tariffs, for that would simply aggravate the already existing trouble. The new industries should be normal, natural ones. The field of possibilities is almost unlimited.

One of the richest of these new possibilities lies in the field of mining, a field that has hardly been scratched. The Andean range and several other regions of Argentina are rich in metals and other minerals. Extensive iron deposits have been discovered recently in La Rioja Province. During 1941, 110,708 metric tons of metals were produced with a total value of 27,206,000 pesos ($6,529,440), according to the annual report of the Bureau of Mines and Geology, tungsten and wolfram being the two principal products. Argentina's total production of mineral products during 1941, including petroleum and other non-metallic products, was 11,534,944 metric tons with a total value of 183,051,000 pesos ($43,-932,240).

The economic position of the United States toward Latin America as a whole is sound. The United States buys more in goods and services than it sells, thereby producing more dollar exchange than is required by the Latin American countries to pay for their purchases in the United States. This economic position is strongest in the northern part of the continent and weakens as it moves southward until it reaches its weakest point in Argentina, where the United States in normal times sells a great deal more than it buys. It is no mere coincidence that Argentina is the weakest and most dangerous point in the whole Latin American policy of the United States, including hemisphere defense.

In the northern part of the South American continent, embracing Colombia, Venezuela, and Brazil, the United States takes from 35 to 50 per cent of the total exports. In the southern part of the continent, embracing Chile, Argentina, and Uruguay, the United States buys only from 20 to 25 per cent of the export production, and sometimes it falls as low as 15 per cent.

Argentina already has enough foreign debts which it must repay in the years to come. What it needs most of all is bigger and better markets. If the United States cannot find a way to fill that need, the totalitarian countries will, and no amount of political loans will make any difference, except that they will render it more difficult for American exporters to sell in the Argentine market because the service charges on such loans will deprive Argentina of just that much money which it might otherwise use for the payment of imports. The loss of American trade in Argentina will mean the loss of American prestige, because it is trade and influence, not money, that gives prestige in international relations.

28. WHERE IS ARGENTINA GOING?

ARGENTINA shifted from a pastoral to an agricultural economy at the turn of the century. Nearly 5,000,000 immigrants had entered the country during the fifty years from 1865 to 1914. Many of them were golondrina harvest hands who, like the swallows which gave them their name, came and went with the seasons. But more than half of them remained, mainly as grain-growers, and the cultivated area, which had been only 373 square miles in 1865, increased 250 times. Argentina ceased living by hunting wild cattle and developed into one of the greatest agricultural countries in the world. During the next forty years from 1900 to 1940 the country grew and progressed at an almost dizzy rate. But this development was confined nearly exclusively to the pampas and the cities on the rivers Paraná and Uruguay, with the great capital of Buenos Aires literally sucking the lifeblood out of the whole country.

At the beginning of the Second World War, one of Argentina's most pressing needs was population. Practically all the serious problems—political, economic, and social—could be solved by doubling or, better still, trebling the population and distributing it intelligently throughout the sparsely settled territory. The most glaring of these problems in 1942 were a reactionary government of force in the hands of a minority party, an overspecialized agrarian economy with an almost helpless dependence on foreign markets, an unhealthy concentration of population in the cities, an exploited farming class that was not settled on the land it worked, a falling birth rate, and a high rate of illegitimacy and illiteracy.

The country's resources hardly have been tapped. Even the restricted area of the pampas could provide many times the amount of foodstuffs now being produced. During the ten years before the outbreak of war the government was encouraging the widespread cultivation of cotton as a new export crop and there are many other ways in which Argentina could strengthen her economic position in the world without ever getting beyond the stage of agricultural and pastoral pursuits. The country easily could support a much larger population. Some authorities mention 25,000,000 as the number that could be accommodated comfortably; others place the figure as high as 70,000,000.

The wise immigration policy during the half-century following the establishment of constitutional government not only transformed the population; it changed the pampas from a shambles of rotting carcasses, from which the hides and horns had been removed, to one of the world's greatest gardens of wheat, linseed, and other grains. But it also made democracy possible during the fourteen years from 1916 to 1930. Consequently, one of the first acts of the Conservatives after their successful revolution of 1930 was to halt immigration. No one knows better than the oligarchy of landowners that, if Argentina had a population of 40,000,000, the country would not put up with the kind of government which they give it.

Much as the country needs population, it is certain that as long as the Conservatives are in power the government will not revert to the former system of virtually free entry of immigrants. Irigoyen's democratic party, the Unión Cívica Radical, got its support from the masses and in many cases encouraged immigration for purely political reasons. Since labor was not organized at the time of the 1930 revolution, there was almost no opposition to immigration as a threat to the wage level. Immigration was stopped because the Conservatives did not want to add further to the majority which was in opposition to them. They did want, however, to increase the size of the middle class by the creation of a "farm-owner" group which never has existed in Argentina. Such a group would tend to offset the growing labor class which is concentrated in Buenos Aires and which eventually must organize and become an important factor in politics.

After the economic depression of 1929–30, Argentina began developing a highly protected industry in an effort to free itself from the disadvantage of a purely agricultural economy. But in 1942 the country still remained essentially agricultural and pastoral. During the ten years preceding the outbreak of the war, agricultural and pastoral products comprised 90 per cent of the exports, with grain representing an average of 55 per cent of the total, and animal products 35 per cent. The investment in agriculture and grazing was still six times the amount invested in industry, being estimated at $8,500,000,000, as compared with the $1,430,000,000 invested in industry, as shown by the industrial census of 1935. The agrarian investment is an Argentine investment, whereas most of the industrial investment is foreign. Consequently, agriculture and the cattle business are likely to have an important political advantage over industry at any time that their interests may conflict. Furthermore, in spite of the rapid growth of the towns and cities, agriculture still remains a nation-wide interest to a far greater extent than it ever has in the United States, where the farmer always has represented a distinct and segregated section of the population.

The Conservatives are opposed to a further influx of southern Europeans because they fear a spread of the various "isms" which are associated with Europe. They would like to attract farmers with some capital from northern European countries such as Denmark, Holland, and Switzerland, with which to create the "farm owner" class. Unfortunately, rural life in Argentina is not likely to attract this type of European settler. The present system of land tenure based on large estates with tenant farmers working the soil on short leases is difficult to overcome, and there is little privately owned agricultural land available for sale to small farmers. Aside from this difficulty, northern Europeans, being accustomed to a fair standard of living, could not compete with the Spanish and Italian sharecroppers, whose standard of living is very low because of their background and lack of education.

Any future attempt to encourage the immigration of agricultural population must face the important fact that the population as constituted in 1942 was an optimum population for the economical production of agricultural commodities to compete in the world's export markets. If the number of grain farms is increased, it must come either from a decrease in the size of the farms or from bringing under cultivation land now under pasture. In the former case, the costs of production will increase; in the latter, there will be overproduction.

Doubling the population and, consequently, the consuming capacity of the country would remove this threat of overproduction. Also, it would solve the meat problem by making Argentina independent of the British market. Doubling the population would mean a rapid development of both commerce and industry, and much of the production which now has to be exported would be consumed locally. Doubling the population would tend to create new centers of activity outside of Buenos Aires and to develop new sources of wealth, such as mining, industries, and production of agricultural commodities other than grain.

The great industrial power of the United States lies in the fact that it has an internal market of 130,000,000 consumers. Argentina needs a much denser population before it can take the next step in national development and shift from an agricultural to an industrial economy. But vegetative growth is not sufficient to increase the population to the required density. Although better health has lowered the death rate, there

has been a constant decline in the birth rate, and in the late 1930's sociol-
ogists predicted that the population would begin to decline about 1960
if immigration is not renewed.

When the Conservatives closed the ports to immigration, they also
began an active campaign for a larger birth rate, with the obvious desire
of increasing the population as it was constituted in 1930. Unfortunately
for their dream, the birth rate cannot be forced under a democratic
form of government. This perfectly futile attempt to preserve the Argentine race and the national spirit as it was constituted on a fixed date
has been part of the narrow nationalism which has accompanied the
return of the Conservatives to power. They fear the effect of immigration on Argentine nationality, forgetting that Argentine nationality
has been built on immigration.

One of the first things that impresses a newcomer in Argentina is
the extent to which the various European nationalities have been assimilated. All speak Spanish. Even the newly arrived immigrants begin
to speak it at once. With the exception of the Russian settlements in
the provinces of Entre Rios and Buenos Aires, there are no colonies,
even in the rural districts, speaking their own language, as in Brazil,
Chile, and Peru. This is due on one hand to the concentration of the
population in Buenos Aires and on the other hand to the isolation of
the farm workers on the large estates. As the latter are nearly all tenant
farmers and move frequently, it is impossible for them to maintain
close or permanent contacts with their own people.

Not only do the foreigners speak Spanish, but they almost immediately become ardent Argentines. They are too appreciative of the freedom they enjoy in their new home to remain very loyal to their father-
lands. But, unfortunately for the Conservative elite, they also immediately become enthusiastic democrats.

Argentina undoubtedly will attract European settlers whenever the
authorities remove the restrictions from immigration. The country offers attractive possibilities for southern Europeans; the prospects for
northern Europeans are less certain. But as the Immigration Bureau of
the Department of Agriculture pointed out in one of its reports, "No
greater misfortune can be feared than the fact that our population may
stop at the present twelve million scattered over a territory of potential
wealth which can provide work and comfort for forty or fifty million
people, only out of agricultural work."

Extensive acreage and favorable climate have combined to give Argentina an enormous agricultural production with a comparatively small rural population. The care of 10,000 head of cattle which are being raised in Argentina only for their meat, hides, etc., requires only 15 or 20 men, whereas in Germany, France, Belgium, and Great Britain, where cattle also are raised for dairy products, it requires 1000 persons to look after 10,000 head. In Argentina a family of three or four working persons can cultivate 500 acres of land and produce 180 tons of wheat. In the European countries cited, the work of 12 or 16 persons is required for the same production. Argentina's 3,300,000 rural inhabitants produce as much as 14,000,000 people engaged in agriculture and cattle-raising in Europe. While this gives Argentina an envied position of privilege as an agrarian producer, it obviously is not a healthy situation that the rural population should show no increase during a quarter of a century in which the urban population doubled. The rural population actually decreased by a quarter of a million in the eight years from 1930 to 1938 as farmers and their families drifted to the cities in search of better living conditions and educational facilities for the children. But city dwellers experienced no urge to try life in the great open spaces.

The concentration of nearly 70 per cent of the population in the cities, however, has been an important element in the rapid growth of secondary industries, as it creates a uniformity in demand and lowers the costs of distribution. These new manufacturing industries are confined largely to the city of Buenos Aires and have been developed by artificial protection in the form of the government's tariff policy and control of foreign exchange operations. The number of people engaged in industries more than doubled from 1914 to 1940, when they totaled 2,770,000 and represented 48 per cent of the 5,730,000 persons gainfully employed throughout the country. Likewise, the number of people engaged in business doubled during the same period to 750,000, which was 13 per cent of the total.

Government expenditures—national, provincial, and municipal—totaled 603,000,000 pesos in 1914. By 1940 they had more than trebled, and totaled nearly 2,000,000,000 pesos. The 1914 government expenditures represented 15 per cent of the national production; the 1940 expenditures were 31 per cent of the production. This tremendous increase of government spending was distributed almost entirely in the cities, much of it going as salaries to the rapidly growing army of government clerks who live in the cities and larger towns. These employees were one of the forces being created by the Conservatives to counteract the voting strength of the democratic masses. Their expenditures, in turn, have tended to develop the towns and cities rather than the rural districts.

This continued neglect of the rural districts has produced some of Argentina's most serious social problems. The Province of Santiago del Estero, for example, with its population of 462,000, gives almost as many new babies to the nation every year as does the city of Buenos Aires, with five times the population. But 38½ per cent of the babies born in Santiago del Estero are illegitimate. The Argentine statistician Alejandro E. Bunge, in his book *Una Nueva Argentina* and in articles published in *La Nación* and *La Prensa*, points out that the rate of illegitimacy is on the increase, while the birth rate itself is declining. The rate of illegitimate births in the city of Buenos Aires is 12 per cent and it reaches 43, 44, and 46 per cent in the provinces of Tucumán, Salta, and Jujuy, respectively. In several of the national territories more than half the births are illegitimate, and in the Territory of Formosa the rate is 66 per cent. The rate for the country at large was 28 per cent in 1938. With the exception of the other South American nations, this is one of the highest rates in the world and compares with 2 per cent of the white population in the United States, 3.7 per cent in Canada, 5.7 per cent in Japan, 7 per cent in France, 4.4 per cent in Great Britain, and 6 per cent in Norway, as reported to the League of Nations.

This high rate of illegitimacy is one of Argentina's most serious social problems. The people of Buenos Aires always have been inclined to shrug their shoulders and dismiss the difficulty as being beyond remedy because of the ignorance of the people in the interior. But Dionisio Caravias Vera, in a study published in *La Nación* on October 31, 1940, showed that there has been a similar increase in the illegitimate births in the city of Buenos Aires, where the rate rose steadily from 10.6 per cent in 1935 to 12.1 per cent in 1939. This is another of the difficulties that undoubtedly could be solved, or at least ameliorated, by increasing the population and raising the standard of civilization in the outlying districts. Increasing the population and making it possible for farm workers to own the land they cultivate would tend to create a family society on the land instead of the present one of frustrated, wandering men who leave the women and children behind them as they move unhappily from place to place.

The statistical bureau of the National Labor Office (Departamento Nacional del Trabajo) has become an excellent laboratory for the study of the country's economic and social problems. It carries on a constant study of the cost of living as compared with wages, providing the statistical basis without which it would be impossible to correct the problems. Wages are incredibly low. Skilled mechanics earn the equivalent of 30 cents an hour; printers, 38 cents; laborers, 14 cents; cotton textile workers, 13 cents; and woolen textile workers 28 cents. Semi-skilled workers earn from 125 to 150 pesos a month ($30–$36). Laborers get less than 100 pesos ($24) and skilled workers something more than 200 pesos. Census data on 113,922 peons show that three-fourths of them earn from 25 to 100 pesos a month, with an average of 50 pesos ($12).

An investigation of workmen's living conditions in 1936 showed that the average workman's family in the city of Buenos Aires is composed of a man and his wife, with three children under fourteen years of age; that the average wage is 127.26 pesos ($30.54) a month; and that this family lives in one room 12 by 13½ feet, for which the rent is 30.92 pesos, or one-fourth of the family income. The room opens onto a patio, but has no garden, balcony, or terrace, the only source of light and ventilation being the door that opens onto the patio. Sometimes this door has a transom. The family shares with other tenants the use of a kitchen, water closet, and shower bath, but there is no tub bath. Of the 3000 cases studied, 59 per cent lived in one room, 30 per cent in two rooms, 8 per cent in three rooms, and 3 per cent in four rooms.

In reporting its findings, the Labor Office was careful to emphasize that its study did not indicate that five persons could live on 127 pesos a month; that it indicated only how they have to live when that is all the money at their disposal. A typical budget for this family provided 56 per cent for food, 21 per cent for housing, 10 per cent for clothing, 8 per cent for general expenses, 5 per cent for fuel and cleaning. But this typical budget provided 164.19 pesos as the minimum cost at which the family could live, leaving a deficit of 36.93 pesos, or 22½ per cent, "which must be covered by other means" than the father's wages.

The industrial census of 1935 showed that of 472,152 laborers employed in industry 216,080 worked in the city of Buenos Aires. The census also showed that their average wage was 110 pesos a month, not 127. The Buenos Aires newspaper *Noticias Graficas* on September 14, 1940, reported that 500,000 families throughout the country live in one room, pointing out that this crowding is as prejudicial to health as it is to morals.

During the twenty years following 1922 there was a constant increase in professional and intellectual unemployment. Physicians, lawyers, and teachers were finding it more and more difficult to find employment in

CONGRESS BUILDING FACING THE PLAZÀ DEL CONGRESO,
BUENOS AIRES

THE CIVIC LEGION, ARGENTINA'S STORM TROOPERS, MARCHING
IN A NATIONALIST DEMONSTRATION IN BUENOS AIRES

LAKE LACAR IN THE ANDES

AERIAL VIEW OF BUENOS AIRES

line with their intellectual preparation, indicating that the professions were overcrowded. Also, a large number of young men and women who had completed their secondary education, but without specializing, were unable to fit themselves into positions in keeping with their education and aspirations. Nevertheless, industrial establishments were continually petitioning the immigration authorities to permit the entry of foreign experts because they could not find experts in the country. Argentina aspires to a gradual but constant industrial evolution which she hopes eventually will free her from dependence on imports. If she is determined to maintain the restrictions against immigration, she will have to prepare industrial technicians and educate young men and women for activities in which they can make careers for themselves.

Education is more highly developed in Argentina than anywhere else in South America. There are 14,000 institutions of higher learning, including 24 universities, and more than 300,000,000 pesos ($72,000,000) are spent annually on education. But this public instruction has not been organized to meet the country's practical needs. The universities turn out hundreds of new physicians, lawyers, civil engineers, and doctors of literature every year, but not enough economists, industrialists, and technicians trained to make a living by developing the country's almost untapped natural resources.

In education, as in other activities, there still is too much concentration in the larger cities and too much neglect of the interior. When all the young men who have reached the age of eighteen are registered for military service every year it is found that those provinces which report the highest rates of illegitimate births also report the highest illiteracy. While the rate of illiteracy in Buenos Aires is only 2 per cent, it is 39 per cent in the Province of Corrientes, 37 per cent in Santiago del Estero, and 35 per cent in Mendoza. Military authorities report the rate for the country at large to be 18 per cent. They also report a steady increase year by year both in the illiteracy of the conscripts and in the physical incapacity of the youths who are called up for registration.

Argentina's social laws are not on a par with the country's economic progress. Labor unions are not recognized by law and there is no law regarding collective contracts between employers and labor organizations. The general movement toward the organization of labor is indicated, however, by the increase in the number of union members from 270,000 in 1936 to 437,000 in 1940. Of the latter figures, 270,230 were enrolled in the Confederación General de Trabajo (General Federation of Labor), 27,000 in the Unión Sindical Argentina, 18,500 in the Catholic unions, and 121,000 in autonomous unions which are not associated with the federations. As this membership is nowhere near the total number of people employed in industry and as the membership of the General Federation includes several thousand longshoremen and transport workers not included among the industrial workers, it is apparent that industry has just begun to be unionized. But labor is one of the strongest democratic forces in the country and as it becomes more efficiently organized it will become an increasingly active instrument of opposition to the Conservatives.

Any attempt to study these political, economic, and social conditions in 1942 immediately posed the questions: "Where is Argentina going? Is she capable of stable government? Can the aristocratic pride of the porteños and their feeling of superiority over the numerically superior criollos be eradicated to permit a truly democratic government?"

All the answers lay hidden in the historical fact that the revolution of September 1930 turned back the hands of Argentina's clock to 1890, suppressed democracy, and put the reactionary Conservatives back into power. The political set-up in 1942 was almost identical with the one which led to the organization of the Unión Cívica Radical and the constant revolt of the masses until President Saenz Peña gave them effective democracy by means of the secret ballot. Again, the Conservative minority was keeping itself in office by electoral frauds. Again, the country was being ruled by the 2000 families of landowners. Since these landowners considered themselves to be especially endowed by Heaven and their wealth to rule over the majority, the one most certain fact in the situation was that, as in 1890, democracy could not be achieved except by revolution. But in 1942 the democratic forces had no Leandro Além or Hipólito Irigoyen to lead them. All the indications were that the country was in for a long period of Conservative rule.

The Conservatives were much concerned over the country's economic problems and were endeavoring to solve them by creating new markets among the other American nations. It seemed probable that these efforts would meet with considerable success. It was doubtful, however, that any effective steps would be taken toward solving the social problems, since those problems were the direct consequence of the long period of Conservative rule before 1916. It always has suited the Conservatives to keep the people of the interior ignorant and suppressed and so prevent the formation of that educated public opinion which is so vital to the efficient operation of democracy.

But the masses in Argentina have known real political freedom. They have fought and suffered for democracy in a way that never was necessary in the United States, where democracy is taken for granted. Having achieved political independence once, it seemed doubtful that they would remain passive under the Conservative rule they once had overthrown. The eventual outcome seemed to depend largely on whether democracy or fascism would win the war.

29. WHY ARGENTINA IS PRO-FASCIST

WHEN the United States entered the Second World War, Argentina's attitude toward that conflict was identical with that of the American isolationists who until the Japanese attack on Pearl Harbor had argued that it was Great Britain's war and so did not concern the United States. Argentines readily saw the dire consequence which an Axis victory in Europe and Asia would have on the world position of the United States. But the men who were in control of the government at Buenos Aires did not believe that Argentina would suffer similarly from an Axis victory. On the contrary, they were firmly convinced that the victory of Germany in Europe would be beneficial to their country.

Since Argentina is dependent on European markets for the disposal of her raw materials, many Argentines honestly believed that a totalitarian trade empire in Europe under Hitler would offer them greater prosperity than they had been able to achieve under the democratic system of free competition in world markets. This attitude was a tribute to the effectiveness of German diplomacy, which had succeeded in making the Argentines believe its side of the story.

Argentines are accustomed to looking at world affairs as observers but not as participants. They have much information, but feel no sense of responsibility in world affairs. Here again they resembled the isolationists of the United States.

It is a widely acknowledged truism that allies are held together in war by their common hatred of the enemy rather than by their love for one another. Argentina not only did not love the United States; she did not share the American hatred of the totalitarian powers and what they stood for. Moreover, the reactionary Conservative class which had seized the government by revolution in 1930 and was holding it by force against a much superior democratic majority did not want democracy in Argentina and was doing everything possible to prevent its revival. The defeat of the democracies in the war against the Axis powers would greatly strengthen the position of this class, since the pseudo-Fascist regime which it desired to impose upon the country would fit much better into a totalitarian world than into a democratic one.

The question naturally arises: "What is behind this pro-Fascist attitude?"

The Argentine Republic was built by a middle class population which gave the country its juridical and social structure and consolidated its democratic institutions. Just when this had been accomplished, about 1890, Argentina began its era of great export trade in meats and wheat to Europe. This middle class improved its condition so rapidly that almost overnight it became a great aristocracy of wealth. With its wealth, it became an exploiter of the masses. The fourteen-year experiment in democracy from 1916 to 1930 convinced this class that democracy means the end of its control of the country. Consequently, it welcomes fascism as a way of retaining its position of privilege. But, as already related in Chapter XVI, this fascism, if it comes, will be a pseudo-fascism designed to keep the wealthy landed class in power at the expense of the masses, rather than to abolish all class distinctions, as fascism attempts to do in Europe.

This class conflict in Argentina dates clear back to colonial times when the Spanish government made vast grants of land to the court favorites. Many of these landed properties have remained in the hands of the same families down to the present. After the wars of independence, the Buenos Aires governments rewarded army officers with large grants of land that were measured by leagues (nine square miles) instead of by acres. Some of these estates contain 1,000,000 acres or more, and it is not unusual for ten or twelve large estates to be in the hands of one family. Of the nation's total area of 691,552,000 acres, 10 per cent is under cultivation and 45 per cent devoted to grazing, a total of 379,500,000 acres. Fifteen families own 8,620,000 acres, or 1¾ per cent of all the producing land. The agrarian census of 1937 showed 2072 holdings of more than 25,000 acres, with an aggregate of 134,316,000 acres and an average holding of 65,000 acres. Thus, approximately 2000 families own one-fifth (19.46 per cent) of the country. In the Queen Province of Buenos Aires, the most fertile and most prosperous of all the provinces, 230 families own 38½ per cent of the land, their average holdings being 46,000 acres.

These 2000 landowning families constitute the backbone of the Conservative Party and insist upon their right to rule the country's 13,000,-000 inhabitants. Obviously they could not exercise this right under a democratic form of government. The corporate form of the Fascist State offers exactly the pattern they need for insuring their permanence of control and for crushing for all time the political power of the masses. Hence their refusal to join the democracies in their efforts to crush fascism.

Whereas German national socialism and Russian communism are systems of revolution, fascism is a system of government. In the two revolutionary systems the State is merely a means toward larger revolutionary ends—racial in the case of nazism; economic in the case of communism. In fascism, however, control of the State is the ultimate objective. Therefore, fascism makes the strongest appeal to the wealthy landowners of South America and to the political "ins," both of whom are seeking a system of government that will guarantee their position of privilege against the ever-present threat of the poverty-stricken masses and the political "outs." By the time the Fascist State has been firmly established by revolution and force, all the dangers of democratic controls or changes in administration have been thoroughly eliminated and the clique in power is more secure than it ever could be under democracy. At the same time, wealth and privilege do not face the risks that would confront them under either the German or Russian systems.

Argentina's cattle barons and other conservatives seem really to believe that with a Fascist State established in Argentina and a New Order set up in Europe under Hitler, Argentina would be ideally situated.

One of the most reactionary members of this Conservative class in 1942 was the Acting President, Ramón S. Castillo, who had devoted his entire public life to fighting democracy. In the presidency he had surrounded himself with a group of pro-Fascist collaborators who were convinced that the Axis was going to win the war. Some of them fervently hoped for an Axis victory because they thought the defeat of the United States would enable Argentina to assume its rightful position of leadership in Latin American affairs, a position which they felt the United States had usurped.

The minister of foreign affairs, Enrique Ruiz Guiñazú, was an admirer of General Franco and as ambassador to the Vatican had lived in Rome and become convinced that fascism is a better way of life than democracy. He made himself internationally famous at the Rio de Janeiro conference of American foreign ministers by opposing any move by the American republics that might give offense to Germany, Italy, or Japan. He, too, was convinced that the United Nations could not win the war, even with the help of the United States. In this conviction he was strongly supported by the Nazi sympathizers among the army officers.

When the war broke out in Europe, 20 per cent of theArgentine army officers were rabidly pro-Nazi, according to government sources in Buenos Aires. Another 20 per cent were just as strongly democratic. The remaining 60 per cent were described as being "more interested in their stomachs than in politics." They waived other considerations in favor of the question of holding onto their rank, their seniority, and their right to a lifelong pension. Consequently, they followed whichever of the two political tendencies happened to be in the ascendancy. Under Castillo the Nazi clique was in control of the army.

The Japanese attack on Pearl Harbor and the entrance of the United States into the war were a great boon for Castillo. For several months he had been looking for some event to serve as justification for declaring a state of siege under which to squelch the democratic forces, which rapidly were getting out of hand. Nine days after the attack on Pearl Harbor, Castillo proclaimed a state of siege in order that the government might have power "to fulfill its international pledges" and to suppress "biased propaganda," according to the decree he issued.

Having assumed the dictatorial powers granted him under a state of siege, Castillo was able to prevent the democratic forces from discussing his refusal to join with the other American republics against the Axis powers, which was the most important point at issue in the elections of March 1, 1942. But to have declared a state of siege because of the local political situation would have put Castillo down in history as a dictator. By blaming the dictatorship on his earnest desire to comply with Argentina's inter-American pledges, as he did, he was able to forget those pledges completely and devote his attention to home politics, which he also did. The "biased propaganda" of the United Nations was crushed effectively. That of the Axis was permitted complete liberty on the ground that interference with it would be a violation of Argentina's neutrality in the war. It was a perfect set-up for Castillo's lifelong cynical political habit of pretending one thing while doing another.

Under his dictatorship Castillo immediately established that censorship which is so dear to all Argentine authorities, and blamed that, too, on the international situation. After being censored, letters were resealed with a sticker bearing the legend: "Opened by Censor. Continental Defense."

During the debate in the Senate on June 16, 1942, Senator Laurencena of Entre Rios charged that the real reason for the declaration of the state of siege was to restrict the activities of the government's political opponents and prevent the strengthening of organized labor. When Congress had convened in May, Castillo had prohibited the newspapers and radio stations from reporting congressional debates in which there was any discussion of the government's foreign policy.

One of Castillo's first dictatorial acts after putting the country under a state of siege was to prohibit several hundred rallies throughout the country at which Argentine democrats planned to declare their sympathy for the United Nations and to pay their homage to President Roosevelt as the world leader of the democratic cause. A message from President Roosevelt was to have been broadcast to the rallies. Even if Castillo's dictatorial regime were not attacked directly, any democratic rally or any homage to Roosevelt could not help but be an indirect reflection against his anti-democratic government, so he refused to let them take place. Again he hid his real motives behind the international situation and said such meetings would be a violation of neutrality. Yet the minister of foreign affairs openly supported anti-democratic rallies by attending them and by delivering orations in favor of Franco, according to declarations made in the Chamber of Deputies during the debate on June 10, 1942.

It probably was natural that the Argentines should want to be on the winning side of the war, and Castillo's position was strengthened considerably in the months immediately following the Rio de Janeiro conference, even among Argentines who were not pro-Fascist, by the failure of the United Nations to halt the Japanese offensive. It seemed fairly certain that until such time as the United Nations could make it apparent that the Axis was going to be defeated, the democracies could shout criticism at Castillo to their heart's content. His attitude toward the criticism of the other American nations was the same that it had been toward the students when he was dean of the law school and unconcernedly played with his watch chain while they were insulting him.

Castillo, however, did not represent the majority opinion of the country. The great mass of the Argentine people still were democratic, just as they always have been. They admired President Roosevelt, whom they considered the world's apostle of democracy. They admired the social policies of the New Deal because they believed they signified the end of the influence of wealth. They desired to co-operate with the people of the United States in the war because they believed that Americans were fighting for the same democratic ideals to which they aspire. But in 1942 the great mass of the Argentine people had no voice in the government. Castillo's guiding motive in declaring the state of siege had been to silence them and to curb their activities in favor of democracy.

Finally on June 24 President Ortiz sent his resignation to Congress, explaining that his physicians had decided that his diabetes made it impossible to attempt an operation to restore his sight. He said that he had not resigned sooner because as long as there had been any hope that he might be able to resume the presidency he felt that it was his duty to do so. Now that there was no such hope, it was his duty to resign the office he could not occupy. This action made Castillo the nineteenth constitutional President of the Argentine Nation until the expiration of Ortiz's term on February 20, 1944. Ortiz wrote a letter to Castillo saying that their differences over democracy and international policy had not affected in the slightest the high personal esteem in which he always had held the Vice-President.

By the time Ortiz resigned, Castillo's efforts to keep Argentina neutral were being made exceedingly difficult by the refusal of the Nazis to treat Argentina as a neutral. Buenos Aires had become the headquarters for German diplomacy, propaganda, and plotting in the western hemisphere; there was unrestricted telegraphic and telephonic communication between Buenos Aires and Berlin; and German banks in Buenos Aires were free to finance the Nazi machine throughout Latin America. Instead of taking jealous care of this enviable position which Castillo's foreign policy had given them, the Nazis torpedoed three Argentine steamers, sinking two of them with the loss of several Argentine lives. Furthermore they formally warned Argentina that any Argentine vessels entering the submarine blockade zone around the United States would be sunk on sight. Even Nazi admirers in Argentina considered this to be poor reward for their support. Argentina had risked the friendship of all the nations of the western world to maintain a friendly and co-operative policy toward Nazi Germany and so felt that she was not being unreasonable in expecting in return that she be treated as a neutral and permitted to sail the seas without having her vessels treated as belligerents.

On the day that Ortiz resigned, a mob of patriotic Argentines stoned the German Embassy, Congress demanded that Argentina comply with the obligations assumed at the Rio de Janeiro Conference and sever diplomatic relations with Germany, and the leading newspapers defined the restrictions of the state of siege and vigorously attacked Castillo's foreign policy, declaring that Argentine self-respect could no longer tolerate the repeated Nazi insults to the Argentine flag. Castillo, the ultraconservative, found himself in a position almost identical with that of Irigoyen, the arch-democrat, during the First World War when he defied both Congress and public opinion to keep Argentina neutral. But the failure of the Nazis to recognize the value of their position in Argentina and to co-operate with Castillo had aroused such widespread and violent revulsion against Castillo and his foreign policy that his position was much more difficult than Irigoyen's had been. Castillo and his pro-Fascist backers now had the government in their hands but were faced with a raging storm of public opposition that had not existed two years earlier when they were plotting to get Ortiz out of the way. There were many people in Argentina who believed that the Nazis themselves were providing the salvation of democracy in Argentina.

Although Castillo prided himself on being a criollo, he had allied himself in politics with the porteños, who always have insisted on the right of Buenos Aires to rule the country. Castillo's government in 1942 was inspired by the same political ideas that had inspired the unitarians of Buenos Aires to fight the federalists of the interior for fifty years after the revolt from Spain. The porteños and criollos were still at war, just as they have been all through the country's history. The heavy immigration from Europe during sixty years failed to decrease the distinction between criollos and porteños. The immigrants settled in the interior and immediately adopted the criollos' attitude toward Buenos Aires.

Juan Curuchaga Hernandez, writing in Argentina's most popular magazine, *El Hogar*, as recently as April 8, 1938, said:

I admit the truth of most of the charges which the provincials make against the porteños. It is true that the typical man of Buenos Aires feels too "high hat" because of the city's material splendor and is inclined to ignore and look down upon the rest of the republic. It is also true that this attitude arouses the resentment of the people of the interior.

He went on to explain that while the porteño was inclined to be overly proud and superior and to make fun of the people of the interior, he did not feel any hostility toward them. The criollos on the other hand, he said, made no attempt to hide their hostility toward the people of Buenos Aires and even put an inflection into the phrase "you porteños" which made it sound like an insult. It is high time, he said, that effective measures be taken to wipe out this hostility between the interior and the capital, but he did not make any suggestions as to what those measures should be.

The sparseness of the population in the interior and the unstable nature of the social structure in the more distant provinces are among the main reasons why federalism has not worked successfully in Argentina. Buenos Aires has managed to force a strongly centralized government upon the country in spite of the federalist Constitution, and the Presidents have assumed a tutelage over the provinces which the framers of the Constitution did not intend them to exercise. Between the framing of the Constitution and 1940 there were one hundred and thirty-five "interventions" in the provinces by the Buenos Aires governments, or an average of nearly two a year. This interference with the government of the provinces has prevented that civic development which comes only from political liberty and experimenting. Consequently, the provinces are far behind Buenos Aires in their political development. So the Conservatives favor reforming the Constitution to establish a centralized form of government—the old unitarian system they always have wanted. Acting President Castillo hinted at such a revision of the Constitution in his annual message opening Congress in May 1941, when he said:

Once our democracy was organized on the great model which was chosen by the builders of the Nation, it became necessary to run the risk of a strong Executive because up to that time anarchy in its various forms had constituted the predominating evil in America. The conversion of this regulating power into an instrument for the formation of legislative majorities has caused a visible deformation in our constitutional structure, a deformation which it is imperative to eradicate through the more moderate use of the executive faculties until the time arrives for the revision of the Constitution.

This was his alibi for refusing to intervene in several provinces where the election frauds had become a national scandal.

Whenever the Conservatives gain control of the number of provinces necessary to insure ratification of a new Constitution it is fairly certain that they will frame one designed to perpetuate their control of the government.

In their attitude toward the war the Conservatives had abandoned their best customer, Great Britain, and were supporting Germany, which never had bought more than a fifth or a sixth as much as Great Britain. This was because the Germans had succeeded in convincing the cattle barons and the wheat kings that as soon as the Führer had won the war and established the New Order in Europe, Argentina would not need the British market. Until the outbreak of the war, Argentina had belonged to Great Britain's trade empire, which embraced several areas outside the colonial empire. The Germans had convinced the Argentines that both these British empires were doomed. Furthermore, there had been a growing resentment against the British ever since the Ottawa Agreement of 1932 established Empire preference in Britain's import trade. British purchases in Argentina dropped from the equivalent of $282,000,000 in 1929 to $136,000,000 in 1938. And the British had been so sacrilegious as to put a quota on Argentine beef. By the time the war began, the Argentines had learned that the Roca-Runciman Treaty had brought them more troubles than benefits. Also, the British government had found it desirable to freeze Argentine credits for the duration of the war. German propaganda agents were making effective use of all these factors, largely through the pro-Fascist nationalist youth movement. These young nationalists also were conducting a bitter fight against the British railroads, picturing them as a huge vampire absorbing the country's strength.

If the United Nations should lose the war, Argentina was all set to profit by their loss and actually was convinced that the defeat of democracy would not mean for her what it had meant for the defeated democracies of Europe. She expected to fit smoothly into the New Order.

If Great Britain and her democratic allies should win the war, then of course there will be a great rush and scramble in Argentina to get onto the victory bandwagon.

If we want to hold the allegiance of Latin America and so unite the Western World as a political and military balance against war-crazed Europe and Asia, we shall have to get down to the serious business of winning the lasting friendship of our southern neighbors. That means winning the friendship of Argentina. This is largely a problem of trade and economics. We must find some way to relieve Argentina of her economic dependence on Europe. One way is to help Argentina establish new industries to manufacture with the raw materials she has been exporting to manufacturing countries. That means not competing with her for South American markets in those products which she can produce cheaper than we can.

Argentines who were inclined to be sarcastic about the good-neighbor policy in 1942 argued that it had failed to provide practical remedies for the war emergency. This argument usually boiled down to the major fact that the United States had failed to buy up all the surpluses of export products which the closure of European markets left on their hands. The Argentines were being unreasonable in believing, or pretending to believe, that instantly upon the outbreak of hostilities the United States should have provided markets for everything which they formerly had sold in a dozen European markets. But the Nazi propaganda machine was working day and night to convince them that as soon as the "present unpleasantness" could be terminated (which always was going to be within the next few months) Germany gladly would provide an outlet for all their products, in contrast to the United States which "refused" to buy from them. So the Argentines refused to be impressed by the argument that the United States government had been paying bounties to American farmers not to produce many of the commodities that they wanted the United States to absorb in tremendous quantities. Regardless of the unreasonableness of this attitude, however, the problem is ours and if we fail to solve it, they will look elsewhere for help. And their allegiance is very likely to be extended to the source of whatever help they get.

This problem cannot be dismissed with an impatient wave of the hand and the exclamation that we cannot import goods which compete with our own farmers, miners, and cattle- and sheep-raisers. We shall have to face the fact that efforts to increase our purchases of almost any important South American commodity which is now shut out by a high tariff will offend some section of the United States and arouse its political opposition. It is a question of the larger general interest being opposed by selfish private interests. We must reconcile ourselves to some commercial sacrifices for the sake of our political and military safety and permit the importation of Argentine and other South American products in quantities sufficient to save the southern nations from economic collapse, or we must surrender them and their allegiance to the Axis, with all the political and economic disaster that such a step will mean to the United States.

Argentines complain that we never have had a long-view, continuing policy toward them; that our policy, when there has been any policy at all, has been one of expediency, usually looking toward large and quick profits. They argue that we should have been engaged in some such far-sighted policy during the twenty years following the First World War and say that if Great Britain and Germany can help them when they are in economic trouble, we ought to be able to find some way to do so.

The Argentine Republic is destined to become a great nation. It has the natural resources, the temperate climate, and the progressive, energetic, and ambitious people necessary to make it so. The shortcomings in government, which are part of the country's Spanish heritage, probably will be remedied with time and education. If not, Argentina will become great in spite of its bad government. The country's potential wealth is so great that its tremendous progress and prosperity during the first forty years of the twentieth century were achieved under governments that would have bankrupted a less vigorous land. It behooves the United States, government and people, to regain Argentina's confidence and friendship, remembering that nations love one another only when it is

mutually profitable for them to do so. The United States once occupied
the leading position in the minds, lives, and economy of the Argentines.
The recovery of that position would be the most effective way of winning Argentina away from fascism. The Germans have had the advantage
in Argentina because they knew very clearly what they wanted and
went after it ruthlessly and in accordance with a definite plan. We have
had only a vague idea as to what we want and no idea of how to get it.

APPENDICES

BIBLIOGRAPHY

INDEX

AREA AND POPULATION

	Area (sq. mi.)	*Population* [1]
FEDERAL DISTRICT		
Buenos Aires City	74	2,364,263
PROVINCES		
Buenos Aires	118,764	3,486,430
Catamarca	30,077	149,766
Córdoba	65,212	1,271,494
Corrientes	33,544	516,671
Entre Rios	29,537	737,300
Jujuy	18,726	113,144
La Rioja	36,086	110,537
Mendoza	58,224	513,527
Salta	49,961	212,307
San Juan	34,910	216,844
San Luis	28,906	196,677
Santa Fé	51,127	1,546,880
Santiago del Estero	56,243	484,649
Tucumán	8,817	530,664
TERRITORIES	460,342	678,570
	1,080,550	13,129,723

INDUSTRIAL CONTROL BOARDS

(Listed in the order of their creation, with their official names in Spanish and the number and date of the law or decree establishing them.)

National Sugar Commission (*Comisión Nacional del Azúcar*), Decree No. 702, May 11, 1928.

National Industrial Development Commission (*Comisión Nacional de Fomento Industrial*), Decree No. 58, January 15, 1931.

National Potato Commission (*Comisión Nacional de Patatas*), Cabinet resolution of July 8, 1931.

National Textile Fibers Commission (*Comisión Nacional de Fibres Textiles*), Decree No. 1401, November 14, 1931.

National Quebracho Extract Commission (*Comisión Nacional del Extracto de Quebracho*), Decree No. 25,092, July 15, 1933.

National Bureau of Grain Elevators (*Dirección Nacional de Elevadores de Granos*), Law No. 11,742, October 7, 1933.

National Meat Board (*Junta Nacional de Carnes*), Law No. 11,747, October 7, 1933.

---

[1] National Government's official estimate as of January 1, 1940.

National Yerba Mate Board (*Junta Nacional de Yerba Mate*), Decree No. 30,854, November 8, 1933. Converted into Yerba Mate Production and Trade Control Commission (*Comisión Reguladora de la Producción y Comercio de la Yerba Mate*) by Law No. 12,236, October 4, 1935.

Grain Control Board (*Junta Reguladora de Granos*), Decree No. 31,864, November 28, 1933.

Dairy Industry Control Board (*Junta Reguladora de la Industria Lechera*), Decree No. 40,140, April 12, 1934. This board was abolished by Decree No. 125,201, February 11, 1938, which created a Dairy Industry Bureau (*Dirección de la Industria Lechera*) in the Ministry of Agriculture. By a new decree on April 5, 1939, a National Dairy Industry Commission (*Comisión Nacional de la Industria Lechera*) was created with an Honorary Consulting Commission (*Comisión Consultiva Honoraria*).

National Oil (Edible) Commission (*Comisión Nacional del Aceite*), Decree No. 42,621, June 5, 1934.

National Food Products Commission (*Comisión Nacional de Productos Alimenticios*), Decree No. 44,423, June 30, 1934.

Meat Export Promotion Board (*Junta para Promover las Exportaciones de Carne*), Decree No. 44,299, July 27, 1934. Abolished by Decree No. 119,263, October 30, 1937.

National Wine Industry Commission (*Comisión Nacional de la Industria Vitivinícola*), Decree No. 46,837, August 11, 1934. Law No. 12,237, December 24, 1934, created the Wine Control Board (*Junta Reguladora de Vinos*) with an Honorary Consulting Commission (*Comisión Asesora Honoraria*).

National Unemployment Board (*Junta Nacional para Combatir la Desocupación*), Law No. 11,896, August 21, 1934.

Flour Commission (*Comisión de Harinas*), Cabinet resolution, April 13, 1935.

National Cotton Board (*Junta Nacional del Algodón*), Decree No. 59,802, April 27, 1935.

National Grain and Elevators Commission (*Comisión Nacional de Granos y Elevadores*), Law No. 12,253, October 5, 1935.

Fruit Commission (*Comisión de Fruticultura*), Cabinet resolution, December 12, 1935.

Seed Loan Commission (*Comisión de Préstamos de Semillas*), Decree No. 77,114, February 22, 1936.

Petroleum and Other Hydrocarbides Commission (*Comisión de Petróleo y demás Hidrocarburos*), Decree No. 82,162, May 8, 1936.

National Forests Consulting Commission (*Comisión Consultiva Nacional de Bosques*), Decree No. 83,731, June 3, 1936.

National Transport Co-ordination Commission (*Comisión Nacional de Co-ordinación de Transportes*), Law No. 12,346, January 5, 1937.

National Charcoal Commission (*Comisión Nacional del Carbón Vegetal*), Decree No. 107,529, June 12, 1937.

Milling Industry Consulting Board (*Junta Consultiva de la Industria Molinera*), Decree of May 14, 1938.

Wool Consulting Committee (*Comité Asesor de Lanas*), Decree of May 24, 1938.

Provisions Control Commission (*Comisión de Control de Abastecimientos*), Decree No. 40,980, September 8, 1939. This commission was created to enforce Law No. 12,591, fixing prices. By decree No. 53,249, January 17, 1940, its functions were transferred to the Bureau of Provisions, Industry, and Commerce (*Dirección de Abastecimiento, Industria, y Comercio*) of the Ministry of Agriculture.

National Agrarian Council (*Consejo Agrario Nacional*), Law No. 12,636, August 21, 1940.

Appendix III

NEW TRADE TREATIES

LISTED IN THE ORDER OF THEIR SIGNING

Country	Date	Classification
Great Britain	May 1, 1933	Trade and Exchange
Chile	June 3, 1933	Trade
Great Britain	September 26, 1933	Supplementary Convention
Brazil	October 10, 1933	* Trade and Navigation
Belgium and Luxembourg	January 16, 1934	Trade and Exchange
Netherlands	January 31, 1934	* Trade and Exchange
Switzerland	May 18, 1934	* Trade and Exchange
Germany	September 28, 1934	Trade and Exchange
Spain	December 29, 1934	* Trade and Exchange
United States	May 24, 1935	Sanitary Convention
Brazil	May 29, 1935	* Trade and Navigation
Chile	July 2, 1935	Frontier Traffic
Rumania	December 14, 1935	* Trade
Uruguay	December 30, 1935	* Trade
Finland	December 31, 1935	** Trade and Exchange
Austria	August 27, 1936	* Trade and Exchange
Great Britain	December 1, 1936	Renewal of 1933 Treaty
Peru	February 3, 1937	Commercial *modus vivendi*
Italy	March 4, 1937	* Additional Protocol to the Convention of 1894
Italy	March 4, 1937	Trade and Exchange
Czechoslovakia	May 20, 1937	* Trade and Exchange
Bolivia	September 17, 1937	Frontier Traffic
Hungary	December 24, 1937	* Trade and Exchange
Chile	February 18, 1938	* Additional Protocol to 1933 Treaty
France	February 18, 1938	* Additional Protocol to 1892 Treaty
Poland	August 31, 1938	* Trade
Greece	November 23, 1938	* Trade and Navigation
Lithuania	November 25, 1938	** Trade
Brazil	April 13, 1939	Protocol on Exchange
Denmark	April 18, 1939	Trade and Exchange
Paraguay	July 5, 1939	Frontier Traffic

Appendix III (Continued)

Country	Date	Classification
Brazil	October 6, 1940	Declaration and Recommendations for Improving Commercial Relations
Japan	March 15, 1940	Exchange of notes intended to increase trade reciprocally
Colombia	October 17, 1940	* Trade
United States	October 14, 1941	** Trade and Exchange

* With most-favored-nation clause.

** Excluded from most-favored-nation concessions granted to South American countries.

Appendix IV

PUBLIC DEBT

Total Bonded and Floating Debt of the Nation, Provinces, and Municipalities on June 30, 1940. Compiled by the Corporation of Bond and Stock Holders.

(In paper pesos)

	Bonded	Floating	Total [1]
Nation	4,973,348,580	318,133,163	5,291,381,743
PROVINCES			
Buenos Aires	1,019,794,441	67,220,341	1,087,014,782
Santa Fé	139,534,869	30,303,909	169,838,778
Córdoba	99,032,025	60,000	99,092,025
Mendoza	18,285,800	1,600,000	19,885,800
Tucumán	38,563,717	6,040,312	44,604,029
Entre Rios	46,860,636	31,998,212	78,858,848
Santiago del Estero	23,996,331	5,323,924	29,320,255
Corrientes	11,967,528	8,911,883	20,879,411
San Juan	5,042,791	1,705,063	6,747,851
Salta	15,344,715	473,452	15,818,167
San Luis	6,081,910	814,912	6,896,822
Catamarca	1,792,081	388,404	2,180,485
La Rioja	1,794,999	937,079	2,732,079
Jujuy	85,539	452,821	538,360
Totals	1,428,177,382	156,230,312	1,584,407,694

[1] The difference in exchange is included in the total debt, the foreign debt having been calculated at the official buying rate for foreign currencies on June 30, 1940.

Appendix IV (Continued)

	Bonded	Floating	Total
MUNICIPALITIES			
City of Buenos Aires	502,060,601	99,107,655	601,168,256
Municipalities of Prov. of Buenos Aires	26,333,671	17,631,773	43,965,444
Santa Fé	18,206,332	6,910,868	25,117,200
Rosario	73,137,390	18,966,462	92,103,852
Rafaela	3,547,306	1,068,890	4,616,195
Córdoba	32,473,185	11,724,850	44,198,035
Municipalities of Prov. of Córdoba	3,068,750	1,111,444	4,180,194
Mendoza	——	948,273	948,273
Godoy Cruz	——	6,155	6,155
Tucumán	——	14,611,483	14,611,483
Paraná	6,042,100	862,464	6,904,564
Municipalities of Prov. of Entre Rios	2,923,750	440,412	3,364,162
Santiago del Estero	1,344,700	878,147	2,222,847
Corrientes	——	1,129,967	1,129,967
San Juan	186,684	——	186,684
Salta	1,196,885	247,326	1,444,211
San Luis	236,640	428,767	665,408
Catamarca	1,333,619	300,225	1,633,844
La Rioja	——	28,845	28,845
Jujuy	169,091	80,501	249,592
Totals	672,260,703	176,484,507	848,745,210
Grand Total	7,073,686,665	650,847,982	7,724,534,647

Appendix V

VALUE OF EXPORTS TO THE UNITED STATES

(F.O.B. values in U.S. currency) [1]

	1941	1940	1939
Wool	68,076,327	32,804,586	16,482,732
Hides and skins	37,188,520	16,109,084	13,785,821
Other animal by-products	10,050,330	1,748,766	1,792,016
Meat and meat products	11,783,147	4,328,109	5,262,750
Dairy products	5,571,260	1,426,748	366,815
Linseed	15,614,486	13,244,324	16,519,955
Other inedible seeds	100,134	20,174	26,314
Forage and garden seeds	483,492	160,950	243,132

[1] Declared values on American consular invoices.

Appendix IV (Continued)

	1941	1940	1939
Quebracho extract	7,130,259	2,890,365	3,976,922
Other inedible vegetable products	1,935,980	231,568	52,003
Fruits and preparations	2,343,552	1,152,600	654,902
Vegetables and preparations	2,396,182	106,952	15,948
Cereals and preparations	517,484	2,800,248	646,692
Other vegetable products	13,813	12,104	1,376
Animal hair	3,241,459	1,143,139	515,561
Other textile products	1,373,595	267,590	170,337
Minerals and metals	3,480,072	2,534,902	1,647,517
Fertilizers	3,322,372	1,820,722	2,352,220
Other chemical products	2,624,893	1,234,707	339,668
Miscellaneous	282,920	38,553	25,637
	177,530,277	84,076,191	64,878,318

Appendix VI

TREATY OF FRIENDSHIP, COMMERCE AND NAVIGATION WITH THE UNITED STATES OF AMERICA

Signed at San José de Flores, July 27, 1853, by the Plenipotentiaries of the Confederation, Salvador María del Carril and José Benjamin Gorostiaga, and the Envoy Extraordinary and Minister Plenipotentiary of the United States of America in Brazil, Robert C. Schenck, and the Chargé d'Affaires of the United States of America in the Argentine Confederation, J. S. Pendleton.

Ratified by Law No. 17 of December 3, 1854.

Ratifications exchanged in Paraná, December 20, 1854, by the Minister of Foreign Relations of the Confederation and the Minister of the United States, J. A. Peden.

Commercial intercourse having been for some time established between the United States and the Argentine Confederation, it seems good for the security as well as the encouragement of such commercial intercourse and for the maintenance of good understanding between the two governments, that the relations now subsisting between them should be regularly acknowledged and confirmed by the signing of a Treaty of Friendship, Commerce and Navigation. For this purpose they have nominated their respective Plenipotentiaries, that is to say:

The President of the United States, Robert C. Schenck, Envoy Extraordinary and Minister Plenipotentiary of the United States in Brazil, and John S. Pendleton, Chargé d'Affaires of the United States in the Argentine Confederation; and His Excellency the Provisional Director of the Argentine Confederation, Dr. Salvador María del Carril and Dr. José Benjamin Gorostiaga;

Who, after having communicated to each other their Full Powers, found in good and due form, have agreed upon the following articles:

Article 1. There shall be perpetual amity between the United States and their citizens on one part, and the Argentine Confederation and its citizens on the other part.

Article 2. There shall be between all the territories of the United States and all the territories of the Argentine Confederation a reciprocal freedom of Commerce. The citizens of the countries respectively shall have liberty, freely and securely, to come with their ships and cargoes to all places, ports and rivers, in the territories of either, to which other foreigners, or the ships or cargoes of any other foreign nation or state, are or may be permitted to come; to enter into the same, and to remain and reside in any part thereof, respectively; to hire and occupy houses and warehouses for the purposes of their residence and commerce, to trade in all kinds of produce, manufactures, and merchandise of lawful commerce; and generally to enjoy in all their business the most complete protection and security, subject to the general laws and usages of the two countries respectively. In like manner the respective ships of war, and post office or passenger packets of the two countries shall have liberty, freely and securely, to come to all harbors, rivers and places to which other foreign ships of war and packets are or may be permitted to come; to enter into the same, to anchor and remain there and refit, subject always to the laws and usages of the countries respectively.

Article 3. The two High Contracting Parties agree that any favor, exemption, privilege, or immunity whatever, in matters of commerce and navigation, which either of them has actually granted, or may hereafter grant, to the citizens or subjects of any other Government, Nation or State, shall extend, in identical cases and circumstances, to the citizens of the other Contracting Party gratuitously, if the concession in favor of that other Government, Nation or State shall have been gratuitous, or, in return for an equivalent compensation, if the concession shall have been conditional.

Article 4. No higher or other duties shall be imposed on the importation into the territories of either of the two Contracting Parties, of any article, of the growth, produce or manufacture of the territories of the other Contracting Party, than are or shall be payable on the like article of any other foreign country; nor shall any other or higher duties or charges be imposed in the territories of either of the Contracting Parties on the exportation of any article to the territories of the other than such as are or shall be payable on the exportation of the like articles to any other foreign country; nor shall any prohibition be imposed upon the importation or exportation of any article of the growth, produce or manufacture of the territories of either of the Contracting Parties, to or from the territories of the other, which shall not equally extend to the like article of any other foreign country.

Article 5. No other or higher duties or charges on account of tonnage, light or harbor dues, pilotage, salvage in case of average or shipwreck, or any other local charges shall be imposed, in the ports of either of the two Contracting Parties, on the vessels of the other than those payable in the same ports on its own vessels.

Article 6. The same duties shall be paid and the drawbacks and bounties allowed upon the importation or exportation of any article into or from the territories of the United States, or, into or from the territories of the Argentine Confederation, whether such importation or exportation be made in vessels of the United States or in vessels of the Argentine Confederation.

Article 7. The Contracting Parties agree to consider and treat as vessels of the United States and of the Argentine Confederation, all those which, being furnished by the competent authority with a regular passport or sea letter, shall under the then existing laws and regulations of either of the two governments, be recognized fully and bona fide as national vessels by that country to which they respectively belong.

Article 8. All merchants, commanders of ships and other citizens of the United States shall have full liberty, in all territories of the Argentine Confederation, to manage their own affairs themselves, or, to commit them to the management of whomsoever they please, as broker, factor, agent, or interpreter; nor shall they be obliged to employ any other persons in those capacities than those employed by citizens of the Argentine Confederation, nor to pay them any other salary or remuneration than such as is paid in like cases by citizens of the Argentine Confederation. And absolute freedom shall be allowed in all cases to the buyer and seller to bargain for the price of any goods, wares or merchandise imported into or exported from the Argentine Confederation, as they shall see good, observing the laws and established customs of the country. The same rights and privileges, in all respects, shall be enjoyed in the territories of the United States, by the citizens of the Argentine Confederation. The citizens of the two Contracting Parties shall reciprocally receive and enjoy full and perfect protection for their persons and property and shall have free and open access to the courts of justice in the said countries respectively for the protection and defense of their just rights, and they shall be at liberty to employ in all cases such advocates, attorneys or agents as they may think proper and they shall enjoy in this respect the same rights and privileges therein as native citizens.

Article 9. In whatever relates to the police of the ports, the lading and unlading of ships, the safety of the merchandise, goods and effects, and to the acquiring and disposing of property of every sort and denomination either by sale, donation, exchange, testament, or in any other manner whatsoever, as also to the administration of justice, the citizens of the two Contracting Parties shall reciprocally enjoy the same privileges, liberties and rights, as native citizens, and they shall not be charged, in any of those respects, with any higher imposts or duties than those which are paid or may be paid by native citizens, submitting, of course, to the local laws and regulations, of each country respectively. If any citizens of either of the two Contracting Parties shall die without will or testament, in any of the territories of the other, the Consul General or Consul of the nation to which the deceased belonged or the representative of such Consul General or Consul, in his absence, shall have the right to intervene in the possession, administration and judicial liquidation of the estate of the deceased, conformably with the laws of the country, for the benefit of the creditors and legal heirs.

Article 10. The citizens of the United States residing in the Argentine Confederation, and the citizens of the Argentine Confederation residing in the United States, shall be exempted from all compulsory military service whatsoever, whether by sea or by land, and from all forced loans, requisitions or military exactions; and they shall not be compelled, under any pretext whatsoever, to pay any ordinary charges, requisitions, or taxes greater than those that are paid by native citizens of the Contracting Parties respectively.

Article 11. It shall be free for each of the two Contracting Parties to appoint Consuls for the protection of trade, to reside in any of the territories of the other party; but before any Consul shall act as such, he shall, in the usual form, be approved and admitted by the Government to which he is sent, and either of the Contracting Parties may except from the residence of Consuls such particular places as they judge fit to be excepted. The archives and papers of the Consulates of the respective Governments shall be respected inviolably and under no pretext whatever shall any magistrate or any of the local authorities seize or in any way interfere with them.

The Diplomatic Agents and Consuls of the Argentine Confederation shall enjoy in the territories of the United States whatever privileges, exemptions, and immunities as are or shall be granted to Agents of the same rank belonging to the most favored Nation; and in like manner, the Diplomatic Agents and Consuls of the United States in the territories of the Argentine Confederation shall enjoy, according to the strictest reciprocity, whatever privileges, exemptions and immunities as are, or may be, granted in the Argentine Confederation to the Diplomatic Agents and Consuls of the most favored Nation.

Article 12. For the better security of commerce between the United States and the Argentine Confederation, it is agreed that if at any time any interruption of friendly commercial intercourse, or any rupture, should unfortunately take place between the two Contracting Parties, the citizens of either of them residing in the territories of the other, shall have the privilege of remaining and continuing their trade or occupation therein without any manner of interruption, so long as they behave peaceably and commit no offense against the laws; and their effects and property, whether entrusted to individuals or to the State, shall not be liable to seizure or sequestration or to any other demands than those which may be made upon the like effects or property belonging to the native inhabitants of the State in which such citizens may reside.

Article 13. The citizens of the United States, and the citizens of the Argentine Confederation, respectively, residing in any of the territories of the other party, shall enjoy in their houses, persons and properties, the full protection of the Government.

They shall not be disturbed, molested nor annoyed in any manner on account of their religious belief, nor in the proper exercise of their peculiar worship, either within their own houses, or in their own churches or chapels, which they shall be at liberty to build and maintain, in convenient situations, to be approved by the local government, interfering in no way with, but respecting the religion and customs of the country in which they reside. Liberty shall also be granted to the citizens of either of the Contracting Parties to bury those who may die in the territories of the other, in burial places of their own, which in the same manner may be freely established and maintained.

Article 14. The present Treaty shall be ratified on the part of the government of the United States within fifteen months from the date; and within three days by his Excellency the Provisional Director of the Argentine Confederation, who will also present it to the first legislative Congress of the Confederation for their approval.

The ratification shall be exchanged at the seat of Government of the Argentine Confederation within the term of eighteen months.

In witness whereof the respective Plenipotentiaries have signed this Treaty and affixed thereto their seals.

Done at San José del Uruguay on the twenty-seventh day of July in the year of Our Lord one thousand eight hundred and fifty-three.

(Seal) Robert C. Schenck
(Seal) John Pendleton
(Seal) Salvador María del Carril
(Seal) José B. Gorostiaga

Appendix VII

CONSTITUTION OF THE ARGENTINE NATION

We, the representatives of the people of the Argentine Nation, in General Constituent Congress assembled by the will and election of the Provinces composing said Nation, in fulfillment of existing covenants, for the purpose of establishing national unity, insuring justice, consolidating domestic peace, providing for the common defense, promoting general welfare, and securing the benefits of liberty to ourselves, our posterity, and to all people in the world who may wish to inhabit the Argentine soil; invoking the protection of God, the source of all reason and justice, ordain, decree, and set up this Constitution for the Argentine Nation.

DIVISION I

FIRST AND ONLY CHAPTER

Declarations, Rights, and Guarantees

1. The Argentine Nation adopts for its Government the Federal Republican Representative form, as established by this Constitution.

2. The Federal Government supports the Roman Catholic Apostolic Church.

3. The authorities who conduct the Federal Government shall reside in the city [1] which, by a special law of Congress, is to be declared the Capital of the Republic upon cession, by one or more of the Provincial Legislatures, of the territory to be federalized.

4. The Federal Government shall defray the expenses of the Nation out of funds of the National Treasury, formed of the proceeds of import and export duties; the proceeds of the sale or lease of nationally owned lands; of the postal revenues; of any other taxes which the General Congress may levy equitably and in proportion to the population, and of any loans and credit operations which said Congress may decree to provide for urgent needs of the Nation or for enterprises of national utility.

5. Each Province shall, under the republican representative system, in accordance with the principles, declarations and guarantees of the National Constitution, frame for itself a Constitution which shall insure its administration of justice, its municipal government, and primary education. Upon these conditions, the Federal Government guarantees to each Province the enjoyment and exercises of its institutions.

6. The Federal Government intervenes in the territory of the Provinces to guarantee the republican form of Government, or to repel foreign invasions, and, on request of their constituted Authorities, to support or re-establish such Authorities, if they have been overthrown by sedition or invasion from another Province.

7. The public acts and judicial proceedings of each Province enjoy full faith in every other Province; and Congress may determine by general laws

---

[1] Buenos Aires; declared the capital by Law No. 1029 of September 21, 1880.

the manner in which such acts and proceedings shall be proved, and the legal effects they shall produce.

8. Citizens of any Province enjoy all the rights, privileges, and immunities inherent in citizenship in all others. The extradition of criminals is a reciprocal obligation among all the Provinces.

9. There shall, throughout the territory of the Nation, be no custom-houses other than the national custom-houses, and in them the tariffs enacted by Congress shall rule.

10. The circulation of articles of national production or manufacture, as well as that of goods and merchandise of all classes entering through the custom-houses for foreign trade shall, in the interior of the Republic, be free from duties.

11. Articles of national or foreign production or manufacture, as well as livestock of all kinds, passing from the territory of one Province into another, shall be exempt from the so-called transit dues, as shall the vehicles, vessels, or beasts used for transporting them; and no other duty shall, under any name whatsoever, hereafter be imposed on them for the act of their passing through the territory.

12. Vessels bound from one Province to another shall not be compelled to enter, anchor, and pay duties by reason of transit; and in no case shall any preference be granted to one port over another by means of commercial laws or regulations.

13. New Provinces may be admitted into the Nation; but no new Province may be erected in the territory of one or more other Provinces, nor may one Province be formed from a number of others, without the consent of the Legislatures of the interested Province and of Congress.

14. All the inhabitants of the Nation enjoy the following rights, subject to such laws as regulate the exercise thereof: to work and engage in any lawful industry; to navigate and trade; to petition the authorities; to enter, remain,[2] or travel in, or leave Argentine territory; to publish their ideas through the Press without previous censorship; to use and dispose of their property; to associate for useful purposes; to profess their religious faith freely; to teach and to learn.

15. There are no slaves in the Argentine Nation; the few slaves now existing are enfranchised as from the moment this Constitution is sworn to; and a special law shall settle the compensation to which this declaration may give rise. Any contract for the purchase and sale of persons is a criminal act for which the contracting parties, as well as the notary or official authorizing it, shall be held liable; and slaves introduced therein in any manner whatsoever shall become free by the mere act of setting foot on the territory of the Republic.

16. The Argentine Nation does not admit prerogatives of blood or birth; no personal privileges or titles of nobility obtain therein. All its inhabitants are equal before the law, and may hold office subject to no condition other than fitness. Equality is the basis of taxation and all public charges.

17. Property is inviolable, and no inhabitant of the Nation may be deprived thereof except by virtue of a judgment founded on law. Expropriation on a ground of public utility must be provided by law and compensation previously made. Congress alone may levy the taxes set forth in Article 4. No personal service can be required of anyone, except by virtue of a law or a

[2] See the Residence of Aliens Law, Appendix VIII.

judgment founded on law. Every author and inventor is the exclusive owner of his work, invention, or discovery, throughout the term granted him by law. Confiscation of property is forever struck out of the Argentine Penal Code. No armed body can make requisitions, nor demand assistance of any kind.

18. No inhabitant of the Nation may be punished without previous trial founded on a law prior to the act for which he is tried nor may he be tried by special commissions, or removed from the jurisdiction of the Judges specified by law before the act giving rise to the proceedings was committed. No one may be compelled to bear witness against himself; nor be arrested except by virtue of a written order from a competent authority. The defense, in Court, of persons and of rights is inviolable. The home is inviolable, as are correspondence by letter and private papers; and a law shall specify in what cases and upon what grounds they may be entered or searched, and seized. The penalty of death for political causes, torture of all kinds and flogging are forever abolished. The prisons of the Nation shall be sanitary and clean, for the safekeeping and not for the punishment of the prisoners detained therein, and any measure which, under pretext of precaution, leads to their suffering more hardships than those required for their security, shall render liable the Judge allowing it.

19. The private acts of man which do not in any way offend against public order or morals, or injure third persons, are reserved to God alone, and removed from the authority of magistrates. No inhabitant of the Nation shall be compelled to do what the law does not command, nor denied what it does not forbid.

20. Aliens enjoy in the territory of the Nation all the civil rights of citizens; they may engage in their industry, commerce, or profession; possess real estate and purchase or dispose of it; navigate on the rivers and along the coasts; freely practice their religion; make wills and marry in accordance with the laws. They are not bound to accept citizenship, or to pay forced extraordinary taxes. They obtain naturalization by residing two consecutive years in the Nation; but the authorities may reduce this period in favor of an applicant claiming and proving services to the Republic.

21. Every Argentine citizen is bound to take up arms in defense of the country and this Constitution, in accordance with the laws which Congress may enact to this end and with the decrees of the National Executive Power. Citizens by naturalization are free to render or refuse this service during a term of ten years from the day they obtain their letters of citizenship.

22. The people do not deliberate nor govern, except by means of their representatives and authorities created by this Constitution. Any armed body or any gathering of persons attributing to itself the rights of the people and petitioning on their behalf, commits the crime of sedition.

23. In case of domestic disturbance or foreign attack, endangering the observance of this Constitution, and the activities of the authorities created by it, the Province or territory in which the disturbance of order takes place, shall be declared in a state of siege and the constitutional guarantees shall be suspended therein. But during such suspension, the President of the Republic shall not be enabled by himself either to sentence anyone or to inflict punishments. His power shall be limited in such cases, with respect to persons, to arresting them or transferring them from one part of the Nation to another, should they prefer not to leave Argentine territory.

24. Congress shall promote the reform of the existing legislation in all its branches, and the establishment of trial by jury.

25. The Federal Government shall encourage European immigration; and it shall not restrict, limit, or impose taxation of any kind upon the entry into Argentine territory of aliens coming to it for the purpose of tilling the soil, improving industries, or introducing and teaching sciences and arts.

26. The navigation of the inland rivers of the Nation is free to all flags, subject solely to the regulations which the National Authority may enforce.

27. The Federal Government is bound to insure its relations of peace and commerce with foreign Powers, by means of treaties consistent with the principles of public law established by this Constitution.

28. The principles, guarantees, and rights recognized in the foregoing Articles may not be altered by any laws regulating their operation.

29. Congress may not confer on the National Executive Power nor the Provincial Legislatures on the Governors of the Provinces, any extraordinary faculties, or the fullness of the public power, or grant them acts of submission or supremacy whereby the lives, the honor, or the property of Argentines are placed at the mercy of any government or person whatsoever. An unremediable nullity shall be inherent in acts of this nature and such acts shall subject those who formulate them, consent thereto or sign them, to the liability and penalty of infamous traitors to their country.

30. Either the whole or any part of the Constitution may be amended. The necessity of such amendment must be declared by Congress by a vote of at least two-thirds of its members; but the amendment shall not be made except by a Convention summoned for that purpose.

31. This Constitution, the laws of the Nation which Congress may enact in pursuance thereof, and the treaties with foreign Powers are the supreme law of the Nation; and the authorities of every Province are bound to abide thereby, notwithstanding any provision to the contrary contained in the Provincial laws or constitutions, excepting, as to the Province of Buenos Aires, the treaties ratified after the Covenant of November 11, 1859.

32. The Federal Congress shall not pass any law restricting the liberty of the Press or setting federal jurisdiction over it.

33. The declarations, rights, and guarantees specified in the Constitution shall not be understood as a denial of other rights and guarantees not specified, but arising out of the principle of the sovereignty of the people and the republican form of government.

34. The Judges of the Federal Courts cannot at the same time be judges of the Provincial Courts, nor does the Federal Service, either civil or military, give residence in the Province in which it is performed, when it is not the habitual place of residence of the employee, this provision being understood to apply for the purposes of his seeking office in the Province in which he may temporarily be stationed.

35. Any or all of the names successively adopted since 1810 and up to the present time, namely: "United Provinces of the River Plate," "Argentine Republic," "Argentine Confederation," shall hereafter be official names for the designation of the Government and territory of the Provinces, the words "Argentine Nation" being employed in the drafting and sanction of the laws.

Authorities of the Nation

PART I: FEDERAL GOVERNMENT

Subdivision I: The Legislative Power

36. A Congress composed of two Chambers—one a Chamber of Deputies of the Nation and the other a Chamber of Senators of the Provinces and of the Capital—shall be vested with the Legislative Power of the Nation.

CHAPTER I: The Chamber of Deputies

37.[3] The Chamber of Deputies shall be composed of representatives elected directly and on a simple majority of votes by the people of the Provinces and of the Capital, which shall be considered for this purpose as electoral districts of a single State. The number of representatives shall be one for every 33,000 inhabitants or fraction thereof not less than 16,500. After the taking of each census, Congress shall determine the representation in accordance therewith, and may increase but may not reduce the basis fixed for each deputy.

38. The Deputies to the first Legislature shall be chosen in the following proportion: For the Province of Buenos Aires, 12; for that of Córdoba, 6; for that of Catamarca, 3; for that of Corrientes, 4; for that of Entre Rios, 2; for that of Jujuy, 2; for that of Mendoza, 3; for that of La Rioja, 2; for that of Salta, 3; for that of Santiago, 4; for that of San Juan, 2; for that of Santa Fé, 2; for that of San Luis, 2; and for that of Tucumán, 3.[4]

39. For the second Legislature a general census shall be taken and the number of Deputies determined in accordance therewith; but such census may be repeated only every ten years.

40. A Deputy is required to have attained the age of 25 years, to have enjoyed four years' active citizenship, and to be a native of the Province in which elected, or have been resident therein for the two years next preceding election.

41. For this occasion the Legislatures of the Provinces shall prescribe the means whereby the direct election of the Deputies of the Nation shall be effected; for the future, Congress shall enact a general law.

42. Deputies shall serve for four years and are re-eligible, but one-half of the Chamber shall be renewed every two years, to which end the deputies elected to the first Congress shall, after meeting, draw lots to decide who shall retire at the end of the first period.

43. In case of vacancy, the Government of the Province or of the Capital shall cause a new member to be legally elected.

44. Laws relating to taxes or recruiting of troops are to be introduced by the Chamber of Deputies exclusively.

45. The Chamber of Deputies alone has the right to impeach, before the

[3] The version here given is that of the article as amended by the National Convention in the capital on March 15, 1898.

[4] Article 3 of the Law of September 1919, provides: "As from the biennial renewal of 1920, the number of Deputies shall be one for every 49,000 inhabitants or fraction not under 16,500; consequently, the Federal Capital shall elect 32 Deputies, Buenos Aires 42, Santa Fé 19, Entre Rios 9, Corrientes 7, Córdoba 15, San Luis 3, Santiago del Estero 6, Tucumán 7, Mendoza 6, San Juan 3, La Rioja 2, Catamarca 2, Jujuy 2, Salta 3."

Senate, the President, the Vice-President, their Ministers, and the members of the Supreme Court and of any lower Tribunals of the Nation, in causes brought against them concerning their responsibility for malfeasance, or for criminal offenses committed in the discharge of their functions, or for common crimes, after cognizance has been taken and a declaration made, by a vote of a majority of two-thirds of the members present, that proceedings should be instituted.

CHAPTER II: The Senate

46. The Senate shall be composed of two Senators from each Province elected by their Legislatures by a majority of votes; and of two from the Capital, elected in the form prescribed for the election of the President of the Nation. Each Senator shall have one vote.

47. The following are requisites for election as Senator: to have attained 30 years of age; to have been a citizen of the Nation for six years; to enjoy an annual income of 2000 *pesos fuertes* [5] or its equivalent and to be a native of the Province which elects him or to have been a resident therein during the two next preceding years.

48. Senators shall serve for nine years and are re-eligible for an indefinite number of years; but one-third of the Senate shall be renewed every three years, those who are to retire after the first and second triennium being determined by lot after all have met.

49. The Vice-President of the Nation shall be President of the Senate; but he shall have no vote unless there be a tie.

50. The Senate shall choose a Provisional President to preside in the absence of the Vice-President, or when he is acting as President of the Nation.

51. The public trial of persons impeached by the Chamber of Deputies falls within the province of the Senate, and its members shall, for such purposes, take oath. When the person impeached is the President of the Nation, the President of the Supreme Court shall preside over the Senate. No one shall be convicted except by a two-thirds majority of the members present.

52. Its judgments shall have no other effect than the removal of the person impeached from office, and, further, to declare him disqualified from holding any office of honor, trust, or remuneration in the Nation. But the party convicted shall nevertheless be liable to indictment, trial and punishment, according to law, before the ordinary tribunals.

53. It shall also fall within the province of the Senate to authorize the President of the Nation to declare one or more points of the Republic in a state of siege, in case of foreign attack.

54. When the seat of a Senator becomes vacant on account of death, resignation, or any other reason, the Government to which the vacancy corresponds shall immediately cause a new member to be elected.

CHAPTER III: Provisions Common to Both Chambers

55. Both Chambers shall assemble every year in ordinary session from May 1 to September 30. They may also be convened in extraordinary session by the President of the Nation, or their session may be extended by him.

---

[5] The *peso fuerte* was a gold coin, now obsolete, minted under Law No. 733, of September 23, 1875, which contained 1⅔ grams of gold 900 fine. It was succeeded by the *peso oro* of Law No. 1130, of November 3, 1881, containing 1.6129 grams of gold 900 fine. Thus the *peso fuerte* was, on the gold content, equivalent to 1.033 *pesos oro*. With regard to paper currency, the ratio of the fiduciary issue

56. Each Chamber is the judge of its own members' elections, rights, and titles so far as concerns the validity thereof. Neither Chamber shall open a session without an absolute majority of its members; but a smaller number may, in such manner and under such penalties as each Chamber may provide, compel absent members to attend the sessions.

57. Both Chambers shall open and close their sessions simultaneously. Neither Chamber shall, while they are in session, adjourn for more than three days without the consent of the other.

58. Each Chamber shall make its own regulations, and may, by a two-thirds vote, discipline any of its members for disorderly conduct in the discharge of his duties, or remove him on account of physical or moral inability occurring subsequently to his admission, and even expel him from its body; but a majority of one over one-half of the members present shall suffice for decisions on voluntary resignations from office.

59. Senators and Deputies shall, when being admitted, take an oath duly to discharge their offices and to act in all matters in accordance with the provisions of this Constitution.

60. No member of Congress can be indicted, judicially questioned, or molested for the opinions expressed or speeches made by him in the performance of his duties as a legislator.

61. No Senator or Deputy can be arrested as from the day of his election up to the day when his term expires, except in case of being surprised *in flagrante delicto* in the commission of a criminal offense punishable by death, a dishonoring penalty, or some other afflictive punishment, of which fact a report shall be sent to the respective Chamber with a record of the summary proceedings.

62. If a complaint is filed in writing before an ordinary Court against any Senator or Deputy, the respective Chamber may, after consideration at a public hearing of the merits of the preliminary proceedings, suspend the accused by a two-thirds vote and surrender him to the competent Judge for trial.

63. Each Chamber may cause the Ministers of the Executive Power to appear before it in order to receive such explanations and reports as it may deem advisable.

64. No member of Congress can receive any office or duty from the Executive Power, without the previous consent of the respective Chamber, excepting appointments constituting promotions in a service.

65. Regular ecclesiastics cannot be members of Congress, nor can the Governor of a Province be a member for the Province under his control.

66. The services of Senators and Deputies shall be remunerated by the Treasury of the Nation with an endowment to be fixed by law.[6]

CHAPTER IV: Powers of Congress

67. Congress shall have power:
   1. To legislate in regard to custom-houses for foreign trade and to fix the import duties, which, as well as the rates of appraisement on which they are to be based, shall be uniform throughout the Nation; it being

---

was fixed at 44 centavos gold to the paper peso (i.e., 2.272 paper pesos are equivalent to 1 *peso oro*) by Law No. 3871 of October 1899. Unless otherwise indicated, pesos unqualified means paper pesos.

[6] Senators and Deputies in 1941 received a remuneration of 1500 paper pesos per month.

understood, however, that these duties as well as all other national taxes may be paid in the money current in the respective Provinces at its just equivalent. Likewise to fix export duties.[7]

2. To levy direct taxes for a specified time and proportionately equal throughout the territory of the Nation whenever the defence, common safety or general welfare of the State so requires.

3. To contract loans of money on the credit of the Nation.

4. To provide for the use and disposal of nationally owned lands.

5. To establish and make regulations governing a National Bank in the Capital and its branches in the Provinces, with power to issue bank notes.

6. To arrange the payment of the internal and external debt of the Nation.

7. To fix annually the budget of the expenses of the administration of the Nation, and approve or reject the statement as to the application of funds.

8. To grant subsidies to be paid out of the National Treasury to those Provinces whose revenues, according to their budgets, are insufficient to meet their ordinary expenses.

9. To make regulations for the free navigation of inland rivers, create such ports as it may deem expedient, and erect or abolish custom-houses, but no custom-house for foreign trade which existed in a Province at the time of its incorporation, may be abolished.

10. To cause money to be coined, determine its value and that of foreign currency; and to adopt a uniform system of weights and measures for the entire Nation.

11. To enact the Civil, Commercial, Penal, and Mining Codes, but such Codes may not modify local jurisdictions, the application thereof being vested in the Federal or Provincial Tribunals, according to the respective jurisdiction under which the things or persons may come; and especially to enact general laws for the whole Nation on naturalization and citizenship, based on the principle of natural citizenship; as well as laws on bankruptcy, the counterfeiting of currency and public securities of the State, and those which the establishment of trial by jury may necessitate.

12. To regulate maritime trade and commerce by land with foreign nations, and of the Provinces among themselves.

13. To arrange and establish the post-routes and general mails of the Nation.

14. To settle definitively the boundaries of the territory of the Nation, to fix those of the Provinces, to create new Provinces, and to determine by special legislation the organization, administration, and government of any national territories left outside the limits assigned to the Provinces.

15. To provide for the security of the frontiers; to maintain peaceful intercourse with the Indians, and to promote their conversion to Catholicism.

16. To provide for everything conducive to the prosperity of the country, the advancement and welfare of all the Provinces, and the progress of enlightenment, by establishing plans of general and university instruction, promoting industrial enterprise, immigration, the construction

---

[7] The version here given is as amended by the law of September 12, 1866.

of railways and navigable canals, the colonization of nationally owned lands, the introduction and establishment of new industries, the importation of foreign capital, and the exploration of inland rivers, by laws protecting these ends and by temporary concessions of privileges and rewards for purposes of encouragement.

17. To establish tribunals inferior to the Supreme Court of Justice; to create and suppress offices, to determine their nature and scope; to grant pensions, decree honors, and grant general amnesties.

18. To accept or reject the grounds for the resignation of the President or Vice-President of the Republic; and to declare when a new election shall be held; to scrutinize and correct the returns.

19. To approve or reject treaties concluded with other nations, and Concordats made with the Apostolic See; and to regulate the exercise of the ecclesiastical patronage throughout the Nation.

20. To admit into the territory of the Nation religious orders in addition to those now existing.

21. To authorize the Executive Power to declare war or make peace.

22. To grant letters of marque and reprisal and make rules concerning prizes.

23. To fix the strength of the land and naval forces in times of peace and of war; and to make regulations and ordinances for the government of such forces.

24. To authorize the calling out of the militia of any or all the Provinces, when the enforcement of the laws of the Nation so requires and when it is necessary to suppress insurrections or repel invasions. To provide for organizing, arming, and disciplining said militia, and for managing and governing such parts thereof as may be employed in the service of the Nation; reserving to the Provinces the appointment of their respective field and other officers, and the care of establishing in their respective militia the discipline prescribed by Congress.

25. To permit the entry of foreign troops into the territory of the Nation, and the departure of the national forces therefrom.

26. To declare one or more points of the Nation in a state of siege in case of domestic disturbance, and to approve or suspend a state of siege declared by the Executive Power during the recess of Congress.

27. To exercise exclusive legislation throughout the territory of the Capital of the Nation, and over all other places acquired by purchase or assignment in any of the Provinces, for the erection of forts, arsenals, depots, or other establishments of national utility.

28. To make all laws and regulations which may be advisable for putting into execution the foregoing powers and all other powers granted by this Constitution to the Government of the Argentine Nation.

CHAPTER V: The Formation and Sanction of the Laws

68. Laws may originate in either Chamber of Congress by means of bills presented by their members or by the Executive Power; except, however, such as relate to the objects set forth in Article 44.

69. When a bill has been passed by the Chamber in which it originated, it is sent to the other Chamber for discussion. If approved by both Chambers, it is sent to the Executive Power for examination; and if also approved by it, the Executive Power promulgates it as law.

70. Any bill not returned within a term of ten working days shall be considered as approved by the Executive Power.

71. No bill wholly rejected in one Chamber shall be introduced again during the sessions of that year. But if only additions or amendments are made by the revising Chamber, it shall be returned to the Chamber of origin; and if the additions or amendments are approved in the latter by an absolute majority, it shall pass to the Executive Power of the Nation. If the additions or amendments are rejected, the bill shall return a second time to the revising Chamber, and if they are therein agreed to again by a majority of two-thirds of its members, the bill shall pass to the other Chamber, which shall not be taken to reject such additions or amendments unless two-thirds of the members present concur in such rejection.

72. When a bill is disapproved either in whole or in part by the Executive Power, it returns with the objections to the Chamber of origin; the latter discusses it afresh and, if confirmed by a majority of two-thirds, the bill passes again to the revising Chamber. If the bill is approved by both Chambers with the aforesaid majority, the bill is law and passes to the Executive Power for promulgation. The voting in this case shall, in both Chambers, be by roll-call and by aye or nay; and the names of the persons voting, as well as the reasons for their votes, and the objections of the Executive Power shall immediately be published in the Press. If the Chambers disagree in regard to the objections, the bill cannot be reintroduced in the sessions of that year.

73. In the sanction of the laws, the following formula shall be used: "The Senate and Chamber of Deputies of the Argentine Nation, in Congress assembled, etc., decree or sanction with the force of law."

Subdivision II: The Executive Power

CHAPTER I: Nature and Duration

74. The Executive Power of the Nation shall be exercised by a citizen having the title of "President of the Argentine Nation."

75. In case of illness, absence from the Capital, death, resignation, or removal of the President, the Executive Power shall be exercised by the Vice-President of the Nation. In case of removal, death, resignation, or inability to act of both the President and Vice-President of the Nation, Congress shall determine what public official shall then act as President, until the cause of inability shall have ceased or a new President shall have been elected.[8]

76. In order to be elected President or Vice-President of the Nation, a person is required to have been born in Argentine territory, or to be the

---

[8] Law No. 252 of September 19, 1868, provides:

1. In case the Republic is without a Head on account of there being no President or Vice-President, the Executive Power shall be exercised in the first place, by the Provisional President of the Senate, in the second, by the President of the Chamber of Deputies, and in default of these, by the President of the Supreme Court.

2. Thirty days before the closing of the ordinary session, each Chamber shall choose its President for the purposes of this law.

3. The official called on to exercise the National Executive Power in the cases of Article 1 shall, within thirty days of his entry into office, summon the people of the Republic to elect a new President and Vice-President, provided always that their inability to act is permanent.

4. The official who is to exercise the Executive Power in the cases of Article 1 of this Law shall, upon assuming office, take the oath prescribed in Article 80 of

son of a native citizen, if born in a foreign country; to belong to the Roman Catholic Apostolic faith; and to have the other qualifications required for election as Senator.

77. The President and Vice-President shall continue in office for six years, and may not be re-elected except with an interval of one term.

78. The President of the Nation ceases to be in power the very day on which his term of six years expires, and no event of any nature whatsoever which may have interrupted it shall be a cause for his completing it later.

79. The President and Vice-President receive a salary,[9] paid out of the Treasury of the Nation, which cannot be modified during the term for which they have been appointed. During the same term they shall not be permitted to fill any other office or receive any other emolument from the Nation or any Province whatsoever.

80. Upon assuming office, the President and Vice-President shall, with Congress assembled, take an oath in the following terms, to be administered by the President of the Senate (the first time, by the President of the Constituent Congress):

"I, So-and-So, do swear, before God our Lord and by these Holy Gospels, to execute with loyalty and patriotism the office of President (or Vice-President) of the Nation, and faithfully to observe and to cause to be observed, the Constitution of the Argentine Nation. Should I not do so, may God and the Nation call me to account therefor."

Chapter II: The Manner and Time of Electing the President and Vice-President of the Nation

81. The election of the President and Vice-President of the Nation shall be carried out in the following manner: The Capital and each of the Provinces shall, by direct vote, appoint a board of electors equal to twice the total number of Deputies and Senators they send to Congress, with the same qualifications and under the same forms as prescribed for the election of Deputies.

Neither Deputies, Senators, nor salaried employees of the Federal Government can be electors.

Upon the meeting of the electors in the Capital of the Nation and in that of their respective Provinces four months before the period of the outgoing President ends, they shall proceed to elect a President and Vice-President of the Nation, by signed ballot-papers, stating on one of them the person for whom they vote for President and on another separate one the person they choose for Vice-President.

Two lists shall be made of all persons chosen for President, and two more of those nominated for Vice-President, with the number of votes cast in favor of each. These lists shall be signed by the electors, and two of them (one of each class) shall be sent closed and sealed to the President of the Provincial Legislature, and, in the Capital, to the President of the Municipality, in whose archives they shall remain deposited unopened; and the other two to the President of the Senate (the first time, to the President of the Constituent Congress).

---

the Constitution, before Congress, and, in its absence, before the Supreme Court of Justice.

5. Be is communicated, etc.

[9] The President's salary is 8000 paper pesos per month, and the Vice-President's 3000 paper pesos per month plus allowances granted for necessary expenses annually by the budget.

82. The President of the Senate (the first time, the President of the Constituent Congress) shall, after all the lists have been assembled, open them in the presence of the two Chambers. Four members of Congress, selected by lot, shall, in association with the Secretaries, proceed immediately to count the votes and announce the number of votes in favor of each candidate for the Presidency or Vice-Presidency of the Nation. Those receiving in each case an absolute majority of all the votes, shall be immediately proclaimed President and Vice-President.

83. If, because the voting is divided, there is no absolute majority, Congress shall choose between the two persons who have received the highest number of votes. If the highest majority obtained proves to be in favor of more than two persons, Congress shall choose from among them all.

If the highest majority obtained proves to be in favor of only one person, and the next highest in favor of two or more, Congress shall choose from among all the persons who have obtained the highest and next highest majorities.

84. This election shall be made by absolute majority of votes and on a roll-call. If, on the first ballot, no absolute majority is shown, a second vote shall be taken, the voting being limited to the two persons who obtained the highest number of votes on the first ballot. In case of a tie, the voting shall be repeated, and, if a tie again results, the President of the Senate (the first time, the President of the Constituent Congress) shall decide. These elections may not be scrutinized or rectified unless three-fourths of the total number of members of the Congress are present.

85. The election of President and Vice-President of the Nation must be concluded at a single sitting of Congress, and the result thereof and the electoral minutes shall be published immediately in the Press.

CHAPTER III: Powers of the Executive

86. The President of the Nation has the following powers:

1. He is the Supreme Head of the Nation and has the general administration of the country under his charge.
2. He issues the instructions and regulations necessary for putting the laws of the Nation into practice but shall see to it that their spirit is not altered by exceptions made by the regulations.
3. He is the immediate and local Head of the Capital of the Nation.
4. He takes part in making the laws in accordance with the Constitution, and sanctions and promulgates them.
5. He appoints the Magistrates of the Supreme Court and of the lower Federal Tribunals, with the consent of the Senate.
6. He may grant pardons or commute penalties for crimes subject to federal jurisdiction, after obtaining a report from the Tribunal in question, except in cases of impeachment by the Chamber of Deputies.
7. He grants superannuation and retirement pay, leave of absence, and pensions in conformity with the laws of the Nation.
8. He exercises the rights of the National Patronage in the presentation of Bishops for Cathedral Churches, on the recommendation in ternary of the Senate.
9. He grants or refuses passage to the Decrees of the Councils, Bulls, Briefs, and Rescripts of the Supreme Pontiff of Rome, with the concurrence of the Supreme Court; a law being required when they contain general provisions of a permanent character.

10. He appoints and removes Ministers Plenipotentiary and Chargés d'Affaires with the consent of the Senate; and he alone appoints and removes the Ministers, the officials of his Secretariats, Consular Agents, and other employees of the Administration, whose appointment is not otherwise provided for by this Constitution.

11. He opens the sessions of Congress every year, with both Chambers assembled for this purpose in the Senate Hall, on which occasion he shall report to Congress on the state of the Nation, on the reforms promised by the Constitution, and recommend to their consideration such measures as he shall judge necessary and expedient.

12. He extends the ordinary sessions of Congress, or convenes it in extraordinary session, when some grave interest of order or progress so requires.

13. He causes the revenues of the Nation to be collected and decrees their disbursement in accordance with the law or budgets of national expenses.

14. He concludes and signs treaties of peace, commerce, navigation, alliance, boundaries, and neutrality, concordats, and carries through all other negotiations required for the maintenance of friendly relations with foreign Powers; he receives their Ministers and admits their Consuls.

15. He is the commander-in-chief of all the land and naval forces of the Nation.

16. He fills the military offices of the Nation, with the consent of the Senate, when filling higher offices and grades in the Army or Navy, and by himself on the field of battle.

17. He controls the land and naval forces and has charge of their organization and distribution according to the needs of the Nation.

18. He declares war and grants letters of marque and reprisal with the authorization and approval of Congress.

19. He declares one or more points of the Nation to be in a state of siege in case of foreign attack, and for a limited period, with the consent of the Senate. In cases of domestic disturbance, he shall have this power only when Congress is in recess, such power being vested in this body. The President exercises it with the limitations prescribed in Article 23.

20. He may call on the heads of all the Branches and Departments of the Administration, and through them on all other employees, for such reports as he may deem advisable, and they shall be bound to furnish them.

21. He cannot leave the territory of the Capital except by permission of Congress. When the latter is in recess, he may do so without permission only for some grave object of the public service.

22. The President shall have the power to fill vacancies occurring while the Senate is in recess in offices requiring the consent of the Senate, by granting commissions which shall expire at the close of the next ordinary session.

CHAPTER IV: The Ministers of the Executive Power

87. Eight Ministers [10] shall have charge of the dispatch of the affairs of the Nation, and shall countersign and legalize the President's acts by their sig-

[10] The version here given is as amended by the National Convention of the Capital of the Republic on March 15, 1898.

nature, without which requirement such acts shall have no effect. A special law shall define the branches of the proper business of the Ministries.[11]

88. Each Minister is personally liable for the acts he legalizes, and liable *in solido* for those in which he concurs with his colleagues.

89. Ministers can in no case make decisions by themselves, excepting as to matters concerning the economic and administrative government of their respective Departments.

90. As soon as the sessions of Congress are open, the Ministers shall present to it a detailed report of the state of the Nation, in so far as the business of their respective Departments is concerned.

91. They cannot be Senators or Deputies without first resigning their offices as Ministers.

92. The Ministers may attend the sessions of Congress and take part in the debates, but not vote.

93. They shall receive for their services a salary fixed by law, which may not be increased or reduced in favor or against them during their continuance in office.

Subdivision III: The Judicial Power

Chapter I: Its Nature and Duration

94. The Judicial Power of the Nation shall be exercised by a Supreme Court of Justice and such other lower Tribunals as Congress may establish in the territory of the Nation.

95. In no case may the President of the Nation exercise judicial functions, take it upon himself to hear pending cases, or to reopen those already closed.

96. The Judges of the Supreme Court and of the lower Tribunals of the Nation shall continue in office during good behavior, and shall receive for their services a remuneration fixed by law, which shall not be reduced in any manner whatsoever while they continue in office.

97. No person may be a member of the Supreme Court of Justice unless he be a lawyer of the Nation, with eight years' practice, and have the qualifications required for being a Senator.

98. When the Supreme Court assembles for the first time, the persons appointed thereto shall take an oath, to be administered by the President of the Nation, to discharge their duties by the proper and legal administration of justice and in conformity with the provisions of the Constitution. Thereafter the oath shall be administered by the President of said Court.

99. The Supreme Court shall make its own internal and economic regulations, and shall appoint all its subordinate employees.

Chapter II: Powers of the Judiciary

100. It is within the province of the Supreme Court and the lower Tribunals of the Nation to take cognizance of and decide on all causes involving points governed by the Constitution and the laws of the Nation, with the reservation set forth in Section 11 of Article 67, and by treaties with foreign nations; causes concerning foreign Ambassadors, public Ministers, and foreign Consuls; causes of admiralty and maritime jurisdiction; matters to which the Nation is a party; causes arising between two or more Provinces; between a Province or residents in another Province; between residents of

---

[11] Law No. 3727 divides the business into: Interior, Foreign and Religious Affairs, Finance, Justice and Public Education, War, Marine, Agriculture and Public Works.

different Provinces; and between a Province or its residents against a foreign State or citizen.

101. In these cases the Supreme Court shall have appellate jurisdiction according to the rules and exceptions prescribed by Congress; but in all matters concerning foreign Ambassadors, Ministers, or foreign Consuls, and in cases in which a Province is a party, it shall have original and exclusive jurisdiction.

102. All ordinary criminal causes other than those arising out of the right of impeachment granted to the Chamber of Deputies, shall be tried by jury, as soon as this institution is established in the Republic. Such trials shall be held in the Province in which the crime was committed; but when committed outside the limits of the Nation, against international law, Congress shall determine by a special law the place where the trial is to be held.

103. Treason against the Nation shall consist only in taking up arms against it, or in joining its enemies, giving them aid and comfort. Congress shall establish the punishment for this crime by a special law; but such punishment shall not extend beyond the person of the offender, nor shall the infamy of the criminal be transmitted to his kindred in any degree.

PART II: PROVINCIAL GOVERNMENTS

104. The Provinces retain all the power not delegated by this Constitution to the Federal Government, and that which they may have expressly reserved by special covenants at the time of their incorporation.

105. They provide their own institutions and are governed thereby. They elect their Governors, their Legislators, and other Provincial officials, without the intervention of the Federal Government.

106. Each Province shall enact its own Constitution, in accordance with the provisions of Article 5.

107. The Provinces may conclude partial treaties for the purposes of the administration of justice, economic interests, and works of common utility, with the knowledge of the Federal Congress; and promote their industries, immigration, the construction of railways and navigable canals, the colonization of lands of Provincial ownership, the introduction and establishment of new industries, the importation of foreign capital, and the exploration of their rivers, by laws protecting said ends, and with their own resources.

108. The Provinces do not exercise the power delegated to the Nation. They may not conclude partial treaties of a political character; nor enact laws relating to home or foreign trade or navigation; or establish Provincial custom-houses; or mint money; or establish banks with the power to issue notes, without authorization from the Federal Congress; or enact Civil, Commercial, Penal, or Mining Codes after Congress has sanctioned them; or especially enact laws on citizenship and naturalization, bankruptcy, counterfeiting of money or State documents; or establish tonnage dues; or arm warships or raise armies—except in case of foreign invasion or a danger so imminent as to admit of no delay, when they shall at once report the matter to the Federal Government; or appoint or receive foreign agents; or admit new religious orders.

109. No Province shall declare or wage war against another Province. Their complaints shall be submitted to the Supreme Court of Justice and be settled by it. Acts of hostility on their part shall be deemed acts of civil war, and classified as seditious or riotous, which the Federal Government shall stifle and repress according to law.

110. The Governors of the Provinces are the natural agents of the Federal Government for the enforcement of this Constitution and the laws of the Nation.

Appendix VIII

THE RESIDENCE OF ALIENS LAW

No. 4144
of October 11, 1864

1. The Executive Power may order any alien condemned or pursued by foreign Tribunals for common crimes or misdemeanors, to leave the Territory.

2. The Executive Power may order any alien to leave, whose conduct compromises the national security or disturbs public order.

3. The Executive Power may prevent the entry into the Territory of the Republic of any alien whose antecedents authorize it to include him amongst those to which the two preceding Articles refer.

4. An alien against whom expulsion has been decreed shall have three days in which to leave the country, and the Executive Power may, as a measure of public safety, order his detention until the time of embarkation.

5. Be it communicated, etc.

Appendix IX

FORMS OF GOVERNMENT SINCE THE REVOLUTION OF 1810

JUNTAS

May 25, 1810	First Junta
December 18, 1810	Second Junta

TRIUMVIRATES

September 23, 1811	First Triumvirate
October 8, 1812	Second Triumvirate

DIRECTORS OF THE UNITED PROVINCES

January 31, 1814	Gervasio Posadas
January 10, 1815	Carlos M. de Alvear
April 20, 1815	Alvarez Thomas
April 16, 1816	Juan Ramón Balcarce
July 29, 1816	Juan Martín de Pueyrredon
June 11, 1819	José Rondeau

ANARCHY
GOVERNORS OF THE PROVINCE OF BUENOS AIRES
IN CHARGE OF FOREIGN AFFAIRS

February 17, 1820	Manuel Sarratea
May 1, 1820	Ildefonso Ramos Mexia
June 23, 1820	Miguel Estanislao Soler
July 4, 1820	Manuel Dorrego
September 26, 1820	Martín Rodriguez
April 2, 1824	Juan Gregorio Las Heras

UNITARIAN PRESIDENTS

February 8, 1826	Bernardino Rivadavia
July 5, 1827	Vicente Lopez y Planes (acting)

ANARCHY (Second Period)
GOVERNORS OF THE PROVINCE OF BUENOS AIRES
IN CHARGE OF FOREIGN AFFAIRS

August 13, 1827	Manuel Dorrego
December 1, 1828	Juan Lavalle
August 24, 1829	Juan José Viamonte (Provisional)
December 8, 1829	Juan Manuel de Rosas
December 17, 1832	Juan Ramón Balcarce
November 4, 1833	Juan José Viamonte
October 4, 1834	Manuel V. Maza (acting)

TYRANNY

March 7, 1835	Juan Manuel de Rosas

PROVISIONAL DIRECTOR OF THE CONFEDERATION

February 3, 1852	Justo José de Urquiza

PRESIDENTS OF THE CONFEDERATION

March 5, 1854	Justo José de Urquiza
March 5, 1860	Domingo Derqui

PRESIDENTS OF THE NATION

1862–68	Bartolomé Mitre
1868–74	Domingo F. Sarmiento
1874–80	Nicolás Avellaneda
1880–86	Julio A. Roca
1886–90	Miguel Juarez Celman
1890–92	Carlos Pellegrini
1892–95	Luis Saenz Peña
1895–98	José Evaristo Uriburu
1898–04	Julio A. Roca
1904–06	Manuel Quintana
1906–10	José Figueroa Alcorta
1910–14	Roque Saenz Peña
1914–16	Victorino de la Plaza
1916–22	Hipólito Irigoyen
1922–28	Marcelo T. de Alvear
1928–30	Hipólito Irigoyen

1930–32   José F. Uriburu
1932–38   Agustín P. Justo
1938–44   Roberto M. Ortiz

Appendix X

EXCHANGE AGREEMENT WITH GERMANY

Buenos Aires, September 28, 1934

Article 1. The Argentine Government undertakes, as long as it maintains a system of exchange permits for imports, to take all necessary measures to enable the importers in Argentina of merchandise of German origin to obtain exchange at quotations which shall not be less favorable than those granted for imports of other origin, and to permit the corresponding remittances of their funds to Germany until such remittances are equivalent to the value, in Reichsmarks, of the regular exports of Argentine products to Germany, after deducting a reasonable sum annually.

Article 2. The German Government undertakes, as long as it maintains a system of exchange control, to take all necessary measures to enable importers in Germany of merchandise of Argentine origin to obtain exchange at quotations which shall not be less favorable than those granted for imports of other origin, and to permit the corresponding remittance of their funds.

Article 3. The Government of the German Reich, as long as it maintains a system of import quotas, will grant to merchandise of Argentine origin equitable treatment and the most favorable possible, taking into account the figures of the normal commercial interchange between the two countries and the total value of the quotas to be fixed for each product.

Article 4. For the purposes of the application of the present agreement, as well as for the purpose of settling any differences of interpretation which may arise, both governments will appoint a mixed commission to sit in Buenos Aires. For this purpose, both governments will communicate with due anticipation the names of their respective delegates, in accordance with the procedure which shall be established at a future date by the ministries of foreign affairs of the two contracting countries.

Article 5. The customs duty on Argentine grapes entering Germany is established as follows:

Item No. 45 of German Tariff: Fresh table grapes imported otherwise than by parcel post packages of 15 kilograms (33 lbs.) or less, between January 1 and June 30; 7 Reichsmarks per quintal (220 lbs.).

Article 6. The origin of the products of either of the contracting parties entering the other shall be established by a certificate of origin issued or visaed by the consular representative of the importing country accredited to the country of origin.

When it is not possible to issue the certificate of origin in the country of origin, it shall be issued or visaed by the consular representatives of the importing country accredited to third countries, or the origin can be certified before the authorities of the importing country, who will issue certificates thereto. In both cases, the consular authority of the country of origin shall intervene in the manner to be agreed upon in the future by the contracting governments.

During such time as it is not possible, for practical reasons, to enforce the obligation regarding the certificate of origin, this may be replaced by other reliable documents which the contracting countries agree to accept. Both governments will reciprocally communicate the names of the offices or authorities authorized to issue such documents.

Article 7. The present agreement shall be ratified as soon as possible in accordance with the constitutional procedure of each of the contracting countries and the exchange of the ratifications shall take place in the city of Buenos Aires.

The present agreement shall remain in force for one year from October 20, 1934, and shall enter into effect provisionally as from that date.

If it should not be denounced two months before its expiration it shall be considered in force for a new period of one year.

(Signed) Carlos Saavedra Lamas
(Signed) Otto Kiep

Annexed List of Argentine Products on Which Germany
Promised Equitable Quotas

Cotton (unginned), turnip seed, butter, entrails (salted or dried), quebracho extract, quebracho logs, barley, rye, wheat, oats, crackles, edible fats, meat extract, eggs, lard, salted cattle hides, dry cattle hides, salted and dried horse hides, sheepskins (with or without their wool), goat and kid skins, skins of wild animals, fish skins, reptile skins, corn, and Guinea corn.

Appendix XI

ROCA-RUNCIMAN TRADE TREATY

The Government of the United Kingdom of Great Britain and Northern Ireland and the Government of the Argentine Republic;

Affirming their common determination to uphold and carry out the Treaty of Amity, Commerce and Navigation signed at Buenos Aires on the 2nd February 1825; and

Considering it to be expedient, in order to increase and facilitate trade and commerce between the Argentine Republic on the one hand and the United Kingdom of Great Britain and Northern Ireland on the other, to supplement the said Treaty of 1825 by certain additional provisions relating to trade and commerce between these two countries; and

Being desirous of concluding an agreement for this purpose, accordingly agreed as follows:

ARTICLE I

(1) The Government of the United Kingdom, fully recognizing the importance of the chilled beef industry in the economic life of the Argentine Republic, will not put any restriction on the importation into the United Kingdom of chilled beef coming from Argentina during any quarter of the

year which reduces the imports to a quantity below that imported in the corresponding quarter of the year ending 30th June 1932, except and solely when in the opinion of the Government of the United Kingdom, and after having consulted with the Argentine Government and exchanged with it all the pertinent information, such a step becomes necessary to insure a level of remunerative prices in the markets of the United Kingdom; such restriction shall not be maintained if the imports so excluded are replaced by increases in the imports into the United Kingdom of other classes of meat (always provided that these are not experimental shipments of chilled beef from other parts of the British Commonwealth of Nations) which tend to neutralize the desired effect on prices.

(2) If, due to unforeseen circumstances, the Government of the United Kingdom considers it necessary that the imports of chilled beef from Argentina into the United Kingdom be reduced below the quantity imported during the year ending 30th June 1932, it shall consult with the Argentine Government and with the Governments of the other principal exporting countries (including those which form part of the British Commonwealth of Nations) with the object of agreeing upon the reduction in the imports of chilled and frozen beef from all the producing countries. The Government of the United Kingdom shall not reduce the imports of chilled beef from Argentina by more than 10 per cent below the quantity imported in the year ending 30th June 1932, unless the imports of chilled beef (excluding reasonable shipments of an experimental nature) or frozen beef into the United Kingdom from all the exporting countries which form part of the British Commonwealth of Nations are also reduced by a percentage equal to the percentage of the reduction in Argentine chilled beef below 90 per cent of the quantity imported in the corresponding quarter of the year ending 30th June 1932. The Government of the United Kingdom agrees not to put any restrictions on the imports into the United Kingdom of frozen beef or frozen mutton greater than the restriction specified in Schedule H of the Convention celebrated between the Government of the United Kingdom and the Government of the Australian Federation on the 20th August 1932, unless the imports of such meats from the countries which form part of the British Commonwealth of Nations are also restricted, in which case Argentine meat will be accorded fair and equitable treatment and all the pertinent circumstances will be taken into account.

ARTICLE II

(1) Whenever any system of exchange control is in operation in Argentina, the conditions under which foreign currency shall be made available in any year shall be such as to secure that there shall be available, for the purpose of meeting applications for current remittances from Argentina to the United Kingdom, the full amount of the sterling exchange arising from the sale of Argentine products in the United Kingdom after deduction of a reasonable sum annually towards the payment of the service of the Argentine public external debts (national, provincial and municipal) payable in countries other than the United Kingdom.

(2) Subject to the aforesaid provision for the service of the public external debts, the order in which the sterling exchange so made available shall be distributed among the various classes of applicants for remittances to the United Kingdom shall be settled by agreement between the Argentine Government and the Government of the United Kingdom.

(3) Of the sterling exchange that remains available, in accordance with foregoing Paragraph 1, for Argentine remittances to the United Kingdom during the year 1933, there shall be set aside in pounds sterling the equivalent of 12,000,000 paper pesos for the purpose of making payments in cash up to an amount to be fixed between the Government of the United Kingdom and the Argentine Government, with respect to each case of peso balances which up to the 1st May 1933, were awaiting sterling exchange in order to be remitted to the United Kingdom.

(4) The Argentine Government will issue sterling bonds in exchange for the peso balances that may remain on the 1st May 1933, awaiting sterling exchange to be remitted to the United Kingdom after the exhaustion of the 12,000,000 paper pesos referred to in the preceding paragraph. These bonds will be issued at par for a term of twenty years, sinking fund payments to begin five years after issuance, and they shall draw 4 per cent interest per annum.

(5) The Argentine Government undertakes that in no event shall applications for exchange for remittance to the United Kingdom, whether in respect to peso balances or current transactions, be less favorably treated than similar applications for exchange for remittances to any other country.

(6) The Government of the United Kingdom will co-operate with the Argentine Government to the best of its ability in order to secure that the amount of sterling exchange, realized in Argentina by the export of Argentine products to the United Kingdom, shall correspond as closely as possible with the value realized for such products on the United Kingdom market, due account being taken of the necessary deductions for freight, insurance, &c.

ARTICLE III

(1) Between the contracting parties there shall be concluded as soon as possible a supplementary agreement which shall be considered as an integral and essential part of this Convention, which shall contain provisions relating to duties and similar charges, as well as the quantitative regulations to be applied to the merchandise of the United Kingdom in the Argentine Republic and the similar measures to be applied to Argentine merchandise in the United Kingdom.

(2) If such supplementary agreement shall not have been realized before the 1st August 1933, either of the contracting parties may, in spite of the provisions of Article VI, terminate this Convention at any later time by giving one month's notice.

ARTICLE IV

(1) Nothing in the present Agreement shall be deemed to affect the rights and obligations arising out of the Treaty of Amity, Commerce and Navigation signed at Buenos Aires on the 2nd February 1825.

ARTICLE V

(1) The contracting Governments agree that any dispute which may arise between them relating to the proper interpretation or application of any of the provisions of the present Agreement shall, at the request of either of them, be referred to the Permanent Court of International Justice unless in any particular case the contracting Governments agree to submit the dispute to some other tribunal or to dispose of it by some other form or procedure.

ARTICLE VI

(1) The present Agreement shall be ratified and the ratifications exchanged in London as soon as possible. The Agreement shall come into force on the date of the exchange of ratifications and shall remain in force during three years from the date of entering into force and shall remain in force thereafter unless one of the contracting parties advises the other, through diplomatic channels, of the termination of the Agreement. In this case, the Agreement shall continue for a period of six months from the date on which notice of its termination shall have been given.

In witness whereof the undersigned, being duly authorized to that effect, have signed the present Agreement and affixed thereto their seals.

Done at London this 1st day of May 1933, in duplicate in English and Spanish, both texts being equally authentic.

Julio A. Roca
Walter Runciman

Appendix XII

TRADE AGREEMENT WITH THE UNITED STATES

(Signed October 14, 1941)

The President of the United States of America and the Vice-President of the Argentine Nation in the exercise of the Executive Power, being desirous of strengthening the traditional bonds of friendship existing between the two countries through the maintenance of the principle of equal treatment in its unconditional and unlimited form as the basis of commercial relations and through the granting of mutual and reciprocal concessions for the promotion of trade, have resolved to conclude a Trade Agreement so providing and have appointed for this purpose as their Plenipotentiaries:

> The President of the United States of America:
> Norman Armour, Ambassador Extraordinary and Plenipotentiary of the United States of America to the Argentine Republic; and
> The Vice-President of the Argentine Nation in the exercise of the Executive Power: His Excellency Señor Doctor Don Enrique Ruiz Guiñazú, Minister of Foreign Affairs and Worship;

Who, after having exchanged their full powers, found to be in good and due form, have agreed upon the following provisions:

ARTICLE I

1. The United States of America and the Argentine Republic will grant each other unconditional and unrestricted most-favored-nation treatment in all matters concerning customs duties and subsidiary charges of every kind and in the method of levying duties, and, further, in all matters concerning

the rules, formalities and charges imposed in connection with the clearing of goods through the customs, and with respect to all laws or regulations affecting the sale or use of imported goods within the country.

2. Accordingly, articles the growth, produce or manufacture of either country imported into the other shall in no case be subject, in regard to the matters referred to above, to any duties, taxes or charges other or higher, or to any rules or formalities other or more burdensome, than those to which the like articles the growth, produce or manufacture of any third country are or may hereafter be subject.

3. Similarly, articles exported from the territory of the United States of America or the Argentine Republic and consigned to the territory of the other country shall in no case be subject with respect to exportation and in regard to the above-mentioned matters, to any duties, taxes or charges other or higher, or to any rules or formalities other or more burdensome, than those to which the like articles when consigned to the territory of any third country are or may hereafter be subject.

4. Any advantage, favor, privilege or immunity which has been or may hereafter be granted by the United States of America or the Argentine Republic in regard to the above-mentioned matters, to any article originating in any third country or consigned to the territory of any third country shall be accorded immediately and without compensation to the like article originating in or consigned to the territory of the Argentine Republic or the United States of America, respectively.

ARTICLE II

1. Articles the growth, produce or manufacture of the United States of America or the Argentine Republic, shall, after importation into the other country, be exempt from all internal taxes, fees, charges or exactions other or higher than those payable on like articles of national origin or of any other foreign origin.

2. The provisions of this Article relating to national treatment shall not apply to taxes imposed by the Argentine Republic on alcohols, alcoholic beverages, beers, natural mineral waters, and fabrics containing 40 per centum or more of silk or artificial silk.

ARTICLE III

1. No prohibition or restriction of any kind shall be imposed by the Government of either country on the importation of any article the growth, produce or manufacture of the other country or upon the exportation of any article destined for the other country, unless the importation of the like article the growth, produce or manufacture of all third countries, or the exportation of the like article to all third countries, respectively, is similarly prohibited or restricted.

2. No restriction of any kind shall be imposed by the Government of either country on the importation from the other country of any article in which that country has an interest, whether by means of import licenses or permits or otherwise, unless the total quantity or value of such article permitted to be imported during a specified period, or any change in such quantity or value, shall have been established and made public. If the Government of either country allots a share of such total quantity or value to any third country, it shall allot to the other country a share equivalent to the propor-

tion of the total imports of such article supplied by that country during a previous representative period, and shall make such share available so as to facilitate its full utilization, unless it is mutually agreed to dispense with such allotment. No limitation or restriction of any kind other than such an allotment shall be imposed, by means of import licenses or permits or otherwise, on the share of such total quantity or value which may be imported from the other country.

3. The provisions of the preceding paragraph shall apply in respect of the quantity or value of any article permitted to be imported at a specified rate of duty.

ARTICLE IV

1. If the Government of either country establishes or maintains any form of control of the means of international payment, it shall accord unconditional most-favored-nation treatment to the commerce of the other country with respect to all aspects of such control.

2. The Government establishing or maintaining such control shall impose no prohibition, restriction or delay on the transfer of payment for any article the growth, produce or manufacture of the other country which is not imposed on the transfer of payment for the like article the growth, produce or manufacture of any third country. With respect to rates of exchange and with respect to taxes or charges on exchange transactions, articles the growth, produce or manufacture of the other country shall be accorded unconditional treatment no less favorable than that accorded to the like articles the growth, produce or manufacture of any third country. The foregoing provisions shall also extend to the application of such control to payments necessary for or incidental to the importation of articles the growth, produce or manufacture of the other country. In general, the control shall be administered so as not to influence to the disadvantage of the other country the competitive relationships between articles the growth, produce or manufacture of the territories of that country and like articles the growth, produce or manufacture of third countries.

3. Notwithstanding any of the provisions of Paragraphs 1 and 2 of this Article, the Government of each country may adopt such measures as it may deem necessary for the protection of its essential interests in time of war or other national emergency.

ARTICLE V

1. In the event that the Government of the United States of America or the Government of the Argentine Republic establishes or maintains a monopoly for the importation, production or sale of a particular article or grants exclusive privileges, formally or in effect, to one or more agencies to import, produce or sell a particular article, the commerce of the other country shall receive fair and equitable treatment in respect of the foreign purchases of such monopoly or agency. To this end such monopoly or agency will, in making its foreign purchases of any article, be influenced solely by considerations, such as those of price, quality, marketability and terms of sale, which would ordinarily be taken into account by a private commercial enterprise interested solely in purchasing on the most favorable terms.

2. The Government of each country, in the awarding of contracts for public works and generally in the purchase of supplies, shall accord fair and equitable treatment to the commerce of the other country as compared with the treatment accorded to the commerce of other foreign countries.

ARTICLE VI

1. Laws, regulations of administrative authorities and decisions or administrative or judicial authorities of the United States of America or the Argentine Republic, respectively, pertaining to the classification of articles for customs purposes or to rates of duty shall be published promptly in such manner as to enable traders to become acquainted with them.

2. No administrative ruling by the United States of America or the Argentine Republic effecting advances in rates of duties or in charges applicable under an established and uniform practice to imports originating in the territory of the other country, or imposing any new requirement with respect to such importations, shall be effective retroactively or with respect to articles either entered for consumption or withdrawn for consumption prior to the date of publication of notice of such ruling in the usual official manner. The provisions of this paragraph do not apply to administrative orders imposing anti-dumping duties, or relating to regulations for the protection of human, animal or plant life or health, or relating to public safety, or giving effect to judicial decisions.

ARTICLE VII

1. Articles the growth, produce or manufacture of the United States of America, enumerated and described in Schedule I annexed to this Agreement and made an integral part thereof, on their importation into the Argentine Republic, if now exempt from ordinary customs duties, shall continue to be so exempt or, if now dutiable, shall be exempt from ordinary customs duties in excess of those set forth and provided for in the said Schedule, subject to the conditions therein set out.

2. The said articles shall also be exempt from all other duties, taxes, fees, charges or exactions, imposed on or in connection with importation, in excess of those imposed on the day of the signature of this Agreement or required to be imposed thereafter under the laws of the Argentine Republic in force on that day.

ARTICLE VIII

1. Articles the growth, produce or manufacture of the Argentine Republic, enumerated and described in Schedules II and III annexed to this Agreement and made an integral part thereof, on their importation into the United States of America, if now exempt from ordinary customs duties, shall continue to be so exempt or, if now dutiable, shall be exempt from ordinary customs duties in excess of those set forth and provided for in the said Schedules, subject to the conditions therein set out.

2. The said articles shall also be exempt from all other duties, taxes, fees, charges or exactions, imposed on or in connection with importation, in excess of those imposed on the day of the signature of this Agreement or required to be imposed thereafter under the laws of the United States of America in force on that day.

3. The Government of the United States of America reserves the right to withdraw or to modify the concession granted to any article enumerated and described in Schedule III at any time after the termination of hostilities between the Governments of the United Kingdom and Germany, on giving six months' written notice to the Government of the Argentine Republic.

ARTICLE IX

The provisions of Articles VII and VIII of this Agreement shall not prevent the Government of either country from imposing at any time on the importation of any article a charge equivalent to an internal tax imposed in respect of a like domestic article or in respect of a commodity from which the imported article has been manufactured or produced in whole or in part.

ARTICLE X

In respect of articles the growth, produce or manufacture of the United States of America or the Argentine Republic enumerated and described in Schedule I or in Schedules II or III, respectively, imported into the other country, on which ad valorem rates of duty, or duties based upon or regulated in any manner by value, are or may be assessed, it is understood and agreed that the bases and methods of determining dutiable value and of converting currencies shall be no less favorable to importers than the bases and methods prescribed under laws and regulations of the Argentine Republic and the United States of America, respectively, in force on the day of the signature of this Agreement.

ARTICLE XI

1. No prohibition, restriction or any form of quantitative regulation, whether or not operated in connection with any agency of centralized control, shall be imposed by the Argentine Republic on the importation or sale of any article the growth, produce or manufacture of the United States of America enumerated and described in Schedule I, or by the United States of America on the importation or sale of any article the growth, produce or manufacture of the Argentine Republic enumerated and described in Schedules II or III.

2. The foregoing provisions shall not apply to quantitative regulations in whatever form imposed by the United States of America or the Argentine Republic on the importation or sale of any article the growth, produce or manufacture of the other country, in conjunction with governmental measures or measures under governmental authority operating to regulate or control the production, market supply or prices of like domestic articles, or tending to increase the labor costs or production of such articles, or to maintain the exchange value of the currency of the country.

ARTICLE XII

1. If the Government of either country should consider that any circumstance, or any measure adopted by the other Government, even though it does not conflict with the terms of this Agreement, has the effect of nullifying or impairing any object of this Agreement or of prejudicing an industry or the commerce of that country, such other Government shall give sympathetic consideration to such representations or proposals as may be made with a view to affecting a mutually satisfactory adjustment of the matter. If no agreement is reached with respect to such representations or proposals, the Government making them shall be free to suspend or terminate this Agreement in whole or in part on thirty days' written notice.

2. The Governments of the two countries agree to consult together to the fullest possible extent in regard to all matters affecting the operation of the present Agreement. In order to facilitate such consultation, a Commission consisting of representatives of each Government shall be established to study the operation of the Agreement, to make recommendations regarding the fulfillment of the provisions of the Agreement, and to consider such other matters as may be submitted to it by the two Governments.

ARTICLE XIII

The provisions of this Agreement relating to the treatment to be accorded by the United States of America and the Argentine Republic, respectively, to the commerce of the other country shall apply, on the part of the United States of America, to the continental territory of the United States of America and such of its territories and possessions as are included in its customs territory. The provisions of this Agreement relating to most-favored-nation treatment shall apply, furthermore, to all articles the growth, produce or manufacture of any territory under the sovereignty or authority of the United States of America or the Argentine Republic, imported from or exported to any territory under the sovereignty or authority of the other country. The provisions of this Article shall not apply to the Panama Canal Zone.

ARTICLE XIV

1. The advantages now accorded or which may hereafter be accorded by the United States of America or the Argentine Republic to adjacent countries in order to facilitate frontier traffic, and advantages accorded in virtue of a customs union to which either country may become a party, shall be excepted from the operation of this Agreement.

2. The advantages now accorded or which may hereafter be accorded by the United States of America, its territories or possessions or the Panama Canal Zone to one another or to the Republic of Cuba shall be excepted from the operation of this Agreement. The provisions of this paragraph shall continue to apply in respect of any advantages now or hereafter accorded by the United States of America, its territories or possessions or the Panama Canal Zone to one another, irrespective of any change in the political status of any of the territories or possessions of the United States of America.

ARTICLE XV

1. Subject to the requirement that, under like circumstances and conditions, there shall be no arbitrary discrimination by either country against the other country in favor of any third country, and without prejudice to the provisions of Paragraphs 1 and 2 of Article XVI, the provisions of this Agreement shall not extend to prohibitions or restrictions

(a) relative to public security;
(b) imposed for the protection of public health or on moral or humanitarian grounds;
(c) imposed for the protection of plants or animals, including measures for protection against diseases, degeneration or extinction as well as measures taken against harmful seeds, plants, or animals;
(d) relating to prison-made goods;
(e) relating to the enforcement of police or revenue laws and regulations; and
(f) imposed for the protection of national treasures or artistic, historic or archaeological value.

2. Nothing in this Agreement shall be construed to prevent the adoption or enforcement of such measures as the Government of either country may see fit (a) relating to the importation or exportation of gold or silver; (b) relating to the control of the export or sale for export of arms, ammunition, or implements of war, and, in exceptional circumstances, all other military supplies; (c) relating to neutrality.

3. It is understood that the provisions of this Agreement relating to laws and regulations affecting the sale, taxation or use of imported articles within the United States of America and the Argentine Republic are subject to the constitutional limitations on the authority of the Governments of the respective countries.

ARTICLE XVI

1. The Government of each country will accord sympathetic consideration to, and when requested will afford adequate opportunity for consultation regarding such representations as the other Government may make with respect to the operation of customs regulations, quantitative regulations or the administration thereof, the observance of customs formalities, and the application of sanitary laws and regulations for the protection of human, animal or plant life or health.

2. In the event that the Government of either country makes representations to the other Government in respect to the application of any sanitary law or regulation for the protection of human, animal or plant life or health, and if there is disagreement with respect thereto, a committee of technical experts on which each Government shall be represented shall, on the request of either Government, be established to consider the matter and to submit recommendations to the two Governments.

ARTICLE XVII

This Agreement shall be proclaimed by the President of the United States and shall be ratified by the Government of the Argentine Republic. It shall enter definitely into force thirty days after the exchange of the instrument of ratification and the proclamation, which shall take place in Washington as soon as possible.

ARTICLE XVIII

Pending the definite coming into force of this Agreement as provided in Article XVII, the provisions thereof shall be applied provisionally on and after November 15, 1941, subject to a right to terminate the provisional application of the Agreement pursuant to the provisions of Paragraph 1 of Article XII or upon six months' written notice.

ARTICLE XIX

Subject to the provisions of paragraph 1 of Article XII, and of Article XVIII, this Agreement shall remain in force until November 15, 1944, and, unless at least six months before November 15, 1944, the Government of either country shall have given notice in writing to the other Government of intention to terminate the Agreement on that date, it shall remain in force thereafter until the expiration of six months from the date on which such notice shall have been given.

In witness whereof the respective Plenipotentiaries have signed this Agreement and have affixed hereto their seals.

Done in duplicate, in the English and Spanish languages, both authentic, at the City of Buenos Aires, this 14th day of October 1941.

For the President of the United States of America:
Norman Armour
For the Vice-President of the Argentine Republic
in the exercise of the Executive Power:
E. Ruiz Guiñazú

Appendix XIII

BALANCE OF PAYMENTS

(In millions of pesos)

Normal Movements	1927	1928	1929	1930	1931	1932	1933	1934	1935	1936	1937
Credits:	2,629	2,693	2,301	1,914	1,581	1,354	1,190	1,811	1,924	2,210	2,619
Exports	2,324	2,428	2,196	1,414	1,475	1,305	1,141	1,618	1,726	1,851	2,484
New foreign investments	285	244	80	483	68	15	15	150	150	310	90
(a) Private investments	51	185	80	245	68	15	15	150	150	310	90
(b) Public loans	234	59	—	238	—	—	—	—	—	—	—
Various	20	21	25	17	38	34	34	43	48	49	45
Debits:	2,293	2,561	2,600	2,282	1,773	1,396	1,422	1,588	1,760	1,783	2,212
Imports	1,668	1,902	1,959	1,680	1,174	836	911	1,110	1,175	1,183	1,557
Service on public debt	122	132	135	158	203	189	176	212	194	184	161
Expenditures abroad	70	69	24	31	21	16	16	21	36	52	91
Dividends on private investments	317	336	354	310	280	270	250	270	278	285	300
Private remittances	116	122	128	103	95	85	69	75	77	79	103
Balance:	336	132	−229	−368	−192	−42	−232	123	164	427	407
Extraordinary Movements											
Credits:	—	—	403	151	562	18	298	123	19	—	—
Gold exports (net)	—	—	403	71	562	18	—	61	12	—	—
"Thawing" loans	—	—	—	—	—	—	298	62	7	—	—
Return of "hot" funds	—	—	—	80	—	—	—	—	—	—	—
Debits:	196	197	80	45	392	75	28	100	71	36	489
Cancellation of public debt	—	—	—	—	156	—	—	46	19	7	445
Release of blocked funds	—	—	—	—	145	40	28	54	52	27	44
Gold imports (net)	196	197	—	—	—	—	—	—	—	2	—
Funds seeking investment abroad	—	—	80	—	—	—	—	—	—	—	—
Retirement of capital	—	—	—	45	91	35	—	—	—	—	—
Balance:	−196	−197	323	106	170	−57	−270	23	−52	−36	−489
NET BALANCE	140	−65	24	−262	−22	−99	−38	146	112	391	−82

Appendix XIV

DISTRIBUTION OF EXCHANGE SOLD BY EXCHANGE CONTROL OFFICE

(In millions of pesos)

	IMPORTS		DIVIDENDS OF PUBLIC UTILITIES		VARIOUS		GOVERNMENT REMITTANCES		
	Amount	*%*	*Amount*	*%*	*Amount*	*%*	*Amount*	*%*	*Total*
1932	788.9	58.16	141.3	10.41	61.0	4.50	198.0	14.60	1,356.4 [1]
1933	722.3	66.22	91.0	8.34	24.0	2.20	191.2	17.53	1,090.8 [2]
1934	826.4	62.06	201.8	15.16	47.8	3.59	223.6	16.79	1,331.6 [3]
1935	912.7	65.35	205.2	14.69	103.6	7.42	175.2	12.54	1,396.7
1936	945.3	67.22	208.7	14.84	66.2	4.71	185.9	13.23	1,406.1
1937	1,338.4	64.16	167.4	8.03	39.1	1.87	541.0	25.94	2,085.9 [4]
1938	1,305.3	73.27	156.9	8.81	182.9	10.27	136.3	7.65	1,781.4

[1] In 1932, remittances of private individuals totaled 167,200,000 pesos and accounted for 12.33% of the total exchange sold.

[2] In 1933, remittances of private individuals totaled 62,300,000 pesos and accounted for 5.71% of the total exchange sold.

[3] In 1934, remittance of private individuals totaled 32,000,000 pesos and accounted for 2.40% of the total exchange sold. After 1934, the Exchange Control Office ceased selling exchange for private remittances.

[4] Government remittances in 1937 included 372,200,000 pesos sent to New York for the conversion of dollar bonds into internal loans.

BIBLIOGRAPHY

HISTORY AND INTERPRETATION

Aikman, Duncan. *The All-American Front*. New York, 1940.

Alvarez, Juan. *Las Guerras Civiles Argentinas*. Buenos Aires, 1936.

Astolfi, J. C., and Migone, Raúl C. *Historia Argentina*. Buenos Aires, 1939.

Beals, Carleton. *America South*. Philadelphia, 1937.

—— *The Coming Struggle for Latin America*. Philadelphia, 1939.

—— *Pan America*. Boston, 1940.

Brady, George S. *Railways of South America (Argentina)*. (Dept. of Commerce Report.) Washington, 1926.

Chandler, Charles Lyon. *Inter-American Acquaintances*. Liverpool, 1917.

Darwin, C. R. *The Voyage of H.M.S. Beagle*. Various eds.

Dominguez, Manuel. *El Alma de la Raza*. Asunción, 1918.

Gillespie, Alejandro. *Buenos Aires y el Interior*. Buenos Aires, 1921.

Haring, C. H. *South American Progress*. Cambridge, 1935.

Herring, Hubert. *Good Neighbors*. New York, 1941.

Inman, Samuel Guy. *Latin America, Its Place in World Life*. Chicago, 1937.

Jefferson, Mark. *Peopling the Argentine Pampas*. New York, 1926.

Kirkpatrick, F. A. *The Argentine Republic*. Cambridge, 1931.

Leguizamón, Martiniano. *La Cuna del Gaucho*. Buenos Aires, 1895.

Levene, Ricardo. *A History of Argentina*. (Trans.) Chapel Hill, 1937.

López, Vicente Fidel. *Manual de la Historia Argentina*. Buenos Aires. Various eds.

Mitre, Bartolomé. *The Emancipation of South America*. (Trans.) London, 1893.

—— *Ensayos Históricos*. Buenos Aires. Various eds.

Oliveira Cezar, F. de. *Güemes y sus Gauchos*. Buenos Aires, 1895.

Palacios, Alfredo L. *Las Islas Malvinas*. Buenos Aires, 1934.

Rodney, Caesar A., and Graham, John. *Report on the Present State of the United Provinces of South America*. London, 1819.

Sarmiento, Domingo Faustino. *Facundo*. Buenos Aires. Various eds.

Siegfried, André. *Impressions of South America*. New York, 1933.

Weddell, Alexander W. *Introduction to Argentina*. New York, 1939.

Whitaker, John T. *Americas to the South*. New York, 1940.

Ybarra, T. R. *America Faces South*. New York, 1939.

GOVERNMENT AND POLITICS

Alberdi, Juan Bautista. *Bases y Puntos de Partida para la Organización Política de la República Argentina*. Buenos Aires. Various eds.

Amuchasteguí, Nicolas R. *La Constitución Nacional Argentina*. Buenos Aires, 1939.

Fernández Artucio, Hugo. *The Nazi Underground in South America*. New York, 1942.

Foreign Policy Association. *Argentina's Revolution and Its Aftermath*. (Bulletin.) New York, 1931.

Gonzalez Calderón, Juan A. *Instrucción Cívica*. Buenos Aires, 1939.

Gunther, John. *Inside Latin America*. New York, 1941.

Matienzo, J. N. *La Revolución de 1930 y los Problemas de la Democracia Argentina*. Buenos Aires, 1930.

Moreno, Mariano. *Doctrina Democrática*. Buenos Aires. Various eds.

Rojas, Ricardo. *El radicalismo de mañana.* Buenos Aires, 1930.
Rowe, Leo S. *The Federal System of the Argentine Republic.* Washington, 1921.

FINANCE AND ECONOMICS
Bunge, Alejandro E. *Una Nueva Argentina.* Buenos Aires, 1940.
Central Bank of the Argentine Republic. *Memoria Anual del Ejercicio 1939.* Buenos Aires, 1940.
Dept. of Agriculture (U.S.). *Agriculture in the Argentine Trade Agreement.* (Bulletin.) Washington, 1941.
Dept. of State (U.S.). *Trade Agreement with Argentina.* (Bulletin.) Washington, 1941.
Elder, George J. *Current Trends in International Trade in Argentina.* (International Conciliation Bulletin.) New York, 1931.
Foreign Policy Association. *U.S. Trade Ties with Argentina.* (Bulletin.) New York, 1941.
Garcia-Mata, Rafael, and Llorens, Emilio. *Argentina Económica.* Buenos Aires, 1940.
Guaresti, Juan José (*hijo*). *Economía y Finanzas de la Nación Argentina.* Buenos Aires, 1933.
Migone, Raúl C. (editor). *Inter-American Statistical Yearbook* (in English, Spanish, Portuguese and French). New York and Buenos Aires, 1940.
Minelli, Pablo M. *Las Inversiones Internacionales en America Latina.* Buenos Aires, 1940.
Normano, J. F. *The Struggle for Latin America.* Boston, 1931.
Phelps, Dudley Maynard. *Migration of Industry to South America.* New York, 1936.
Phelps, Vernon L. *The International Economic Position of Argentina.* Philadelphia, 1938.
Putnam, George E. *Supplying Britain's Meat.* London, 1923.
Southard, Frank A., Jr. *Foreign Exchange Practice and Policy.* New York, 1940.
Storey, W. N. *Report on Economic and Commercial Conditions in the Argentine Republic.* London, 1939.
Velez, Mariano. *La Situación Agrícola de la Pampa.* Buenos Aires, 1934.

SOCIOLOGY
Bunge, Alejandro E. *Una Nueva Argentina.* Buenos Aires, 1940.
Ingenieros, José. *Sociología Argentina.* Buenos Aires, 1918.
Oddone, Jacinto. *La Burguesía Terrateniente Argentina.* Buenos Aires, 1936.
Sarmiento, Domingo Faustino. *Conflictos y Armonías de las Razas en América.* Buenos Aires. Various eds.

PERSONALITIES
Amadeo, Octavio R. *Vidas Argentinas.* Buenos Aires, 1940.
Bilbao, Manuel. *Historia de Rosas.* Buenos Aires, 1919.
Bucich Escobar, Ismael. *Historia de los Presidentes Argentinos.* Buenos Aires, 1927.
Galvez, Manuel. *Vida de Hipólito Irigoyen.* Buenos Aires, 1939.
Ibarguren, Carlos. *Juan Manuel de Rosas.* Buenos Aires, 1938.
Mitre, Bartolomé. *Historia de Belgrano.* Buenos Aires. Various eds.
—— *Historia de San Martín.* Buenos Aires. Various eds.

Parker, Wm. B. *Argentines of Today*. New York, 1929.
Rojas, Ricardo. *El Santo de la Espada. Vida de San Martín*. Buenos Aires, 1940.

ENGLISH TRANSLATIONS OF ARGENTINE WORKS

Bierstadt, E. H. (editor). *Three Plays of the Argentine*. New York, 1920.
Frank, Waldo (editor). *Tales from the Argentine*. New York, 1930.
Güiraldes, Ricardo. *Don Segundo Sombra* (a novel). New York, 1935.
Holmes, Henry A. *Martín Fierro, an Epic of the Argentine*. New York, 1923.
Mármol, José. *Amalia* (a novel). New York, 1919.
Owen, Walter. José Hernandez's *The Gaucho. Martin Fierro*. New York, 1936.
Wast, Hugo. *Stone Desert* (a novel). New York, 1928.
——— *Black Valley* (a novel). New York, 1929.
——— *Peach Blossom* (a novel). New York, 1929.

INDEX

357

militia, organization of, 60
Miller, William Gilchrist, first **U.S. vice consul** at Buenos Aires, 240
mining resources, 290
Misiones, territory of, 6; boundary dispute settled, 121; German preponderance in, 173
missionaries, American, in Argentina, 266–8
Mitre, Bartolomé, President, 1862–68, 106–9; defeat and rebellion, 119; defeated at Cepeda, 106; first constitutional president, 109; founder of *La Nación*, 123; governor of Buenos Aires province, 108; in Paraguayan War, 116, 117; member of civic union, 131; quoted, 77, 91, 231; statesmanship of, 108–9, 116; victor at Pavon, 108
monarchists and their influence on early government, 89, 91; failure of plan, 91; in search of a kind for Buenos Aires, 63, 90
Monroe Doctrine, Ch. 26; discussed, 270–4; in Falkland Islands case, 274–77; recognized by Argentina, 257, 269–70; repudiated by Argentina, 269, 277; text of, 273
Monroe, James, President, appointment of Rodney as minister to Argentina, 240, 273; recognition of Argentine independence, 240–3; sends mission to River Plate, 244
Monte Protegido, Argentine schooner, torpedoed, 142
Montes, Enrique, conquistador, 28, 29
Montevideo, besieged by patriots, 79; captured by English, 61; Congress of, 152; Regional Conference, 287
Moors, influence on conquistadors, 40; influence on gauchos, 67
Moreno, Mariano, mentor of emancipation, 74, 75; monarchical sympathies, 89; death, 89
Mortgage Bank, National, founding by Roca, 121
most-favored nation clause, 211, 221, 222, 225, 279; granted to U.S., 225, 226; nullified by exchange control, 212; violated by quotas, 212
mountains, Argentine, 5
mourning customs, 20
El Mundo, of Buenos Aires, 183
municipalities, character of, in colonial period, 88
music, 21
Muto, Tony, 196

La Nación, of Buenos Aires, 123, 128; quoted on illegitimacy, 297
Nahuel Huapi, 1
Napoleon in Spain, 61, 75, 82
Napoleonic Wars, European line-up, 58, 61
National Boards, see under respective names
National Democratic Party (Conservatives), 174
National Labor Office, 297
National Recovery Plan, 162, 198, 202, 204–8
nationalism, 156; under Castillo, 178–9, 182; under Uriburu, 159; attitude toward Great Britain, 309
nationalistic movement (*see Federación Patriótica Argentina, Legión Cívica Argentina*)
Nazi activities, 125, 175, 307; concerning Falklands, 277; organizations, 173, 175; penetration, 175; propaganda, 171, 258 (*see* Germans)
Negroes, importation of, 46; in Viceroyalty, 79; population in 1852, 124

Netherlands, loan agreement with, 206; position in Argentine trade, 210; trade agreement with, 213, 317
Neuquen, Territory of, 48
neutrality, Argentine, Axis violations of, 307; in First World War, 142, 261; U.S. effort to break, 261–2
newspapers, circulation of, 187; excellence of, 183, 184; forces for democracy, 174; U.S. influence on, 249, 254; *Los Andes*, 184; *La Capital*, 184; *Crítica*, 158, 183; *Herald*, 183; *El Mundo*, 183; *La Nación*, 123, 183, 297; *La Prensa*, 123, 183–4; *The Standard*, 183 (*see* censorship)

O'Higgins, Bernardo, liberator of Chile, 81, 83
oligarchy of wealth, 133, 154, 156, 293; attitude toward democracy, 302
ombú tree, 4
open cabildo of 1810, 64
Ortiz, Roberto M., President, 1937–42, birth and early life, 163–4; democracy under, 178; democratic support for, 165, 173; friendship with Irigoyen and Alvear, 164; friendship for U.S., 165; ill health and retirement, 166, 179; inauguration of, 164; opposition of Conservatives, 165–6; repudiation of election frauds, 163, 165; resignation, 306–7
Ortiz de Zárate (*see* Zárate)
Juan de Osorio, conquistador, 34
Ottawa Agreement, effect on Argentine trade, 309

packing plants (*see frigoríficos*)
Pack, Colonel, defeated at Buenos Aires, 60
palabra inglés, word of honor, 232, 235, 258
Palacios, Alfredo L., democratic leader, 179–82; attitude toward U.S., 182; foreign policy, 182; on Falkland Islands, 182, 275; social legislation, 182; university reform, 181
Palermo Park, formerly estate of Rosas, 4; conference of governors, 104; livestock show, 189; racetrack, 21
La Pampa, Territory of, 3, 48
Pampa Indians, 13, 24; removal to Entre Ríos, 72; Roca's campaign against, 72
pampas, description of, 2–4; population of, 7
Pan American conferences, 9, 288; Argentine attitude toward, 262–3; treaties and conventions, 262; at Havana, 262; at Mexico City, 262; at Montevideo, 152; at Panama, 288; at Rio de Janeiro, 171
Paraguay, Argentine influence in, 263; in Chaco War, 16; early dominance of, 41, 42, 46; secedes from United Provinces, 78; treaty of peace with, 106; war with, 116
Paraguay River, ascent of, by Ayolas, 37; by Garcia, 27
Paraguayan War, 16, 17, 128
Paramillo, 6
Paraná, capital of Argentina, 1853–61, 105
Paraná River, 26, 29; early settlements on, 36; opening of, to foreign ships, 106
parties, political and election frauds, 155; during revolution, 87; federalist and unitarian, 110; movement to abolish, 161; representing class interests, 120–6 (*see* Conservatives, federalism, Federalists, National Democratic Party, Radical Party, Unitarians)

PERU

Cochabam

VENEZUELA

BRITISH
GUIANA

DUTCH
GUIANA

FRENCH
GUIANA

COLOMBIA

BRAZIL

ECUADOR

PERU

BOLIVIA

PARAGUAY

CHILE

URUGUAY

ARGENTINA

N

E

W

WOODS

S

SCALE OF MILES

0   100 200   500   1000